38.00

(958)

BRITISH DIPLOMACY AND FOREIGN POLICY
1782–1865

British Diplomacy and Foreign Policy

1782–1865

THE NATIONAL INTEREST

JOHN CLARKE
University of Buckingham

London
UNWIN HYMAN
Boston   Sydney   Wellington

Published by the Academic Division of
Unwin Hyman Ltd
15/17 Broadwick Street, London W1V 3FP, UK

Unwin Hyman, Inc.
8 Winchester Place, Winchester, Mass. 01890, USA

Allen & Unwin (Australia) Ltd
8 Napier Street, North Sydney, NSW 2060, Australia

Allen & Unwin (New Zealand) Ltd in association with the Port Nicholson Press Ltd,
60 Cambridge Terrace, Wellington, New Zealand

First published in 1989

British Library Cataloguing in Publication Data

Clarke, John
  British diplomacy and foreign policy 1782–1865 :
  the national interest.
  1. Great Britain. Foreign relations, 1782–1865
  I. Title
  327.41
ISBN 0–04–445040–0

Library of Congress Cataloging in Publication Data

Clarke, John (John Charles), 1947–
  British diplomacy and foreign policy, 1782–1865.
  Bibliography: p.
  Includes index.
  1. Great Britain — Foreign relations — 19th century.
2. Great Britain — Foreign relations — 1760–1820.
I. Title.
DA530.C5   1988   327.41   88–17295
ISBN 0–04–445040–0

Typeset in 11/12 plantin
Printed in Great Britain at the
University Press, Cambridge

Contents

BRITISH DIPLOMACY AND FOREIGN POLICY
1782–1865

1

Britain and the European Pattern

I

Writing in *Foreign Affairs* in July 1931, Austen Chamberlain attempted to prove that his policies as Foreign Secretary had been consistent with the main strands of British foreign policy in earlier centuries. He rather assumed that the demonstration of such consistency would provide adequate justification for his own policies. Perhaps the article is the work of a man at the end of his career trying to provide some intellectual window dressing for his own reputation, yet it raises important questions about British foreign policy and about international relations in general. Chamberlain called his article 'The Permanent Bases of British Foreign Policy'; an apologetic streak runs through the article, as if Chamberlain knew that he was 'thinking like a Continental'. He acknowledged that his title would be meaningless to the average Englishman in that there was a widespread belief that such 'permanent bases' existed only in the minds of envious and paranoid foreigners:

Nothing in foreign comment on British policy surprises an Englishman more than the frequent attribution to British statesmen of all parties and in all times of an almost machiavellian subtlety in the design and in the unalterable persistence in the execution of their plans. Such a picture of ourselves seems to lack even a resemblance of a caricature to the original and to attribute to the conduct of our foreign

relations the one characteristic which whether for good or
evil it most conspicuously lacks. Yet the charge is constantly
made – sometimes with reproach, sometimes with envy – and
is as certainly believed.[1]

If Chamberlain's average Englishman was right, this and
most other books about British foreign policy produced in
the last twenty years could not have been written. The
vogue now is for the systematic and analytical approach,
and system and analysis require common ground on which
comparisons can be made. The 'systematic' study of international relations can be taken to absurd conclusions, so
that the average reader suspects that the average Englishman may have been right after all. Yet it is intellectually
defeatist to reduce a book on foreign policy to mere
narrative. There are some things which cannot be proved
in history; they depend upon certain assumptions about
the human condition in general. The assumptions of the
present writer are similar to those of Austen Chamberlain
– that foreign belief that British policy has had an underlying coherence over time is not essentially wrong headed
and that English scepticism about intellectual structures
of all kinds may serve as a necessary corrective to the
wilder flights of Continental, and more recently of American,
imagination.
   Chamberlain believed that different perceptions about
foreign policy illustrated fundamental differences in the
national character. The English are presented as pragmatic
and empirical to a fault. They find systematic planning
irksome and uncongenial, submitting to it with reluctance,
mistrustful of attempts to visualize hypothetical futures,
and are always ready to fall back on a capacity to adapt to
emergencies as they actually arise. The Englishman is
neither systematic nor logical. He distrusts logic and most
of all in the government of men; instinct and experience
alike teach him that men are not governed by logic, that
it is unwise to treat politics as exercises in logic. Wisdom
more often lies in refraining from pressing arguments
to their logical conclusions and in accepting a workable
though illogical compromise – 'after all, logic lost us

the Thirteen Colonies'. Empiricism and distaste for long prepared schemes make the English reject 'criticisms which impute to us schemes we have never entertained and a subtlety of thought of which we feel ourselves incapable'.[2] Far from being ashamed of their intellectual deficiencies, Englishmen glory in their approach, boasting that they are guided less by logic than by instinct and ready to admit that if something 'feels right' they will do it whether logical or not. Englishmen do not really *think* about foreign policy at all. In part, the refusal to acknowledge that there are underlying principles to foreign policy can be attributed to a mixture of general intellectual laziness and lack of interest. When pressed on the question of the bases of foreign policy, the inquirer will be lucky to get as much as 'Oh, I suppose peace; we are a "nation of shopkeepers", you know'.

According to Chamberlain, the English response to foreign policy difficulties, and to much else – 'Well, I suppose we shall muddle through somehow' – would never escape the lips of a system-loving German or a logic-worshipping Frenchman. Chamberlain is usually correct in appreciating that attitudes to foreign policy reflect other attitudes. He is also correct in acknowledging that, in their aversion to logic and system, the English may deceive themselves about the way their foreign policy has been formulated and implemented. Is it not possible that the underlying unity may be perceived by a Frenchman or by a German rather than by the average Englishman – just as family likenesses are quickly recognized by strangers, whereas members of the family circle see only the individual differences? Of course, British foreign policy is not formulated by 'average' Englishmen, yet even amongst skilled diplomats some of the 'average' attitudes can be discerned. Chamberlain is a generation in advance of academic historians in his belief that divergent ways of thinking, exemplified in national stereotypes, can themselves be a fertile cause of antagonism and dispute. He quotes with approval the words of Salvador de Madariaga, culturally a neutral observer, on the disagreements between England and France in the 1920s.

France and England are often in general at loggerheads. Not that their interests cannot be made to agree. As national interests go, their differences are more often than not bridgeable in themselves, given a little time and good will. Thus it is not altogether impossible to bring the French and British delegates to see eye to eye. Only that their eyes are so different. Time and again I have seen the French nonplussed at the illogical and empirical vagueness of the English and the English shocked and irritated at the unseemly yet unreal clarity of the French. The whole difficulty comes from the particular region in which the centre of gravity of their respective psychologies is situated, which in the Frenchman is above, and in the Englishman, below, the neck. The Frenchman thinks with his head, and with nothing but his head; the Englishman thinks or rather, as he himself says 'feels somehow' with everything but his head, and provided he does not allow his head to meddle with it, he is generally right ... The Frenchman, trusting thought, is apt to distrust life and therefore he endeavours to imprison future life in present thought; while the Englishman, who trusts life and mistrusts thought refuses to foresee and is content to cross the bridge when he comes to it – even at the risk of having to ford the river on finding that there is no bridge at all.[3]

II

Accepting that there is some truth in Chamberlain's picture of a sharp divergence between English and Continental attitudes to foreign policy, we must ask four questions:

(1) When did the divergence become especially marked?
(2) Was the divergence due to 'accidental' or 'real' factors?
(3) If divergences in attitude reflected *actual* differences in foreign policy, were those differences due to 'external', 'internal' or 'institutional' factors?
(4) Despite superficial differences, were there at least some underlying similarities between the British policy and that of certain Continental states? In other words, did Britain really conform to some kind of 'European norm'?

Chamberlain's stereotypes of differing national attitudes to foreign policy originate in the eighteenth century. The first comments on a typically English aversion to abstract or analytical thought are also found at this time. The desire to generalize and to regard all spheres of knowledge as amenable to 'scientific method' is one of the hallmarks of the Enlightenment. There was never much of an English Enlightenment and the English reluctance to 'think serious-ly' about foreign policy compared to the Continental ten-dency to 'systematize' about it to excess, can be attributed to a divergent intellectual climate in the eighteenth century. But the Enlightenment itself was the product of specific social and political factors weaker in England than in parts of the Continent or even in Scotland. Eighteenth-century England did not produce learned works on the *theory* of relations between states, either in the same numbers or at the same level of sophistication that its actual position in the world would lead one to expect. The intellectual tradition, or rather the lack of it, which was visible in the eighteenth century and in the more popular attitudes delineated by Chamberlain, reflect the same thing.

The explanation for the divergence of the English and the Continental traditions implicit in Chamberlain is geo-graphical. English people, whether policy-makers, intel-lectuals or others, do not need to think deeply about foreign policy because the Narrow Seas protect them from attack from the Continent and the same seas banish visions of Continental annexions. Chamberlain omits to add that it is only the *Narrow* Seas which act like this; in reality, aggression and conquest across broader oceans have held fewer terrors. Yet if Britain's geographical position makes it no less ambitious than its Continental neighbours, at least its ambitions are directed away from Europe. Perhaps fear is a more powerful inducement to thought than ambition. The Chamberlain theory is that fear coupled with ambition creates the ideal climate for the 'scientific' analysis of foreign policy. If eighteenth-century Britain was neither particularly fearful nor particularly ambitious, then a happy go lucky approach to foreign policy is understandable. It is even more understandable if, as Chamberlain claims

towards the end of his article, one of the few permanent
bases of British foreign policy has been a desire to preserve
the peace. If the yardstick is thought then, whilst peace may
have been thought about to some extent, this has usually
been outweighed by the thought devoted to winning wars.
Bearing in mind the Continental dictum that diplomacy
is the pursuit of the objectives of war by other means,
it follows that he who does not think deeply about war
will not think deeply about diplomacy, foreign policy
or international relations. Thus, the material implicit or
explicit in Chamberlain's article provides answers to two of
our four questions – that the divergence between English
and Continental attitudes to foreign policy dates, at least
in its modern form, from the eighteenth century, and that
this divergence, stemming from the weakness of the 'Enlightenment way of thinking' is explicable in geographical
terms. But why was it that, in the eighteenth century,
geographical considerations, especially in the shape of the
Narrow Seas, assumed an importance which they did not
have before?

The geographical emphasis points to a liking for 'hard
fact'; the Narrow Seas are pre-eminently factual. Chamberlain typifies, if in an unusual way, an approach to
international relations common amongst writers in the
inter-war period. Many, including the commanding figure
of Harold Temperley, had produced pro-Allied propaganda
during the First World War. They wanted 'hard' evidence
in the shape of the texts of treaties which the accused power,
Germany, could be shown to have violated. With the return
of peace they remained dedicated to the pursuit of 'hard
evidence', in the form of the transcriptions of documents
which in the tradition, if not in the spirit of Leopold
von Ranke, would 'speak for themselves'. One important
work on eighteenth- and nineteenth-century foreign policy
produced in this period, Harold Temperley and Lilian
Penson's *The Foundations of British Foreign Policy from
Pitt to Salisbury* (Cambridge University Press, 1938), is
a collection of documents linked by short commentaries.
The authors assume that the 'foundations' of policy are the
documents themselves. This approach stresses individual

incidents and discourages a belief in 'permanent bases' of policy as propounded by Chamberlain. Indeed, by standards of the 1930s, Chamberlain's approach is modern. Yet we must turn to more recent writers to understand the deeper reasons for the divergence of British and Continental ideas about foreign policy. We shall be forced further towards the modern approach if we seek to explain why that divergence was not absolute.

Historians now pay more attention to the methods of economists, sociologists and political scientists than was usual in the past. In his book *Games Nations Play* (1972), John Spanier argues that the best way to study foreign policy is through three distinct 'levels of analysis': those of the 'states system', 'the nation state' and 'decision making'. The 'states system' approach explains the evolution of one state's role in relation to the roles of other states operating within a definable pattern of international relations. The second level, or 'the nation state' explains foreign policy in terms of internal factors within the state. The third level, 'decision making', concentrates on the effect of institutional features such as the organization of the actual machinery of policy formulation and implementation. Spanier's scheme is not watertight; his levels of analysis overlap and constantly influence each other. Spanier himself refrains from indicating which level of analysis is the most important; clearly their relative significance will vary widely over time and place.

The Spanier approach has important implications for British foreign policy in the eighteenth century, particularly when considering the questions raised earlier. Were Britain and Continental Europe part of a definable 'states system'? If not, total divergence between actual foreign policies, as well as in attitude, is readily understandable. If Britain was part of such a system then the real divergence may have been quite small. Again, if Britain belonged to this system, but occupied a special place within it, the divergence could still be substantial. The second 'level' raises the question of whether 'internal' factors operated in similar ways in Britain and on the Continent. The answer probably depends on the underlying similarity or otherwise of political and social systems. We must also consider how the importance of Spanier's different levels varied between Britain and the Continent and how this changed over time.

According to Roy Jones (1974), the common meaning of 'foreign policy' is 'the actions and purposes of the state in the world beyond its own territorial boundaries'.[4] These actions and purposes will always be affected by conditions elsewhere. To quote Jones again, 'adopting traditional assumptions, foreign policy can be seen as the struggle of the state to secure congenial actions from other states'.[5] The strategies employed, the resources applied and the risks run will depend on whether the state to be influenced is near or far off, more or less powerful, than one's own. This approximates to Spanier's first 'level' of analysis. Although the behaviour of a state may be influenced by political entities physically remote, those nearer at hand will probably play a larger part in its calculations. According to Adam Watson (1982): 'Where a group of states are so involved with each other that, without their losing their independence, what one state does directly or indirectly affects all the others, it is useful to talk of a system'.[6] Although much employed by modern theorists, the concept of 'states systems' has a respectable pedigree and can be traced back at least as far as Samuel von Pufendorf's *De Systemactibus Civitatum* written at the end of the seventeenth century.

III

To what extent, therefore, was Britain part of a 'states system' in the eighteenth century or at other times? Without actually using the term 'states system', Chamberlain discusses Britain's relations with Europe and with the rest of the world largely in these terms. His conclusion appears to be 'half in and half out':

Three geographical facts have been decisive for the course of British history and explain as they dictate the main principles of British policy and the preoccupations of British statesmen. First, Great Britain is an island, but secondly this island is separated only by a narrow streak of water from the Continent of Europe. Thirdly, this island has become the centre of a wide-flung empire whose arterial roads are on the oceans and through the narrow seas.[7]

As an island state, Britain has no land frontiers. Earlier ambitions to become a Continental power, to expand like its rivals, through continental conquest had been abandoned in the sixteenth century. Since then, the sea has been both its defence and its opportunity. Britain's land forces had been kept to a minimum and were always insufficient to wage continental war, except in alliance with a great military power: '... but thrown into the scales on one side or the other in the struggle between the continental giants, their weight and the bull-dog tenacity of the race when once engaged in a fight have more than once been decisive of the issue.'[8] Britain put its defence effort into the navy and jealously guarded its superiority at sea. Its existence, certainly as an Imperial power, depended upon its ability to keep the oceans open to shipping.

The existence of a sea barrier might tempt Britain to adopt an isolationist policy and 'opt out' of any European states system. The ultimate conclusion was that Britain should not react either diplomatically or militarily *whatever* happened on the European mainland. Yet, as Chamberlain appreciated, there were powerful reasons pointing Britain towards such involvement:

The waters which divide her from western Europe are so narrow that she can never for long remain indifferent to what happens on the opposite shores of the Channel or the North Sea. Steam brought the coasts nearer and rendered the movement of ships independent of the winds which played so large a part in the days of Nelson and Cornwallis. The development of aeronautics has further impaired our insular security and given fresh force to the secular principle of British policy that the independence of the Low Countries is a British interest that their frontiers are in fact our frontiers, their independence the condition of our independence, their safety inseparable from our own. It was to secure the independence of the Low Countries that we fought Spain in the sixteenth century, that we fought Napoleon in the

nineteenth and that we fought Germany in the twentieth.
Here, at any rate, we find a permanent basis of British
policy recognized and reaffirmed by the guarantee we have
given in the Treaty of Locarno to the frontiers of Germany
and her neighbours on the West.[9]

In the 1920s, there was concern about new German
designs on the Low Countries. Britain wanted to maintain
the independence of the area, but not out of any rooted
hatred of any other power. Its attitude towards other
countries was determined by their behaviour for the time
being. Those who learned their lesson could look forward
to British forgiveness. Thus the relatively lenient treatment
of France after 1815 provided a precedent for Germany's
admission to the League of Nations and the 'equality of
status' implicit in Locarno. Chamberlain believed that a
truly isolationist foreign policy was an impossibility for
Britain for any length of time. The paradox of isolation
was that it was more likely to lead to war than to preserve
the peace. There was always a danger that a Continental
power might misread Britain's ostensible indifference and
be tempted to aggression in the Low Countries, only to
discover, too late, that Britain was as resolute as ever in
defence of its vital interests.

Yet, if Britain was an integral part of a states system
which embraced the Low Countries, did this mean that
it was also part of a larger structure covering the whole
of Europe? Chamberlain had little patience with the idea
that Britain's interests, even traditions, required involvement over a wider area. Exponents of this view, extending
the argument applied to the Low Countries, contended
that the wider the British involvement and the more extensive its guarantees, the less the probability that Britain
would ever be called upon to honour its commitments;
Chamberlain thought that this was like saying that if only
you ask enough ladies to marry you, you need never
marry at all. Britain had rarely given commitments, much
less involved itself in war on the Continent of Europe, unless
its own interests were directly at stake. There was no reason
why wars or alliance structures based on Central or Eastern

Europe should be of more than marginal concern. There had been times when Britain had gone to the assistance of its oldest ally, Portugal, and it had an interest in the approaches to the Black Sea. Yet involvement in a European states system to the extent of military intervention in support of the status quo, in areas far from Britain itself, as exemplified in episodes such as the Crimean War, was not in accordance with Chamberlain's 'permanent bases'. If Britain was rarely alarmed by territorial change in areas remote from its own shores, it was even less concerned with domestic changes in other states:

> Great Britain makes no pretensions to dictate the form of government which other nations shall adopt, but she expects that nations with which she is in formal relations shall abstain from interference in her domestic affairs, shall respect her institutions and not excite enmity against her either at home or abroad.[10]

Of course, Britain was not just concerned with the affairs of Europe. Even its European policy was influenced by non-European considerations; maintenance of its overseas possessions and communications with them was always a high priority. Sensitivity to developments in the Mediterranean owed as much to Indian as to European considerations. In areas where Britain had no strategic concerns, in places such as China, its interests were purely commercial.

Chamberlain's analysis may be simplistic and even platitudinous. It is doubtful whether British foreign policy was always so benign or so committed to peace. Yet he does provide an interesting point of departure for considering the interaction between British foreign policy and that of the country's continental neighbours. For the historian, his importance is not that he was quite a good Foreign Secretary but that he was writing at the right time. In 1931, he could view the eighteenth and early nineteenth century with some detachment. Equally, writing before the Nazi takeover in Germany, the Second World War and Britain's subsequent decline, he was perhaps closer in spirit to the

foreign secretaries of this period than to policy-makers in
the 1980s. At least he has the merit of facing up to the
problem of how far British foreign policy conformed to
Continental patterns.

The most remarkable feature of Europe in the eighteenth
and nineteenth centuries was that it contained many more
or less sovereign states, geographically in close proximity
to one another, following parallel though conflicting policies and dominated by similar cultural values. Although
regarded as 'normal' by contemporaries, this 'state system'
was unusual.

E. V. Gullick notes in *Europe's Classical Balance of
Power* (1955) that in the Middle Ages 'The vogue was for
imperial solutions of one form or another', and the idea
of a Europe composed of a number of sovereign states
would have been absurd. The power of Kings to conduct
foreign policy was limited by 'Supra-state' institutions like
the Holy Roman Empire and Papacy and by 'sub-state'
factors such as a rebellious baronage and a host of 'feudal'
privileges and anomalies – all against a background of
poor communications restricting contacts between states
at every level.

The Italian Renaissance saw the emergence of entities
displaying some of the attributes of modern states and
the appearance of foreign policy in its modern form.
The notion that the two phenomena were related is a
central theme of Jacob Burckhardt's *Civilization of the
Renaissance in Italy* (1860) and is brilliantly elaborated
in Garrett Mattingley's *Renaissance Diplomacy* (1955).[11]
But the conditions found in fifteenth-century Italy were
not found to the North of the Alps until later. Europe
could not develop a concept of foreign policy as a thing of
calculation, even as an 'art form', until notions of 'Imperial'
control had receded and the notion of the sovereignty of
states had been established. This principle appears inherent
in the Treaties of Westphalia (1648) but traces of earlier
attitudes persisted. Louis XIV aspired to an Imperial role
but his bid for hegemony was successfully resisted. From
1713 until the Revolutionary Wars of the 1790s there were
no serious bids for the 'Imperial' position. For most of

the eighteenth century the idea of Europe as a collection
of many independent and, in some senses, equal states
approximated to reality.

Perhaps the development was retrograde. Under an Imperial system, the entire area covered by the 'states system' is
ruled or dominated by one power – as in the Mediterranean
basin and the Roman Empire, Eastern Asia and Imperial
China or even the non-European world of the nineteenth
century where Britain was pre-eminent. Under this arrangement there will be prolonged periods of peace; armed
conflicts take the form of uprisings against the Imperial
power. It may involve oppressive government, extremes of
exploitation and stifling of initiative. Once established,
an Imperial system usually lasts a long time, but it can
be threatened by rebellion, by the incursion of a power
hitherto outside the system or by the decline of the Imperial
power itself.

The European states system of the eighteenth century was
a 'multiple system', characterized by a number of units of
approximately equal strength which combine and oppose
each other in ever changing alliances. Of course, the members of the system were not of equal strength. There were
five major powers (Great Britain, France, Russia, Prussia
and Austria), four secondary powers (Portugal, Spain, the
United Provinces and Sweden), and a large number of
lesser powers located chiefly in Italy and Germany. Yet
the classic features of the 'multiple system' were usually
visible, including flexibility, uncertainty and a propensity
to endemic warfare, albeit of a limited and inconclusive nature. With the exception of the Revolutionary and
Napoleonic period, the 'multiple system' continued up to
1914, although the number of states involved declined
until the 1870s.

The third or 'bi-polar system' is distinguished by the
predominance of two major powers of equal strengths
around which other smaller powers are grouped. The
system is stable so long as there is an equal distribution
of power between the two predominant members and the
subordinate powers remain subordinate to their respective
masters. There were times in the eighteenth century when

the rivalry between France and Britain came close to a 'bi-polar system', but conditions were always too fluid for the system to become established. The experience of Europe and, perhaps, the world after 1945 provides the best example of the operation of the 'bi-polar system'.

If eighteenth-century Europe was not to be subject to some Imperial figure, how were individual states to behave? The sovereignty of states meant that there was no tribunal before which rulers could be summoned. Subscription to any concept of international law had to be voluntary, not, as in an Imperial system, mandatory. States free to follow their own interests were bound to collide with other states doing the same thing. The successful state appeared to be self-conscious, amoral, absolutist and predatory. Eighteenth-century proponents of national egotism and selfishness found Machiavelli a kindred spirit. It was in Renaissance Italy, too, that a belief first emerged that the destructive tendencies inherent in a system of independent and competing states could be tempered through the operation of a 'Balance of Power'.

IV

If eighteenth-century British observers had been able to read Austen Chamberlain's article, they would have been astonished to discover that, apart from one dismissive aside, there is no mention of the Balance of Power. Most would have deplored the omission and insisted that the maintenance of the Balance of Power should have featured as one of the most important of the 'permanent bases of foreign policy'. Continental observers of the same period would have responded similarly. The maintenance of the Balance of Power became a respectable plank of policy. The Anglo-Spanish Treaty of July 1713, which committed the parties to keep the peace by adjusting their policies to the requirements of the Balance of Power, was typical of many treaties of the time.

In the late seventeenth and early eighteenth centuries, the doctrine of the Balance of Power, as conceived by a man such as William Temple, held that its object was to protect the interests of Europe as a whole. States were free to try to aggrandize themselves – with no moral blame attaching to them – but a kind of natural law would result in a combination of the weaker states resisting any aggression. The great coalition headed by William III against Louis XIV provided the most striking example of the successful working of this mechanism. Although the restraining mechanism operated primarily through war, it could also function through diplomacy. Rivalry between states was unavoidable and gave Europe a diversity and a vitality in contrast to the dead uniformity of great Empires. There appeared a direct connection between cultural achievement and the prevailing pattern of international relations. Periods notable for great achievement had usually been those characterized by acute rivalry between states and the operation of a Balance of Power mechanism. The obvious example was the Italian Renaissance but there was also another 'Happy Age', that of Ancient Greece. Gibbon declared:

> The cities of Ancient Greece were cast in the happy mixture of union and independence which is repeated on a larger scale but in a looser form by the nations of modern Europe; the union of language, religion and manners which renders them spectators and judges of each others' merit; the independence of government and interest which asserts their separate freedom and excites them to strive for pre-eminence in the career of glory.[12]

Rivalry between more powerful states would not lead to the disappearance of weaker and smaller ones. The Balance of Power was thus one of the main props of liberty and independence. Although writing in 1803, Henry Brougham put forward what essentially an eighteenth-century view of the Balance of Power.

> The European powers have formed a species of general law which supersedes in most instances an appeal to the sword, by rendering such an appeal fatal to any power that may infringe upon the others by uniting the forces of the rest inevitably against each delinquent; by agreeing that any

project of violating a neighbour's integrity shall be prevented
or avenged not according to the resources of this neighbour
but according to the full resources of every other member of
the European Community; by constantly watching over the
state of public affairs even in profound peace.[13]

There are obvious affinities between Balance of Power
ideas and the intellectual climate of the period. The word
'balance' has an eighteenth-century ring about it. Here was
a belief that some impersonal force would ensure that,
whatever the foibles of individual rulers, the fundamental
features of the existing state structure of Europe would
last indefinitely. When comparing the present condition
of Europe with the Roman Empire, Gibbon appears com-
placent. Everything was working for the best; some states
might increase their power, others go into decline, but the
essential framework would continue. Contemporaries came
to believe that the Balance of Power would operate in a
predictable way; it would render the fate of nations more certain and diminish the influence of chance, of the fortunes of
war and the caprice of individuals. The eighteenth century
was a mechanistic age – a time when, instead of trusting
in Divine Providence to look after the affairs of men, natural
laws were discovered to do the job better. The Balance of
Power was a product of the same outlook which identified
the operation of the Unseen Hand in economic matters.
In some definitions we find an explicit comparison with
Newtonian physics whose elegance and balance provided
an example for other intellectual disciplines to imitate.
Brougham likened the Balance of Power to the operation of
the Laws of Gravity, whilst Frederick the Great compared
international relations to the workings of a watch.
    Such comparisons may seem absurd but there is some-
thing to them. In some respects international relations
were uncomplicated. The trouble with trying to make
history into a science is that there are too many variables
to take into account. There were not so many variables in
international relations in the eighteenth century. In 1763
the negotiators in Paris redistributed territories amongst the
rulers of Europe without thinking they should consult the

inhabitants. Between the days when religious enthusiasms dominated much of the activities of governments and the time when popular nationalism came to possess so much influence, there was a 'window' when men could think about international relations in an unusually cool and dispassionate way. In such a world, the boast of Prince Kaunitz that he could apply 'arithmetical methods' to his diplomacy probably had some validity.

If the Balance of Power really did exist then we have an explanation for the frequent but inconclusive wars. Anything more would threaten to destroy the Balance, yet the Balance appeared indestructible. By 1720 the concept of international stability achieved through the workings of a system of conflicting forces had become securely established in the political thinking of Europe. If one accepted the existence of a balancing system one could construct one's own policy accordingly. It was obviously foolish to fly in the face of a well-attested law of nature which precluded any state from dominating the rest of Europe.

There appears to be a connection between Balance of Power ideas and eighteenth-century warfare. For all the individual acts of savagery, eighteenth-century wars were probably less horrible than those of earlier or later generations. Perhaps the new mood can be explained by the natural reaction of people who had watched Europe tearing itself apart in the Thirty Years War. The chaos inspired men like Hugo Grotius (1583–1645) to develop international law and the laws of war as means of limiting destruction and loss of life. Grotius's great work *The Law of War and Peace* insisted that there are laws of war and peace, even in a Europe of independent, sovereign and secular governments. The fact that war was held to be subject to legal principles implied a limitation on what could and could not be done. The rules of war were to be discovered from Natural Law, that is from reason, and from the Roman Law of Nations, the *Jus Gentium* which had always been considered as written reason or *ratio scripta*.

Early international lawyers tried to distinguish between wars which were just and lawful and those which were unjust and therefore unlawful. They failed because there was no international authority which could decide which side was in the right. Now they gave up the attempt to distinguish between wars and accepted that 'war is no illegality'. War could be made at the discretion of each sovereign state strong enough to wage it. There was no legal blame involved in an action such as Frederick the Great's attack at Silesia in 1740. The outbreak of war, however, brought into operation the rules of war to mitigate its severities and to protect civilian lives and property. The old practice of the internment of enemy aliens and the confiscation of their property was no longer employed. On condition of reciprocity, merchants' goods were not taken and their owners left free. A similar development took place in the case of enemy wounded and prisoners. Until the end of the seventeenth century the fate of those taken or disabled in battle was left to the discretion of their captors. Now there were treaties which stipulated that these unfortunates should be treated in a humane way. There was a general condemnation of weapons which caused unnecessary suffering in that their use did not bring any extra military advantage. Grotius himself had denounced the poisoning of wells and the use of poisoned weapons. Such a danger could not be met by military strength and would bring war uncomfortably close to those responsible.

International law did not attempt to deal with important matters such as the limitation of armaments or the prohibition of economic policies designed to ruin a neighbour. Yet even in the absence of enforcing agencies, the new ideas were accepted by states also engaged in asserting their absolute sovereignty. International law was entering a new phase. By the time of Emmerich de Vattel (1714–1767) international law became less preoccupied with war as such and more interested in the development of rules of day-to-day relations between government, a development which could reduce the number of occasions for war.

Comments on the beneficial consequences of the Balance of Power, ranging from Temple to Brougham, suggest that British attitudes to foreign policy were more intellectual and conceptual than Austen Chamberlain supposed. Yet if Chamberlain was right in thinking that the preservation of the territorial status quo in Europe normally suited Britain – and that the operation of the Balance of Power did preserve that status quo – then it would not be surprising if the maintenance of the Balance of Power became a prime objective of British foreign policy. The analytical consequences are important. A foreign policy where responses are conditioned mainly by assessments of the strength and weaknesses of other states points to the dominance of 'external' rather than 'domestic' considerations – in other words to that of Spanier's 'state system' level of analysis.

V

British policy can be described in such terms, especially if the idea of the Balance of Power is simplified into a desire to contain or balance the supposedly 'Imperial' ambitions of France. In British eyes the Balance of Power was long regarded as synonymous with an alliance of powers whose chief function was to counter France. Britain's objectives in the War of Spanish Succession were defensive. The country was not really interested in Habsburg claims to the Spanish throne, but feared French control over the Spanish Netherlands would threaten its own security. Subsidiary motives were also defensive: fear for the work of the Revolution, fear for the Protestant succession, fear for commercial interests in Europe and elsewhere. Although most of Britain's aims were secured by the Treaty of Utrecht, a sense of insecurity remained. In the 1720s there was some collaboration with France but underlying suspicion surfaced again in the 1740s. British statesmen thought that France had not given up its desire for European and colonial preponderance; the apparent moderation of France's policy was merely temporary and attributable to exhaustion after 1713.

But France could not pursue all the ambitions of Louis XIV. Cardinal Fleury had planned a decisive struggle with Britain but his plans were thwarted by the death of Charles VI and Frederick's invasion of Silesia. France was sucked into a continental war to establish French hegemony in

Central Europe. The objective was unrealizable and had
to be abandoned in the next war. France escaped with
reasonable terms in 1748 but its position in the Seven Years
War was more unfavourable and, after initial difficulties,
Britain was able to make a clean sweep of the colonial world.
Once the real threat of French hegemony had disappeared,
British foreign policy lost its lodestar: people drew various
conclusions. At one extreme, Britain itself might aspire to
the position of pre-eminence previously claimed by France.
Historians such as Sorel describe the period between 1713
and 1776 as 'the Age of English preponderance'. If such
a period ever existed, however, it was confined to the
headier days of the Seven Years War – the time when Pitt
the Elder declared that it was not enough to bring France
to its knees; the country had to be made totally prostrate.
Such sentiments scarcely suggest Balance of Power ideas.
Perhaps Britain's success in the Seven Years War had been
too great – so that other countries had to combine to cut the
country down to size. French, Spanish and Dutch support
for the American rebels could be justified in these terms.
If this is correct, Britain conformed to the European
patter of bidding for hegemony when circumstances looked
promising. But there was no such bid. The gains of 1763
were modest compared to the scale of military successes.
Britain may have been too generous. Pitt argued that Britain
should have continued fighting and make France accept
terms so severe that it would have no means of avenging
its defeat. As it was, the British desire for a quick peace
left the defeated power still in possession of means to enable
it to reverse the verdict. Britain seems to have accepted a
'Balance of Power' settlement after all.

Yet was the maintenance of the Balance of Power really
the prime objective of British foreign policy? It was always
hard to say how the Balance of Power actually operated.
In order to square with reality the theory had to be made
more elaborate. In addition to an overall Balance, stability
appeared to depend on three regional balances: in the
Baltic, Central Europe and Italy. There was little attempt
to explain how these local balances related to the larger
one. More seriously, how could one assess the strengths

of the states involved in the Balance, something that was surely essential when contemplating changing sides in order to keep things on an even keel? Statistical information was scant or of doubtful reliability but what criteria were to be adopted? Any assessment would be highly subjective – although the size of a state, its population, the revenues and competence of its government, the strength of its armed forces and its strategic position were bound to figure prominently. One assessment was made by Baron J. F. von Bielfeld whose *Institutions Politiques*, published in 1760, divides the powers of Europe into four groups. In the first rank are Britain and France, able to make war by themselves without the help of allies; in the second were Spain, Russia, Austria and Prussia, possessing considerable armed forces but lacking the financial strength to fight prolonged wars without allies; in the third were the Dutch, Portugal and Sweden whose function was to act as the auxiliaries of greater powers; in the fourth, the small states of Italy and Germany. The most difficult problem was that the Balance refused to stay still. The Balance of Power as a 'law of nature' simply refused to function in a way comparable to the orbits of the planets or the precise mechanism of a watch.

VI

The concept of the Great Power emerged soon after the doctrine of the Balance of Power. Although the two share common assumptions, they are difficult to reconcile completely. The states of Europe were never really equal: four or five were pulling ahead of the rest. The Balance of Power came to be thought of as a number of rival political systems each consisting of a Great Power and a variety of client powers. But would the Balance be affected if one or more of those Great Powers actually absorbed the territory of its former clients? The advantages of a multiple system would be diminished if there were fewer states. There would be fewer possible combinations, and the restraints of limited population and lack of resources which preserved a Europe of small states from anything approaching total war would disappear. Even the Peace of Westphalia had reduced the number of states in the German Empire from 900 to 355. For much of the eighteenth century the process of concentration seemed to have been halted sufficiently to make it plausible to argue that rivalry between the powerful states did preserve the independence of weaker ones. After the 1760s, however, the trend resumed again. The *cause célèbre* was the first Partition of Poland in 1772. Although this partition left a Polish state of a kind in existence, it was obvious a further partition resulting in the complete disappearance of Poland was likely in the near future.

The Partition of Poland was evidence of the rise to Great Power status of Prussia and Russia, occupying territory previously on the margins of the European system of international relations. Thus the area of potential conflict was enlarged to include both the colonial world and hitherto relatively uninvolved parts of Europe itself. The Partition could be defended on Balance of Power grounds in that the chief powers in Eastern Europe – Prussia, Austria and Russia – had all received a share of the booty so that the local balance of power was not altered. Yet the Partition of Poland had changed the overall balance; the importance of the Eastern, or 'Northern' Courts had increased without any corresponding increase in the power of the Great Powers of the West. In less than a century Russia, only a half-European power, had broken Swedish power in the Baltic and Turkish power in the South. The country had also done better than her partners in the Partition of Poland. Russia was still backward but was catching up fast. In fundamental ways, Western Europe had reached a hiatus. Economic difficulties were more profound than the mere embarrassment of governments. Agriculture could barely sustain the existing population and further increases would simply be wiped out by starvation. Technology was still dominated by the sheer muscle power of man and beast.

To observers contemplating the vast size of Russia, the land areas of the Great Powers of Western Europe were too small – yet the Balance of Power prevented anything more than marginal increases. There were those who were alarmed by the rise of Russia and, like Frederick the Great, urged the states of Europe to cease their squabblings lest they be overwhelmed by their Eastern neighbour. Only a decade passed between the Partition of Poland and the independence of the United States, this time creating an entirely non-European state possessing the attributes of a potential Great Power. Yet the powers of Europe did not unite to stop the rise of Russia; nor did they unite to help Britain keep her American colonies. Eighteenth-century rulers may have said that they were all part of a great European order: they did not behave as if they were. The 1780s provide the first hint of a world where the multiple system would give place to a bi-polar system dominated by North America and Russia. The implications of a Balance of Power theory, therefore, were uncertain and potentially unpleasant for thinking Europeans. Despite the apparent optimism of the intellectual climate of the eighteenth century there was a melancholy note, especially after 1760. This may be a symptom of social and economic malaise but it may also reflect the state of international relations.

Near equality amongst the Great Powers did not prevent them from following individual objectives with greater determination than ever. The existence of a broad balance resulted in less freedom of action, as enthusiasts for Balance of Power ideas were happy to acknowledge. But this did not reduce tension, rather the contrary. The slightest addition to the strength of one power had implications for the positions of all, and the range of 'knock-on' retaliation was increased. Given the internal trend towards centralization and state-fostered nationalism, restraint resulting from fears about the consequences of wholesale destruction of the broad balance was compensated by greater avidity in the pursuit of limited objectives which would not weaken the overall structure. Yet what one state might regard as adjustments within the general balance could well be seen by others as an attempt to disrupt the whole. There was 'a kind of schizophrenia' about in Europe resulting from the conflict between the desire to expand and the awareness of the need to be careful. In Meinecke's words, 'the States of Europe were ceaselessly agitated and yet always remained in fixed limits'. More and more aggression found fewer and fewer outlets. We see a transition from the headlong aggression of Frederick of Prussia in 1740 to his comment in 1776 that a village on the frontier was worth more than a province sixty miles away. Frederick appreciated that the Balance of Power had become a Deadlock of Power. The deadlock was caused by the relative decline of France, the rise of the Northern monarchies and the fact that once Russia was included there would be an equal number of Great Powers in Continental Europe.

Perhaps Britain should leave the Deadlock to itself. Constant intervention in European affairs might be neither practical nor desirable. An interventionist foreign policy involved alliance. The lack of a large standing army meant that allies were needed for effective action on the Continent. Yet allies were never very attractive. They were usually papistical and despotic, loud in their demands for large subsidies and ready to go over to the other side at a moment's notice. In fact there was a strong streak of isolationism in British foreign policy, which at first sight seems incompatible with any commitment to the Balance of Power in Europe. The English were isolationists of a kind already in that they seemed uninterested in Continental affairs. The Dutch diplomat, Bentinck, was astonished when an English nobleman told him that it mattered no more who was Emperor than who was Lord Mayor of London. Some doubted if 'The Balance of Power' had any meaning. Whatever his later position, in 1745 Pitt the Elder was very isolationist. He declared 'we have suffered ourselves to be deceived by names and sounds – the balance of power, the liberty of Europe, a common cause... without any other meaning than to exhaust our wealth.' Perhaps Britain was too isolationist in the 1760s and 1770s when it should have been forming an alliance against the threat of French resurgence. Even after the American War there was a new type of isolationism, enjoying at least the qualified support of Pitt the Younger.

Yet even a policy of isolationism requires an analysis of the situation in Europe and a conclusion that nothing is likely to happen that can threaten Britain. Earlier in the eighteenth century, Bolingbroke argued that Britain needed to interfere to preserve the European Balance of Power only occasionally and could exploit periods of strife to acquire colonial possessions for itself. Military action would be confined to naval operations; close and binding alliances could be avoided. The next step was to assert that Britain's presence was no longer needed in continental diplomacy because there was now a Balance of Power on the European mainland which could be left to look after itself. France was no longer capable of attempting a position of European preponderance. If the country were to attempt to do so, the other Great Powers would restrain it without British help. Britain would now be free to expand its power in the non-European world without let or hindrance. This analysis, put forward by Israel Maudut in the 1750s, seems at variance with Britain's role in the Seven Years War. Yet Maudut's argument is not totally isolationist. In effect, Britain is free to make continental alliances or not as seems most expedient. It is under no compulsion to seek out allies and can wait for others to approach it and then make its own terms. There are times when intervention on the Continent is attractive, but it is only a means to an end. Britain can encourage quarrels on the Continent, send subsidies to its allies, even make a military effort itself, but the prime objective is for more overseas territories.

In the Seven Years War, Britain sought to evict France from its colonies by tying the country down in Europe, leaving it without sufficient resources elsewhere. The Deadlock of Power which deprived continental states of any room for manoeuvre gave Britain unparalleled freedom of action. Because Britain was not part of that Deadlock, it could do almost as it pleased. Britain could afford to be a little capricious. As there was no danger of French hegemony, it could withdraw from Continental alliances, as it broke with Prussia in 1763, just as it entered into them – without fear of upsetting the underlying balance. The unusual position is clearly revealed in the debates about the desirability of peace or war in the early months of George III's reign.

Advocates of war did not suggest that the fighting should go on because France still had ambitions for European preponderance, neither did advocates of peace insist that the threat was now finally defeated. The issue had ceased to be of importance; it was appreciated that a Balance of Power existed and did not have to be laboriously created and maintained. Britain could regard with satisfaction a Balance in which it was not directly involved but which nevertheless it could exploit to its own advantage. The most subtle of the Renaissance tyrants would have envied Britain's position in 1763. Thus, even where Britain most obviously diverged from the Continental pattern, as in the Seven Years War, this divergence was only possible because of a particular state of affairs on the Continent. By 1782 Britain's position was less enviable. The successful rebellion in North America had so damaged Britain's prestige that some European rulers affected to believe that it was no longer a Great Power. Some supposed that Britain's decline had been long in the making and even the successes of the Seven Years War had merely masked adverse factors. British diplomatic involvement in Italy and in Poland largely ceased after the 1750s. The Diplomatic Revolution of 1756 and the consequent break with Austria meant that the Southern Netherlands were in the hands of an ally of France, an old nightmare come true.

Thereafter problems multiplied. Growing difficulties in North America were compounded by the strength of the Bourbon Family Compact. The Compact seriously weakened British influence in the Mediterranean and allowed France to annex Corsica in 1768. Over Polish Partition and the Swedish Revolution, Britain simply followed the French line. When the American War came, Britain had to fight not only its old enemies, France and Spain, but also a former ally, the Netherlands. Most of Europe rejoiced at Britain's misfortunes; the League of Armed Neutrality embracing the powers of Northern Europe was so hostile that it was almost at war with Britain. By 1780 Britain had learned what it was like to be the victim of the operation of the Balance of Power. Although the system of international relations now worked to its disadvantage, Britain was seen as the embodiment of the defects of this system. Notions of the ideal international order were changing. Even at its best, the Balance of Power theory was mechanistic and amoral. It had nothing to do with the worth of a society in terms of happiness, creativity or liberty. Significantly, anglophilia, common earlier in the century, gave way to anglophobia. Men such as Montesquieu had portrayed Britain sympathetically and presented the country as an example to the rest of Europe. The next generation was more critical. Rousseau's comments on the trickery and corruption inherent in British society were typical of the new mood. Foreign critics could cite the treatment of Wilkes and the writings of Adam Smith. Smith was critical of all European governments but most of his examples were British. A superficial reading of *The Wealth of Nations* gives the impression that the greed of British merchants had caused most of the wars of the century. The overall impression of British policy was one of cowardly reliance on subsidies or bribes, of a readiness to spill the blood of every nation except Britain, of economic greed, of capriciousness, of willingness to redistribute territories regardless of the wishes of the inhabitants. In short, Britain was the epitomy of the old order. Yet the American Revolution pointed the way out of the corruption and despotism which had brought Europe to such a low ebb. For the first time since the religious wars of the seventeenth century, ideology really mattered in foreign policy, a crucial departure from the eighteenth-century pattern. The new ideas had a wider appeal than the arid charms of 'just equilibriums' and 'balances of power'. The chief victim of the new climate was likely to be a Britain closely identified with the old and discredited system. France, however, which had come forward to help the Americans, hoped to benefit from its identification with liberty.

VII

Even in the previous section, devoted primarily to 'external' considerations, it has been difficult to exclude other factors. Perhaps the domestic factors influencing foreign policy were similar everywhere in Europe. It would be convenient if we could establish something like a European norm in terms of social structure, political ambitions and economic priorities, and then examine relations between states in terms of this norm. In other words we should have established a subsection of Spanier's 'states systems' level of analysis, the 'common domestic' level. Surely, the 'states system' approach can be applied only if a common set of domestic factors can be identified. Even allowing for differences in geography, in cultural and intellectual tradition and in economic and political organization, perhaps Britain did conform to some wider European norm. On the other hand, regardless of whether any such norm is applicable to Continental Europe, perhaps Britain differed too much from other countries for the concept to be applied at all on the British side of the Channel. The balance between 'external' and 'domestic' factors may have been radically different in Britain and, more fundamentally still, the nature of the domestic factors may have diverged profoundly from those elsewhere.

If we are to explain the diplomatic tension and frequent wars of the eighteenth century, one obvious area of investigation is in the personalities of the rulers. Personality cannot be excluded from history, especially if there are relatively few real decision makers. Between 1648 and 1789 only a few dozen people occupied the thrones of the leading states of Europe. Louis XIV, Charles XII, Peter the Great, Catherine the Great and Frederick the Great were all outstanding but difficult and aggressive personalities. They and their less remarkable contemporaries devoted much of their energies to foreign affairs. They believed that posterity would judge them to a large extent on their performance in the fields of diplomacy and war. Some at least actively sought war as a means of enhancing their own prestige. On the whole eighteenth-century English monarchs were less forceful and aggressive than most of their Continental counterparts. Yet both George I and George II saw themselves as warrior kings and both took pride in the bravery they displayed on the battlefield. All

of the Hanoverian kings were interested in military matters
and frequently appeared in military uniform. A Hanoverian
monarch who spent his entire reign at peace would have
regarded himself as a poor creature.

But international relations were not just a matter of
personalities. Whilst Charles XII of Sweden may have
wanted war for its own sake, the attitudes of figures
such as Frederick and Catherine were more complex.
Even Louis XIV on his death bed expressed regret for
the wars he had engendered. Many rulers had little option
but to implement policies likely to lead to war with their
neighbours. This view flies in the face of conventional
notions of 'absolute monarchy' and the belief that if there
ever was a time when kings could do what they liked it
was in the eighteenth century. Did not many of them
regard their lands and their subjects as their own private
property to be used as they thought fit? At all levels of
society, however, the family was more important than the
individual. The ruler's job was to administer his family's
inheritance which he was expected to pass on to the next
generation undiminished and preferably augmented. As
head of his family, a king would be failing in his duty
if he did not further the claims of cadet members of his
house to estates, or even countries, elsewhere. Louis XIV
would have been failing in his duty if he had not supported
the claims of the Duke of Anjou to the throne of Spain.
Wars could still be regarded as quarrels between families
over inheritance rights. Tangled family alliances produced
frequent opportunities for conflict, especially when death
removed many direct heirs. Most of the wars of the first
half of the eighteenth century were wars of *succession*: Spanish, Polish, Austrian or Bavarian. Similarly in diplomacy,
dynastic marriage was still of paramount importance. A
'good' marriage could enable a ruler to consolidate existing
territory or to lay the foundations of a claim to some
remote kingdom or duchy. This policy is traditionally
associated with the House of Habsburg but it was virtually
universal in eighteenth-century Europe. Britain seems to
diverge from the Continental pattern but French support
for the Jacobite cause in the 1740s meant that the War of

Austrian Succession was also in some measure the War of British Succession.

There were other 'traditional' factors which increased tensions between states. Religious issues which had proved potent sources of conflict in the past had not lost all their importance. One of the reasons for the Bourbon success in Spain was Spanish hostility to the Protestant troops used by the Habsburg claimant. Irish resistance to English rule was strongly influenced by religion. English hostility to Louis XIV was partly motivated by the identification of Catholicism with absolutism, epitomized by the Revocation of the Edict of Nantes. Religious conflicts were particularly strong in Eastern Europe; the old animosities between Catholic and Orthodox, Christian and Muslim, remained as strong as ever.

But these traditional influences were declining. By previous standards the eighteenth century was a secular age. The Church had less influence on policy-making. The spirit of religious exclusivity and persecution was on the wane. After the Thirty Years War there were no more wars of religion. The examples of England, Holland and Prussia pointed to the advantages of toleration. Even Catholic rulers were less concerned with spreading the Faith than with asserting their authority over the Church within their territories. The decline of religion as a factor in international politics is symbolized by the fate of the Jesuits, once the most militant tool of the Counter Reformation. In the 1760s they were expelled from Spain, Portugal and France, and the Order itself was abolished in 1773. The decline of 'dynastic' influence is harder to trace. Perhaps the decline of religion left the field clear for the unchallenged dominance of dynastic calculations. Many eighteenth-century rulers, however, were influenced by *philosophe* ideas and saw their duties in a different light. They came to see themselves not *as* the state – in the manner of Louis XIV – but as the *first servant of the state* – in the manner of Frederick of Prussia. What mattered now was not so much the private wishes of the king or of his family but the material and political interests of the state itself, measured in terms of territorial expansion and economic success. These rulers accepted that the state had its own rationale transcending all private interests.

We need to explore new factors in order to understand the underlying reasons for interstate rivalries. Many of the most powerful states of the previous century, such as Spain, Poland, the Ottoman Empire and Sweden, were in decline. Great Britain, Prussia and Russia were all to some extent *parvenus*; only France and Austria retained something like their old position. The elbowing aside of the 'older' powers was often achieved by military force. The 'new' states were better organized and the most successful rulers were those who concentrated decision making in their own hands. They were better placed than rulers whose powers were shared with the aristocracy, provinces, towns, estates or the Church. Such rulers tried to integrate the whole of society in their policies and to gain the co-operation of all sectors of the community. They regarded representative institutions abroad as opportunities to meddle in the internal affairs of 'Constitutional' states like Poland or Sweden. Within their own borders, representative institutions, even if permitted at all, were allowed very limited powers. With the exception of Britain, a constitutional monarchy, protected by the sea and a powerful navy and enriched by world trade, the 'rising' powers of the eighteenth century had or at least aspired to an autocratic form of government.

Many eighteenth-century rulers saw themselves as state builders; their task required them to weld together a patchwork of diverse territories with different traditions of religion, language, administration and law into one coherent whole, possessing a common identity and feeling. There were limitations on what rulers and their ministers could achieve, but the overall objective seems clear. Standing armies and large bureaucracies (tightly disciplined bodies) were intended to make their members identify less completely with local traditions and loyalties. Both provided prestigious and lucrative careers to men who in other circumstances might have proved disruptive. The growth in the size of armies could be dramatic; between 1740 and 1780 the Prussian army grew from 80,000 to 200,000 men. There was a conscious calculation that frequent wars would help to foster a national identity, rather than a local or regional one. If Prussia was an extreme case, symptoms of the same phenomenon were visible everywhere.

Another reason for the frequency of collisions between states was that the number of occasions for disputes increased dramatically. Wars were no longer solely concerned with European issues. Throughout the better part of history, several systems of international relations had existed at any one time with little or no contact between them. Thus, until the European discovery of America, relations between the tribes of North America or even the great Empires of central and South America could have had no effect whatsoever on relations between the powers of Europe. The Chinese and Indian systems had only indirect and intermittent contact with Europe. Now the whole world was being drawn into one European-dominated system. The process took a long time to accomplish and was completed only in the nineteenth century. For some time, however, European states regarded colonial wars as distinct from conflicts nearer home. In the seventeenth century, colonies were not yet considered of sufficient value to justify war between the parent states in Europe. Hence states could be at peace in Europe, even when their agents overseas were at war. Equally it was possible for states to be at peace in their colonies when they were at war in Europe.

Yet, in the long run, it was impossible to preserve the old distinctions. Colonial questions became of increasing importance in the determination of the policies of European states. The turning point came with the War of Spanish Succession; when Charles II bequeathed the Spanish Empire there could be no question of separating overseas and European territories. Henceforth the rivalries between European states were fought out on a global scale. Fighting in the West Indies was the chief cause of war between Spain and England in 1739. The Seven Years War was precipitated by fighting both in India and North America between French and British. The assimilation of the colonies into the European state system was itself another manifestation of the growth of the centralizing aspirations of the state – although, of course, such aspirations could provoke powerful, and sometimes successful, resistance from the colonial population as Britain discovered in 1776.

VIII

In the closing years of the eighteenth century, economic factors were seen as a major cause of war. Here the obvious milestone is Adam Smith's *Wealth of Nations*, which argues that the policies of all major European powers had been dominated by a set of beliefs best described as the Mercantile System. The object had been to acquire the maximum share of the world's stock of bullion, originally by straight robbery and later by a favourable balance of trade. Devices such as navigation laws, protective tariffs, export prohibitions on some things, bounties on others, favourable commercial treaties, colonies exploited for the sole benefit of the mother country and a general predilection for monopolistic practices, had all been employed to further this end. The chief beneficiary of the Mercantile System had been the merchant classes. Other groups, even the socially dominant landowners, had suffered as consumers and as taxpayers. Yet the men who determined foreign policy in the eighteenth century were usually landowners and aristocrats rather than merchants. Smith believed that the politicians and diplomats, even rulers, had been duped. They were so conscious of their own ignorance in commercial matters that they accepted the advice of merchants, the supposed experts. Governments had a vague idea that it was important to enrich their subjects, if only to enlarge their own tax revenues, but they had no understanding of the true nature of national wealth. They accepted the merchants' view that wealth could be equated with bullion. The policies consequent on this belief assumed that the amount of bullion – and hence the amount of 'wealth' in the world – was finite; one country could only become richer if other countries became poorer. The objective of governments was literally to beggar their neighbours. According to Smith, the Mercantile System had been the root cause of many of

the wars between England and France which had already
occupied a large proportion of the eighteenth century.

It is now fashionable to question Smith's analysis, and
authors such as A. V. Judges argue that the Mercantile
System was not so coherent as Smith had supposed, and
was certainly never applied in a systematic fashion to actual
policy. But it is foolish to see in the Mercantile System no
more than a figment of Smith's imagination. It is never easy
to separate economic objectives from political ones. Perhaps
Smith's real mistake lay in his failure to understand the
process whereby regional markets were giving way to national markets, and regional identities were giving way to a
degree of national consciousness.

Even in the days of the 'dynastic' state in the seventeenth
century, rulers were aware of commercial interests. Like
other landlords, kings wanted to improve their territories,
especially when experience showed that economic strength
was essential for success in war. Up to the French Revolution, states found one of their chief strengths in money;
Louis XIV declared 'Victory lies with the last gold piece'.
From the days of Colbert, nationalist economic policies and
attempts to expand state power had been closely linked.
Like diplomacy, economic policy was an adjunct of war.
Economic strength could make a state militarily powerful
whilst military power could enable it to capture a larger
share of world trade and hence a larger store of bullion.
Internal administration, economic nationalism and military
might went together. It was no good being strong in one
area and weak in another. A rich country without adequate
force or the means to tap the wealth of its people would
be easy picking. Even a country with a splendid military
tradition but with a creaking machinery of government
and inadequate revenue would find it difficult to maintain
its armed forces. The fate of Poland stood as an example
of what happened to countries which did not look after
themselves properly.

Until the eighteenth century, Western society lacked the
resources to organize stable states on a national scale; only
at the level of the city state had anything like this been possible. There, the smaller distances to be overcome brought

the problems of collecting taxes and maintaining central authority within sight of a practical solution. Concentration of population and small land area had enabled the city states of Renaissance Italy to find the resources required for the essentials of 'modern' government to an extent impossible in the 'sprawling loose-jointed Northern monarchies'.[14] They could pursue foreign policy objectives with greater continuity than Europe could show elsewhere. The presence within the limited space of northern and central Italy of several competitive, agile, efficient and predatory armed states made vigilance in foreign affairs essential to survival. Then, things had been different north of the Alps. The greater space there made the clash of states and of foreign policies less continuous and less menacing. Edward III and Henry V of England may have been aggressive monarchs, capable of conjuring formidable spurts of energy from their people, but these spurts were only occasional. Rulers who could not organize their own internal space were incapable of really sustained aggression.

This situation had changed by the eighteenth century. Europe as a whole came to resemble Renaissance Italy. Improved communications meant that the difficulties of taxation and administration were no greater in large states than they had once been in small ones. As once in Italy, the continental space of Western Europe could now be organized to make sustained military and diplomatic pressure a practical possibility. Political interstices were filling up; the margins and the cushions were shrinking. The states of Europe were being forced into a continuous and suspicious awareness of each other. Where frontiers had once been vague and frequently extensive no man's lands, they were fast becoming *lines* on the increasingly accurate maps of the period.

IX

If there were 'common domestic' factors which made war frequent and inevitable, similar factors also determined the relatively limited and inconclusive matter of such warfare. War and diplomacy were still controlled by a small group of people conscious of belonging to a common culture. After the divisions of Reformation and Counter Reformation the essential unity of European civilization was reasserting itself. The message of the *philosophes* was largely inter-nationalist. There was much talk of Europe as a Republic of Letters whilst the widespread use of French and the institution of the Grand Tour precluded the development of cultural nationalism alongside political and economic nationalism. Nor was the nobility of Europe the mere servant of various Absolute monarchs. There was still a code of honour, part feudal, part humanistic, which would limit what generals and diplomats would agree to do.

Even if they tried, as Frederick the Great tried, it was difficult for rulers of the *ancien régime* to wage total war. Total war demands total control and this was beyond eighteenth-century governments. The most absolute of absolute monarchs found his power restricted on all sides. Despite the intellectual climate of the Enlightenment, eighteenth-century rulers could not escape the remnants of feudalism. They had to contend with anomalies, privileges and immunities. Their authority was restricted by the limitations of technology, by slow communications, by illiteracy, and by the absence of such things as railways, tear gas, television, computers and closed frontiers. An *ancien régime* ruler might well make an example of a dissident nobleman, even of groups of noblemen, but he would be foolish to take on the group as a whole. The increasing difficulties of the French monarchy stemmed largely from its inability to make headway with schemes of reform in the face of noble opposition. Rulers could hardly appeal over the heads of the nobility to the patriotic feelings of the rest of the community. In many places such loyalties were to much smaller units than the state. It was difficult to rouse 'national' feeling for the simple reason that over much of Europe nations did not exist in the modern sense of the word.

There were other reasons why wars were limited affairs. In their state-building activities, rulers often attempted

more than their resources would permit. Perhaps, as contemporary physiocrats alleged, governments erected too
large a superstructure of courtiers, soldiers and bureaucrats
for the productive classes to support; eventually the weight
of taxation became so heavy that it destroyed its own
basis. Perhaps growth in the peasant population produced
a situation where the surplus available for other sections
of the community was smaller than in the past. With
the possible exception of Spain, this explanation is not
convincing. It is more likely that rulers were unable to tap
the wealth of their subjects properly. They might thus be
forced to end wars because their coffers were empty – even
though the underlying condition of their country was reasonably prosperous. Thus, recovery after a war would be fairly
rapid; another war could be undertaken but then the whole
process would repeat itself.

Eighteenth-century governments tended to be 'hard up'
and could not afford to waste their resources and assets.
Most regarded their armed forces as their most precious
asset, almost too precious to use. Quite as much as any
humanitarian motives this accounts for the nature of warfare. Although exaggerated, there is justice in Godechot's
assertion that 'warfare was turning into an affair of dainti-
ness and good manners; strategy and tactics into a pedantic
chess game which left almost no place for battle – the
confrontation of men in the supreme test of strength'.[15]
The art of war had reached an impasse. The 'military revolution' of the seventeenth century, exemplified in the victories of Gustavus Adolphus, was not sustained. Firepower
increased and armies grew in size but movement was
hampered by the dependants, camp followers, civilian
contractors and provision sellers who accompanied armies
on the march. As guns became heavier they became harder
to move along roads, abysmal almost everywhere. Above all,
defence had the edge over offence. This was the chief lesson
of the work of Vauban who developed a scientific method of
fortification. As a result, campaigns often degenerated into
a succession of drawn-out seiges. Strong points could be
taken but the effort was so great that by the time a few
fortresses had fallen the attacking armies were exhausted.

Thus, far from total war, the armed conflicts of the eighteenth century were limited wars involving only a fraction of the total human and material resources of the belligerents. Only a small part of the population was morally identified with these wars or suffered directly from them. Each war was waged for limited objectives, and hence differed profoundly both from the Religious Wars of earlier times and the Revolutionary and Napoleonic Wars later. The significance of Westphalia was that it provided what most people regarded as a permanent settlement. Even the wars of Louis XIV were seen as merely adjustments to a system which had achieved virtually universal acceptance. The crucial development is the emergence of the concept of a system of diplomacy. Wars and peace treaties all took place within that system. The great settlements in 1713, 1748, 1763, even 1783, conformed to this pattern. On the basis of what had been achieved in 1648, to a greater or lesser extent these settlements attempted to produce a European order acceptable to all. It may be difficult to say precisely what constituted the system which prevailed for so long. What matters is that the practitioners of diplomacy believed that a system existed and behaved accordingly. Wars and antagonism were not abolished but, in contrast to the international anarchy that had prevailed from the 1520s to the 1640s, it was now possible not only to systematize but also to civilize relations between states. The perennial disposition towards conflict and violence between societies is one of the distressing features of the human condition. Any period of history which makes even partial progress towards the resolution of this problem deserves attention and respect.

The restraining influences were important in Britain. Whatever the benefit of war to the merchant classes, the politically predominant landowners were required to foot the bill as taxpayers. Although war sometimes brought higher grain prices it did not do so always. Farmers might not object to wars that were short, victorious and cheap, but whenever any of these conditions was absent they tended to be eager for peace. There was little moral objection to war, except amongst Quakers, but taxes, over-enthusiastic recruitment into the army or navy, defeat, or economic distress could make war unpopular.

How far, then, did Britain fulfil the requirements of the European norm in the eighteenth century? The term *'ancien régime'* loses all meaning if applied to Britain. It is not evident that Britain was ahead of the Continent. By Continental standards Britain was modern in some respects and old fashioned in others. Nowhere was this difference more telling than in the field of foreign policy. Yet Britain enjoyed only relative immunity from those pressures which compelled Continental states to be so preoccupied with foreign policy. Even the question of national identity was not entirely absent. There was the problem of the creation of a British, as distinct from a purely English, identity. The Act of Union of 1707 can be seen as the British equivalent of the centralization found on the Continent. The flowering of the Enlightenment in Scotland was caused in part by the need to reconsider a range of political questions in the wake of the Union. In the case of Adam Smith this concern developed into a wider interest in international relations. Whatever he may have said about the Mercantile System, there was no stronger supporter of the Union than Smith, but neither the English nor the Scots accepted a common identity at once. The Jacobite Rebellions of 1715 and 1745 were attempts to reassert a specifically Scottish identity. English policy after 1745, involving the construction of military roads, the suppression of Highland dress and culture and the extensive recruitment of Scottish soldiers into the British army, followed very much the lines one would expect from a Continental Absolutist state in similar circumstances.

The Jacobite risings raised other issues common on the Continent. They showed that the dynastic issues, whether the population regarded Stuarts or Hanoverians as their 'true' kings, had not disappeared. They suggested that England was not so secure as it seemed. There were recurrent fears of invasion from across the Channel and such possibilities were taken seriously enough in the Seven Years War and in the American War to prevent the despatch of fleets to colonial waters. Perhaps the fears of invasion were exaggerated but the Jacobite risings pointed to a back door route into England. The Jacobite attempts would not have been possible without French assistance, however hesitant. The Jacobite cause was dead after the failure of the '45 rebellion, but there remained the more intractable problem of Ireland, with its separate Parliament, its economic grievances and its Protestant and Catholic communities resentful of many features of what they regarded as English rule. Given France's success in humbling Britain by assistance to the American rebels, the Court of Versailles might well apply the same tactics to Ireland. Thus, if Continental powers had no territorial claims on the British Isles they had opportunities in plenty for exploiting internal discontent.

Similarly, Britain had territorial interests of a kind on the Continent. From 1714 to 1837 the King of England was also Elector of Hanover. Other states had designs upon Hanoverian territory and, at least in the days of George I, Hanover wanted more territory for itself. If there had been any amalgamation of all the territories ruled by George I and his successors then the resources of Britain would have been committed to the defence, even aggrandisement, of Hanover. In short, Britain would have been compelled to give the same priority to foreign policy – and all that entailed – as any Continental power. Of course, there was never any possibility of an Act of Union between Britain and Hanover, and the two territories went their separate ways. On occasion George I tried to gain extra help for the Electorate but his British ministers would never agree to participate in a war for the benefit of Hanover but of no conceivable advantage to Britain. Later Hanoverian monarchs accepted and sometimes exploited their split role. There was no obligation upon George III to consult British ministers about Hanoverian policy and his decision to join the Furstenbünd in 1785 undoubtedly annoyed Pitt and Carmarthen. In theory there was nothing to stop George III going to war against himself, and several times in the eighteenth century Hanover made peace with a country still at war with Britain. Yet there were many who believed that the connection between Britain and Hanover was still too close. In 1742 Lord Chesterfield claimed that Hanover deprived Britain of the benefit of being an island, whilst Pitt the Elder was well known for his denunciations of 'that despicable electorate'. But even those who advanced such ideas did not act without regard to Hanover. As Secretary of State in 1747, Chesterfield was to conclude the first Anglo-Russian subsidy treaty to guarantee Hanover against a Prussian attack, a development which, from the standpoint of the later eighteenth century, seemed contrary to the true interests of Britain. The sensitivity to Hanoverian interests reflected the continued importance of the monarchy in British politics. Even Pitt the Elder admitted that British governments could not afford to allow George II to lose his German possessions as a result of a war fought for the benefit of Britain. So long as the king was reasonably effective in British politics and conscious of his obligations to Hanover, governments in London would be reluctant to abandon their master's German homeland.

Concern for Hanover as territory belonging to the King of England was a factor in British policy but there were other reasons for interest in Hanover and neighbouring parts of Europe. As Austen Chamberlain appreciated, the real problem was that the Narrow Seas were too narrow for comfort. It was a fundamental objective of British policy to ensure that as little as possible of the coast opposite its own should be in the hands of a potentially hostile power. In the days of sail the British fleet could be kept in port by adverse winds, the same winds that could carry an invasion force across the Channel or North Sea. The implications of the story of 'the Protestant Wind of 1688' were alarming in the extreme. A high price was often paid to secure British objectives. In 1748 Britain had to give up all its colonial conquests in order to secure French withdrawal from the Low Countries. Some colonial gains were made in the knowledge that they would have to be 'traded in' at the next peace treaty in order to neutralize French gains in the Netherlands. Hanover was almost as important as the Low Countries. Hanoverian territory included the mouths of the Elbe and Weser, giving the Electorate a position of great economic and strategic importance. Under no circumstances could it be allowed to fall into the hands of

the French. In the event, Hanoverian calculations played
an important role in the Diplomatic Revolution of 1756.
As Prussia now thought itself threatened by Austria and
by Russia, Newcastle decided to use a new Anglo-Russian
subsidy treaty to force upon Frederick an agreement safe-
guarding Hanover in return for the lifting of the Russian
Treaty. Once war started the remarkable achievement of
Ferdinand of Brunswick in keeping the French invaders of
Hanover at bay enabled Britain to make sweeping colonial
gains which, unlike the country's experience of previous
wars, she could actually hope to keep.

It was not only the personal connection with Hanover
but the institution of the monarchy itself which brought
Britain closer to the European 'norm'. Despite differences
about the role of the monarch, it was generally agreed that
the king's opinion should carry a great deal of weight in
foreign affairs. This was partly a matter of tradition. There
was also the consideration that many European monarchs
conducted their own foreign policies and wished to deal
directly with other heads of state, not with ministers who
came in and out of office. The Kings of England were
related to many other European royal families and links
were particularly close with Protestant Germany. Family
connections could not be ignored in the formulation of
foreign policy. Although Kings of England never went so
far as to develop a *secret du roi* similar to that of the Kings
of France, they could always employ Hanoverian diplomats
to do things they did not wish their British ministers to
know about.

It was, however, in the role of Parliament that Britain
seemed to differ most sharply from the Continental norm.
Continental observers despaired of making sense of British
foreign policy precisely because there were so many interest
groups represented in Parliament whose votes ministers had
to try to solicit. It was a situation which seemed certain
to produce frequent volte-faces in policy. Governments
had to discuss their foreign policy and even reveal things
they would rather not reveal to ignorant and raucous back
benchers. Experience of Parliamentary debate might cause
a government to change its foreign policy. More likely,

an administration might fall over an unrelated matter and the new set of ministers would bring in a new foreign policy. Opposition leaders rarely considered it wrong to intrigue with foreign ambassadors. The press could be uninhibited in its comments on foreign sovereigns, men who refused to believe that such attacks did not have official approval. In the 1760s foreign policy seemed to change from day to day. The spectacle convinced men such as Frederick the Great that England could not be a reliable ally – that it was *Albion Perfide* precisely because Parliament was so powerful. There were occasions in the eighteenth century when, as with the fall of Walpole in 1742 and the fall of North in 1782, parliamentary opposition to the foreign policy of the government of the day was the major reason for its defeat. In this respect the constitutional system operating in Britain places the country not amongst the more successful of the European states but amongst the least successful. In unsuccessful and visibly declining states such as Poland, for example, foreign policy was controlled by the Diet – many of whose members received bribes from other rulers in order to encourage them to cause the maximum amount of trouble.

Britain's strategic position was more favourable than Poland's and it could afford a measure of political licence dangerous elsewhere. In any case the constitutional position of Britain is open to misunderstanding. The distinction between 'absolute monarchies' and 'constitutional states' frequently applied to eighteenth-century Europe may be too arbitrary. In some respects Britain was not a 'constitutional' state at all. Its central government was more powerful than that of Poland or the United Provinces, and arguably more effective than that of France. In domestic matters Kings of England were subject to all kinds of constraint but their theoretical power over foreign policy remained absolute and unlimited. There was nothing in England to compare to the Swedish Law of 1773 prohibiting contact between the king and Swedish diplomats abroad. The apparent discrepancy between royal power in domestic and foreign affairs was noted by de

Lolme. Much of the power theoretically assigned to the king did not reside in the person of George III but in 'the Crown'. The Crown meant the executive government, ministers and king together. The coherence of British policy might be weakened if the two elements were at variance and the king sought to enlarge his personal power by launching initiatives independently of his ministers. Royal initiatives of this kind, though they did occur, were the exception rather than the rule. Discussions about the relationship between king and ministers should not blind us to the fact that the two elements together possessed a degree of control over foreign affairs which some apparently more absolutist regimes might envy.

The point was made by Blackstone who insisted that by its nature foreign policy could not be conducted by popular assemblies but belonged to the Crown in which had been vested the sole prerogative to make war and peace and to conclude all treaties. The doctrine was uncontroversial, and even those who disapproved of a particular aspect of foreign policy did not dispute the underlying theory. In February 1783 Lord Stormont, speaking against the Preliminary Articles of Peace, pointed out that in limited governments such as Sweden 'before the late revolution' and in Poland, no treaty of peace could be valid without ratification by the Estates. In Britain, however, the prerogative of the Crown alone could conclude a treaty of separation with the American rebels. The Constitution had wisely placed the making of peace or war in the hands of the executive power. God forbid that this privilege should ever be wrested from it!

There was, therefore, a long-standing tradition that foreign policy was a mystery of state with which ordinary MPs should not meddle too much. That there were debates in Parliament about foreign affairs in no way detracts from this point. Many were 'window dressing' debates where ministers gave away as little as possible. In fact the limitations on the executive had weakened. In the days of the Stuarts, Parliaments had at least tried to control foreign policy; after 1714 they gave up except in extreme circumstances. For the most part, governments could pursue their policies unhindered because these policies were seen as fairly successful and conforming to the representations of crucial economic interest groups. The situation would change if these criteria were not met – as in 1782 – but the fact remains that the executive was less restricted in foreign policy than in domestic affairs. Despite appearances to the contrary, it is necessary to include Britain in the generalization that successful states were those where vital decisions were kept in few hands and where foreign policy was not controlled by fractious estates.

X

To a surprising extent, therefore, Britain conformed to a pattern of 'common domestic' factors observable elsewhere, but investigation of Spanier's third 'institutional' level may still lead to the conclusion that British foreign policy could not conform to a 'European' pattern. Apart from anything else, it would be difficult to produce a coherent foreign policy if the structure of decision making was confused. There had been discussion about this earlier in the century. In 1701 the House of Lords suggested that William III should establish a Council to discuss all affairs of importance, both at home and abroad. A few years later, Abraham Stanyan proposed a Council, composed of professional diplomats, which would advise the King on foreign policy. These proposals came to nothing and foreign policy was still determined at the formal level at meetings of the Privy Council. If there was a trend to greater coherence, it was a reflection of the increasing importance of the Cabinet. On the face of it, a small body of professional politicians, having a common interest in its own political survival, should have provided an ideal institution for the discussion and formulation of foreign policy. This body could take executive decisions itself or make unanimous recommendations to the King.

Although more logical and less 'centrifugal' than the cumbersome arrangements found in 'declining' states such as Poland, the system was not ideal. Responsibility for specific areas of government business – or what seem specific areas to twentieth-century eyes – was divided between two or more ministers. The confusion was obvious in the field of foreign affairs, where, until 1782, responsibility was shared between the Secretary of State for the Southern Department and the Secretary of State for the Northern Department. Both appointments carried domestic responsibilities. There was a danger that the two Secretaries, leaders of different political factions, rivals as much as colleagues, would follow diametrically opposed foreign policies. Institutional factors could produce a situation in which it was impossible to identify British foreign policy with certainty. Here at least there seems to be a fundamental disparity between Britain and the Continent where things were better organized. This was precisely the point made by George III when, in 1771, he urged the establishment of a centralized ministry of Foreign Affairs on Continental lines. In the event, it was only after the fall of Lord North's government, when royal influence was much reduced, that the suggestion was implemented. The Rockingham Ministry finally abolished the old system and turned the two Secretaries of State into a Foreign Secretary and a Home Secretary.

How crucial was this reform? Perhaps Britain was catching up with the true 'diplomatic revolution' of the eighteenth century, the trend towards the concentration of foreign policy formulation and co-ordination under a specialized ministry of foreign affairs. This was as important to the establishment of a mature system of international relations as permanent diplomatic contact achieved some two centuries earlier. Yet the institutional disparity between Britain and Europe before 1782 can be exaggerated. George III was not quite correct; there were many states apart from Britain where responsibility for foreign affairs was divided between more than one minister. Similarly it would be foolish to make too much of the significance of the reforms of 1782. The creation of a Foreign Office headed by a Cabinet Minister was a move in the right direction. In the long run it would contribute to the recovery of Britain's influence after its defeat in the American War. But the reform made little difference to the day-to-day conduct of affairs. Until 1793, the Foreign Office was physically divided, as under the old system, part in Cleveland Row, St James's and part at the Cockpit in Whitehall. The two sections were brought under one roof when the Foreign Office moved to Downing Street. Everything about the new establishment was marked by penny-pinching and general philosophy of 'make do and mend'. The actual buildings were leased from Lord Sheffield and Sir Samuel Fludyer. With various piecemeal additions they remained the home of the Foreign Office until they were demolished in 1861. The buildings were not kept in good order and the roof collapsed in 1852. Sir Horace Rumbold gives an unflattering description of the working conditions:

> Dingy and shabby to a degree, made up of dark offices and labyrinthine passages – four houses at least tumbled into one, with floors at uneven levels and wearying corkscrew stairs that men cursed as they climbed – a thorough picture of disorder, penury and meanness.[16]

The staffing of the Home Office was as modest as its accommodation. According to Parliamentary Commissioners who reported in 1786, in addition to the Foreign Secretary, there were two Under-Secretaries, a chief clerk, nine other clerks, two Chamber Keepers and a Necessary Woman. There were also several sinecures, or virtual sinecures, attached to the office. These included the Gazette Writer, the Deputy Gazette Writer, the Keeper of State Papers, the Collector and Transmitter of State Papers and the Secretary for the Latin Language.[17] The Commissioners appear to have missed the existence of two Decipherers and a number of messengers. They explained that the two Under-Secretaries ran the Office whilst the Chief Clerk acted as the accountant. They concluded with an opinion that there was not enough business to keep all the staff fully occupied and recommended a reduction in the number of clerks.

One of the Under-Secretaries was essentially a political appointment, the other filled by a civil servant. The political Under-Secretary was usually a Member of Parliament. Most Foreign Secretaries were Peers and it was useful to have a

man who could act as a government spokesman in the House
of Commons. It took many years before there was a clear
understanding of the roles of the two Under-Secretaries.
They shared responsibilities and operated a type of extended
shift system:

> We are very like the two figures in the Weather House and
> rusticate and labour alternately, so that if the office were left
> vacant for a short time, it would only be if one of the two
> were in the country recovering from his fatigues.[18]

Of the staff of clerks, seven were copyists, a group that
sometimes displayed surprising militancy. At the time of
the Eden Treaty they complained they were being forced to
work beyond their normal hours and successfully demanded
extra payment. The two remaining clerks, the précis writer
and the Private Secretary, were men of greater importance,
usually young and hoping to take up a diplomatic career.
Over the years there was a trend towards greater efficiency
but the general atmosphere remained that of a down-at-heel
family business. Some of the clerkships in the Foreign
Office were virtually hereditary; four generations of the
Bidwell family served in the Foreign Office or its predecessors from 1767 to 1872.

Whatever economies the Commissioners of 1786 recommended, the resources applied to the day-to-day running of
the British foreign policy appear sadly inadequate, especially
when compared to the larger staffs at foreign ministries in
Paris or Madrid. On one occasion Sir James Harris arrived
at the Foreign Office in normal working hours to find the
whole place locked up for no obvious reason. Sometimes
important treaties were mislaid, or pressure of business
meant that British envoys abroad received no instructions
for months on end. Ambassadors frequently disregarded
their instructions or dismissed them as worse than useless.
Harris said that he had never received an instruction worth
reading. Diplomats thought that parliamentary business
took up too much of the clerks' time. The priority given to
political matters could produce a standstill in negotiations
going on abroad. When a session was in progress, a

Foreign Secretary was too busy in Parliament to give much thought to the content of instructions to be sent to ambassadors overseas.

Foreign policy necessarily involves contact with other governments. One channel of communication was between the Foreign Secretary and foreign ambassadors resident in London. This channel was used but it had its drawbacks. It might be impossible to discover if the ambassador concerned had given an accurate version of the British position in reports back to his own masters. Such a system, unlike the more normal procedure of issuing instructions to British diplomats overseas, left no official documents which the Foreign Secretary could 'refer to for the rectitude of his own conduct'. There was too much danger of misunderstanding and accusations of bad faith. Further, contact between the Foreign Secretary and overseas ambassadors was often hampered by language difficulties. Many Foreign Secretaries possessed little more than the rudiments of French whilst many foreign agents in London had no knowledge of English. The first Foreign Secretary, C. J. Fox, spoke excellent French but it is significant that this ability attracted so much notice. As late as 1815, the British delegation at the Congress of Vienna had to call upon Hanoverian assistance to translate some of Castlereagh's papers into French.[19]

To add to problems of institutional weakness and periods of mediocre leadership, there was also the difficulty of slow communications, a difficulty which affected all governments more or less equally – except that in Britain's case the importance of contacts with the non-European world made it worse than for states with purely Continental interests. Letters to and from British representatives abroad took weeks, even months, to reach their destination. By the time the letter arrived, the situation it was supposed to deal with might have changed beyond all recognition. Worse still, diplomatic correspondence was liable to be intercepted and read by interested parties en route. All this points to the crucial importance of British diplomats acting in accordance with broad instructions issued from London but, of necessity, given discretion to act on their own initiative. In the 1780s the activities of ambassadors

such as Eden and Harris were as important to the success
of British foreign policy as any decisions taken in London.
Not everyone approved; Edmund Burke claimed that,
instead of controlling their ambassadors properly, British governments usually allowed these men to determine
actual policy.

Of course, there were only a few who could exercise
power on this level. Those most likely to fit Burke's picture
were the minority with full ambassadorial status. Only the
posts in Paris, The Hague and Madrid were always held by
Ambassadors, although representatives in St. Petersburg,
Vienna and Berlin were increasingly likely to hold this
rank. Other courts had to make do with men of lesser
importance who might be superseded by a fully fledged
ambassador if the political situation required. There were
no British embassies as such, and each envoy had to lease
a suitable property. During his tenancy the house would
be graced with the Royal arms above the door.

It is hard to deny that there was much about the conduct
of British foreign policy that was marked by amateurism
and incompetence, although Britain was by no means
unique in this respect. This is certainly the impression
given by the Select Committee on Diplomatic Salaries which
reported in 1861. The Committee's report stated that, in the
eighteenth century, the conduct of international relations
had been based largely on considerations relating to 'the
social convenience and advantage of the upper classes of
the community'. Political calculations had been paramount
in appointments. Diplomacy had been less of a career than
as an excuse for foreign travel. The entire edifice had been
permeated by corruption and incompetence. The Report's
conclusions seem in accordance with contemporary anec-
dotal evidence, at least for the first three-quarters of
the eighteenth century. When Bute left to take up the
Embassy to Madrid, his secretary observed that he was 'as
fit to be ambassador as I am to be Pope of Rome'. Lord
Chesterfield's view was that:

> Most of our ministers abroad have taken up that department
> occasionally, without having ever thought of foreign affairs

before; many of them without speaking any one foreign language and all of them without the manners which are absolutely necessary towards being well received and making a figure at foreign courts.[20]

If this picture even approximates to the truth, then foreign policy cannot have made much of a contribution to the standing of Britain in world affairs in the eighteenth century, or to her recovery after 1782. Indeed, perhaps the recovery was achieved in spite of the activities of diplomats and foreign secretaries. According to this view, what really mattered in the re-establishment of British influence were such things as the strength of the Navy, the size of the Empire, the stability of political and social institutions and the magnitude of industry and commerce. What was diplomacy compared to these? Without them, a Palmerston, even a Grenville, would have been ridiculous. After all, what does foreign policy involve if not the winning of friends and allies? Surely those countries which wanted to be friends with Britain would have been friends in any case, without all the trappings of embassies and treaties. Perhaps the whole thing was no more than an expensive, elaborate and irrelevant farce.

But such a view is naive and the picture of eighteenth-century diplomacy conveyed by the 1861 Report is misleading. Like many Victorian judgements on the previous century, it makes too sharp a distinction between the efficiency of the present and the incompetence of the past. Few of the witnesses before the 1861 Committee had any idea of what had been normal diplomatic practice before the 1820s.[21] This is not to say that mistakes were never made. Whatever his other qualities, Castlereagh was a poor judge of men and some of his appointments at a crucial stage in the Napoleonic Wars proved singularly unfortunate. But the case for regarding the eighteenth-century diplomatic service, especially as it functioned after 1782, as hopelessly incompetent is not sustainable. The evidence points to a growing professionalism. There was an established system of promotion through a series of grades. There were even retirement allowances regulated by the state. Diplomacy was established as a career and had ceased to be regarded as a temporary job involving residence abroad. Even the political dimension was becoming less important. In the 1780s the most influential member of the diplomatic service was Sir James Harris, later Lord Malmesbury, who was recognized as a specialist and was employed by British governments of all political complexions. In short, the machinery for taking and implementing decisions about foreign policy was being improved. The system still had some odd quirks but, provided the right decisions were taken, there is no reason to suppose that sheer administrative muddle prevented Britain resuming its interrupted career of increasing influence in world affairs. It would be wrong to suppose that the foreign ministers of other European countries were models of efficiency. This is evidenced by the experience of Britain's second Foreign Secretary who, as Ambassador of Spain in the early 1770s, had been able to walk into the Foreign Ministry in Madrid, unstaffed but unlocked on an important religious holiday, and there peruse secret Spanish documents undisturbed!

In many ways, Britain and Continental Europe were very different but diplomats could not be typical reflections of British society; they needed to have some understanding of their host country as well. Diplomacy was a means of linking Britain with the Europe of the *ancien régime*. The very fact of having a foreign policy and a diplomatic service was to subscribe to a European norm. For good or ill, well into the nineteenth century, most foreign secretaries and most diplomats were still imbued with many of the assumptions of the *ancien régime*. Ever since the Renaissance there had been a widespread belief that diplomacy was a proper, perhaps the most proper, career for a gentleman. Those who believed that the upper classes of Europe were united in a common culture naturally wished to meet gentlemen in other countries, to exchange ideas with them and to be attached to brilliant Courts on the Continent. At its lowest level, diplomacy was an ideal way of prolonging the delights of the Grand Tour; at its highest it could be equated with civilization, involving a commitment to a unique way of life and to a social and international order of a very special kind. One thinks of Castlereagh's passionate defence of the gift of expensive presents to foreign ambassadors and their entourages – certainly a matter of observing the social courtesies but also a sign of commitment to the values those courtesies represented.

In the task of linking with the Europe of the *ancien régime*, the role of the diplomat was of central importance. The existence of a diplomatic profession did not imply a universal desire for peace. It was precisely because it was necessary to keep an eye on the activities of other states that permanent diplomatic representation became essential. In the sixteenth century, European rulers regarded ambassadors as little better than spies. There have been few periods when diplomacy has been free from all suspicion of espionage. Yet peaceful contacts between states were necessary; such were the mutual suspicions that if negotiations were to take place, special privileges and protection had to be afforded to the representatives of foreign powers enabling them to go about their business without interference. In earlier periods diplomatic envoys were regarded as subject to the Courts of the host state. This system was based on the notion that it was the duty of all rulers to enforce a universally acknowledged body of law in the area of their own territories. As nation states became more distinct, however, this view was no longer tenable. It became necessary to develop the concept of the extra-territoriality of ambassadors.

In the eighteenth century diplomatic representatives were divided into two categories: ambassadors who were obliged to vie for precedence at Court and senior official agents or chargés d'affaires who were less involved in Court functions and normally had fewer powers. It was then that the complicated business of the protocol, the names, the procedures, the special language, the *ritual* of diplomacy – the surest sign of the emergence of a profession – became established throughout Europe. To later generations this ritual might seem pointless but it did reduce opportunities for dispute and inculcated qualities of patience and tranquillity which were vital to the peaceful settlement of disputes. This process was assisted by the trend towards the establishment of ministries of foreign affairs staffed by professional advisers.

But if diplomacy linked Britain with the Europe of the *ancien régime* it did not make Britain part of that Europe. British conditions were diverging even further from those found on the Continent and British diplomacy would have to reflect that fact. The *ancien régime* had only a few more years to run. Almost everywhere there could be seen evidence of aristocratic, middle-class and even peasant discontent. In 1782 it still seemed possible that Britain might be the chief victim of these pressures. It soon became apparent that it was not Britain but the Europe of the *ancien régime* proper that was the more vulnerable. Britain had the capacity to compromise with the new forces in a way impossible elsewhere. The convulsion on the Continent that followed the collapse of the *ancien régime* threatened to destroy some of the better features of the international system of the eighteenth century. Perhaps there was a danger of a reversion to international barbarism on a scale not seen since the Thirty Years War. It was in Britain's interest, as much as that of the rest of Europe, to show that it was possible to preserve the best features of the old system but alongside a more modern political, economic and social structure than anything found in Continental Europe before 1789. The British example did suggest that such a development might be possible. Even so, the tasks demanded of British diplomacy in the closing days of the *ancien régime* looked formidable in the extreme.

In conclusion, therefore, it would seem that the 'states system, mode of analysis is applicable to the study of British foreign policy in the eighteenth century – perhaps to a greater degree than is usually appreciated. It may be that it should even be given pride of place over other modes. Nevertheless the situation was extremely complex. On the one hand British foreign policy was still in the hands of men who shared many of the values and priorities of their Continental counterparts. There was, perhaps, a greater degree of institutional similarity between Britain and the major Continental states than some historians have been prepared to concede. On the other hand, British society had never conformed completely to the patterns observable on the other side of the Channel, and the difference seemed to be increasing. Soon the pattern of British foreign policy would be complicated by the rise of social and economic groups who might entertain very different ideas about the nature of the national interest. It was not even a question of straightforward recovery of Britain's position after the American disaster; rather, of what form that recovery should take. If Britain was 'evolving' away from the world of the eighteenth century, other forces were at work on the Continent which would soon produce a far more dramatic break with the past. The task of 'making sense' of foreign policy would now become harder than ever.

NOTES: CHAPTER 1

1 Austen Chamberlain, 'The permanent bases of British foreign policy', *Foreign Affairs*, Vol. 9, no. 4, July 1931, pp. 535–46.
2 Ibid., p. 537.
3 Chamberlain, op. cit., quoting Salvador de Madariaga, *Disarmament*, New York, Coward McCann, 1929.
4 Roy Jones, *The Changing Structure of British Foreign Policy*, London, Longman, 1971, p. 11.
5 Ibid., p. 13.
6 A. Watson, *Diplomacy: The Dialogue Between States*, London, Methuen, 1982, p. 6.
7 Chamberlain, op. cit., p. 538.
8 Chamberlain, op. cit., p. 538.
9 Chamberlain, op. cit., p. 538–9.
10 Chamberlain, op. cit., p. 542.
11 Jacob Burckhardt, *The Civilization of the Renaissance in Italy* (1860), (translated by S. G. C. Middlemore), London, Phaidon Press, 1951; G. Mattingley, *Renaissance Diplomacy*, London, Jonathan Cape, 1955.
12 Edward Gibbon, *The Decline and Fall of the Roman Empire*, with notes by J. B. Bury, London, Methuen, 7 vols., 1905–6, Chapter 53.
13 Henry Brougham, *Works*, London and Glasgow, R. Griffen & Co., 1855–61, vol. 8, pp. 11–12.
14 Mattingley, op. cit., p. 59.
15 J. Godechot, *France and the Atlantic Revolution of the Eighteenth Century, 1770–1799*, (translated by Herbert H. Rowen), London, Collier Macmillan, 1965, p. 2.

16 R. Jones, *The Nineteenth Century Foreign Office, An Administrative History*, London, Weidenfeld & Nicolson, 1971, p. 11.
17 *First Report: Secretaries of State*, British Parliamentary Papers, 1806, (309) VII, p. 10.
18 Quoted in C. K. Webster, *The Art and Practice of Diplomacy*, London, Chatto & Windus, 1961, p. 190.
19 D. B. Horn, *Great Britain and Europe in the Eighteenth Century*, Oxford, 1967, p. 15.
20 4th Earl of Chesterfield, *Letters*, (ed. B. Dobree), 6 vols., London, Eyre & Spottiswoode, 1932, vol. 1, p. 114.
21 D. B. Horn, *The British Diplomatic Service, 1689–1789*, Oxford, Clarendon Press, 1961, p. 13.

2

Recovery and War
1782–1801

Many Europeans believed that Britain could never recover from the loss of her American colonies. Those who applied the techniques of the Mercantile System to their own territories could appreciate the consequences of the loss of large protected markets. Once the Americans could make things that were previously prohibited, or import what they needed from any quarter, there might be a drop in British exports and a corresponding crop of British bankruptcies. There would be fewer British vessels crossing the Atlantic, causing a corresponding reduction in the number of trained seamen available for the Royal Navy. Such was the ill-will against the British that the Americans would now trade with their friends rather than their former oppressors. Britain's re-export trade in tobacco and sugar would suffer. The independence of the Thirteen Colonies would affect the rest of the Americas. Even if Britain managed to retain its West Indian islands, planters would not longer obtain supplies from North America, thus increasing costs and making British sugar uncompetitive. Such damage could only reduce the wealth which was the basis of taxation; from now on the British government would be less free with the subsidy treaties which had made it so formidable in the past.

By 1782 the British had abandoned the American theatre but the war with France and Spain continued. The French

Foreign Minister, Vergennes, talked of regaining Canada
and the other losses of the Seven Year War. If the anti-
British alliance could be tightened and the war continued,
Britain could be humbled more completely than France
in 1763. France had recovered and had advantages which
Britain did not possess – a larger population and more
fertile land. The glories of the Seven Years War had been
just a dream; Britain's role in world history was destined
to be marginal. The 'Age of English Preponderance' had
always been a doubtful concept; even the possibility of
this occurring had now disappeared. This development
was not regretted. In the past Britain had deserted Austria
and then Prussia. If the country had no friends it did
not deserve any. In comparison, French policy, the long-
standing alliance with Spain and support for the cause of
liberty, seemed a model of constancy and honour. News of
British defeats in America had been received with delight
everywhere in Europe. There were some, not necessarily
fools, who believed that the future lay with the House
of Bourbon.

The position was not really so bad. Those who predicted
the eclipse of Britain either deceived themselves or lied for
their own political reasons. Britain was still more formidable amongst the nations of Europe than in 1700. It had
acquired a large colonial Empire, impressive even without the Thirteen Colonies. Once Britain had accepted
the loss of America it could warn European enemies that
the war would go on unless they were prepared to leave the
country's empire intact. The military achievements of the
Bourbon powers had been unimpressive. France had gained
a few Caribbean islands whilst the Spaniards had captured
Minorca and Florida. Apart from America, however, the
war was now turning Britain's way. The Spaniards made
their final, unsuccessful attack on Gibraltar. Attempts
by Suffren and Bussy to revive France's power in India
achieved nothing. At one stage it had looked as if Britain
might lose naval supremacy, but on 12 April 1782 Admiral
Rodney defeated the French at the Battle of the Saintes. The
Caribbean was now safe and the French could be expelled
at leisure from their West Indian conquests.

There were many reasons for Britain's strength. The
country had a larger number of trained seamen and a
bigger shipbuilding capacity than either France or Spain.
Whatever happened in the early stages of a war, Britain
could outbuild its enemies who soon found themselves
unable to replace their losses or man their fleets with proper
crews. This had been the reason behind the disastrous
French showing in 1759; by 1782 the story was about to
repeat itself. There was also a financial factor. Either
because or in spite of government policy, Britain had
become much richer during the eighteenth century. It had
a reasonably modern financial system, the capacity to tap
at least some of the nation's increased wealth through the
taxation system and access to loans on reasonable terms.
Britain was better placed than France, the governmental
finances of which were chaotic. Its efforts in North
America had saddled France with a terrible financial burden. Even if opportunities for the further dismemberment
of the British Empire had arisen, France could not have
exploited them for lack of funds. Although Britain was war
weary, its finances were fundamentally sound; if the need
arose, subsidies could still be provided to allies on a scale
France could not match. Britain's position in 1782 was like
a sudden dip on a rising graph. Even so, a foreign policy
demanding care, ability and vigilance would be needed to
effect a complete recovery.

Britain's first Foreign Secretary was Charles James Fox,
notorious for his support of the American rebels and his
denunciations of Lord North and of the King himself.
Paradoxically, the reforms of 1782 represented a belated
recognition of the unity of the European states system
– on the eve of the disintegration of the system in its
old form. In the past, the Baltic powers were treated as
belonging to a states system distinct from Western Europe.
That the distinction was not artificial is attested by the
separate existence of the War of Spanish Succession and the
Great Northern War earlier in the century. The distinction
between 'Northern' and 'Southern' departments was not
just a British eccentricity; it was repeated in the supposedly
more logical Prussian system. In the British case, however,

the amalgamation of the two departments did not resolve the problem of overlapping authority and many anomalies persisted. The Barbary Consuls remained under the Home Office until the middle of the nineteenth century. The reforms did not affect negotiations with the American rebels, France and Spain. Fox was responsible only for negotiations with Europe. Something like American independence might exist in practice, but any dealings with the rebels were still the responsibility of Lord Shelburne, Secretary of State for Home and Colonial Affairs. The long-standing personal animus between Fox and Shelburne, the inevitable problems caused by overlapping responsibility and divergent analyses of the international situation weakened the effectiveness of British foreign policy.

At least Fox knew what he wanted to do – although in some respects his views were surprisingly old fashioned. He hated the Bourbon powers and his economic philosophy was distinctly mercantilist. A mercantilist might not think that the independence of the American colonies had to be resisted at all costs. In economic terms, Fox believed that North America had been an anomaly within the British Empire. Britain needed colonies entirely different from the mother country in climate and produce. North America was too similar to England. It produced too many of the things produced in England and thus, despite the provisions of the Mercantile System, could never provide a proper market for British goods. Equally, it did not produce tropical products such as sugar, unobtainable in Britain itself and so necessary for Britain's re-export trade. Within the Empire, the Americans were rivals for the West Indies trade. From an economic point of view the loss of America – provided the vital Caribbean islands were retained – might turn out a blessing in disguise.

Fox's analysis was defective because he overestimated the re-export of tropical products and underestimated the actual and potential market in North America for British manufactured goods. One could hardly expect to exclude the Americans from the West Indies trade and yet insist that they accept the free import of British goods. Fox was vague on future Anglo-American economic relations, thereby causing much difficulty for his successors. In any case he saw things in political not in economic terms, hoping that an early and generous acknowledgement of independence would restore American affection for Britain. A common cultural and political heritage would permit the development of similar policies on international issues. A sane influence emanating from America would counter the siren song of continental despotism with its alleged appeal to George III. Far from being resisted, American independence should be welcomed as the best thing that had happened since 1688.

Fox had no objection to colonies as such. French defeat in India raised hopes of a new Empire in the East, more complementary to Britain's own economy than the North American colonies had been. Fox's preoccupation with tropical colonies coincided with his hostility to France and Spain. Approval of the American cause did not mean that Bourbon powers deserved any reward for their help to the rebels. Fox totally opposed Vergennes' demand that Britain relinquish most of its 1763 gains; he took advantage of the improving military situation to dismiss Vergennes' threats as empty. Fox said his policy was to clear the decks – give the Americans their independence and modify the British Right of Search to appease the League of Armed Neutrality – and then get on with a good old-fashioned war against France and Spain. French observers, who had received the news of North's fall with delight, grew alarmed. Vergennes commented: 'c'est un fagot d'épines que ce M. Fox'. Fox probably did not plan to continue the war. There was too much war weariness in Britain, yet he had to convince the French that he was serious in order to persuade them to accept terms which gave them no profit for their exertions and which left the British Empire intact. Fox did not want to settle the war at one large conference where all belligerent nations were represented.

This involved a departure from the 'general' settlements which had characterized the end of major wars since 1648. Fox hoped that the Americans would desert their French and Spanish allies if they were offered sufficiently favourable terms. The American–Bourbon alliance was already cracking; Fox hoped to destroy it utterly. The Americans could have no interest in the aggrandisement of France, especially in the colonial field. There were also Frenchmen who distrusted an alliance which threatened to spread subversive views in France itself. As a country with important interests in the West Indies and hopes of recovering Canada, the last thing France wanted was for its erstwhile protégé to become too successful.

Unfortunately, Fox's analysis was not supported by his colleagues. Shelburne insisted that the American War and the war with France and Spain should be settled at one large conference. When the conference assembled, Shelburne's representative, responsible for contacts with the rebels, was treated as more important than Fox's man, Thomas Grenville, representing the Foreign Office in dealings with the European powers. Discussions in Paris had scarcely begun when the Prime Minister, Rockingham, died on 1 July 1782. Rockingham was succeeded by Shelburne; Fox refused to serve in the new government and the Foreign Office was taken over by Lord Grantham whose policies were derived from Shelburne's ideas, not Fox's.

Shelburne was more modern minded than Fox; he was influenced by Dean Tucker and by Adam Smith and declared that he preferred trade to dominion. Unlike Fox, he did not believe that the loss of America could be overcome by acquiring colonies in the tropics and in Asia. The large white population of America, enjoying a high purchasing power, represented a more valuable market than any number of exotic colonies – the inhabitants of which were likely to be extremely poor. Whatever happened, Britain needed to maintain trading links with its former colonies. From an economic point of view, it might pretend that the American Revolution had not happened and continue to trade on the same basis as before independence. If this line seems odd, coming from an admirer of Smith and a critic of the Mercantile System, it is worth remembering that the trading system of the old British Empire had permitted a degree of free trade between its various territories, certainly more than was normal between independent states. These arrangements had suited many in the colonies as well as in Britain. Some people in an independent United States would find life difficult if prevented from trading with neighbouring areas remaining under British rule. Before the Revolution there had been an important trade between New York and the West Indies, yet during the war the sugar islands, faced with a continued threat from France, had remained loyal to Britain. New York merchants did not relish exclusion from the sugar trade. Concessions here might persuade the Americans not to raise tariffs against British imports; debts owed to British merchants by Americans would be honoured; property, confiscated from loyalists, restored. In other words, Shelburne hoped to combine political independence with economic integration, or at least with the absence of mutually destructive 'beggar my neighbour' policies.

Shelburne knew that many Americans would disagree with his analysis; not all Americans thought like New York merchants. In New England and in Virginia, hostility to the 'unfair' features of the old economic relationship – clearly revealed in Book IV of *The Wealth of Nations* – had been fundamental to the desire for political independence. Thus the Americans might reject Shelburne's proposals; many wanted to cut themselves off from Britain entirely and doubted whether trade and dominion were so readily separable as Shelburne supposed. Perhaps Shelburne was merely seeking to remove some of the more objectionable features of the Mercantile System in order to preserve its essentials.

How, then, were the Americans to be persuaded to accept Shelburne's terms? Whereas Fox wanted to bribe the Americans to desert the French and Spaniards, Shelburne wanted to bribe the French and Spaniards to desert the Americans. Fox wanted to settle with the Americans, leaving Britain free for an 'old style' colonial war against its traditional rivals unless they accepted peace on its terms. Shelburne wanted the Americans to fear that, if they did not settle on his terms, Britain would 'square' the Bourbon powers and then turn its undivided attention to the American theatre with better prospects of success. The fact that Shelburne did not really contemplate another campaign in America is beside the point. The prospect of French desertion should have been sufficient to bring the Americans to their senses. To further his plans Shelburne was prepared to be generous to the Bourbon Powers; they might hope for tropical colonies (whose importance Shelburne thought exaggerated), concessions on Britain's maritime claims, and even European strategic points such as Gibraltar. Other concessions could include freer access for European goods into British markets. Best of all, the mutual reduction of barriers to trade would reduce tension and the risk of war. According to the latest theories, this would help the economic development of all European states. Shelburne was more influenced by Smith's ideas in his views on Europe than in his attitude to North America which remained tinged with quasi-'mercantilist' assumptions. In the long run, Shelburne's ideas would help to promote economic growth and thus ensure European hegemony over the rest of the world.

But Shelburne's analysis was too *avant garde* to be readily understood. Fox found it easy to misrepresent it. Talk of continuing economic ties with America was a ploy to reassert Imperial control. Shelburne was prepared to bribe France and Spain with offers of British colonies to persuade them to desert the Americans. If the Bourbon powers withdrew, the Royal campaign to suppress liberty on both sides of the Atlantic could begin again in earnest. Any settlement which gave the Americans less than complete independence would enable George III to claim that the war for America had not been in vain. A revival in Royal prestige was the last thing Fox wanted.

Would Parliament prefer an arrangement which made concessions to the Bourbon powers in return for a favourable settlement with the United States; or would it prefer a settlement with America which, although guaranteeing complete independence, also entailed the possibility of continuing hostilities with France and Spain? The disagreement between Shelburne and Fox can be seen as a classic instance of the clash between 'European' and 'Atlanticist' schools of foreign policy. But a decision would have to be made soon. The negotiations in Paris were making good progress.

Preliminary Articles were signed with the Americans on 30 November 1782 and with France and Spain on 20 January 1783. There is still controversy about which delegation secured the best terms. Some American historians see the discussions as a triumph for Franklin over old style British diplomats; yet American independence was won on the battlefield, not at the conference chamber. The British negotiators achieved a settlement as favourable as could be expected, assisted to some extent by knowledge gained from intercepting Franklin's correspondence. Although the peace terms were obtained during Shelburne's premiership, they cannot be regarded as the practical realization of his analysis. Fox and Shelburne appear to subscribe to mutually exclusive foreign policy programmes, yet peace settlements are seldom wholly consistent. Peace involves compromise not only between states but also between factions within states. Consistency is often the first victim of compromise.

There was much of 'the Fox line' in the peace terms, largely because his evaluation of the situation was substantially correct. It was not difficult to detach the Americans from the French. Franklin and his colleagues were so anxious to gain recognition of American independence that they made what amounted to a separate peace with Britain – just as Fox had wanted – largely ignoring instructions to work closely with Vergennes and the French. The British gave the Americans a favourable boundary between the United States and Canada in order to widen the breach. Large areas south of the Great Lakes were given up, even though there were few American settlers and economic life centred on trade with Montreal and the St Lawrence. British debts were not properly secured and there were inadequate guarantees on the future of American loyalists.

Further, Britain gave away little to the Continental powers. France got Tobago, a few settlements on the Senegal Coast, a tiny enclave in India, an increased share of Newfoundland fishing and permission to fortify Dunkirk – all trifling compared to the losses of 1763. France might make major gains only if joined the British in a partition of the Dutch Empire; the French indignantly

declined the suggestion. French refusal did not prevent
Britain from taking Negapatam from the Dutch and securing the right to navigation in the Dutch East Indies. Although France was offered little of value, Spain seemed
likely to do better. Even in defeat, Britain might be able
to weaken the Bourbon Family Compact. Shelburne and
Grantham were ready to give up Gibraltar, believing that
retention was the chief obstacle to improved relations with
Spain. Vergennes did not want Britain to give up Gibraltar;
he calculated that so long as Spain had a grievance against
Britain, she would stay close to France. Unfortunately for
Shelburne, Gibraltar's resistance to seige made the territory
a symbol of British patriotism. Shelburne and Grantham
were opposed by other ministers and there was talk of
the government breaking up over the issue. In the event,
the Spaniards had to settle for Minorca and Florida. The
treaties offer no support for the claim made by Vergennes'
assistant, Rayneval, that Britain had been 'plucked like a
chicken'. Perhaps without the differences between Fox and
Shelburne, the negotiators could have secured even better
terms. Yet the draft treaties would have been much the
same if Fox had remained Foreign Secretary. This was
not because the key figures were sympathetic to Fox but
because an anti-Bourbon, quasi 'mercantile' attitude was
second nature to them. Indeed, whoever had been in
power the terms would have been similar. This was due in
part to the result of the war and in part to the underlying
assumptions of the negotiators, British, American, French
and Spanish alike.

Fox knew that the range of options was limited yet he
was ready to denounce every facet of his opponents' policy
in an attempt to eject them from office. He proceeded to set
up a 'phoney' attack on the peace terms. There has always
been a hint of untruth and deception about diplomacy and
foreign policy – at the domestic as well as the international
level. In alliance with Lord North, Fox secured the defeat
of the Shelburne government and returned to the Foreign
Office in April 1783. Allegations of unprincipled political
opportunism compelled the Fox–North coalition to make
a show of having distinctive objectives in foreign affairs.

Certainly, neither Fox nor North liked Shelburne's ideas
and both believed in a large British Empire surrounded
by high tariff walls, but beyond that the contradictions of
the alliance were obvious. If Fox believed that Shelburne's
treaties were too unfavourable, he must also believe that
Lord North had not left a hopeless situation for his successors. If there was any ideological justification for the
Fox–North coalition it had to rest upon the premiss that
Fox's diatribes against North from 1778 to 1782 had been
unwarranted.

Denunciations of Shelburne's peace terms – 'a peace
more calamitous, more dreadful, more ruinous than any
war could possibly be'[1] – would seem dishonest if Fox
himself did not do any better. The Fox–North coalition
was such an extraordinary government that few foreign
observers thought that it could last long. The French
strategy was to insist that Fox accept the Shelburne–
Grantham terms; if he refused they would 'stall' until a more
reasonable government came to power. The tactic worked,
and the new terms presented to Parliament in November
1783 contained nothing new.[2] Despite Fox's francophobia
there was even a clause providing for a future commercial
treaty between Britain and France – a stipulation of great
significance for the next few years. Less satisfactorily,
recognition of American independence was not coupled
with any trade settlement between Britain and the United
States. Fox concluded that the quickest way to settle with
the Americans was to sign a peace treaty recognizing their
independence and leave the trade question for a later date.
This was a mistake which the previous administration
would not have made. Although trade with the independent
United States revived, the terms were not settled and
occasioned endless dispute culminating in the war of 1812.
The coalition gained parliamentary approval for its peace
terms but its attempts to reorganize the East India Company
– arising in part from Fox's exaggerated assessment of the
economic potential of the East – proved unpopular. This
unpopularity gave the king the chance to dismiss the
coalition and to appoint a new administration headed by
William Pitt the Younger.

II

The period between the end of the American War and the outbreak of the French Revolution was not propitious for serious discussion about British foreign policy. Attention was mainly devoted to domestic affairs. In the aftermath of an inglorious war, the new Prime Minister understandably preferred a low profile in foreign policy, hoping that Britain would be able to enjoy the blessings of peace for some years. Yet the 1780s were not a 'barren patch' in foreign policy. As we have seen, 'ideological' elements had not been prominent in 'classic' foreign policy. When they surfaced, as in the American Revolution, they appeared to threaten British interests, at least as understood by traditionalists. Moreover, most of the new ideological factors originated outside Britain and found domestic support only in opposition circles which, on past form, would probably drop them when they came to power. After 1782, however, ideological interests became more important, especially as they gained the attention of some of the administration's own followers. The appearance of ideological pressure groups, exercising political leverage on those in power, was bound to alter the way in which foreign policy was determined. In Spanier's terms, these groups would produce a shift towards 'domestic' rather than 'states system' considerations.

The cause attracting most attention in the 1780s was the abolition of the slave trade. As Oliver Furley notes in C. J. Bartlett's *Britain Pre-Eminent* (London, Macmillan, 1969) attacks had been made on the slave trade in the seventeenth and eighteenth centuries, but it was only when the British Abolition Committee enrolled William Wilberforce and Henry Thornton to engender parliamentary support that there was a prospect of action. Evangelicals such as Wilberforce and Thornton, leaders of the Clapham Sect, proved capable lobbyists. Furley declares:

> Their methods set the pattern for most humanitarian campaigns... thereafter a flow of books and pamphlets, numerous public meetings, societies with branches all over the country, addresses and petitions to Parliament all became regular

features, and the influence of the pulpit, especially in non-conformist churches, was perhaps the greatest power of all.

Yet it is dangerous to examine the formulation of foreign policy through 'case studies' of individual pressure groups. For every group advocating change in one direction, another would argue the opposite. The power of the Anti-Slavery group in Parliament was balanced by the West India Committee protecting the planters. Yet although the slave trade was not abolished until 1807, Pitt's sympathy with Wilberforce's objective was a symptom that things were changing. Indeed, the abolition of the slave trade in the midst of a major war is a testimony to the power of Evangelicals. The step would have seemed insane to men of the 1740s and 1750s. Evangelicals no doubt believed that slavery was sinful, that it was essential to destroy the trade regardless of the economic consequences. Powerful as the Evangelicals were, however, it is unlikely that their campaign would have progressed if politicians had believed that Abolition would destroy the British economy. Slavery was part and parcel of the Mercantile System and the fixation on sugar colonies. It is significant that the 1780s saw the emergence of another, if more nebulous, pressure group promoting the ideas of Adam Smith. The ideas of the humanitarians, supposedly representing Christian love and charity and those of the Political Economists, supposedly representing enlightened self-interest (as opposed to the short sighted self-interest of the Mercantilists) were to come into conflict, but they had much in common. Pitt the Younger, though too much of a pragmatist to be fully committed to either sect, had sympathy with both.

In the 1780s Pitt's objective was to avoid another war. The new 'ideological' pressure groups were broadly in sympathy. In theory at least, the Evangelicals regarded war between Christians as wicked. Political Economists, reacting against the mercantilist obsessions, often realizable only through war, wanted domestic reform and more open trading with other states, a development which Smith insisted would benefit the majority of people in Britain and render war less likely. But the economic climate was changing. In the 1780s there occurred the first noticeable acceleration in economic growth, later described as the Industrial Revolution. This change was both the cause and the reflection of changes in society and the value system of the nation. The change was not sudden; in the long run, however, the transformation altered the priorities of foreign policy dramatically. Could the middle-class values and aspirations be reconciled to the aristocratic ethos in which international relations were conducted? If British society diverged more markedly from Continental Europe, the already difficult task of preserving a system of diplomacy based on common values and assumptions might become impossible. For the time being, the profundity of the change left the nation with little energy for foreign affairs.

On a more personal level, the low priority given to foreign policy reflected the standing of Lord Carmarthen, Foreign Secretary from December 1783 to June 1791. Although not a nonentity, Carmarthen's importance was reduced by his lack of application, excessive vanity, unstable political conduct and generally 'capricious disposition'. For much of the period Pitt took little interest in diplomatic matters. Carmarthen was allowed to initiate discussions with Austria, Spain, Prussia, Russia and Denmark in search of alliances to counteract what he perceived as the French dominance of Europe. There was little chance of weakening the ties between France, Spain and Austria but Frederick of Prussia was interested, although he played hard to get. Yet Frederick demanded support for his policies in Eastern Europe. Carmarthen was ready to give such undertakings but they were unacceptable to Pitt. The initiative collapsed and a similar fate befell approaches made to Russia. Carmarthen had to content himself with some increase in British influence in Denmark, a poor return on a year's work to find an ally amongst the great powers of Europe.[3]

It is not surprising that there was some tension between Carmarthen and Pitt. Their disagreement involves one of the fundamental dilemmas of foreign policy. Carmarthen thought that Britain should enter close alliances whose collective strength would deter potential aggressors and thus keep the peace. Pitt feared that membership of alliances would make war more likely. He feared that Britain might be drawn into Prussian designs for expansion in Eastern Europe and become committed to a project in which no British interests were involved and which might be disliked by the British public. The peace of Europe, he believed, would be best preserved if Britain avoided binding alliances. Carmarthen, on the other hand, wanted to rush into alliance with any power which showed signs of disagreement with France – regardless of its other policies. If Carmarthen's fear of France was just an outdated reflex then the alliances suggested by the Foreign Secretary were no longer necessary. Now was the time to consider the drawbacks of these entanglements; perhaps Britain and France could forget their differences and unite against common foes.

The new approach was revealed in the Eden Trade Treaty of 1786. As a representative of the younger generation and an associate of Shelburne, Pitt was the obvious proponent of the ideas of Adam Smith. He accepted that many of the wars between Britain and France had resulted from 'beggar-my-neighbour' tariff policies. A mutual reduction in duties diminished the danger of wars, whilst the proximity of the two countries meant that Anglo-French trade would support more people than could be sustained by long distance colonial trade. Settlement of trade matters could lead to a general *rapprochement*. It was pointless to argue whether the American War had damaged France more than Britain. What mattered was that the Eastern European powers had avoided involvement and were now relatively more powerful. The decline of British and French influence in Eastern Europe was obvious; both had tried in vain to prevent the partition of Poland. It seemed that Britain and France would enjoy more influence if they acted together.

The 'European' aspect of Pitt's policy is illustrated by comparing his interest in the Eden negotiations and his coolness to suggestions for an American trade treaty. He would consider an American trade treaty settlement only on favourable terms, thus effectively destroying the chances of an agreement. Pitt seemed to be 'free trade' towards France but 'mercantilist' towards the United States. Pitt's policy was opposed by Fox and was uncongenial to Carmarthen who feared 'the present rage for Commercial Treaties' would weaken Britain's influence on the Continent and who persisted in regarding France as 'our natural and inveterate rival'. Mercantile prejudices were still powerful and, whatever his own inclinations, Pitt appreciated that it was necessary to proceed cautiously to avoid political damage resulting from a sweeping attack on vested interests.

It would be wrong to exaggerate Pitt's attachment to free trade ideas. The initiative for the Treaty was as much French as English, and Pitt was probably more interested in the potential for improved relations between London and Paris than in free trade principles. In any case Pitt was too much of a pragmatist to believe that lowering tariff barriers would remove all occasion for dispute between Britain and France.[4]

The next two years must have been disappointing for a man who wished for better relations. Success depended on the new approach being adopted in both capitals. If not, the traditionalists, convinced francophobes and protectionists, would say they had been right all along. Despite the new cordiality in commercial matters French policy towards the Netherlands was worrying. Carmarthen believed that Vergennes was trying to increase French influence so that Dutch foreign policy would be directed from Paris. Given the continuation of the Franco-Austrian Alliance, Britain would face French dominance of the entire Low Countries. If the French succeeded, Britain would have to abandon one of the cardinal tenets of its foreign policy. Although overshadowed by subsequent events, the Dutch crisis had great significance. At one level it was merely another episode in rivalry between Britain and France; at another, issues of ideology and popular opinion impinged upon diplomacy in a way not seen since the seventeenth century. The American War had already indicated that the closed, mechanistic world of eighteenth-century diplomacy was breaking up. The Dutch crisis produced the same symptoms in Europe and also provided a hint of the pressures that British diplomacy would have to cope with after 1789. It was significant that 'progressive' elements in the Netherlands were pro-French and anti-British. There seemed a danger that the people of Europe would view Britain as the natural ally of anti-popular forces and the mainstay of an antiquated and constricting European order. In the past, Britain had faced the resentment of élites because it had been too successful in tipping the Balance of Power in its own favour. Now the resentment was spreading and Britain might be portrayed as the enemy of the people of Europe. If this sentiment could be exploited by Bourbon France, how much more might be feared if there was ever a more popular régime in Paris? The Dutch crisis provided a mild foretaste of the Revolutionary and Napoleonic Wars.

Carmarthen's francophobia would have led to war if he had been in charge of British policy. Yet the crisis was solved without direct hostilities, surely the mark of successful diplomacy. Indeed, the Dutch affair was a model of successful crisis management. It also offered valuable lessons for subsequent and more difficult crises. French strategy depended on the support of elements opposed to the pro-British House of Orange. The potential allies included both Amsterdam merchants and the more advanced and intellectual *Patriotten* groups. Pitt's response was one of 'wait and see'. It would be foolish to enter commitments which made war more likely, especially as French designs might collapse of their own accord. It would be necessary to reconsider the position only if Vergennes's schemes looked like coming to fruition.

Successful management of the crisis required Britain to maximize its advantages. The anti-Orange groups distrusted each other and were unlikely to co-operate for long. Although claiming to speak for the people, few of these elements had genuine contact with the masses. There was a considerable fund of popular support for the House of Orange but this had to be organized to produce a popular Orangist party. This objective could be realized only by employing diplomats whose concept of their duties was not confined to contacts with the political and social élite. These traditional attitudes had to be replaced by a readiness for greater involvement in the internal politics of the host country. Fortunately for Britain, Sir James Harris, the ambassador at the Hague, possessed a talent for such activities and was also plentifully supplied with funds to facilitate his task.[5] The new fashion for popular involvement in politics could seriously alter the nature of the diplomatic profession, even if external aspects of the traditional style were preserved.

French influence in the Netherlands could be also countered by more old-fashioned stratagems. The French portrayed themselves not only as the friends of certain groups and of Dutch interests in general. Their task was made more difficult by their desire to preserve the Franco-Austrian alliance. Too much attention to the Dutch might drive Joseph II of Austria towards Britain, whilst acquiescence in Austrian schemes would discredit the pro-French party in the United Provinces and pave the way for a revival of pro-British sentiment. Thwarted in his desire for Bavaria in exchange for his possessions in the Low Countries, Joseph decided to develop the potential of the Austrian Netherlands. He intended to repudiate articles XIV and XV of the Treaty of Westphalia which closed the Scheldt to ocean-going vessels and thus destroyed the prosperity of Antwerp. The revival of Antwerp, the cornerstone of Joseph's scheme, would be unwelcome both in Amsterdam and in London. The scheme seemed tailor-made for driving Britain and the United Provinces together again.

In Vergennes, Britain encountered a skilful adversary, although he tended to overplay his hand. Vergennes took the first trick; he persuaded Joseph to abandon his Antwerp scheme and successfully presented France as the true friend of Dutch and Austrian alike. Vergennes' success seemed total when most of the powers remaining to the Stadtholder, William V of Orange, were abolished and the Dutch made a defensive treaty with France. Miscalculation now could lead to war or to a humiliating acceptance of French dominance in the Low Countries. The two perils were separated by a narrow path, too narrow for a man of Carmarthen's temperament. Foreign policy decisions were largely taken by the Prime Minister and by George Grenville who had assumed most of Carmarthen's responsibilities before becoming Foreign Secretary in name as well as in fact in June 1791.

Together Grenville and Harris made a powerful team whose methods reflected the transitional nature of the crisis. Harris successfully promoted a popular Orangist back-lash and exploited divisions amongst other groups. He also took advantage of the fact that Frederick William, the new king of Prussia who had succeeded his uncle in August 1786, was the brother of the Princess of Orange – the traditional 'dynastic' side of international relations. Frederick William was appalled at the insults offered to his sister and was determined to restore the power of his Orange relations.

Whereas Carmarthen had contemplated unilateral action to restore British influence, this purpose could now be effected by Prussia, thus reducing the chances of a direct clash between Britain and France which, on other grounds, Pitt was anxious to avert. Frederick William II's anger at the behaviour of the *Patriotten* militia towards his sister suited British interests. In September 1787 Prussia invaded the Republic whilst a squadron of the Royal Navy was sent to Dutch waters. Prussian intervention was successful and the Orangists returned in triumph to The Hague. Britain's calculation that France would accept reduced influence in the Netherlands proved justified. The vindication of British policy was not the result of chance. It recognized the advantages of magnanimity; the triumphant Orangists were induced to make concessions to their opponents, thus weakening the pro-French party. Further, there was an appreciation of the connection between French foreign policy and domestic affairs. Foreign wars can sometimes paper over divisions. If the crisis had been 'forced' earlier, as Carmarthen intended, Bourbon France might have lasted a few more years. Yet when internal dissension reaches a certain point, a resolute foreign policy can no longer shore up a decaying régime; by Autumn 1787 this point had been passed. As early as January the bellicose Carmarthen had pointed out to George III that events in France, culminating in the *Convocation des Notables*, 'renders a proper degree

of exertion on the part of England less dangerous than in
other times'.[6] Finally, the blow to French policy caused by
Vergennes' death in February 1787, together with problems of government finances, meant that Britain achieved
its objectives by means of the gallantry of the King of
Prussia and with small risk of French counter attack.

There had been no war, the funds spent by Harris
had not been excessive, a traditional objective of British
policy had been upheld, relations with France had not
been damaged beyond hope of improvement and British
prestige in Europe was demonstrably rising again. Although
the crisis was a triumph for Pitt rather than for Carmarthen,
the Foreign Secretary's warnings on the dangers of isolation
had not been in vain. In June 1788 Britain entered into
an alliance with Prussia and the new Orangist government
in The Hague. A mixture of resolution and caution, old
and new diplomacy, coupled with intelligent anticipation
of French responses, had produced a satisfactory result.
Compared to later crises the Dutch affair was insignificant
but it was important in restoring self-confidence to British
foreign policy. For those with eyes to see it provided
valuable but alarming hints of how things might develop
in the future.

III

The years between 1788 and 1793 form a curious interlude
in British foreign policy. There had always been some
who claimed that France posed no serious threat to British interests but these assertions had been unconvincing.
Memories of French support for the American rebels and
Dutch *Patriotten* were still fresh but French inability
to respond to Anglo-Prussian intervention in the United
Provinces, coupled with the rapidly deteriorating internal
situation, induced more people to conclude that France
had ceased to be a great Power and could be excluded
from diplomatic and military calculations. In October 1789,
William Eden predicted that France would be 'very interesting as to its interior, but probably for a long time of

little importance with regard to its external policies'. As a result, British attention turned away from Western Europe. Perhaps diplomats were playing with irrelevant disputes to pass the time until the major crisis with Revolutionary France was ready to explode.

Diplomacy often defines itself in terms of actual or potential enemies. Countries, like the psalmist, seem to need an adversary. With France out of the way, British policy lost its direction. Superficially, the crises of 1787–1791 suggest a shrinking world where all conflicts had implications for Britain, thus resembling disputes of modern times. In later disputes serious British interests were at stake, but in the 1780s the interests affected were minute and it would have been foolish to go to war over them. Unfortunately ridiculous disputes can lead to war. During France's temporary eclipse there were two main candidates for the role of Britain's natural enemy. Some observers raised the spectre of Spain, England's chief adversary in the days of Philip II but now hardly a plausible threat. Others with more perception discerned the immense potential of Russia as the real threat. Although Russia had a promising future as a natural enemy, its hour was not yet. Those unable to make sense of their own time, therefore, either indulged in historical fiction set in the sixteenth century or in some kind of science fiction which has been partially fulfilled in the twentieth century.

In February 1790 news was received of the Spanish seizure of the British commercial base at Nootka Sound on the Pacific coast of America. In demanding the return of British property and the modification of the Spanish claim to exclusive trade and settlement, Carmarthen half hoped for a war. He believed that the Triple Alliance would support Britain; Austria was occupied elsewhere and France too distracted to help Spain. As in the Dutch crisis, Pitt interposed a less bellicose policy, initiating negotiations which produced compensation for British losses and the possibility of trade and settlement from California to Alaska. Pitt's skilful use of 'brinkmanship', combined with offers of negotiations, brought as much benefit as a long and expensive war. In his handling of the Dutch crisis and the Nootka Sound incident Pitt had apparently evolved a successful technique of crisis management.

The success of British policy can be attributed to the domestic problems of the Bourbon powers, but Britain was worsted by Russia during the Ochakov crisis of 1791. As a member of the Triple Alliance, Britain was obliged to support Frederick William of Prussia's demand that Russia give up the fortress of Ochakov on the Black Sea captured from the Turks in December 1788. Russia stood firm against Pitt's usual mixture of threats and offers of negotiation. Britain had to decide whether to back down or to go to war. It was difficult to contend that British interests were affected by the ownership of a remote fortress, although Ochakov provides the opening chapter to the 'Eastern Crisis' which haunted British diplomats in the next century. In the event Pitt had no option but to allow the Russians to keep Ochakov, a decision which provoked Carmarthen's resignation.

It would have been convenient if Russia had given way but the outcome was hardly a serious reversal for Britain. Whatever Carmarthen may have said in the heat of the moment, refusal to go to war in 1791 was consistent with Pitt's earlier policy. Pitt was not an isolationist but neither was he ready for frequent armed interventions in European, specifically Eastern European, affairs. He was reluctant to embark upon steps which might endanger the tranquillity and economic progress Britain had achieved since 1783.

The Ochakov crisis resulting from Britain's membership of the Triple Alliance suggested that it might have to pay a high price for the strength and security the alliance had provided. Prussia's welcome intervention in the Dutch crisis had been at variance with the prevailing eastward orientation of its policy. The affair suggested that resolute backing for a central European ally would be unpopular with British public opinion, whilst weakness in dealings with Russia renewed Prussian doubts about Britain's value as an ally. According to Harris, British acquiescence in the Russian retention of Ochakov had 'broken our Continental system and let us down from that high station in which we stood'.[8] Prussian suspicions of Britain's unreliability had unfortunate results in the Revolutionary Wars. Yet Britain had had a merciful escape; one can only speculate as to what might have happened if it had been fighting an unpopular war with Russia when events in France reached their climax.

The change of Foreign Secretary did not imply a move to isolationism. Grenville believed that Prussian firmness in the Ochakov crisis was the prelude to a Prusso-Turkish alliance directed against Austria and Russia. Britain hoped to gain Austrian friendship as internal developments in France weakened the ties between Paris and Vienna. Grenville had no desire to antagonize Prussia but imagined he could reconcile Berlin and Vienna in an expanded Triple Alliance which would thus become the Quadruple Alliance, strong enough to guard against Russian expansion in the East or any unexpected consequences of the situation in France. The new policy was too clever by half. By trying to expand the Triple Alliance and involving himself in Eastern problems he did not understand, Grenville risked breaking up the alliance and destroying the understanding with Prussia. Britain alienated the Prussians without winning the Austrians who decided to strengthen their ties with the Russians. The Austro-Russian alliance posed a threat to Prussia, yet in the face of British duplicity the country had no option but to try to join Austria and Russia. British diplomats were shocked by the Vienna Convention between Austria and Prussia signed on 25 July 1791. If Britain's position was better than in 1782, there had certainly been a decline since 1788. Despite subsequent disputes, the new agreement between Austria, Prussia and Russia prepared the way for new Partitions of Poland: the Second Partition of 1793 which reduced the country to one third of its original dimensions and the Third Partition of 1796 which resulted in its complete destruction.

IV

The temporary eclipse of British influence in Eastern Europe had implications for events leading to the outbreak

of war with France. The British government now had little
contact with the counter revolutionary spirit in Vienna
and Berlin which sought to destroy revolution in the
name of monarchical solidarity. Ever since 1789 the British
government had been uncertain about its response to events
across the Channel, and even the outbreak of war between
France and Austria in August 1792 did not clarify matters.
Edmund Burke might insist that a policy of neutrality
was tantamount to sanctioning the outrages in France,
but the Prime Minister and Foreign Secretary looked
forward to a period of peace. Even concern for the safety
of the French royal family was qualified by a reluctance
to indulge in 'meddling with internal disturbances of that
ill-fated kingdom'.[9] Yet the French declaration of war on 1
February 1793 should not have caused surprise. Britain and
France maintained that they wanted to preserve peace but
these protestations were unconvincing. Some blame may
be placed on Pitt's haughty attitude but war was probably
inevitable. The early stages of the French Revolution
had created little concern in Britain. Some had seen the
Revolution as divine punishment for French support to the
American rebels. Others believed that France would now
develop a constitutional monarchy on British lines which
would assist better relations. Most were gratified to learn of
the misfortunes of Britain's traditional rival which promised
to remove French influence from European affairs.

An ideological element was present in 1793 but British
involvement in war was determined by traditional considerations. Unexpected French victories over Prussia and
Austria in the Autumn of 1792 allowed the revolutionary
armies to enter the Austrian Netherlands, thus threatening
the United Provinces. As in 1787, Britain prepared to take
action to protect its interests in the Low Countries. Unlike
1787, however, the French had powerful armies in the field
and also enjoyed the support of a much larger section of
the population. If Britain had been unwilling to ignore the
dangers in 1787 it is hard to see how they could have been
ignored in 1792. Perhaps the perceived danger of France
was greater than the reality; nevertheless, a man like Pitt, so
concerned with harbouring British resources and fostering

economic growth, would not have entered a war without being convinced of its necessity. Given the military situation at the beginning of 1793, Britain would have gone to war even if there had been no French Revolution.

Some responded to the French Revolution with bewilderment tinged with hysteria. France had thrown aside the assumptions and values which had informed European military and diplomatic behaviour since 1648. The enthusiasm of the revolutionaries portended a return to the passions of the Thirty Years War. Thus the French Revolution represented a visitation from a different epoch, some appalling Dark Age from the remote past or some equally ghastly future. Many in Berlin and Vienna thought it was an affront to the laws of nature that such a monstrosity should be permitted to exist. Yet events in France did not mark such a departure from recent trends. The partition of Poland in 1772 began a new and more brutal phase in international relations. Similarly, the experience of the American Revolution and the Dutch crisis should have prepared British statesmen for the potency of ideology and popular sentiment in foreign policy crises. Despite their comments on revolution, statesmen in Britain and Central Europe did not adjust their conduct to the new situation. They behaved as if the old system of war and diplomacy was still operative. In 1793 Britain prepared for the same war it had always fought against Bourbon France. The real change came not with the outbreak of war against France – after all, a frequent enough occurrence – but with the gradual realization that the war against revolutionary France required new concepts of war and diplomacy.

British plans envisaged a classic 'limited liability' conflict. There might have to be a British expeditionary force on the Continent but this would contain many German mercenaries. Treaties were made with the smaller German states and, by August 1793, seventeen thousand German troops were fighting under the command of the Duke of York in the Netherlands. The armies of Prussia and Austria would be the chief instruments of French defeat. Britain would co-ordinate the objectives of the powers in arms against France, a task facilitated by careful distribution of loans and subsidies. Britain's activity at sea would be of greater importance. The shipbuilding programme of the 1780s would be sufficient to guarantee victory' over the French Navy and thus prepare the way for the painless acquisition of colonies in the non European world. Despite protestations of hatred of revolution, Prussia and Austria had their own versions of this 'low risk, high profit' approach. The behaviour of some of the German rulers was even more typical of earlier wars; London suspected the Hessian Landgraves encouraged their soldiers in British pay to desert – so that they would enlist again and thus secure double payment for their masters. The persistence of such behaviour helps to explain the fate of the First Coalition.

The idea of a Coalition of smaller powers to oppose French hegemony had a long history; a structure similar to that created by William III against Louis XIV seemed needed. Austria and Prussia were linked by their war pact of 1792 but Britain's only tie with the belligerents was the largely moribund Triple Alliance. Thus British policy hinged on the assumption that the way to frustrate revolutionary France lay in the expansion of an alliance begun to thwart the Bourbons. An attempt to expand that Alliance in the easier circumstances of 1791 had failed. Now, all that could be achieved was a string of separate treaties with Prussia, Austria, Spain, Portugal, Naples and Sardinia. The resulting 'Coalition' looked impressive, but events demonstrated that an alliance consisting of separate treaties was too weak to withstand the shock of French victory.

The problem was that the members of the Coalition, especially those in Central Europe to whom the French armies posed no immediate threat, were not single-minded in their desire to destroy revolutionary France. The Eastern powers were suspicious of each other and their first priority was to acquire the largest share of Poland. Had they been united, France might have been crushed in 1793 or 1794. Russia was lukewarm about a campaign against France and had no intention of doing anything without subsidies from Britain. Although both Prussia and Austria were fighting the French, relations between the two were strained. Both limited their military commitment in the West because of their ambitions in Poland. Britain had gone to war to ensure that the Austrian Netherlands were not annexed by France yet it appeared that the Austrians were ready to give the territory up in return for compensation elsewhere. Other powers, notably Sardinia, simply pocketed British subsidies and then failed to produce the forces they had promised. British acquisitions in the colonial field and the small scale of its military efforts in the Netherlands added to the general uncertainty which surrounded the Coalition.

Despite initial successes by the Coalition, the French armies regained the initiative in the Autumn of 1793, and by the beginning of 1794 were ready for a new offensive. Some members of the Coalition were almost as hostile to each other as they were to the enemy, and the war against France seemed certain to fail unless there was greater commitment and unity. Each power called on others to contribute more whilst showing little willingness to extend its own efforts. The withdrawal of some of the smaller powers as a result of French military successes only made the larger powers more concerned to protect their own interests. Prussia transferred part of its forces on the Rhine to Poland and proceeded to blackmail its allies. It was hinted that the country might withdraw from the war altogether unless Britain gave more generous help and guaranteed Prussia's Polish lands against attack by another power. Such an undertaking could involve Britain in a war against Austria.

Initially, Britain rejected this tactic and Grenville upbraided Prussia for reneging on Prussian obligations under the treaty of 1788. The Prussians pointed out that this treaty had been made obsolete by Britain's failure to meet its own obligations during the Ochakov crisis. Prussia was confident that the deteriorating military situation would compel Britain to accept its demands. As the French armies moved forward into Holland, Britain wavered; whilst refusing to give any guarantees over Poland it offered Prussia one million pounds per year to keep an army of 20,000 men in the field against France. After protracted negotiations a subsidy treaty was signed by Britain, the United Provinces and Prussia on 19 April 1794.[10]

The treaty marks an important development. In 1793 Britain had been prepared to provide financial assistance only to the smaller powers because it was hoped that Prussia and Austria would have sufficient resources and dedication to defeat France without British assistance. The British knew that Austrian and Prussian resources were limited; their expectations were based on the belief that victory could be achieved in one campaigning season. Yet the French were proving a match for their opponents, and Prussian and Austrian treasuries were emptying. The struggle against France could only be continued if the entire allied effort was underpinned by British gold. On the principle of 'he who pays the piper' Britain might hope to deflect its allies away from the maddening distraction of Poland and keep them resolute against France.

Thus, Britain needed to enter into something more serious than the limited liability war envisaged in 1793. The country's financial strength, greatly enhanced by the economic growth of the 1780s, was a major asset to the allies, yet the commitment implicit in the Prussian treaty was frightening and ministers recoiled from its implications. Its significance was appreciated by Fox who told Parliament: 'I know that in every war to be carried on by a confederacy, we must pay the weaker powers whom we engaged in that confederacy.'[11] There was a danger that Britain would become a 'milch cow' for allies who took subsidies and then refused to keep their promises. Despite his British subsidy, rebellion in Poland gave Frederick William an excuse for doing nothing on the Rhine; his armies failed to stem the French advance after the Austrian defeat at Fleurus on 25 June 1795. British impatience resulted in the suspension of further instalments of the Prussian subsidy. Prussia now withdrew from the war on 5 April 1795 and made peace with France at Basel.

As at other times in the eighteenth century, there was much debate whether Austria or Prussia should be England's closest ally. Protagonists of Prussia argued that that country was the only power which really wanted to keep France out of the Low Countries. This argument became more insistent as the French achieved complete success and the

Dutch warned that, short of a miracle, they would have to accept peace on French terms. Only the Prussians could provide that miracle. Others had reservations about Prussian good faith. The country had proved unreliable in the past and, more than any other power, its greed for more Polish territory had fatally weakened the allied effort at the beginning of the war. Perhaps Austria would make the more reliable friend because its dedication to the destruction of Revolution was more genuine. The debate was brought to an end by the capitulation of the Dutch and by the Franco-Prussian treaty. Spain was also negotiating with France and peace terms were agreed in July 1795. Austria was now the only important power on the European mainland still at war with France. If the Coalition were to be continued, Britain would have to help Austria on terms at least as generous as those given to Prussia.

On 4 May 1795 a new agreement was signed whereby, in return for financial support, Austria promised to maintain an army of 120,000 men in Germany.[12] There seemed to be grounds for optimism: French successes in the Low Countries necessitated a change in military strategy. The war could now be fought in Germany, in areas closer to Austria's vital interests than the campaign in Belgium had been. Perhaps the Austrians would fight with greater determination. There would be fewer disagreements between London and Vienna; the British expeditionary force in the Netherlands could return home and German mercenaries in British service would join the Austrian armies. The new strategy involved an Austrian attack on France's eastern frontiers and a British invasion of the French Atlantic coast in collaboration with French royalists. France would face a war on two fronts and allied chances of success would be substantially improved. New overtures were also made to Russia. Exotic presents were dispatched to the Empress, Russian ships were promised to assist the Royal Navy and there were hopes that Russia would commit its inexhaustible reserves of manpower to the struggle.

New realism pervaded British foreign policy. The early days of the war had demonstrated the difficulty of reconciling the ambitions of Prussia, Austria and Russia. It would be easier to make an effective combination with two of the three Eastern powers. Although the war against France remained the chief priority, an alliance between Austria and Russia, sustained by British gold, would work to Prussia's disadvantage. The Prussians would have no one to blame but themselves. Indeed, the prospects of gains at Prussian expense, implicit in the new arrangement, afforded the best hope of keeping the alliance together. Whereas the arrangement with Prussia had entailed financial commitments as the price for maintaining the war, the new arrangements with Austria and Russia involved further loss of innocence. Britain no longer expected her European allies to continue the war because of their hatred of Revolution. Another stimulus was needed: that of national acquisitiveness. In short, the other European powers would not take the anti-French crusade seriously unless there was something in it for them.

Yet had prospects improved? Expectations of extensive help proved ill-founded. The Russians refused to send troops to the West and their contribution remained minimal. Problems also arose with Austria, resembling earlier difficulties with Prussia. Austrian ministers were suspicious of Russian intentions in Poland, thus hampering their military contribution to the West. Like the Prussians the Austrians demanded ever larger financial support whilst, to British eyes at least, doing little in return. The military story was unedifying. The French had already been victorious against Savoy and Sardinia. The Austrian Netherlands had been incorporated into metropolitan France and the United Provinces transformed into the Batavian Republic in alliance with the French. Now the British invasion of Brittany failed and, after initial success, the counter-revolutionary movement in the Vendée was suppressed. In the late summer of 1795 the French crossed the Rhine and the Austrian armies fell back in chaotic retreat.

This sorry state of affairs appeared due to the brilliance of French arms, the appeal of the Revolutionary creed and, above all, to the short-sighted selfishness of the Eastern powers. This analysis appealed to the British government, but it was not the whole story. British policy was open

to criticism and some Continental observers thought that it
was Britain, not Prussia or Austria, that was half-hearted.
Britain's commitment to the defeat of France could be
demonstrated only by the despatch of substantial armies
to the Continent. This step had not been taken. Financial
assistance was all very well but Britain was reluctant to seal
treaties with allies by a readiness to sacrifice British lives on
the scale demanded by Continental warfare – exemplified in
the modest scale and mediocre performance of the Duke of
York's expedition to the Low Countries. Britain refused to
make more than a minor military contribution to the war
in Europe. On 30 April 1794 Grenville told the House of
Lords that it was 'certainly cheaper and more politic to
pay foreign troops than to take our own youths from the
plough, and the loom, and thereby not merely put a stop
to all domestic industry, but also drain the island of its
population and diminish our natural strength'.[13] In recent
years British economic growth had exceeded that of other
countries. Here was clear assertion that Britain would
not allow the war to interfere with a continuation and
acceleration of that growth. It was hinted that it would be
no disaster if other countries bled themselves white while
fighting the French – they would damage their economic
potential in the process. Some saw in British foreign policy
a cunning of satanic dimensions. Perhaps the whole war
against revolutionary France was no more than a British plot
to extend its economic lead over its 'allies' and rivals.

The British claimed that they had a special part to play
in the war. The small size of their military contribution
was determined by a dislike of standing armies as a threat
to liberty. The chief British contribution would be in the
naval and colonial fields. Success would have important
consequences. If France were deprived of its colonial and
seaborne trade economic distress was sure to follow. This
distress might lead to internal rebellion thus compelling
the French to withdraw from Germany and elsewhere.
British action would damage the already precarious financial
position of the French government and diminish its capacity
to wage war. At least, colonial conquests by Britain would
provide the allies with bargaining counters to be used to

persuade the French to disgorge their Continental conquests if a compromise peace ever became necessary.

Colonial considerations were important in the outbreak of war and British naval victories in the ensuing months contrasted with French success on land. The fact that the French were unable to create a 'citizen navy', capable of standing up to the Royal Navy, was important to the allied cause. Revolutionary ideas might spread to the French colonies, to the colonies of countries such as the Batavian Republic under French dominance and even to British territories. The danger was exemplified by the events in St Domingue where the slave population had risen in August 1791. Far from seeking to suppress the insurrection the authorities in Paris only encouraged the slaves to murder their masters.

Britain alone could stop such outrages. Ideally, its navy would destroy the French fleet in home waters, blockade French ports and thus interdict communication between France and the non-European world. Other squadrons of the Royal Navy would then be free to roam the seas. With a minimum of cost, British forces in the Caribbean could assist the beleaguered French planters who, disgusted by the Revolution, would willingly put themselves under British protection. Servile revolts could then be suppressed. In the early days of the war Britain sought to act in collaboration with Spain, a country with reason to fear slave revolt. With Spanish capitulation, Britain had to carry the burden on its own. French success in Europe made it essential to bring Dutch colonial possessions under British protection. Britain was not always successful and the campaign to liberate St Domingue from the former slave, Toussaint, failed dismally. Even so, the ideological contagion of revolution found it difficult to overcome the quarantine of the Royal Navy. Slave revolts in Jamaica caused concern but, without sustenance from St Domingue, they never seriously threatened British possession of the island. Above all, Dutch possessions in Africa and India were taken with little or no resistance, as were some of the smaller French islands in the Caribbean.

Britain's allies seemed ungrateful for these services – what more could the country be expected to do? Perhaps Britain was not doing too little but too much. Success in the colonial sphere contrasted suspiciously with feeble efforts on the Continent. Perhaps Britain was merely using the war against France to enlarge its own empire and wanted to prolong the war so that territories taken under its protection became so integrated into its Empire that it would be impractical to return them to their rightful owners. There is little point in distributing blame for the failure of the First Coalition, but British preoccupation with the colonies may have weakened the war effort in Western Europe in a way comparable with the activities of the Eastern powers in Poland. Those with doubts about Britain's real motives might feel vindicated when on 8 December 1795, Parliament in London approved the opening of peace negotiations with France. It was expected that Britain would take its fill of colonial conquests and leave its allies, or former allies, to their fate.

Between 1795 and 1797 three major initiatives were launched, but they offer only partial confirmation of the suspicions of Britain's detractors. It is true that the initial proposals were unrealistic and that the Foreign Secretary for one was never enthusiastic for peace. Yet the mood was deeply pessimistic. It is difficult to say whether the net effect of the war was advantageous to Britain, but it was believed to be destroying the prosperity of the 1780s which was the government's proudest achievement. Much of the distress of 1794 and 1795 was caused by bad harvests and by the down-turn of the trade cycle, but people blamed the war. Some proclaimed their sympathy for the revolutionary cause and hoped that it would triumph in Britain. The continuation of the war strengthened their following. More immediately, the payment of subsidies to Continental allies brought the Bank of England's gold reserves to a low level. To a government which took commercial indicators seriously, this was a powerful argument for peace. Financial assistance to Prussia and Austria had resulted in betrayal and no military return. Even if the Austrians fought with vigour in Southern Germany, what was that to Britain? Britain's strategic concern on the Continent had been in the Low

Countries and the Low Countries had been lost. Perhaps
it would be wise to make the best of a bad job and accept
what terms could be had from the French.

IV

There had been no point in negotiating with a Jacobin
government because of its contempt for the conventions
of diplomacy and its missionary enthusiasm for revolution. Calls upon France to provide 'assistance' to peoples
labouring under monarchal oppression were likely to prove
irresistible – regardless of promises made in treaties. The
case for negotiations would be enhanced if a more 'respectable' government emerged in France. The establishment
of the Directory in November 1795 seemed to meet this
condition. The British government had never defined its
position on the re-establishment of the monarchy. Early
in the war a monarchist posture had been adopted. It
seemed unlikely that a Republican régime would accept
terms which included a French withdrawal from the Low
Countries. A readiness to abandon the French royalists to
their fate might not necessarily bring a settlement any
nearer and would certainly outrage the Austrians. Yet the
manifesto to the people of France drawn up in October 1793
merely described monarchy as the best, but by implication
not the only, means of establishing 'some legitimate and
stable government' with which Britain would be ready
to negotiate.

Prospects for peace were not good. Some in Britain were
unconvinced of the Directory's moderation; in July 1794
Portland Whigs had entered Pitt's Cabinet and exercised
great influence over the Foreign Secretary. The Portland
Whigs' distaste for the French Revolution was more fundamental than Pitt's approach. The peace initiative came
from Pitt rather than Grenville but, whereas it had been
easy to set aside Carmarthen's policies, Grenville was a
more important figure. Although Grenville agreed to the
negotiations he probably wanted them to fail. He agreed
with Burke that the strategic threat from France was

secondary to the ideological and that Britain's chief war aim should be the restoration of the Bourbons. In 1796 there could be no insistence on the return of the Bourbons but Grenville asked that France abandon its European conquests, accept British annexation of French colonies and give favourable treatment to Austria in a general peace settlement. These unrealistic demands were countered by French proposals stipulating a return of all colonies and acceptance of a substantial enlargement of French territory in Europe. The failure of the negotiations was inevitable and the Foreign Secretary probably saw them as a public relations operation to prove that French demands left no alternative but to continue the war with renewed vigour.

Another attempt was made to reinvigorate the remnants of the Coalition by bribing Prussia back into the war. British policy was learning the lessons of *real politik*. Even in 1795 Grenville had been prepared to sacrifice Eastern Europe to the ambitions of stronger powers. Now the principle was extended to the West. Belgium would be given to Prussia whilst Austria gained Bavaria. Prussia was not interested and Austrian resolution was failing in the aftermath of the new French victories. As a last throw negotiations were re-opened with Russia but the Russian price was believed to be beyond Britain's resources. In October 1796 Spain's declaration of war on the French side meant that parts of the Spanish Empire could be attacked cheaply. Yet acquisitions of Spanish colonies seemed a roundabout road if the real objective was still the overthrow of the French Revolution. The other extreme, that of a direct invasion of France, though supported by Grenville, was rejected by Pitt; such plans had failed in the past and would achieve no more if they were tried again.

There was no alternative but to renew peace negotiations, this time offering serious concessions. But Britain's readiness to accept French annexations on the Continent and to restore captured French colonies was still qualified by an insistence that France relinquish the Austrian Netherlands, her most significant acquisition, whilst Britain would not only lose no territory but might actually make colonial gains at the expense of France's allies. Britain claimed to have gone to war to protect the Dutch but now she proposed to take the Cape and Ceylon from them. Grenville gave the game away when he said that he did not really expect the Directory 'to accept a peace contrary to its interests'.[14]

In many ways 1797 was the worst year of the entire war. The death of Catherine in November 1796 meant that the French no longer feared Russian armies aiding the Austrians and could thus prepare a knock-out blow. An anti-British peace party flourished in Vienna. After the Austrian armies collapsed in February 1797 it was obvious that Austria was going the way of Prussia. The consolation that Austrian departure from the war would open the way for Prussia's return was exploded by the revelation that Prussia had recently made another secret treaty with France. Britain would soon be totally isolated.

As Europe fell under French dominance, Britain looked for friends elsewhere in the world but the United States, the most considerable extra-European power, proved unsympathetic. The American politician and diplomat, Gouverneur Morris, warned Grenville that Americans believed Britain was prolonging the agony of Europe, by putting forward unrealistic peace terms, so that it could complete its colonial conquests. Morris suggested that Britain should promise that seizures of French, Dutch and Spanish colonies were war measures to protect neighbouring British territories, thus stressing that colonial gains were not Britain's chief objective which remained the protection of Germany and the Low Countries.[15]

It was partly with an eye on America and partly to prevent a separate Franco-Austrian peace that Grenville indicated Britain would 'sacrifice certain of her colonial conquests in order to assure the welfare and security of her Ally on which His Majesty holds that of Europe essentially to depend'.[16] Britain would even accept the Austrian Netherlands as an integral part of France and the Dutch Republic as a French satellite. For the first time British proposals were consistent with the military situation and stood some chance of acceptance. Even this self-sacrifice proved insufficient, however. For Austria an arrangement with France, although involving loss of territory, could be made palatable by a share in the partition of Venetian Republic – the main feature of the Treaty of Campo Formio between France and Austria signed in October 1797.

Britain was now alone. The country had failed to prevent French domination of Western Europe and had lost far more completely than in 1783. There was not even the consolation of retaining colonial conquests. However humiliating the peace, an end to the war was preferable to its continuation. Even amongst the political nation, support for the war was ebbing. In Parliament, Fox's criticisms were beginning to tell. The French could exploit a number of vulnerable spots, as demonstrated by their despatch of an army to Ireland in December 1796. In England economic distress, coupled with bad harvests, was causing growing unrest. The widespread adoption of the Speenhamland System of Poor Relief can be seen as a panic response to the threat of civil commotion and even revolution.

Revolutionary ideas manifested themselves in the Royal Navy, the supreme symbol of British power. Without an obedient navy, the British government was impotent to the point of absurdity. Crews at Spithead and the Nore mutinied and blockaded the Thames estuary. This devastating news, coupled with rebellion in Ireland, prompted financial panic, a run on the Bank of England and suspension of cash payments, the touchstone of financial orthodoxy. The vaunted financial and economic miracle of the 1780s was evaporating. A total reconstruction of the government seemed inescapable; Pitt would go and a new administration make peace on French terms. One section of the Cabinet led by Grenville argued that the war could still be continued by detaching Austria from France, but a majority including the Prime Minister recognized the inevitable. Malmesbury was sent to France again – with instructions to give way to the French in almost all disputed matters.

Why, then, did peace not break out in 1797? The Directoire was alarmed at the growing prestige and political ambitions of its army commanders; peace with Britain might help to prolong its own existence. Unfortunately the civilian politicians had let matters go too far and the situation was transformed by the *coup d'état* of 18

Fructidor (4 September 1797). The new régime was more intransigent and would make no face-saving concessions to the British. Malmesbury was informed that he must accept all of the French demands or depart from Lille within twenty-four hours.

But there was another reason for the failure. Grenville was one of the more intransigent members of the government yet he was not old fashioned in his philosophy of diplomacy. He remembered the lessons of the Dutch crisis of 1787, that the French could be fought with their own weapons, with opinion 'out of doors'. Grenville appreciated the importance of public opinion and also recognized that public opinion could be managed. The most important opinion to manage was not French or Austrian but British. If the British public could be persuaded that the war must continue and get, as it were, a second wind, then all was not lost. Grenville found newspaper editors to help him. Every development in the negotiations suggesting 'French insolence and English humiliation' was magnified in the effort to maintain the determination of the British government and people to resist French aggression. Malmesbury's rejection of the French ultimatum had political sense behind it. In his use of the press to widen his debate in Cabinet, to conduct foreign policy through the columns of newspapers, Grenville bears an unmistakable resemblance to Palmerston half a century later.

After an interlude of trying to come to terms with France, whether sincerely or not, Britain now seemed to gain a new determination. Grenville's gamble might have failed. The continuation of the war could have brought further military disaster, revolution in Britain and French invasion resulting in the overthrow of the political and social system. Yet luck was with Britain – or at least with the Britain Grenville believed in. The months following the collapse of the Lille negotiations saw a resurgence in British power. Although there were setbacks in the future, even a short-lived peace with France, the nadir of British fortunes came in the summer of 1797. Thereafter things improved. Discipline in the navy was restored and morale boosted by the defeat of the Dutch at Camperdown on 12

October 1797. French intervention in Ireland, although troublesome, did not yield the desired results. Above all, the suspension of cash payments did not destroy commercial confidence. Bank of England notes, at least, were accepted as 'real' money. Indeed, the suspension proved a blessing in disguise, giving the government greater financial flexibility and an ability to spend substantially more than it received in taxation without encountering immediate disaster. In any case, revenue rose sharply from £23 million in 1797 to over £35 million in 1799, a record which prepared the ground for new military and diplomatic initiatives. The French were finding that they were not welcome everywhere and the ferocious opposition they encountered in Switzerland was the first sign that the cause of revolution was not universally popular.

The way now appeared open for a new coalition distinguished by greater firmness of purpose than the ramshackle alliances of 1793–95. The obvious targets were Prussia and Russia, and even in Vienna many resented Campo Formio and looked forward to renewing the war against France. Hopes were raised by the death of Frederick William II of Prussia in November 1797. Frederick William III did not share his father's suspicion of Austria. Grenville told him that if France had not yet threatened North Germany this was only because it wanted to lull Berlin into a false sense of security. The French armies would invade the neutral zone established by the Treaty of Basel and then Prussia would appreciate that her true friend had been England. No nation in Europe was safe from French aggression.

The plan was for an Anglo-Prussian alliance which would later expand to include Austria and Russia. It was essential that all members should agree on objectives. Without that agreement the project was liable to be wrecked by an individual member accepting a tempting offer from France. The proposals were far-sighted and similar to the arrangements adopted in the final stages of the war against Napoleon. A key factor in the strategy was the attempt to bring Russia into the coalition. Apart from the military advantages, Russian membership would make it difficult for Prussia to remain neutral. The Czar might even impose some discipline on the German members of the alliance and thus reduce the danger of the whole enterprise being ruined by Austro-Prussian antagonisms. Russia had been a lukewarm ally in the past but in 1793, even in 1795, she had not felt threatened by the French who were still far from her own borders. By 1798, however, France was influential in Germany and the Russians felt genuine alarm at French attempts to revise the boundaries of the Holy Roman Empire.

Progress with the Russians was encouraging. The French invasion of Switzerland, the annexation of Geneva, the occupation of Rome and the acquisition of the Rhineland provided more evidence – if more were needed – of the French lust for conquest. The new Czar agreed to send a personal emissary to Berlin to win Prussia to the cause. True to Grenville's prediction that the Austrians would not dare to stay out of such a powerful combination, Vienna despatched an envoy to London to discuss an alliance. Things seemed to be going so well that there was a danger that Britain would regard the alliance as signed and sealed. Hopes of Frederick William III were too optimistic and the king quickly demonstrated his tendency to paralyzing indecision. The king of Prussia became the most courted man in Europe. British, Austrian and Russian ambassadors urged him to join them in a counter-revolutionary crusade, whilst the French put forward plausible arguments for him to stay neutral. Frederick William simply tried to keep discussions going on as long as possible whilst avoiding any decision. At least some of the Prussians exposed the false optimism of the British plans and Haugwitz ridiculed Grenville's assertion that the creation of a powerful coalition would probably compel a French climb-down without re-sorting to force. The French would give nothing without a fight.

Grenville was running ahead of reality and beginning to think of ways of maintaining peace even *after* France had been defeated. There was indeed a danger that the alliance of anti-French powers would disintegrate as soon as its objectives had been realized, thus leaving the French free to resume their career of conquest. It was necessary to guard against this by making the wartime alliance virtually permanent. Grenville even argued that countries should pledge themselves to interfere in the internal affairs of their neighbours if they believed that changes in the style of government presented a potential threat to international peace. The Great Powers would be committed to using their joint resources to strangle revolution at birth wherever this monstrosity appeared. These proposals anticipated the ideas of the Holy Alliance nearly a generation later. Grenville also anticipated the future in another respect. To be effective, the new alliance could not afford to waste time sending despatches between London, Vienna, Berlin and St Petersburg. A central Council of Ministers was needed, empowered to direct the master plan which would finally overwhelm the French.

Grenville appreciated that the arrangements of previous wars could not succeed against revolutionary France. As the French Revolution marked a new step in European history, so a new style of diplomacy had to evolve in concert with a new style of warfare. But it was one thing to speculate about how the new alliance should operate and another to make it a reality. Despite the obdurate neutrality of Prussia and obstacles to a closer understanding with Austria stemming from British insistence on repayment of loans, Britain and Russia drew closer together. The French capture of Malta in June 1798, followed by Bonaparte's attack on Alexandria, raised fears of a French Empire in the Near East and removed any remaining Russian hesitation. Czar Paul prepared to send a fleet into the Mediterranean and despatched troops to help Austria. Britain was able to demonstrate significant military capacity. Nelson's victory at the battle of the Nile showed that once the French armies were out of Europe they were vulnerable to British naval power. Some of France's best soldiers were trapped in Egypt; it seemed that the moment had come to settle accounts with the forces of revolution. Britain and Russia made a formal alliance in December 1798.

Grenville still expected Austria and Prussia to play a major role. His plan possessed a geometrical elegance. The Anglo-Russian alliance involving two powers at the periphery of Europe would control the disputes of the powers in the middle. There was a way to reconcile these disputes. Austria would receive large areas of Italy, a direction of expansion to which Prussia could hardly object. Prussia would be allowed to expand in Germany. Austria had clearly lost interest in the Southern Netherlands and the best way of dealing with this area would be to add it to the United Provinces under a restored Stadtholder.

For the time being, however, continued Prussian prevarication and disputes over finance between London and Vienna prevented the full implementation of Grenville's Grand Design. Although falling short of hopes entertained in more optimistic moments, the fact that Britain could construct a Second Coalition by the Spring of 1799 was an impressive achievement and represented a significant recovery from the dark days of 1797. Britain and Russia made joint treaties with Naples and with the Turks. Now that the war was entering a Mediterranean phase, prospects were brighter. A Mediterranean war was bound to be something of a side show and offered no immediate solution to the problem of the French domination of the heartland of Europe. None the less, a war which was a cross between a colonial war and a European war could dent the legend of French invincibility. Even in the Continental theatre proper there were grounds for hope. Although not directly linked with Britain, Austria was now in alliance with Russia and in March 1799 a Russian army appeared in Vienna. France obligingly declared war on Austria and initial allied success culminated in the capture of Turin on 20 May 1799.

The hopes of the Second Coalition were soon dashed. The Russians believed that they had captured Turin in order to restore the king of Sardinia, whilst the Austrians intended to annex much of Northern Italy for themselves. Grenville hoped to arrange a compromise by encouraging the Austrian and Russian armies to move into Switzerland. If the French could be ejected from the Alps their whole position in Italy would have been lost and the allied armies excellently placed to launch an attack on France itself through Franche Comte. Yet the Austrians, who wanted to stay in Northern Italy, were unenthusiastic especially as they were not receiving any direct financial help from Britain. Austrian failure to support the Russian advance was a major factor in the Russian defeat by the French at Zurich in September 1799.

A further project also met with disaster. Since 1795 the original objective of the war, the security of the Low Countries, had been largely forgotten. Grenville proposed to rectify this. The early victories of the Second Coalition forced the French to withdraw most of their troops from the Low Countries. An attack on this area by Britain, Prussia and Russia might have succeeded. The Prussians refused to take part, although an Anglo-Russian invasion went ahead. The expedition turned out to be a complete failure and the Duke of York was forced to withdraw both British and Russian armies on 18 October.

One reason for allied optimism had been the chaotic situation in France. The return of Bonaparte in October 1799 and the establishment of the Consulate gave France its most resolute government since 1794. Embittered by the disasters in Switzerland and the Netherlands and feeling betrayed by their allies the Russians withdrew from the war early in 1800. The Austrians entered an alliance with Britain in return for a generous subsidy, but after a brief and disastrous campaign they accepted an armistice with the French and on 9 February 1801 signed the Treaty of Luneville which followed closely the terms of Campo Formio. Britain was back in the position of 1797; despite its early promise, the Second Coalition had achieved even less than the First.

It is hard to avoid an impression of *deja vu* when examining the events of 1797–1801. On the intellectual level, British policy had advanced since the early days of the war. There was a clearer appreciation of the necessity of closer union between the Coalition partners. Unfortunately, the gap between Grenville's imagination, so fertile in stratagems for defeating the French, and the actual state of affairs in Europe was too wide. British strategy presupposed a degree of collaboration between allied armies which had never been achieved in the past and assumed that the fortunes of war would favour Austria and

Russia. Grenville may have been a perceptive observer of European politics but he had little military understanding; in particular, he had no notion of the difficulties likely in a campaign in the Alps. Greater attention to detail and closer co-ordination between diplomats and military men was urgently required; several years were to elapse before these conditions were met.

V

A history of British foreign policy is not the place for a detailed discussion of the effects of the French wars upon Britain. This topic has been admirably discussed in Clive Emsley's *British Society and the French Wars 1793–1815* (London, Macmillan, 1979). Yet it is relevant to examine the effects of war on attitudes towards foreign policy; the very fact of war on an unprecedented scale demanded more thought to the question. There can be no doubt that there was much discontent in England, and perhaps even more in Scotland, during these years. It is possible that a majority of lower-class opinion was against the war. Apart from any ideological identification of the revolutionary cause there was a widespread belief, largely justified, that the poor were carrying a heavier share of the tax burden than the rich. Of course, it is never easy to separate the consequence of war from what might have happened in any case, particularly during a period of rapid economic change. People were probably inclined to blame the war for hardship to a greater extent than circumstances really justified. It is easy to understand that the cry of a wicked war could be more comprehensible than denunciations of an emerging economic system, the operations of which were beyond the analytical powers of even the most radical of contemporary thinkers. Indeed, it is difficult to advance firm conclusions about popular attitudes to the war at all. Opponents attract more attention than Church and King men but were not necessarily more numerous. In this debate, perhaps more than in most historical controversies, the analysis put forward depends in the last resort on the ideological standpoint of the individual historian – ranging from Arthur Bryant's picture of a nation united against an ancient foe, now more repellent than ever, to the Hammond's portrayal of widespread hostility to the war and sympathy with the French.

Upper-class opinion generally favoured the war, as might be expected, and, although on occasion the majority in Parliament supporting Pitt shrank sharply, the government was normally in no danger – especially after the defection of the Portland Whigs to Pitt in 1794. The Whigs were divided and the opinions of their leaders fluctuated markedly. In fact, the Whigs produced the most interesting theories of international relations during these years in the shape of young Brougham. Despite his advanced views on some domestic matters, however, Brougham's theories were not radically different from those put forward by adherents of Balance of Power theories before 1789. However much he might criticize specific aspects of the war against France, Brougham's commitment to such theories made it difficult for him to repudiate the war in principle. In 1803, in an important article in *The Edinburgh Review* he declared:

> Whenever a sudden and great change takes place in the internal structure of a State, dangerous in a high degree to all neighbours, they have a right to attempt, by hostile interference, the restoration of an order of things safe to themselves; or at least, to counter balance by active aggression, the new force suddenly acquired.
> The right can only be deemed competent in cases of sudden and grand aggrandization, such as that of France in 1790, endangering the safety of the neighbouring powers, so plainly as to make the consideration immaterial of the circumstances from whence the danger has originated.[17]

Of course, the war affected many economic interest groups – some advantageously others not – with the former rather better represented in Parliament. For bankers, government contractors and some colonial trades the war brought increased profits. For traders with Europe and those whose businesses suffered from the effects of war taxation, peace must have seemed an attractive prospect. Perhaps the most

powerful support of all came from the landowners, partly
for ideological reasons and partly because the war seemed
to create high food prices and rising rent rolls.

In many ways the most interesting question concerns the
attitude of the middle-classes whose numbers and importance were increasing as a result of economic change. Quite
apart from their personal economic interest, which could
point in either direction, this group was faced with conflicting ideological pressures. The Anglican Evangelicals,
already well represented in Parliament, had a considerable
following amongst the 'old' or established middle-classes
and to a lesser extent across a much broader social spec-
trum. They remained in favour of the war almost without
exception, fully committed to a hierarchical social order
and appalled by the godlessness of the French Revolution.
Another group, again with a large following in the middle-
classes, occupied a more complex position. In the 1780s,
the supporters of the new ideas of Political Economy generally supported the government; they could hardly align
themselves with Fox and his denunciations of the Eden
Treaty. Now, however, although large numbers remained
loyal to Pitt and his policies, the more thorough-going began
to identify with the Whigs and to regard the war with
misgivings. As régimes in France became more respectable,
they found it difficult to approve of a war for the defence
of the social values – and, by implication, the economic
system – of the European *ancien régime*. As far as Britain
was concerned, they feared that the war might postpone
reform in the domestic sphere which had been part of Pitt's
appeal in the past. Now, lavish government expenditure,
with considerable possibility for the misappropriation of
public funds and the political leverage inherent in government contracts, conflicted with their ideas relating to the
virtues of cheap and clean government. In the 1780s a start
had been made, if only that, in dismantling the worst
features of the Mercantile System so brilliantly exposed
by Smith. There was a danger that the process would be
reversed. War is bound to create vested interest groups
which become difficult to remove subsequently. It must,
of necessity, distort the 'natural' operation of the economy

by increasing taxation and unproductive expenditure as well as enlarging the sphere of government regulations and direction. Indeed, A. H. Imlah shows that the degree of protection enjoyed by British industry during the war was substantially higher than in the 1780s. Tariffs were introduced by hard-pressed governments for seemingly innocuous purposes, but they had much the same effects as the protective duties of earlier times – the establishment of 'sheltered' industries charging consumers excessive prices. Similarly, although the conquest of French, Dutch or Spanish colonies might be undertaken for strategic rather than mistaken economic motives, the effect would be to strengthen the 'colonial lobby' which had been seen as the main adversary in the past.

Amongst the middle classes, probably the most significant factor in determining attitudes towards the war was religious affiliation. Anglicans supported the war. Although their lower-class 'tail' might embrace radical opinions and the Methodist movement itself encounter much official hostility, the more respectable Methodists took a line similar to the Anglicans. But the case was different for other Nonconformists. J. E. Cookson's *The Friends of Peace: Anti War Liberalism in England 1793–1815* (Cambridge University Press, 1982) shows that middle-class Nonconformists, particularly the Unitarians, were the core of opposition to the war. The leaders were often men of standing in their local communities, possessing important links with the press. Although never centrally organized, Cookson claims that they became the first Nonconformist pressure group operating in the flanks of the Whig party, giving it a new, popular and liberal character. Historians usually assume that attitudes to foreign policy are 'secondary' responses to values derived from domestic experience. Cookson hints, however, that in the case of the Friends of Peace the process worked in the opposite direction. He believes that it was precisely because of their opposition to the war, in contrast to the strident support of other groups, that these men came to develop a truly distinctive middle-class value system, the orthodoxy of the future. He insists that it was this, rather than the more conventional 'effects of the Industrial Revolution' which determined new attitudes. If Cookson is right, then Britain was conforming to Continental norms in one sense – that foreign policy considerations play an important part in the creation of the general ethos of society. Yet in Britain's case, unlike that of the Continent, it was apparently not the official foreign policy but the 'unofficial', the 'anti' foreign policy which performed this role.

Although in 1800 the full implications of these developments lay in the future, more perceptive politicians may have appreciated that one day they would have to pay more heed to middle-class opinion. Either they would have to make peace with France or they would have to fight a different war and present their policies in more attractive ways. It may seem strange to arrange this chapter to include the 1780s and 1790s, rather than to treat the 1780s separately and then to have a chapter devoted entirely to the Revolutionary and Napoleonic wars. Yet in many ways the 1790s were a hangover from the 1780s. The period from 1801 to 1815 would see a far more determined attempt to get to grips with fundamental problems, old and new alike.

NOTES: CHAPTER 2 .

1 Debates in *Parliamentary History*, 17 and 21 February 1783, vol. 23, pp. 485–9; 526–43.
2 *Parliamentary History*, 14 November 1783, op. cit., pp. 1156–87.
3 Sir A. W. Ward and G. P. Gooch (eds.) *The Cambridge History of British Foreign Policy*, Vol. 1, 1783–1815, Cambridge, Cambridge University Press, 1922, p. 146.
4 J. H. Ehrman, *The British Government and Commercial Negotiations with Europe, 1783–1793*, Cambridge, Cambridge University Press, 1962, p. 185.
5 *Cambridge History of British Foreign Policy*, Vol. 1, pp. 161–4; 172–5.
6 Carmarthen to the King, 9 January 1787. *Political Memoranda*, op. cit., p. 66.
7 William Eden to Morton Eden, 20 October 1789. Quoted in J. H. Clapham, 'Pitt's First Decade 1783–92', in *Cambridge History of British Foreign Policy*, p. 190.
8 R. Lodge, *Great Britain and Prussia in the Eighteenth Century*, Oxford, Clarendon Press, 1923, p. 212.

9 George III in *The Dropmore Papers: The Mss of J. B. Fortescue of Dropmore*. Historical Mss Commission 10, Vols 1892–1927, Vol. 2, p. 317.
10 *Cambridge History of British Foreign Policy*, Vol. 1, p. 245.
11 *Parliamentary History*, 30 April 1794, vol. 31, pp. 442–51.
12 J. M. Sherwig, *Guineas and Gunpowder: British Foreign Aid in the Wars with France 1793–1815*, Cambridge, Mass., 1969, p. 65.
13 *Parliamentary History*, vol. 31, pp. 452–5.
14 Morris to Grenville, 5 October 1796, H. M. C. Dropmore Papers, 10 vols., London, 1892–1927, vol. 3, p. 258.
15 *Cambridge History of British Foreign Policy*, Vol. 1, p. 272.
16 Grenville to Eden 4 April 1797. Quoted in *The Cambridge History of British Foreign Policy*, Vol. 1, op. cit., p. 274.
17 *Edinburgh Review*, vol. 2, April 1803, pp. 19–20.

3

The Road to Victory, 1801–1815

The early nineteenth century was a confusing time for British foreign policy, owing partly to the rapid turnover of foreign secretaries and partly to more fundamental factors. The 1790s had exposed some of the basic problems. How far could Britain ignore events on the Continent in order to concentrate on the rest of the world? If it could not, how serious was the threat posed to its vital interests by any particular Continental power? If the threat was serious, was the danger significantly increased by the nature of the régime in that state? Again, if the threat was serious, could Britain rely on the enthusiastic collaboration of other European states to contain and destroy it? If this collaboration was available, to what extent would it be undermined by the divergent interests and by different values? If collaboration was not forthcoming, could Britain make a satisfactory agreement with its enemy? So far, none of these questions have been resolved.

The 1790s had had their achievements. The French had never dented Britain's naval superiority, as in the American War; Britain's position in the non-European world was virtually unassailable. There had been an impressive recovery from the dark days of 1797 when Britain itself could have taken the revolutionary path. Above all, despite acute problems, the remarkable transformation of British society continued unabated. But Britain had neither defeated the French nor come to terms with them. Two coalitions had been destroyed by a combination of French military might, poor co-ordination and the survival of attitudes more appropriate to the pre-revolutionary world. The Second Coalition had shown greater realism than its predecessor and Grenville, at any rate, appreciated the need for closer collaboration between the allies, but the actual achievement was minimal. With the withdrawal of Austria and Russia, the Second Coalition was at an end. The capture of Malta in September 1800 was encouraging but it angered Czar Paul who now established a new League of Armed Neutrality opposed to British maritime claims to stop and search neutral shipping. In response, a naval expedition was despatched to the Baltic. The destruction of the Danish fleet at Copenhagen, the death of Czar Paul and the enthusiastic reception of the British fleet in some Baltic ports led to the collapse of the League. However welcome, these successes, together with other victories, did not detract from the reality of French hegemony over most of Western Europe.

The only thing to do was to explore again the various options that had been tried in the 1790s. The first option was peace. Although the collapse of Pitt's ministry in February 1801 arose through issues not directly connected with foreign policy, war weariness played some part. Negotiations began immediately after the Addington ministry took office. Peace preliminaries were signed on 1 October 1801 and later formalized into the Treaty of Amiens. Britain agreed to return all its overseas conquests made since 1793. Trinidad and Ceylon were the only gains. Malta was to be restored to the Knights of St John whilst France promised to withdraw from Naples, the Roman States and Egypt. The essentials of French domination of Europe – control of the Low Countries, Western Germany, Switzerland and Northern Italy – remained untouched.

The debate on the Peace Preliminaries held on 3 and 4 November 1801 reflects different views of Britain's position

in the world. The new Foreign Secretary, Lord Hawkesbury, claimed that the peace was based on terms similar
to those offered to France in 1797 – though Grenville
denied this. Hawkesbury was reluctant to pledge that the
peace would last but it was both honourable and advantageous; it might not be popular with fervent supporters of
the Bourbons but at least the Consulate was better than
the Committee of Public Safety. The manners, opinions
and habits of the French people had recently improved
dramatically. The Consulate might have conquered even
more than the Jacobins but it was less of a social threat.
Thus France could now be treated as a 'normal' power, not
the terrifying alien which had ignored all the conventions
and assumptions of civilized relations between states. If
Britain's war efforts really had brought about a return
to partial respectability in France then in a profound
sense it had saved European civilization. With this task
accomplished, relations with France could be conducted on
a more normal basis. Any future wars would be more like
the wars against the Bourbons than the 'no holds barred'
conflicts of the 1790s.

After the failure of the First and Second Coalition
there was little chance of constructing another. If the
war continued, what harm could Britain do to France and
what harm could France do to Britain? The answer was
'very little'. Britain could not break French domination of
Europe and France could not challenge Britain's maritime
supremacy. There was no point in going on. Hawkesbury
compared his work with the treaties of 1713, 1748, 1763
and 1783. Britain had made large gains only in 1713 and
1763 and many of the supposed gains of 1763 proved
illusory. The settlement arranged now resembled that of
the Treaty of Aix-la-Chapelle in 1748 which had at least
given Europe seven years respite from war. Of course,
critics might argue that neither in 1748 nor in 1801 had a
proper balance of power been re-established and therefore
peace was bound to be short lived. Hawkesbury countered
that, whilst the idea of a balance of power remained valid,
it should be restated in modern terms. The balance was
not just in terms of population and territory – although

this was still important – but was also about commercial
and industrial strength. On this basis, France was not as
all powerful as it seemed:

> ...In appreciating the power of France we must consider
> the diminution sustained by her commerce, the ruin of her
> manufacturers, and an incalculable loss of wealth, while, if
> we consider the real increase to the substantial power of Great
> Britain, it will be found in proportion to the Continental
> increase of France.[1]

Hawkesbury's emphasis on Britain's commercial and industrial power suggests that the war had not impeded the
upswing in the British economy. Despite the pessimists
of the 1790s, Hawkesbury was probably correct. The
statement also implies a partial acceptance of the French
interpretation of the Balance of Power theory, exemplified in the works of the French propagandist, Hauterive,
asserting that Britain's economic expansion required a
corresponding territorial expansion on the part of France.
There is also an isolationist strand in Hawkesbury's words
hinting that what happened on the Continent is not of
paramount importance, that Britain's economic strength
insulates it from the effects of European convulsions, a
sort of commercial version of the North Sea.

Hawkesbury's statement suggests changed assumptions
about foreign policy. Here we find a paradox. Before 1789,
although the bases of British policy differed somewhat from
those of other states, it was still possible to see a common
denominator. This unity had been destroyed by the French
Revolution. Yet just when France allegedly showed signs
of coming into line, social and economic changes in Britain
were producing a philosophy of foreign policy which, in
its own way, differed as much from the European norm
as anything arising from the French Revolution. Perhaps
it would soon be Britain, not France, that would be the
odd man out.

Hawkesbury's peace proposals were carried by a large
majority but were criticized by speakers such as William
Windham and Thomas Grenville. Windham's emphasis

on honour and prestige seemed to represent old fashioned values. He quoted with approval Junius's assertion
that any departure from the highest standards of honour
was as dangerous to a nation as it was to female virtue.
The woman who permits one familiarity seldom knows
where to stop. In the affairs of nations, one humiliating
submission to a threatening neighbour only encourages
further demands and eventually brings the weaker state
into universal contempt; in short, Hawkesbury was turning
England into the whore of France. Despite its colourful
language, Windham's analysis is quite sophisticated, a
classic indictment of the appeasing belief that concessions
to an already stronger power will satisfy its appetite and
guarantee the weaker power against attack in the future.
He saw that Hawkesbury's argument depended on the
good behaviour of France. But was France now a reformed
nation? The country's appetite for world domination was
clearly as sharp as ever and it was obviously moving
towards a military despotism. Although he did not use
the precise words, Windham was asking whether a right-
wing dictatorship was any more reliable than a left-wing
dictatorship. Windham's argument was not really one of
ideology but of interest. In 1793 Britain had gone to war
over a strategic rather than an ideological issue – and had
been right to do so. It did not signify what ideology the
authorities in France used to justify their own existence.
What mattered for Britain was that France was too strong
and that it was essential to contain this strength. Windham
was proposing an important theory of international relations
– that ideology is rarely important in contacts between
states and that alliances and enmities are usually based on
substantive struggles for power and territory.

The most interesting part of Windham's speech discusses
Hawkesbury's claims about the protection afforded to Britain by her wealth and economic strength. Hawkesbury
seems the typical economist, believing that the future must
develop in a certain way, indifferent to specific details and
all the while assuming that everyone else accepts his own
premisses. The French Revolution may have produced
economic liberation in some fields but it certainly did not

do so universally. If Napoleon had presided over a state where the laws of the market were allowed to operate freely, Britain might indeed be safe. Windham admitted this but he thought like an historian not an economist, suspicious of generalization and aware of fundamental differences in outlook. With one sentence he demolished Hawkesbury's optimism: 'But the competition will not be left to its natural course. This game will not be fairly played.'[2] British commerce would be excluded from European markets or subjected to crippling disadvantages. The power of economic advantage could so easily be thwarted by political and military measures.

II

The renewal of war with France in May 1803 suggests that one option of the 1790s, that of peace, had been taken to its logical conclusion of a settlement on French terms. But even this had failed and the only available course was to go to the other extreme and construct another Coalition. This conclusion was implicit in Pitt's return to power in May 1804. The new ministry coincided with the proclamation of the French Empire and it was hoped that Bonaparte's usurpation would unleash a storm of indignation from the surviving 'legitimate' monarchs. The British plan was to make a firm alliance with Russia and then use Russian influence in Berlin and Vienna to complete the task – in other words, the strategy of the Second Coalition. But Russia was now more involved in the structure of European diplomacy; Czar Alexander's opinions may have been clouded with romantic mysticism but at least his concept of Europe overlapped with Pitt's more prosaic appreciation of the need for greater unity. Exchanges between Alexander and Pitt produced an important policy statement contained in a letter to the Russian ambassador on 19 January 1806. Pitt made explicit what had only been half perceived in the past – that a Coalition would fail unless there was prior agreement on how Europe should be ordered after France had been defeated. Pitt had three main objectives:

1st   To rescue from the Dominion of France those
        countries which it has subjugated since the beginning
        of the Revolution, and to reduce France within its
        former limits, as they stood before that time.
2nd   To make such an arrangement with respect to the
        territories recovered from France, as may provide
        for their Security and Happiness, and may at the
        same time constitute a more effectual barrier against
        Encroachments on the part of France.
3rd   To form, at the Restoration of Peace, a general
        Agreement and guarantee for the mutual protec-
        tion and Security of Different Powers and for the
        re-establishing of a general system of Public Law
        in Europe.[3]

These clearly enunciated aims marked a step forward
from the piecemeal approach of the 1790s, yet they lacked
sufficient detail and Coalitions could still be destroyed by a
combination of defeat and disloyalty. The intellectual basis
of the Coalition might be new, but the performance was
depressingly familiar. As Britain prepared for more active
hostilities, her high-handed measures at sea angered other
powers. Thus, war with Spain early in 1805 gave rise to
rumours of an impending attack on Spanish America and
conjured dreams of new El Dorados. This response showed
that attitudes had changed little since the 'traditional' wars
of the eighteenth century. The action did not advance the
war against France and was potentially exhaustive of manpower and liable to disperse the navy, making it vulnerable
to attack in home waters. An Anglo-Russian alliance was
achieved in June, and Austria joined in August. At this stage
there were the usual protestations of solidarity and promises
not to make separate treaties with the French. Unfortunately the Russians still harboured their own ambitions, the
Austrians were too weak and the Prussians could not make
up their minds and always distrusted Austria. The British,
though prepared to give financial help to their allies, were
still reluctant to make a major contribution to the land
war and at the same time were dangerously distracted to
colonial side shows.

Before the tragedy of the Third Coalition unfolded there was one moment of triumph. The Battle of Trafalgar on 21 October 1805 destroyed the fleets of France and Spain and made British supremacy in the non-European world unassailable, again the logical conclusion of earlier developments – although not fully appreciated at the time. Thereafter there was little but disaster. The Austrian armies were destroyed at Austerlitz and the terms of the ensuing Treaty of Pressburg hinted of an economic blockade of Britain. The Prussians who had hesitantly joined the Coalition in return for the promise of Hanover made a separate peace with France. Of the major powers, only Britain and Russia remained at war with France, and Russian resolution was increasingly suspect. In more ways than one Pitt's death in January 1806 was the end of an era. In recent years both the course of peace and the course of more vigorous prosecution of the war had been tried unsuccessfully. There was no obvious answer to the question of what British foreign policy should do next.

There was no reason to suppose that there was more chance of lasting peace in 1806 than in 1801. The negotiations that now took place resulted more from changes in the domestic situation than from any alteration in the international scene. After a lapse of twenty-three years, Charles Fox returned to the Foreign Office. Yet Fox's negotiations were different from earlier discussions, even those culminating in the Treaty of Amiens, which had been conducted by men who regretted that they were compelled to try to find some accommodation with régimes they loathed. Fox had been the arch proponent of an alternative foreign policy, applauding the French Revolution and declaring that it was the oppressive monarchies of Europe who had been the real aggressors in the revolutionary wars. He had welcomed the French conquests because they had brought liberty to the peoples of Europe. He had denied that France posed any threat to England, certainly no threat at all to the people of England. He had portrayed the war as an excuse to suppress liberty in England through draconian treason laws and other repressive measures. He was an admirer of Bonaparte and had once described him as 'afraid of war to the last degree'. If anyone could bring lasting peace between England and France, Fox was surely the man.

Fox's failure to secure a peace settlement indicates the realities of international power politics. Despite the problems of an alliance with Russia, Fox appreciated that the Czar was the only man who could balance Bonaparte in Continental Europe and insisted that any peace settlement must involve Alexander. The French wanted a bilateral treaty which would leave the British supreme in the colonial world and the French in control of Europe. Despite his earlier support for the American rebels, Fox was convinced of the value of Empire, yet he also appreciated that Britain's position in the non-European world depended on preventing any one power dominating Europe. In the last week of his life, Fox told Grey – who was to succeed him at the Foreign Office – that he must not forsake the Russian connection.

Although some like Samuel Whitbread insisted that a settlement with Napoleon could be achieved without damaging essential British interests, the failure of the 1806 negotiations marked a new phase in the war. The cyclical pattern of coalition, defeat, disintegration and negotiations was broken. After 1806 British governments, if not opposition spokesmen, knew that a compromise peace was impossible. Some new and more effective ways of waging war had to be found.

1806 produced a new option for British foreign policy – although characteristically it was a French invention. So far the French had been unable to inflict crippling damage on the British economy, yet unless they could do this Britain would keep on organizing coalitions against them. Economic warfare was the obvious answer. The French as much as the British were looking for a way out of deadlock. They decided that they needed to develop a strategy which would deprive Britain of the means of providing subsidies to the other powers of Europe. Even better, such warfare might inflict so much damage that Britain itself would be compelled to seek peace on any terms. Economic collapse would make the war unpopular and increase the chances of social disruption. In a country where commercial men and commercial values were gaining ground over aristocratic notions of honour, the pressure to withdraw from the war would become irresistible.

In the debates of November 1801 Hawkesbury had asserted – in the face of Windham's incredulity – that the French could never exclude British trade from the Continent of Europe. Now the French believed they had found the answer. French readiness to deprive Prussia of Hanover and the proclamation of the Confederation of the Rhine in July 1806 brought about yet another *volte face* in Berlin. The Prussians went to war only to see their armies destroyed at Jena-Auerstadt on 14 October 1806. Bonaparte then occupied Berlin and on 21 November issued the Berlin Decrees in which the British Isles were placed under blockade. All commerce and communications with British ports were forbidden and British property in the territory of France or her allies subject to confiscation. Despite the move towards 'total war' which had been such a marked feature of the French Revolution, economic contact had continued between the belligerent states. Now the French moved to plug this loophole. The Decrees were to be carefully implemented by France's satellite states to close most European ports to British trade. Prussia and Austria were soon persuaded to join 'The Continental System'. The Ottoman Empire was now moving closer to France so it was decided in London to send a fleet to the Straits to warn the Turks not to attack Russia and thus convince the Czar of the continued value of the British alliance. The Russians drew their own conclusions from the ignominious withdrawal of the British fleet in the face of fire from Turkish shore batteries. At Tilsit, Czar Alexander agreed to join the Continental System and undertook to persuade Portugal, Denmark and Sweden to co-operate in the French scheme. If these countries refused to co-operate they would be treated as enemies and their fleets seized for use by the French.

The completion of the Continental System had serious consequences for Britain, but in 1806 and 1807 no one, either in Britain or in France, could predict the likely outcome of a trade war. Indeed, the trade war exposed the falsity of established assumptions about Britain's economic priorities. In some respects the Tilsit agreements were less serious than anticipated, even after Russia declared war on Britain on 7 November 1807. It had been thought that the two countries were natural allies because of their long-standing commercial ties; any breaking of those ties would harm both. Yet Britain was able to manage without the supposedly essential naval stores from Russia and British exports to Russia had been declining as a proportion of total exports for some years. If foreign policy was to be determined by trade then Russia was irrelevant. If foreign policy was to be determined by considerations of military means then Russia was crucial. Britain had no obvious means of regaining the Russian alliance. The best hope was that the trade war would do more harm to Russia than to Britain but, for the time being, all that Britain could do was to hope that renewed French expansionism would drive the Czar to reconsider his position.

The Continental System proved less effective than its authors had hoped. It was based on an out-of-date view of the British economy. European markets had been the chief destination of re-exported colonial goods which had been so vital to Britain in the eighteenth century. Now re-exports were being over-shadowed by exports of manufactured goods. Here, the dependence on European markets was less acute. In 1805 only a third of manufactured exports went to European destinations. Not even this trade could be stopped entirely. There were loopholes in the Continental System in the Mediterranean, and even in Northern Europe some British goods managed to evade Bonaparte's coastguards. Even assuming complete closure of European markets, Britain would not be really crippled so long as it retained access to markets elsewhere. Britain now exported almost as much to the United States alone as it did to the whole of Europe.

The British counter measures to the Berlin Decrees were contained in the Orders in Council of 7 January 1807 and aimed at stopping ships of other nations trading to the ports of France or her allies. Unfortunately, these counter measures caused more resentment than the French decrees amongst the neutral powers and damaged relations with the United States. President Madison replied with Acts of Non-Intercourse and Embargo directed against Britain. In 1808 and 1809, therefore, British goods were excluded both from United States' and European markets. Despite evasions, some 60 per cent of British manufactured exports were now excluded from their normal destinations. With the decisive addition of American assistance, the Continental System might achieve its objective of bringing Britain to its knees. Distress and discontent was rising at an alarming rate. Yet even at this crucial juncture British exports were able to find new outlets: in South America, in India and in former Dutch territories such as Java, captured in 1810.

The Continental System was also misconceived in that it failed to stop essential British imports. The first decade of the nineteenth century witnessed a rapid population growth in Britain, combined with a run of poor harvests. In bad years there was a deficiency of food. Yet the Continental System made no attempt to stop grain imports from the Baltic, a step which might have produced serious social protest in a Britain reduced to near starvation. The Continental System did cause major problems: a deterioration in the balance of payments and increased inflationary pressures. But the response of the British economy which became far more world-oriented during these years meant that it never succeeded in its chief objective of forcing Britain to seek peace on French terms. Further, the assumptions of both the Continental System, and of the Orders in Council, centred on the overriding importance of foreign trade. Significant as exports and imports were, the most crucial development was the growth of the internal economy of Britain, involving British raw materials and British consumers. Here the French could do nothing, apart from hoping that heavy wartime taxation would inhibit growth.

The chief effects of the Continental System and the Orders in Council were not felt in Britain but in the French satellite territories, particularly in Holland and North Germany. The economic dislocation felt in ports such

as Hamburg made the French unpopular, even amongst
people who had initially regarded them as liberators. The
more completely the Continental System was enforced –
the chief purpose of Bonaparte's annexation of Holland
into metropolitan France in July 1810 – the more unpopular
the French would become. By the beginning of 1811,
relations between France and Russia were deteriorating.
The Czar imposed tariffs on French goods and allowed a
resumption of trade with Britain. The Continental System
was crumbling and by the following year was in such
disarray that the Orders in Council could be repealed.
Even in France itself there were signs of discontent. Britain
held most of the cards in a war of economic attrition. It
was not just a matter of Britain's industrial might; the
country's entire trading system was based on the greater
efficiency and lower costs of sea transport compared to
land transport. A Napoleon with railways would have been
a more formidable opponent.

The other new feature of the war effort was a belligerent
populism evident during George Canning's tenure of the
Foreign Office from 1807 to 1809. The British reaction to
Tilsit was vigorous. In 1806 and 1807, defence resources
had been scattered in expeditions to the Straits, to Egypt,
to the Cape, even to Buenos Aires. An expedition to Mexico
was being prepared but this plan was countermanded and
in September 1807 the force was despatched to Copenhagen
to forestall the French and thus open a large hole in the
Continental System. Canning's solution involved 'gunboat
diplomacy' of the crudest kind. Aristocratic restraint and
respect for international law which had constituted at least
one strand of traditional British foreign policy was being
discarded. Britain was showing some of the ruthlessness
which had become the hallmark of French behaviour.
Canning's only justification was success. Canning had only
scorn for opposition spokesmen who denounced the procedure as a violation of international law. The government
was being called to account, not for disaster and disgrace
– as so often in the past – but for success.

The new vigour and belligerence was especially manifest
in Spain. The passage of French troops across Spain to

attack Portugal – a kind of Copenhagen in reverse – alerted Bonaparte to a grander project, once attempted by Louis XIV. If he could acquire Spain and the Spanish Empire and infuse French efficiency and enthusiasm into this ramshackle and under-developed estate, he might break out of the European sphere to which the British had confined him. Called on to arbitrate between Charles IV and his heir, Ferdinand, Napoleon compelled both to renounce their rights and then proclaimed Joseph Bonaparte as king of Spain. Little seemed to stand in his way; British sea power could hardly stop the French crossing the Pyrenees. At worst, Britain might confine the French to the Peninsula and deny them the Spanish Empire. But events in Spain offered Britain an exciting opportunity; outbursts of Spanish nationalism in response to the imposition of a French puppet monarch culminated in the Madrid rising of 2 May 1808. Ever since 1793, French conquests had been defended on the grounds that, whatever aristocrats might say, ordinary people preferred the principles of the French Revolution to those of the *ancien régime*. The French cause, even in its Napoleonic guise, had been identified with the liberation of Europe, while Britain was linked to a spiteful but inevitable futile opposition to the will of the people. Now the time had come to turn the tables; no one could pretend that the régime of Joseph Bonaparte represented the wishes of the people of Spain.

The situation raised wider issues. If Britain gave whole-hearted supported to Spain's 'patriots', could it show that monarchs were more representative of the peoples of Europe than French 'liberators' whose objective was to destroy all traditional identities and establish a centralized dictatorship? In Spain at least, radical patriots and tradition-alists could unite against the French. Although Napoleon seemed as strong as ever, May 1808 was the beginning of his downfall. On the ideological level the initiative was passing from French hands. Canning was quick to appreciate this, declaring that any people who took to arms against the French immediately became the ally of Britain. The way was open to a position which had eluded Britain even before the French Revolution; idealists everywhere might look to

Britain rather than to France as their natural ally. The idea
of the wars against Napoleon as wars of liberation began
to enter popular mythology. In 1830, Palmerston gave his
version of what had happened in a way that would have
caused astonishment in the 1790s:

> When Bonaparte was to be dethroned, the Sovereigns of
> Europe called up their people to their aid; they invoked them
> in the sacred names of Freedom and National Independence:
> the cry went forth throughout Europe: and those, whom
> Subsidies had no power to buy, and Conscription no force to
> compel, roused by the magic sound of Constitutional Rights,
> started spontaneously into arms. The long suffering Nations
> of Europe rose up as one man, and by an effort tremendous
> and wide spreading, like a great convulsion of nature, they
> hurled the conqueror from his throne.[4]

Thus, sympathy for the aspirations of others appeared
compatible with a more strident assertion of self-interest.
National independence whether in Europe or elsewhere
– and prospects in South America looked favourable –
could remove the commercial restrictions which had limited
British exports and trade in the past. Economic interests
had always been important in foreign policy but the change
from a trading to an industrial economy could have major
consequences. In its new 'popular' dimension British policy
might appear to have more in common with the French
approach than with that of the other Great Powers. Yet
if Britain were to defeat France she still had to make a
common cause with traditional monarchies, a collaboration
which might prove even more difficult to sustain than
in the past.

Commitment to Spain could be demonstrated only by
sending British forces to the Peninsula. It required substantial financial outlay at a time when the effects of
the Continental System were most severe. The expedition
could be despatched, however, because of Britain's underlying financial strength and because the injection of funds
elsewhere usually brought the money back to Britain in the
shape of increased orders for goods. It was not a question of
money but of men. Britain's allies had always complained

that its short lived, small-scale and usually inglorious interventions into Continental warfare cast doubt on its determination and motives. The fact that British forces in the Peninsula actually won battles against French regulars was a sign that Britain had the capacity to become a major power on land as well as at sea. The French forces in Portugal may have escaped lightly under the Convention of Cintra but the improvement of British prospects had been so dramatic that what would have recently passed for a triumph now seemed a disgrace. A new foreign policy based on economic warfare and vigorous nationalism at home and abroad had transformed the situation in Britain's favour.

III

Yet how much had things really changed? There were appalling losses and defeats in Spain to come. Attempts to strike at the heart of French power, as in the Walcheran expedition of 1809, failed catastrophically. After Canning left the Foreign Office there were even unofficial peace negotiations involving the French Minister of Police, Joseph Fouché, negotiations later repudiated by Napoleon. Relations with the United States were so mishandled as to lead to the outbreak of an unnecessary war in 1812. Disproportionate effort was spent to little avail in cultivating Sweden. The new policy was largely the product of French success; Britain had no option but to appeal to popular sentiment because so many legitimate rulers had become French clients. There was no alternative but to give more attention to the Mediterranean, South America and the East, because prospects of reviving the war in the heart of Europe were uninviting. Britain may have shown commendable flexibility in producing a less European-orientated policy but this resulted from her effective expulsion from Europe. Despite its brave face, Canning's policy reflected the fact that Britain had had no allies of importance since Tilsit. If such allies became available again it would be necessary to modify some of the 'newer' features of British foreign policy, evident in the period of enforced isolation from the

Continent. Castlereagh, who became Foreign Secretary in March 1812, understood this point.

Castlereagh appreciated that the best hope of constructing another coalition lay in the deterioration of Franco-Russian relations. The imminence of the French invasion of Russia made it imperative to convince the Russians of the value of British help. On 24 June 1812 the French Army crossed the River Niemen; on 17 July the Treaty of Obero was signed forming an alliance between Britain, Russia and Sweden. A coalition of sorts existed once more. The Russians' defence of their country made Alexander I a popular hero in Britain and revived enthusiasm for the war. Perhaps the retreat from Moscow brought the final defeat of Napoleon in sight, yet even in victory the British contribution might be regarded as only marginal. Even in Spain, British troops were only a small proportion of the anti-French forces. In any case, the war in Spain would soon be seen as a side show compared to the great battles needed to defeat Napoleon in the heartland of Europe. In every sense of the word, the British role would be regarded as peripheral. At the extremities of Europe, in the Mediterranean and in the Baltic, British naval power might make some difference but the country seemed incapable of influencing the areas of the decisive battles. If this 'landsman's view' of the war gained ground it would be difficult to secure proper attention to British interests. French dominance might be replaced by Russian dominance; a prospect highly unwelcome in London where, at least in official circles, Alexander was regarded with suspicion. Although receiving substantial financial help from Britain, he continued to support the Americans against their former masters. Perhaps, having fought France far longer than the other countries of Europe, Britain would be excluded from the final settlement; the efforts and sacrifices since 1793 might become entirely wasted.

Even the result of the war was not assured. The French armies in Russia contained units from Prussia and Austria, whose rulers, together with the other German princes, showed no signs of throwing off their shackles. The French still had huge forces in the field. German rulers who had tried to escape from their French masters in the past had been severely punished for their pains. For the time being they were unwilling to repeat the experiment. Unless the war spread westwards into Germany, France would still dominate Europe; all that would happen would be a return to the position before Tilsit. News from Spain brought welcome relief. By the summer of 1812 the French were in retreat and the British prepared to invade France itself. This news attracted interest in Germany where nationalist sentiment was rising. French exactions had impoverished the people of Germany, yet Napoleon had trained many of the same people in the use of arms – an ideal combination for a mass rising. If the German rulers proved obdurate in their loyalty to France, perhaps Britain should appeal over their heads to their subjects. But Germany was not Spain. The British army was too heavily involved in the Peninsula to be spared and the terrain of most of Germany was unsuited to guerilla warfare. German nationalism was more likely to succeed if a German ruler put himself at the head of the movement and provided a professional army as the nucleus for a popular crusade. Sooner or later a major German ruler would become more frightened of nationalist insurrection than of French retribution. Already, units of the Prussian army were refusing to serve alongside the French. The King of Prussia took the hint and in February 1813 made an alliance with Russia at Kalisch. Alexander insisted that Prussia give up its claim to Hanover, making co-operation with Britain easier. In turn, Britain made treaties with Russia and Prussia at Reichenbach on 14 June. Further British victories in Spain, together with French rejection of its compromise peace proposals, persuaded Austria to join the war on 12 August. It seemed that the new Coalition, the Fourth, was shaping up well.

Yet the position of August 1813 had been reached in the past only to disintegrate in the face of divergent interests and French victories. Castlereagh had a difficult path to tread. He had to secure an unbreakable allied unity – which implied flexibility – yet he could not afford to be so flexible that Britain's own interests were sacrificed. These included recognition of special Maritime Claims, French withdrawal from the Low Countries, Spain and

Southern Italy and British annexation of various colonial territories. Many of these 'maritime' objectives were
either not understood in Continental countries or were
regarded with suspicion. Certainly as compared to earlier
wars Britain enjoyed powerful advantages. The growth of
the British economy meant the country could afford to be
more generous with financial help, whilst the expansion of
its manufacturing base enabled the provision of substantial
amounts of war material. Castlereagh exploited Britain's
position as paymaster, informing the Russian ambassador
in London that the availability of munitions and subsidies
would depend on the other members of the alliance falling
in with British plans.

The fact that threats of this kind were usually sufficient
reflected more than Castlereagh's personal standing. Britain
had provided loans and subsidies for its allies throughout
the Revolutionary and Napoleonic Wars but J. M. Sherwig
demonstrates that, at least under Pitt the Younger, the
country was not significantly more open handed than in
earlier wars – in other words that the legend of 'Pitt's gold' is
mythical. Reluctantly Britain came to accept that she would
have to be the paymaster of the allied war effort. Arguably,
the implications of the new warfare launched by France in
the 1790s were only grasped in about 1810. Sherwig stresses
that, of the £66 million given to allied powers between 1793
and 1815, £33 million was concentrated between 1810 and
1815. In the three years before Waterloo, Britain's subsidy
payments were never less than £71/2 million per annum,
whereas under Pitt the Younger they had never been more
than £21/2 million.[5] Similarly, thanks to the increased
efficiency of the Ordnance service, London was able to
send large quantities of armaments to the Russians, Swedes,
Austrians and Prussians – over one million muskets in 1813
alone. Small wonder that the rulers of Europe paid more
attention to Castlereagh than they had to Grenville.

On 18 September 1813 Castlereagh sent despatches to
Britain's overseas representatives asserting that there was no
point in regarding the struggle against Napoleon as different
wars. Success would come only with the recognition that
the wars in Spain and in Germany were part of a greater

whole. Bilateral treaties between the allied powers were not enough. There would have to be a common binding instrument setting out precise objectives to which all subscribed. It was vital that the Eastern European powers should pledge their support for Britain in matters regarded as crucial in London, but which might be seen as unimportant in Berlin, Vienna or St Petersburg. Reverting to the ideas of 1805, Castlereagh saw his scheme as the basis for the long-term stability of Europe involving the maintenance of a perpetual defensive alliance. Despite the success of allied arms at the Battle of Leipzig on 18 October 1813, Austria and Prussia were still interested in a peace in which British interests would be virtually ignored.

In part, the problem arose from poor communications and bad feeling between the principal British representatives on the Continent, some of whom came to identify too closely with the interests of their host countries. In Vienna, Aberdeen came near to accepting the idea of a compromise peace based on Metternich's Frankfurt Proposals which left the Low Countries under French control. In order to overcome these problems Castlereagh left England for the Allied headquarters in Germany in December 1813. British foreign policy would now be determined by a Foreign Secretary resident abroad, no longer having to work through the distorting piles of reports and despatches and able to deal with Continental rulers, politicians and generals face to face. Yet he would also be removed from personal contact with the Cabinet in London, with the nuances of British politics and with public opinion. He would be surrounded by 'Continental' influences to an unprecedented degree. Success would depend to some extent on personal qualities and values; it was as well that Castlereagh had something of the *ancien régime* about him.

With the French armies in retreat, the allies faced the problem of the 'liberated areas'; there was hopeless confusion about Poland, Italy, Germany and the Netherlands. At the end of the war, as at the beginning, the Low Countries preoccupied the British government. In his priorities, as well as in style, Castlereagh seemed 'European' compared to Canning. Colonial acquisitions were secondary when a vital strategic objective was at stake. In return for allied acceptance of the independence of the Netherlands, he conceded that no colonies would be retained for purely commercial reasons but it was essential to retain key points which might otherwise threaten Britain's existing empire. Yet Castlereagh knew that the recent economic changes had expanded the potential of Britain's international trade and thus placed maritime issues in the first order of importance. He argued that although essential to Britain's own prosperity and security, naval power was defensive and, unlike an army, posed no threat to other nations. The only 'teeth' Britain required was acceptance of her maritime claims – the right to stop, search and, if necessary, confiscate the vessels of other nations carrying war contraband; this system, together with the Orders in Council, had played a vital part in weakening the Napoleonic Empire. Castlereagh was adamant that Britain must retain these rights, so advantageous to its own economy and so damaging to others, whatever the other powers might say.

Apart from protecting Britain's own interests, Castlereagh tried to preserve a common front with Austria, Russia and Prussia. He went out of his way to cultivate Metternich whom he regarded as the allied leader most prone to seek a compromise with the French. He emphasized that Britain and Austria were traditional and natural allies. Due to its land-locked position Austria had less interest than other powers in contesting Britain's maritime claims. With Russia, on the other hand, Britain had considerable disagreements and, once France was defeated, Russia might become Britain's main adversary in world affairs. Yet Castlereagh endorsed Alexander's current 'hard' line that there could be no compromise peace which left Napoleon in control of France. The trouble was that Alexander might change his mind and Metternich insisted that one more attempt should be made to secure a settlement with Napoleon. Reluctantly, Castlereagh agreed, although he hoped the negotiations would fail. Despite his fears about Metternich, Castlereagh was also growing more suspicious of Russia. Alexander was hostile enough to Napoleon but alarmingly open minded on the question of French frontiers. Perhaps Alexander did not really want to weaken France because he wanted to put Bernadotte of Sweden, then under strong Russian influence, upon the French throne. If Bernadotte replaced Napoleon, France and Russia would dominate Europe. Another soldier Emperor in Paris – but able to call on Russian armies of incalculable size – was a truly alarming prospect. The last thing Castlereagh wanted was to have to make a choice between Metternich and Alexander.

Fortunately for Castlereagh, an interruption to the recent run of allied victories by a successful French counter attack in February 1814 threw Alexander into panic. A few days earlier he had been the most uncompromising of the allied leaders, now he spoke as if all were lost. This reaction lowered the Czar's standing in the eyes of other leaders, especially when the setbacks to the allied advance proved only temporary – as Castlereagh had insisted they would. Yet without Castlereagh's steadying influence, Alexander's panic might have proved infectious and the other allies rushed to protect their own interests by being first to make peace with Napoleon. According to Charles Stewart, even at this late stage of the war, the mood had been one of 'Devil take the hindmost'. The short-lived French recovery had another beneficial effect. Flushed with his recent victories, Napoleon instructed his representatives to reject even the most generous of allied terms. Thus the Chatillon negotiations proved abortive and gave Castlereagh the proof needed to convince Metternich that there could not be any peace with Bonaparte.

Castlereagh's influence was at its peak in March 1814 and he was the dominant figure in discussions between the allies at Chaumont, forcing acceptance of his blue print for the future. The Treaty of Chaumont, signed on 9 March, stipulated that France should be restricted to her 1789 frontiers. In addition to earlier pledges not to make separate treaties with France – Britain, Prussia, Austria and Russia agreed to maintain at least 60,000 men under arms until victory was achieved. Britain would also provide generous financial assistance. Even more strikingly, the four powers each undertook to contribute 60,000 men if the French tried to overthrow the new European order at any time in the next twenty years. This was a major breakthrough, although it meant unprecedented commitments by Britain who, unlike the Continental powers, had no tradition of a large army in peace time. Castlereagh's promises had disturbing implications for the British taxpayer and, some would say, for British liberty.

The Great Powers had drawn a sharp distinction between themselves and weaker states; even Sweden was only invited to accede to the Treaty, not to take part in the negotiations. Britain, Austria, Prussia and Russia, probably joined in the future by a France in safe hands, would take all the important decisions and the smaller nations would have no option but to do as they were told. The phrase 'the Great Powers' was a recognized feature of the language of diplomacy. Castlereagh would not even make exceptions in favour of Hanover. That state's interests, like those of any smaller German state, could be bargained away to secure agreement between Britain and the major partners in the alliance.

The four Great Powers were now committed to the overthrow of Napoleon, and their armies prepared to march on Paris. It was one thing to decide to get rid of Napoleon, however, and another to agree on who should follow him. Britain alone favoured a Bourbon restoration, but the Bourbons were virtually unknown to a whole generation of French people and a crude attempt to impose Louis XVIII on an unwilling France might provoke popular resistance. The British view was accepted, however, when the declaration of the Mayor of Bordeaux in favour of the Bourbons provided evidence of some popular support. The next question to be resolved was the nature of the government under a restored monarchy. Despite his reactionary reputation in England, Castlereagh did not want to recreate every feature of the *ancien régime*. British experience in Spain suggested that the allied cause, and certainly British interests, might be better served by a constitutional rather than an autocratic régime, whilst English history since 1660 indicated the wisdom of a restored monarchy accepting many of the features of the preceding system.

Louis XVIII promised to rule constitutionally, recognize the validity of the Revolutionary land settlement, accept responsibility for the public debt and maintain Napoleonic officials in their jobs.

On 29 March 1814 the allied armies reached Paris. By the end of April, after a delay caused by an attack of gout, Louis XVIII crossed the channel in the British Royal Yacht to occupy the throne of his martyred brother. Although mistakes had been made, Castlereagh had brought a degree of skill to the formulation of policy rarely witnessed in the past. There could be no doubt that Britain would play a major role in determining the shape of the postwar world.

The return of a 'respectable' government in France complicated the diplomatic situation by increasing the number of possible 'permutations' of collaboration and enmities between the powers. Castlereagh was still afraid of a Franco–Russian understanding, a danger increased by the rapport established between Alexander and Talleyrand who emerged as chief adviser to Louis XVIII. Such was Talleyrand's skill in exploiting what amounted to a competitive appeasement of France that the allies were soon talking of 1792 rather than 1789 frontiers. A settlement was achieved quite swiftly, although at first Louis XVIII declined to accept territory in Savoy and asked for compensation on his northern frontiers. Castlereagh vetoed this as incompatible with British interests. Louis was compelled to swallow his scruples and take Savoy whilst giving up Belgium and the left bank of the Rhine. Negotiations on the former French colonies were handled directly by Castlereagh and Talleyrand. Castlereagh only insisted on the retention of Malta, the Cape, Mauritius and Tobago, although St Lucia was added to the list under pressure from London. Castlereagh made one major concession to Talleyrand. Having renounced the slave trade, Britain wished other countries to do the same. The French West India lobby claimed that Britain's West Indian sugar trade had been falling off and had been overtaken by the French, even before the Revolution. Espousal of the abolitionist cause sprang from a desire to cripple competitors and assure the profitability of sugar from the East Indies which did not depend upon slave labour. Castlereagh allowed the French to re-establish the slave trade in their West Indian islands for five years, even in territories where it had been abolished under British occupation. This arrangement infuriated the anti-slavery group at Westminster and did little for Castlereagh's long-term reputation.[6] Yet on the whole the colonial arrangements were sensible. Britain secured what was needed to guarantee its naval supremacy, whilst the French and Dutch regained much of their old empires.

Castlereagh was also accommodating over financial indemnities. Despite protests from Prussia, the allies accepted Castlereagh's argument that France could not pay a large indemnity. The French were even allowed to retain the art treasures they had looted from occupied Europe. In part, this generous treatment sprang from a desire to facilitate the second stage of the settlement. It was now conceded that France should be treated as a full Great Power. Much would depend on the French attitude towards Central and Eastern Europe and each of the allied powers wanted to win France to their point of view. The situation gave Talleyrand the chance to show that clever diplomacy could do much to mitigate military defeat.

Castlereagh hoped that all important decisions would be taken at a meeting in London before a great Congress assembled in Vienna to produce the definitive settlement. But little was achieved in London; European rulers were still too euphoric at Napoleon's defeat to attend to the task of reconstruction, although the Czar's behaviour confirmed the suspicions of the British government. Dynastic marriages were still important in diplomacy and the engagement of the Regent's daughter, Charlotte, to the Prince of Orange was a crucial element in the British plan for the Dutch annexation of the former Austrian Netherlands. Due to the influence of the Czar's sister, Catherine, who had accompanied Alexander to England, Charlotte broke off the engagement. Russian interference in the affairs of the royal family, jealousy of the Czar's popularity with Londoners and anger at his open friendship with Whig politicians turned the Prince Regent into an ardent Russophobe.

Fortunately it proved possible to repair relations with the Dutch. By 14 June 1814 Castlereagh obtained the agreement of the other powers to Dutch administration of the Austrian Netherlands. The Dutch colonies in the East Indies and the Caribbean were to be returned, although the Cape was to remain in British hands.

The problem of the Peninsula was more complex. In 1812 anti-French forces in Spain proposed a Constitutional monarchy but the restored Ferdinand VII refused to accept restrictions on his power. Castlereagh disapproved of this repudiation of the 1812 Constitution and pressed Ferdinand to grant a new, if more restricted, constitution in its place. Castlereagh managed to conclude a rather vague treaty with Spain but the Spaniards were infuriated at their exclusion from the ranks of the Great Powers and Talleyrand's promise to support their claims in Italy boded ill for the future.

When the Congress of Vienna assembled in September 1814, however, Britain had secured most of its own objectives and could concentrate on the establishment of a lasting peace in Europe. If the job was bungled, war would probably break out again and Britain could hardly avoid involvement. Whatever interest Britain may have had in fomenting war in the past, the country's dedication to peace in 1814 was genuine. It had enough power; although Britain's territorial gains in the colonial fields were modest, it was by far the most powerful country in the non-European world. The empire was different to that of the eighteenth century. Its centre of gravity was in India rather than in North America. In the East, the empire was a matter of trade routes rather than territory. Britain did not need to take on the burden of the administration of huge areas. Provided control of the sea lanes was achieved, the country could sell goods wherever it liked. Further wars could not improve its situation and might make it worse. The British economy, having established a substantial lead over potential rivals, required an extended period of peace to consolidate its gains. Industry would benefit from the lower taxes promised by the return of peace. As the effective motor of world trade, Britain had an interest in the free flow of commerce which would be interrupted by any renewed outbreak of hostilities. The British message was one of harmony, but how was harmony to be achieved? The best arrangement would be to produce a Europe in which no power was predominant and where no state felt that it had been cheated. If all states, or at any rate all powerful states, were happy with the territory apportioned to them, then they would be less likely to resort to war. Alone of the Great Powers, Britain had no territorial ambitions on the Continent and was thus especially well placed to act as mediator.

The main difficulty was in Poland and Germany, although disputes there would 'echo' in Italy. The fundamental problem concerned the overlapping ambitions of Austria, Prussia and Russia. In the next few months Britain was to find all these 'Northern' powers greedy and intransigent. Eastern Europe had been a breeding ground for trouble ever since Poland had been weakened and then eliminated. The treatment of Poland by the Northern Powers still troubled men of conscience, and even conservatives such as Castlereagh regarded Poland's tragedy as the source of many of the evils which had afflicted Europe since the 1770s. One way of bringing stability to Eastern Europe, so essential for the peace of the Continent as a whole, was to press for the restoration of an independent Poland. Three of the four Chaumont powers had a vested interest in preventing Polish independence. There was no hope of securing that independence except in collaboration with France. Now that France was no longer a serious rival it might make a useful partner. Under Louis XVIII, France would have a constitutional government which, even if limited compared to Britain, still gave greater liberty to Frenchmen than anything enjoyed by Austrians, Russians and Prussians. Collaboration between Britain and France following the fairly generous treatment of France in defeat would weaken the case of Frenchmen who called for revenge. It would increase the popularity of the Bourbon dynasty and reduce the chances of another revolution. The French sympathized with the Poles and in the Napoleonic period there had been a phantom of Polish independence in the shape of the Grand Duchy of Warsaw. An independent Poland would give the map of Europe a more 'French' look about it than anything envisaged by the Northern powers. Anglo-French collaboration to obtain an independent Poland would also drive a wedge between France and Russia.

Yet the choice of France as Britain's partner in the reconstruction of Europe involved unacceptable risks. The Bourbon dynasty was not secure and disunity amongst France's former enemies might facilitate a Bonapartist restoration. Even after its defeat, France was potentially the strongest of the Continental powers with a strong sense of national unity and a military tradition which no other country could rival. France had been cut down to a size where it could be accommodated within a European Balance of Power, but the fetters which held it back from a new career of conquest looked feeble. British and French ideas on the proper ordering of Europe were not identical. French sympathy for the Poles was a symptom of a grander design. Even in the France of Louis XVIII some people believed that the proper way to secure peace and justice was to break up existing large states, or amalgamate smaller ones, to produce a Europe based on units of cultural and linguistic traditions. The French Revolution and the French conquests had tried to achieve this admirable objective only to be stopped by an evil alliance between the rulers of 'unnatural' multi or sub-national states with a Britain infected with a paranoid suspicion of France, a cynical desire to expand its economic lead over its rivals and to 'clean-up' in the rest of the world. Of course, as the one large true nation and the dominant culture, France would be the lynch pin of this new Europe, the supreme embodiment of national independence which others humbly imitated. There could be no place for an Austrian Empire in such a Europe.

Sympathetic as the country was to the national cause in particular instances, Britain could not make this a general rule. It could not consent to the weakening of the Northern monarchies, because they were the natural counterweights to France. They had won the war and Britain wished to gratify at least some of their aspirations as a guarantee against future wars. A Europe of Nations was incompatible with a Europe that was properly balanced. This balance could only be achieved if there was a small number of roughly equal states. A balanced Europe would be of Great Powers – Britain, Austria, Prussia, Russia and France – where, regardless of national sentiments, a substantial part of the peoples of Europe would be divided up between a handful of rulers. Britain hoped that those rulers would prove kindly and sympathetic to their new subjects, but there was little that it could do to ensure their good behaviour.

At Vienna the disagreement between Britain and France centred on the concept of the Great Powers. Talleyrand argued that the 'Great Powers' was a concept without legal standing and insisted that the smaller states of Europe should be fully consulted before anything was decided, asserting that Britain, Prussia, Russia and Austria were conspiring against the rest of Europe whose only protector was now France. If doubts about Poland led to this, then Poland was best forgotten. Talleyrand's policy endangered the whole edifice of diplomatic theory evolved over the previous two years; it threatened to produce appalling delays before a definitive settlement could be reached and introduced an element of uncertainty about the future which could endanger the peace which Britain earnestly desired. The road to a new European order based on closer collaboration with France was not one that could be taken in 1814.

Once this decision had been taken, there was no alternative to working with the Northern monarchies. This meant acceptance of the partition of Poland and annexations and extended spheres of influence in Germany and Italy. But could this be achieved in a way that would satisfy the powers concerned and pose no threat to British interests? Britain feared Russia and wished to keep Russian gains to a minimum. If close collaboration with France and Russia was ruled out, Britain had to achieve close partnership with Austria and Prussia and thus construct a barrier against France on the West and Russia on the East. Unfortunately, Austrian and Prussian ambitions overlapped; there was acute suspicion between Berlin and

Vienna, whilst relations between Berlin and St Petersburg were cordial.

The best way to resolve differences between Austria and Prussia was to point them in different directions. Prussia would be allowed, even encouraged, to dominate Northern Central Europe, whilst Austria could begin a new career as master of Italy. Of course, it would be easier to accommodate Prussia if Russia could be persuaded to give the former a larger share of Poland. Castlereagh may have hoped that the Czar would make this concession in order to retain Prussian good will. Russia refused but, such was the country's influence in Berlin, that Prussia accepted this refusal and demanded territory which Castlereagh had intended for the Austrian sphere of influence. Prussia's desire to annex Saxony was strongly resisted by Austria. If Britain was to weaken the ties between Berlin and St Petersburg and reunite Austria and Prussia, some alternative to Saxony had to be found. The only solution was to allow Prussia to take the Rhineland, allowing this country to advance further westwards than Castlereagh had intended. The prospect of a Prussian Rhineland might pose a threat both to Hanover and the Dutch – although the interest of these lesser powers had to be subordinated to the more important objective of avoiding trouble between Austria and Prussia. The Rhineland solution had the important advantage of giving Prussia a stronger interest in opposing any future French expansion. At least the Prussians agreed to new proposals, though with little enthusiasm. In the long run, Castlereagh's solution, satisfactory as it appeared at the time, was one of the most unfortunate of the arrangements made in 1814. The Rhineland had enormous economic potential which, two generations later, was to provide Prussia with the resources to take over the rest of Germany. It would be foolish, however, to blame Castlereagh for taking the first step on the road to Bismarck and the wars of the twentieth century. In 1815 Prussia was the weakest of the Great Powers and any price seemed worth paying to secure Europe against French aggression in the West and, through the achievement of amity between Berlin and Vienna, to stop Russian expansion in the East.

Austria would not accept Prussian gains in Germany and Russian control over most of Poland unless it received compensation in Italy. This, the broad objective of British policy, proved difficult to achieve. British troops had been in Sicily for some years and their commander, Lord William Bentinck, was an enthusiast for constitutional government and Italian national unification, aspirations incompatible with an autocratic and Austrian-dominated future. Constitutional governments and national movements had been useful against Napoleon, but in the postwar world they became an embarrassment. Bentinck could be dismissed, but the problems of Italy did not end there. A desire to improve relations with Spain and to keep some lines open with France suggested the desirability of a Bourbon restoration in Naples. Yet Austria did not want to see its annexation of Northern Italy compromised by the presence of a Spanish Bourbon dynasty closely linked to France. Rather than permit this it was prepared to allow Joachim Murat, Napoleon's brother-in-law, to continue as King of Naples. The Austrians had to be convinced that Murat was totally untrustworthy. Discussions about the future of Naples coincided with Napoleon's escape from Elba. Murat seized this opportunity to launch a campaign for Italian unification under his own leadership. This initiative threw Murat into conflict with the Austrians. Murat's defeat and subsequent execution removed an unwelcome complication.

Napoleon's advance through France and his entry into Paris on 19 March 1815 gave Britain more to think about than the future of Naples. The news confirmed the wisdom of not becoming too closely involved with France or too far separated from other Great Powers. Britain, Austria, Prussia and Russia announced that Napoleon had placed himself outside 'the pale of civil and social relations'. As an enemy and a disturber of the tranquillity of the world he had rendered himself liable to public vengeance. The Treaty of Chaumont was renewed and no hint of recognition given to the Imperial régime. Fortunately for Britain the hostilities were of short duration and by 23 June Castlereagh, who had returned to England in March, was able to introduce a vote of thanks to Wellington and the allied armies following their victory at Waterloo.[7] It was as well that most of the fundamental questions about the future of Europe had been resolved before the escape from Elba.

The British government reluctantly accepted the responsibility of acting as Napoleon's gaoler, and Castlereagh regretted that Louis XVIII did not have the courage to have him shot. A more serious question was what difference should the Hundred Days make to British foreign policy? By welcoming the return of Napoleon, the French had shown little gratitude for the lenient treatment they had received in 1814. In some respects British policy did harden.

The ideal in 1814 had been of a Europe of restored monarchies which incorporated many of the social and political changes of the revolutionary period. The failure to come to a better understanding with France, and the need to work with the Northern powers, had gradually pushed British policy away from any chance of co-operation with Continental liberals, radicals and nationalists. The experience of the Hundred Days completed the process. There was now a greater readiness to countenance a much more thoroughgoing return to the ways of the *ancien régime*.

Castlereagh now declared that he wanted to return to 'that ancient social system which had long predominated in Europe and of the enjoyments of which we had been too long deprived'. Castlereagh's concern now was to enhance the slender authority of Louis XVIII; he urged Talleyrand to make an example of those who had taken an oath of loyalty to the Bourbons and then rushed to join Napoleon.[8] Others drew different conclusions. The success of Napoleon's return indicated that Louis XVIII had inspired little affection. Even if Napoleon was sent to the other end of the world, the Bourbons could not provide stability. Castlereagh's argument that there were two alternatives for France – the old social order or military tyranny – appeared dubious. A more popular and progressive government than Louis's might have provided a better guarantee of peace and stability. The Czar, a friend of liberty everywhere except in his own country, was already flirting with the idea of an Orleanist dynasty or even a moderate Republic.

As far as the boundaries of France were concerned, British policy was unchanged. Excessively harsh treatment would prevent France playing its proper role in European affairs. Indeed, a vindictive peace would only weaken the Bourbons further and increase the chances that France would soon welcome a new military régime pledged to restore its lost territories. Castlereagh managed with difficulty to persuade other members of the Cabinet, as well as Austria and Prussia, that France should lose only relatively small areas such as the Saar, Landau and part of Savoy. Although parts of France would be occupied by allied armies until an indemnity was paid, Britain insisted on a scheme which would allow payment in three years.

Castlereagh was finally free to concentrate on his most important objective, the establishment of machinery to safeguard the achievements of the past two years. The creation of a 'balance of equilibrium' at Vienna needed to be supplemented by a positive commitment to maintain that equilibrium. He urged the Great Powers to declare their determination to uphold and support the arrangements agreed upon. Initially the scheme had been thwarted by Russian opposition, but Castlereagh's proposals underlined his readiness to commit Britain to active intervention in European affairs. Castlereagh's aim came nearer to realization on 1 October 1815 when Britain, Russia, Austria and Prussia renewed the Treaty of Chaumont with the additional clause that the exclusion of Napoleon and his family from the throne of France should become part of the law of Europe. The parties to the Treaty would invade France at once if Bonaparte ever returned.

Castlereagh's slow progress was eclipsed by Alexander's proposal that the rulers of Europe should come together in what was later to be known as the Holy Alliance. His suggestion that the sovereigns of Europe should pledge themselves to base their policies on the principles of Christianity struck Castlereagh as so absurd that he had doubts about the Czar's sanity. Britain would not join such a body but all the other rulers of Europe, except the Pope and the Sultan, signed a treaty as the Czar had proposed. Castlereagh's own intentions were revealed in the Quadruple alliance – all the Great Powers except Russia – signed in November 1815. Apart from stressing allied unity in the face of aggression the treaty provided for regular meetings, either under the immediate auspices of the sovereign or by his ministers. So much of Castlereagh's own achievement had depended on face-to-face contact with Metternich and the Czar; it seemed sensible to continue this direct contact.

IV

The arrangements made in 1814 are open to serious criticism. It was not entirely clear what Britain's precise obligations were to the new European order created in Vienna. This uncertainty was made worse by Castlereagh's reticence in Parliament. Samuel Whitbread suspected that Castlereagh had entered into secret agreements which would not be brought before Parliament. Some of Whitbread's points, that secret undertakings may be a fertile cause of wars, foreshadow the critique of 'secret diplomacy' popular in the aftermath of the First World War. There was criticism, too, of the way in which Britain had abandoned the cause of national freedom. Everywhere, people were being forced to submit to foreign powers after being encouraged by Britain to rise up against the tyranny of Bonaparte. Castlereagh had sacrificed their interests to gratify the rulers of Austria and Prussia who, as late as 1812, had been allies of Napoleon. Castlereagh's hopes of a long-lasting peace would prove illusory if the settlement paid no heed to the considerations of justice. Rulers who installed repressive régimes and refused to keep pace with 'the improved judgement' of their subjects faced an early day of retribution. It is hard not to sympathize with Whitbread's criticism. In some ways British policy was short-sighted. Castlereagh's ideas about a 'just equilibrium' were too imprecise and it was as difficult as ever to *measure* the Balance of Power. The parcelling out of the people of Europe amongst a small number of generally traditionalist states, whilst continuing the fragmentation of Italy and Germany, was not a good recipe for economic growth, and thus against Britain's interest. Above all, the refusal to pay sufficient attention to aspirations to national independence created a situation in which the chief features of the Vienna settlement became more objectionable to more people with the passing of each year.

There is much to be said in favour of Castlereagh. There is always danger in peace settlements which ignore the realities of power. The arrangements of 1814 were overwhelmingly realistic. Realistic peace treaties are the ones that survived. In the face of the actual power of the conservative monarchies, it is hard to see how a Europe of nation states could have been created, much less survived. Nor was the denial of national independence likely to encounter immediate and overwhelming objection. In 1815, national sentiments were still largely confined to the European middle-classes. The peasantry, who made up the bulk of the population and provided the foot soldiers of the armies of Continental Europe, were rarely imbued with nationalist ideas. Again, variations in levels of social and economic development, as well as the diversity of tradition, precluded the establishment of British style constitutions everywhere. Castlereagh was justified in claiming that the decisions reached in Vienna were in broad accord with the objectives announced in the closing stages of the war. Some cynical compromises were made but it would have been näive to expect that discussions between the Great Powers would yield immediate agreement, much less a system which corresponded to the aspirations of all the peoples of Europe. Castlereagh believed that the first priority was to restore the power of Prussia and Austria, countries which had been virtually destroyed during the previous twenty years. The rights of smaller states or aspirations to unity and independence could not be allowed to stand in the way of this goal. The real question was whether a system had been established which would enable Europe to enjoy a period of tranquillity.

The Vienna settlement did not represent a return to the international order of the eighteenth century. Then, the independence of most European states had been preserved through the operation of the balance of power, but, as we have seen, it could not ensure peace. The eighteenth-century order had only been possible because of the relative 'under achievement' of France which, despite the failure of Louis XIV's attempts to achieve European hegemony, remained the most populous and potentially the most disruptive of the Great Powers. The French Revolution swept away the old order and prepared the way for a new 'imperial solution' headed by Napoleon. Napoleon's supporters claimed that, once French victory had been achieved, a new European order could emerge in which overall French dominance would be combined with peace and with personal liberty and social progress in the various satellite kingdoms. The earlier coalitions had represented little more than an attempt to restore the lost world of the eighteenth century – and had failed for reasons similar to those which had produced so much instability before 1789.

By 1815, however, a new dimension had been added. Although the idea of the Balance of Power was still important, the 1815 settlement did contain an element of the 'Imperial' solution. But instead of the Imperial position being occupied by one single power, the solution adopted a collective or collegiate Imperium presiding over the nations of Europe and composed of five Great Powers – including France. In a sense, therefore, the new system represented a compromise between the Balance of Power solution and the Imperial solution, retaining the best features of both. It kept the principle of the independence of states which had been the chief feature of the eighteenth century, whilst avoiding the likelihood of frequent and disruptive wars. It offered the peace which the Imperial system promised without the associated danger of total subordination.

Whether by luck or judgement, the peace makers had hit upon a successful formula. The achievement was all the more remarkable when one remembers that the revolutionary and Napoleonic wars had lasted for a generation and that the longer wars go on the harder it is to dispel the animosities they have produced. Although the term and its meaning were open to disagreement, the settlement of 1815 had created the Concert of Europe. Initially the arrangements may have inclined too much towards repression and the status quo, but it is hard to disagree with the verdict of Adam Watson:

> The proof of the pudding was a century of near peace in Europe, during which major adjustments were made and great material prosperity developed. The minor European wars of the following hundred years were little more than campaigns, fought by professionals for limited objectives, which did not noticeably interrupt material progress and the development of civilisation and the arts, or the expansion of European dominance over the rest of the Old World. No tragedy on the scale of the destructive American Civil War afflicted the competitive but diffused and balanced power structure of the nineteenth century European society or states. To a considerable extent this must be attributed to the flexibility of the concert of great powers set up as a result of the Congress of Vienna.[9]

In 1815 the real problem was not that the settlement was wildly anachronistic; rather its essential defect was that Castlereagh and the other peace-makers assumed a static world. The French Revolution may have convulsed Europe, but change was less important than continuity in a world still dominated by agriculture and village life. Things were changing in England but even England was still in the early stages of the Industrial Revolution. What the Vienna Settlement did not do, perhaps could not do, was to provide explicitly for the implementation of appropriate political change when this great social and economic revolution spread first throughout England and then over Continental Europe.

Europe faced two opposite perils. Without appropriate adjustment from time to time, a settlement which began life as a highly realistic arrangement would become divorced from reality and thus the source of anger and ultimately of war. Equally, a failure to perceive the real merits of the settlement and a consequent readiness to destroy it root and branch in pursuit of a totally different and probably highly impractical European order could prove no less disastrous. Having made a major contribution to the settlement of 1815, the task now facing Britain was to steer a middle course between the two extremes. Perhaps Britain was uniquely qualified for this role. There was at least the possibility that the country could preserve the essentials of its social and political order by piecemeal adaptation to changing economic circumstances. If it could do this, then it might be able to do the same in international relations. In 1815, however, Britain's capacity to fulfil this role, whether at home or abroad, still remained uncertain.

NOTES: CHAPTER 3

1 *Parliamentary History*, vol. 36, p. 46.
2 ibid., p. 100.
3 Printed in C. K. Webster (ed.) *British Diplomacy, 1813–1815*, London, G. Bell & Sons, 1921, Appendix 1.
4 *Hansard's Parliamentary Debates*, New Series, Vol. 33, p. 10.
5 J. Sherwig, *Guineas and Gunpowder: British Foreign Aid in the Wars with France 1793–1815*, Harvard University Press, 1969, p. 279.
6 *Hansard*, Vol. 30, p. 997.
7 *Hansard*, Vol. 31, pp. 980–6.
8 *Cambridge History of British Foreign Policy*, Vol. 1, p. 506.
9 A. Watson, *Diplomacy: The Dialogue between States*, London, Methuen, 1982, p. 110.

4

Peace and its Problems, 1815–1830

The end of the war raised the fundamental question of whether foreign policy issues are really important in peace time. Britain had grown apart from the Continent since 1793 and once Napoleon had been defeated many Englishmen became indifferent to European affairs. During the Congress of Vienna, Liverpool complained that there was little interest in the negotiations, except in so far as they were connected with expense. Yet men like Castlereagh found it difficult to move to a peace-time outlook and still believed that foreign policy was all important – even though many people regarded the alliances and antagonism of European states as irrelevant to their real problems. Few now favoured an administration which concentrated so much on foreign policy that it neglected pressing domestic matters. In 1819, when speaking against an opposition motion of 'No Confidence', Castlereagh accepted that most of the criticisms of the government's economic policy were 'perfectly sound and warranted by facts' but then proceeded to vindicate his foreign policy as if this were the only thing that mattered. But the foreign policy to be pursued was also a matter of controversy. In the period after 1815 the state of the economy became the chief topic of political debate. Despite its underlying strength, the British economy faced serious problems, perhaps worse than during the war itself. Neither could work be found for demobilized soldiers and sailors to re-absorb them into civilian society. Distress mounted as spending on armaments diminished and overgrown war industries faced painful contraction. So price and wage levels fell and the real burden of taxation, mainly devoted to the payment of interest on war debts, increased. If a foreign policy was to be popular it had to be seen to be doing something to alleviate the social and economic problems of the postwar world. Some, like G. R. Porter, argued that Castlereagh had been too generous to the foreign powers. He should have been only concerned with the national interests of Britain in the manner of his eighteenth-century predecessors. It had been folly to give up colonial territory such as the Dutch East Indies which *de facto* had become a part of the British Empire and which had provided promising markets for British goods. These tangible assets had been thrown up in pursuit of an insubstantial abstraction called the Balance of Power. British policy appeared to rest on snobbery which regarded trade as vulgar, a sentiment exploited by foreigners who duped Castlereagh into thinking that he should not tarnish the laurels won on the field of slaughter with any desire for reward. For Porter at least, unless there was some reward then the slaughter had been useless. Castlereagh's sympathy for old fashioned régimes only strengthened the authority of states maintaining barriers against British goods, barriers which would not exist if Europe and the world had been organized differently.

A policy of maintaining an active involvement in European affairs carried the risk that one day Britain would have to fulfil its engagements in war. Even if war was avoided, the policy led to a higher level of military spending than would otherwise be the case – and thus to higher taxation which interfered with the natural workings of the economy and impeded economic recovery. Ironically this taxation would probably take the form of duties on imports, thereby damaging relations with other countries and making war more likely. Even leaving aside the generals, admirals and armaments, diplomacy itself was expensive business. The ritual of diplomacy and the social round with which it was inextricably connected might cost more than it would ever achieve. For theoreticians and middle-class tax payers, the parties, not to mention the illicit amours, associated with the Congress of Vienna seemed unconnected with Britain's real needs. By the exacting standards of utilitarianism, British foreign policy appeared sadly deficient.

There was an even more alarming allegation. Economic distress produced agitation and the government responded with repressive legislation on an unprecedented scale, measures regularly defended by Castlereagh in the House of Commons. The apparatus of spies, informers, *agents provocateurs* and gagging legislation has led writers like the Hammonds to conclude that no other British administration came so close to the spirit of Czarist Russia. Perhaps domestic and foreign policy were of a piece. Europe experienced a wave of reaction in which Britain played a major part. Shorn of high-sounding verbiage, in reality the rulers of Europe were taking their revenge on their subjects for their behaviour since 1789. The kings and princes were trying to erase the humiliation they had suffered at the hands of the French by re-establishing the most objectionable features of the *ancien régime*. The British government, supposedly the defender of individual and parliamentary liberties achieved through centuries of struggle, was busily betraying its unique heritage. The Foreign Secretary, an enemy of liberty in his native Ireland, had become tainted with Continental ideas and, in conjunction with the odious Metternich, wished to set up despotisms in England and elsewhere on Austrian lines.

Most of the European rulers now believed that it was essential to be firm with their subjects; even modest concessions to critics would only encourage further demands and probably end in republicanism. The restored monarchs were thus united and believed in a policy of rigid repression. Yet, unlike their eighteenth-century predecessors, who had seen war as a necessary instrument of state building, they were now in a peaceful frame of mind. They wanted no unnecessary excitement. They eschewed war because it might arouse dangerous passions. If they went to war against each other they would have to put guns in the hands of men who might turn these weapons against them. The rulers of Europe saw that they had more in common with each other than they had with their subjects. What was needed was a 'monarchs' club' or 'trade union of monarchs'.

Like other similar bodies this 'trade union' – the Holy Alliance – imposed implicit and explicit rules on its members. These included respect for the territorial division of Europe achieved by the peace treaties – even if co-operation with discontented elements in other states might appear advantageous to the particular country concerned. It was absolutely forbidden for one ruler to stir up discontent amongst another's subjects. There had to be no concessions to liberals, nationalists and other trouble-makers in one's own state; apart from the folly of such proceedings, they might provide an example for more dangerous movements elsewhere. Repression and absolutism at home were both in the given country's own interest and part of a duty to fellow monarchs. Thus, the chief function of the armed forces and intelligence services of each state would be the control and elimination of internal rather than external enemies. Above all, the only time that the forces of a state should cross frontiers was when a fellow monarch faced opposition or insurrection which looked like getting out of hand. In these circumstances it was the duty of other states to provide all possible assistance to the régime in difficulties. If such a system could be implemented, the territorial and ideological status quo in Europe, perhaps even in the world, might be preserved for evermore.

Did Castlereagh really subscribe to this view of postwar Europe now canvassed by Metternich? If he did, the consequences were terrifying. Europe might enjoy a period of freedom from conventional wars, but the peoples of Europe would rise time and time again against the iniquities of the system. Constant armed interventions would be needed to suppress their wishes and aspirations. If fears about Castlereagh were correct, British troops would be involved in these deplorable activities. Such misuse of British forces was bound to provoke opposition, which might serve to justify further curbs on liberty in Britain.

In the eyes of opposition spokesmen, Europe would be far more disturbed and agitated than if timely concessions were made to popular demands. A more liberal Europe would be a more tranquil Europe, and it was genuine tranquillity that Britain needed. Castlereagh and Metternich actively encouraged the extremists. Their intransigence could only weaken the influence of sensible men who combined a belief in progress with a healthy respect for property.

In foreign affairs, as in the other fields, judgements are often made more on the basis of style than upon deeds. Castlereagh certainly seemed haughty and to care little for public opinion, declaring that he preferred unpopularity to popularity because unpopularity was more gentlemanly. He gave the impression of having something to hide; restraint in the revelation of foreign policy matters may be necessary at all times but Castlereagh took caution too far. He did not appreciate that it is harder in peace than in war to plead reasons of state for withholding information. Indeed, the appetite for information was growing sharply and technological innovations such as steam printing were providing the means of gratifying it. A minister so consistently uninformative as Castlereagh was unlikely to be a favourite of the press.

After Whitbread's death, Henry Brougham became the chief parliamentary critic of Castlereagh's foreign policy. Brougham appreciated the importance of the press and knew how to present Castlereagh's reticence in the most sinister light. On 9 February 1816 Brougham moved for copies of 'The Christian Treaty', establishing the Holy Alliance. Castlereagh admitted that a copy of the treaty produced by Brougham was accurate but still accused him of indulging in 'unfounded imputations and groundless suspicions' that were calculated to disrupt the good understanding recently established among the sovereigns of Europe.[1] Although the Prince Regent was not a formal member of the Holy Alliance, Castlereagh's British government intended to conduct its policy in harmony with the 'Christian Sovereigns'. Radical papers such as *Black Dwarf* spoke of 'Castlereagh and the Holy Leaguers' and Brougham constantly asserted that the Liverpool administration was infected with the spirit of the

Holy Alliance, determined 'to make the Government of this country less free – and permanently so'. As if to confirm the conspiracy theory, Castlereagh was always advocating European Congresses. In some strange and tyrannical land, he would plot and scheme against liberty. Beyond the eye of Parliament, perhaps even without the knowledge of other ministers, pledges might be given which would commit British influence, treasure and blood to the cause of oppression.

Yet the real objectives of British foreign policy were different from what so many imagined. Few remembered that Castlereagh had once toasted 'Our Sovereign Lord – the People'. Although his views changed as he grew older, he never wanted to restore the *ancien régime* in its entirety, and dismissed the Holy Alliance as a 'piece of sublime mysticism and nonsense'. He certainly did not regard the Congress system of diplomacy as just a device to permit rulers to go back on their promises of amnesty to the supporters of former régimes. Policies such as these would only drive men who might have been reconciled to the return of kings into desperate measures. Castlereagh's real task was to defend the rulers of Europe from ill-informed criticism in Parliament and at the same time warn them that British support was conditional on their behaving with sense and moderation. It was necessary to disabuse any ruler who thought that he could count on British gold and armed intervention when faced with a revolution provoked by his own intransigence and vindictiveness. The mood of Parliament probably pushed Castlereagh further towards the liberal position than he would have liked, but he was also disappointed by the operation of the Congress System. He was walking an uncomfortable tightrope; in England he appeared very reactionary whilst on the Continent he looked dangerously liberal.

There were many reasons why Britain could not behave even as an 'informal member' of the Holy Alliance. The Christian Treaty might mean everything or it might mean nothing at all. Such treaties had never commended themselves to British diplomats. General statements of intent were too vague. The British preferred a diplomacy based on specific commitments to act in specific ways in specific circumstances. This approach may have reflected the down-to-earth traditions of Common Law, in contrast to the greater propensity to generalize inherent in the Roman Law traditions of the Continent. The British approach may have been limited, but it allowed each country to know exactly where it stood. In accordance with this tradition, Castlereagh's preferred instrument for keeping the peace was the Quadruple Alliance, basically a continuation of the wartime coalition and concerned with what to do in the event of renewed French aggression. This was the only formal obligation that Britain entered into. The general consensus was that the country would do what it had promised to do and nothing more.

The Holy Alliance also contained a strong ideological element and an implicit assumption that absolute monarchies were the best form of government. The British system was constitutional rather than absolutist and even the most conservative of ministers would have been appalled – understandably – at the thought of allowing the Prince Regent to decide everything. In any case, ideology had rarely figured prominently in British calculations. Protestant England had never had any qualms about taking on Catholic Austria as its closest ally. Castlereagh himself often pointed out that Pitt had gone to war against revolutionary France more for strategic than ideological reasons. Britain's primary concern was usually with the strategic and economic implications of a particular régime rather than with the régime itself. An important distinction began to be made. Britain certainly wished to uphold the *territorial* divisions of 1814 and 1815, yet even in this case the country might not intervene militarily unless the threat came from France. There was less commitment to the *ideological* status quo. If other countries wished to change their governments, and the matter could be confined to their domestic affairs, then Britain was inclined to let them do as they pleased.

Thus, Castlereagh's foreign policy differed relatively little from that advocated by his critics. Britain was not really committed to keeping Europe and the world in a strait jacket. There was room for change as circumstances required without jeopardizing the crucial achievement of the Peace – the re-establishment of a Balance of Power necessary to protect Europe from future French, perhaps Russian, aggression. Yet if this is what Castlereagh stood for, why is it that contemporaries and others should have been so mistaken? There are three possible explanations. We may place the chief emphasis on Castlereagh's own ineptitude, his association with other repressive policies, his unwillingness to explain his policies properly and the skill with which his shortcomings were exploited by his opponents.

Perhaps Castlereagh *did* have some sympathy with the absolutist powers or believed that co-operation with them to preserve peace was a price worth paying even if it did involve Britain in some morally questionable activities. Castlereagh's actual policy could then be explained as the retreat of a realist who, on returning to Britain, was forced to recognize that Parliament would never swallow the medicine he had concocted whilst on the Continent with Austrian and Russian absolutists. On the other hand, perhaps Castlereagh never had any real sympathy with Austria and Russia but recognized that in order to influence them he had to appear more sympathetic than he actually was – even at the cost of appearing as an ogre in England. Perhaps the 'style' was deliberate after all. In Castlereagh's case there is probably some truth in all three explanations. Whichever position seems the stronger, all point to the same conclusion – that public opinion would be increasingly important and that the wishes of the electorate and middle-classes might be hard to square with what an essentially aristocratic diplomatic service considered to be the permanent interests of Britain and Europe.

The arrangements made at the end of the Napoleonic wars may have had intrinsic merit of their own, but peace is maintained more by the continuing desire of statesmen to avoid war than by clauses in a treaty. The long peace after 1815 was largely the result of this desire. In other words, peace is never automatic. No system of international relations can guarantee peace; peace must be managed as new situations arise. Although the Great Powers recognized that they had interests in common, the selfishness inherent in the great states remained. The rulers of Europe had been given a fright but they retained their eighteenth-century propensity for expansion. The emphasis on state building was as strong as ever. Indeed, war and French conquest had assisted the process by sweeping aside feudal obstacles to centralized authority. In many instances identification between subjects and states became closer. Everywhere writers produced books about the role of their country's 'destiny' – always grander than the present. These forces were very strong in Prussia, still apparently the weakest of the Great Powers. After the disaster of Jena the reaction was 'never again'. Greater loyalty, greater self-sacrifice, more careful planning, more profound scholarship – all combined in a greater ruthlessness to achieve desired objectives – would be available to the state. There was an inherent conflict between these developments and professions of monarchical solidarity.

Even conservative régimes aspired to manipulate the 'just equilibrium' of Europe, especially in areas they claimed were 'unimportant'. Others might think differently, in which case war ensued. For the moment Russia and France appeared the most 'revisionist' of the Great Powers, a revisionism counter to British interests. Perhaps the Czar's emphasis on the 'Christian' aspects of the Holy Alliance was a ploy to exclude the Sultan so that the guarantee of the territorial status quo inherent in the alliance would not apply to the Turkish Empire. It was hard to understand Russian policy. In Southern Italy, Russia favoured constitutional government, the same view as France yet, in Spain, the Czar urged a tough line against all liberal ideas. Perhaps Alexander was creating confusion to distract attention from a projected Russian invasion of Turkey and aiming at an alliance with either France or Spain to give him a presence in the Mediterranean.

Many in France would respond. Compared to later settlements, the arrangements of 1815 looked generous to the vanquished, but Frenchmen found their treatment unjust. Even the Bourbons did not believe that a 'just equilibrium' had been established. Britain, Austria and Prussia had gained whilst the borders of France had been pushed back. A 'just equilibrium' necessitated the restoration of French influence in Spain, Italy, the Southern Netherlands, the Rhineland and in the world beyond Europe. Britain's unassailable position in the colonial world and Austria's dominant influence in Italy and Germany seemed the main obstacle to French hopes. A Russian invasion of Turkey would threaten the British Empire and, especially if the Austrians came to rescue the Turks, France might join the war on the Russian side. There was a current Anglophobia in Russia. The Foreign Minister, Capo D'Istria, came from Corfu and deplored the British acquisition of the Ionian Islands. To Orthodox Christians, Turkey, Austria and Britain seemed to conspire to keep their brethren in chains. Everywhere in Central Europe, Russian interests collided with Austrian, and behind Austria stood Britain. The Russian plan did not stop at a revisionist alliance with France and/or Spain. Although Britain and the United States had made peace in 1814, most of the issues remained unresolved. If the United States would co-operate with the Czar and the Bourbons, the outlook for Britain would be bleak and present alarming similarities with the American War of Independence.

A number of courses were open to Britain. The country could appeal to Russian memories of wartime solidarity, improve relations between Russia and Austria, strengthen its own ties with Austria, be more conciliatory towards France and Spain or turn the United States away from thoughts of collaborating with Continental powers. Castlereagh announced that he favoured early withdrawal of allied armies from France. Eventually it was agreed that there should be another European congress – at Aix-la-Chapelle – to try to prevent Europe from plunging back into war. The Congress which met in the Autumn of 1818 would test Castlereagh's conviction that peace could be preserved by face-to-face contact between the statesmen of Europe. In the event, the Congress was more concerned with the reality of the revolt of Spanish America than with the possibility of war in the Balkans with all its knock-on implications. Yet the two issues were linked. The revolt in South America could enable Britain to destroy any prospects of a revisionist bloc. Only the assistance of the Royal Navy would allow the Spaniards to defeat the rebels; Russia could be of no use and the Spaniards had to seek Britain's help. The provision of assistance would detach the Bourbon powers from the Czar. Britain had recently signed a treaty with Spain and not to help the latter now could be damaging. Britain would be seen to be retreating from the monarchical solidarity of 1815 and would look as unscrupulous as Russia. Whereas the Czar favoured the territorial and political status quo everywhere except in the Balkans where he might further his own interests, so Britain would be accused of making a similar exception – but a much larger one – of the whole world outside Europe.

Yet a policy of assisting Spain would encounter opposition at home. Apart from any ideological objections, commercial issues were at stake. Trade with South America, which had enjoyed *de facto* independence during the French occupation of the Peninsula, had helped Britain to survive the challenge of the Continental System. Trading and industrial interests would deplore the likely effects of the restoration of Spanish colonial rule and its associated restrictions. Furthermore, the rebel cause was popular in North America and the conflict had the useful effect of deterring the United States from any alliance with the Bourbon powers. British neutrality, or even tacit support for the rebels, would help relations with Washington.

When faced with such conflicting pressures it was sensible to take a low profile; Britain would be courted by both sides because her naval power could decide the outcome. On 19 March 1817 Castlereagh announced that Britain would not endorse attempts to suppress the rebellions, yet he was equally hostile to Brougham's suggestion that Britain send help to the rebels. Castlereagh wanted a peaceful settlement; Spain should give its colonial subjects the same rights as metropolitan Spaniards and allow them to trade freely with other nations.[2] At Aix he presented himself as a mediator between Spain and the rebels. Unfortunately Spain rejected Castlereagh's proposals and demanded military support.

Britain might be seen as an unreliable ally but Castlereagh was prepared to risk an increase in Russian and French influence in Madrid because he thought the rebels would win. In any case, cultivation of the United States, exemplified in an agreement to disarm the Great Lakes, was more important than influence in Spain.

The Anglo-American rapprochement averted Britain's worst nightmare but the Russians could still do immense harm. They claimed that the Quadruple Alliance had worked to the sole advantage of Britain and Austria. They took up the cause of the smaller powers and suggested a dilution of the Quadruple Alliance to include France and Spain and its replacement by an *Alliance Générale* involving all the signatories to the 1815 Settlement. The New Alliance would control the affairs of Europe and guarantee the thrones and territories of existing rulers. The French supported the Russian initiative and refused further co-operation with the Quadruple Alliance. If the 'surveillance' of France to guard against a resurgence of Revolution was to continue it would have to be reciprocal.

Castlereagh disliked these proposals, knowing that Parliament would reject an alliance so bristling with interventionist entanglements. Britain would be completely isolated if the *Alliance Générale* went ahead without it. Fortunately Castlereagh was supported by Metternich, the Russian proposals were defeated and the Quadruple Alliance renewed, although France was to be invited as a full member of future congresses. The triumph was complete when Louis XVIII replaced the pro-Russian Richelieu with a more liberal ministry headed by Decazes. The collapse of the Franco-Russian understanding left Britain and Austria dominant in Europe. Metternich was at the height of his influence between 1818 and 1820. Even Prussia, once the close ally of Russia, moved into the Austrian orbit. The German princes fell into line and, meeting at Carlsbad in August 1819, agreed to co-operate with Metternich in stamping out liberal ideas from the universities and the press. Austrian hegemony in Germany posed no threat to British interests and Castlereagh was not unduly disturbed by the persecution of German professors and journalists.

In terms of traditional analysis of national interest, British foreign policy was highly successful between 1818 and 1820. Unfortunately, opinion in Britain was running ahead of Castlereagh's cautious disengagement from the absolutist cause. Not everyone shared his indifference to the fate of German professors and many wanted a more positive commitment to the cause of liberty. In May 1819 Castlereagh found himself in difficulty when defending the government's Foreign Establishment Bill, which sought to prevent British subjects enlisting in the service of the South American rebels. Castlereagh described the Bill as necessary to support his policy of neutrality; if British subjects fought on the rebel side, Spain would have a valid reason for declaring war on Britain.[3] Several members argued that Spain was in no position to declare war on anybody. Some rejected neutrality altogether. Petitions against the Bill poured in, asserting that the effect of the Bill would not be one of neutrality but of help to Spain. As British merchants were already engaged in lucrative trade with the rebels, passage of the Bill could result in the loss of that trade to the United States.

Castlereagh's policy encountered criticism from members of his own party. Younger Tories had little sympathy with the 'aristocratic' diplomacy of the past and advocated a 'cost benefit' approach, more in tune with a middle-class outlook. On 19 March 1819, William Huskisson criticized Castlereagh's claim for £8,432 expenses incurred at the Congress of Aix-la-Chapelle.

The Government had recently spent £22,510 on presents of snuff boxes to foreign statesmen and their entourages, including their coachmen. Huskisson could see no justification for such extravagance.[4] Castlereagh could not understand the point of Huskisson's criticisms. The practice of distributing presents after the signature of treaties was 'as old as the monarchy and nearly co-extensive with civilized states'.[5] Castlereagh believed that the abolition of snuff boxes and the abolition of monarchies were closely connected. He noted with distaste that only the United States, a republic of course, did not permit its representatives either to give or to receive presents.

Criticism of 'old fashioned' foreign policy did not cut much ice so long as Britain and Austria remained friends. Castlereagh's ability to work with Metternich had preserved the peace, protected British interests and kept France and Russia in check. One could scarcely ask for more. Yet if Anglo-Austrian friendship should ever falter, it would be necessary to develop another policy in a hurry. There were tensions on both sides. Would Metternich's fears of Russia and France outweigh his fears of revolution? If not, the Anglo-Austrian understanding would be endangered. Would Castlereagh's desire to assist Austria be greater than his own dislike of foreign entanglements and Parliament's growing distaste for absolute government? If not, British friendship was hardly worth having. The first test was passed with surprising ease. The Spanish Revolution of January 1820 which forced Ferdinand VII to restore the Constitution of 1812 prompted the Czar to canvass intervention in Spain to restore Ferdinand to his full royal power. Metternich agreed with Castlereagh that Alexander's scheme would only benefit Russia and perhaps re-establish the earlier Franco-Russian co-operation. Thus, Metternich emerged as an unlikely champion of non-intervention. Britain and Austria agreed that Spain could be left to its own confusion.

Yet the Spanish crisis raised issues which required clarification. The result was the confidential State Paper of 5 May 1820. This paper formed the basis of British policy for the rest of Castlereagh's life and even later. The Paper, circulated to most European governments, stressed that the key-note of British policy would be non-interference. There might be circumstances when Britain would consider intervention to prevent one country annexing another, but force would never be used to influence the internal affairs of another state, either to install one kind of régime or to depose another. Castlereagh's enthusiasm for the Congress System, reaffirmed at Aix-la-Chapelle, was evaporating. It would be better for contacts between governments to be of a more traditional kind, 'confidential communications between the Cabinets' rather than be subject to the hazards of a ministerial conference. Castlereagh's new position sprang from a fear that future congresses would not listen to him. A congress which authorized military intervention would be guilty of perverting the purpose of the Quadruple Alliance. Nothing was more likely to destroy the Alliance than pushing its objectives beyond the original intention. The alliance was not a union for the government of the world or for the superintendence of internal affairs. The statesmen of Europe might deplore the spread of democratic principles but existing treaties gave them no right to expect Britain to help them in suppressing these ideas. Ministers had to act in accordance with the wishes of Parliament which, in turn, reflected public opinion. No one would support a policy of spending taxpayers' money to save Ferdinand VII from the consequences of his own folly. Castlereagh's Paper came as a shock to many in Europe. Metternich was now aware, perhaps for the first time, of just how far the British government had diverged from his own views. Castlereagh's balancing act between Austrian friendship and the principles of non-intervention would be hard to sustain any longer.

The British problem was exemplified by events in Italy. Castlereagh's optimism that the Spanish Revolution would not spread elsewhere – an important point in leading Metternich towards non-interference – proved ill-founded. In July 1820, Ferdinand IV of the Two Sicilies was compelled to proclaim a constitution similar to that imposed on Ferdinand VII in Spain. Metternich had not been sorry to see Spain fall into chaos but Italy was a different matter. Although initially dubious about Ferdinand IV's restoration – precisely because Ferdinand was a Bourbon – Metternich's objections disappeared when Ferdinand accepted Austrian supremacy in Italy and moved into the diplomatic orbit of Vienna. So a revolution in Naples was a direct humiliation of Austria and threatened territories under Austrian rule. Thus the revolution in Naples had to be suppressed with the utmost vigour. The twin pillars of Castlereagh's foreign policy were directly opposed to each other.

Castlereagh valued friendship with Austria too much to oppose Metternich directly. Austrian intervention in

Naples had a legal basis under the Austro-Neopolitan Treaty of 1815 and was thus different from Alexander's loose talk of intervention here, there and everywhere. But Castlereagh could not do what the Austrians wanted. Metternich regarded the Neopolitan Revolution as a symptom of an international movement which could be defeated only by concerted action. The best solution would be to despatch troops from various countries, including Britain, to restore the situation. Yet there was no more likelihood of British troops going to Naples than to Spain. Castlereagh, once the most 'European' of Foreign Secretaries, was moving through non-intervention to near isolationism. Metternich began to question a policy based on friendship with a country which was turning its back on Europe and whose government, enmeshed in the embarrassments of Queen Caroline's trial, might soon be succeeded by Whigs enthusiastic for revolution. Austria would have to look elsewhere.

The estrangement between Britain and Austria presented Russia and France with a splendid opportunity. Richelieu, now recalled to power in France, suggested another European congress which might widen the split further and allow France and Russia to run Europe as they wished. When Alexander announced his support, Castlereagh feared the triumph of a 'Holy Alliance' position, which would compel Britain to withdraw from the Quadruple Alliance. But when the Congress assembled at Troppau in October 1820 his worst apprehensions were not realized, because French and Russian views did not coincide. Metternich persuaded the Czar that there was little to choose between moderate and extreme constitutions; the spirit of revolution was still alive in France and even the Bourbon dynasty was infected by it. He induced Alexander to sanction Austrian suppression of the Neopolitan revolution. Austria, Prussia and Russia then signed the Troppau Protocol committing themselves to intervene if revolutionary changes in any state seemed to threaten any other state. British policy was now totally at variance with such views and the solidarity of the Courts of Vienna, Berlin and St Petersburg looked like dominating European politics for the foreseeable future, but at least France did not sign the Troppau Protocol. As far as Britain was concerned, the situation might have been worse, but the loss of Austrian friendship seemed to have brought Castlereagh's diplomacy to ruin.

Fortunately for Castlereagh the breach was healed by the Greek revolt. Russia was bound to be attracted to the Greek cause whilst Britain and Austria would oppose it. Despite the ideological incompatibility between absolutist Austria and parliamentary Britain, their interests as states usually converged. Castlereagh was so alarmed by the news from Greece that he forgot his objections to Congresses. The Czar was forced to accept proposals for a Congress to meet in Vienna in the Autumn of 1822, to be followed by a larger gathering at Verona which Castlereagh was expected to attend in person. In the Spring of 1822 he was busy deciding his 'instructions'. The idea that the map of the entire world could or should be frozen as it was in 1815 was rejected. Spain should be given a time to re-establish its authority in South America. If the country could not do this, Britain would recognize Spain's former colonies as independent states, *de jure* as well as *de facto*. Castlereagh killed himself before the meetings in Vienna and Verona could assemble, but his 'instructions' provided the basis of his successor's policy.

II

George Canning's return to the Foreign Office in September 1822 was once believed to mark a decisive change in British foreign policy. Though currently unfashionable, this view has something to commend it. Part of Castlereagh's problem was that he had taken so large a part in the creation of postwar Europe that he could not be completely detached. The purposes of the Treaty of Chaumont and the Congress of Vienna had been to keep France within its new borders and prevent the return of a Bonaparte dynasty. With the withdrawal of foreign armies France had achieved full Great Power status. The more 'respectable' France became, the less the need for a Quadruple Alliance to keep it under surveillance. If the Alliance of 1814 was no longer needed, two things could happen. It could wither away or develop into an instrument for maintaining the territorial and political status quo throughout the world.

Castlereagh's attitude was ambiguous. He refused to commit Britain to 'abstract and speculative principles of precaution', yet disapproved of intervention less in Italy than in Spain. He did not wish to destroy the Alliance; despite doubts, he remained committed to the Congress System which was its visible embodiment. Castlereagh's policy had reached a dead end. He opposed turning the Alliance into an international counter-revolutionary police force, but had no concrete alternative. All he could do was to put forward his version of intentions in 1815 and draw on a fund of wartime goodwill. Castlereagh's move towards non-intervention, even withdrawal from active participation in European diplomacy, was made with reluctance. For all the disagreements, he had a basic affinity with Metternich and Alexander. He would not part company willingly with the two men in Europe who, together with himself, had played the largest part in the defeat of Napoleon. Canning, however, did not have the same emotional ties with 1814 and had had little contact with either Metternich or Alexander. When he was Foreign Secretary last, both had been allies of Napoleon Bonaparte.

Foreign policy cannot be explained in purely personal terms and 1822 may mark the beginning of a new period for other reasons. Liverpool's government was moving into a new phase. Some of the repressive legislation of recent years was dismantled, new blood was brought into the government, patronage and extravagance were pruned, economic reform undertaken and a start made in reducing import duties. A new type of Toryism needed a new style of foreign policy, more open, more economical, more influenced by commercial considerations, more opposed to despotism, more on the side of liberty and freedom, internationalist in some respects yet with a dash of national self-interest and xenophobia – a policy more representative of the aspirations of the middle-classes than anything

Castlereagh had had to offer. Canning was the embodiment of the new Toryism. He represented a great commercial constituency – Liverpool – and had familiarized himself with economic and financial problems. When last Foreign Secretary he had championed the cause of freedom in Spain. Canning had none of Castlereagh's distaste for popularity. A superb performer in Parliament, there would be no danger that the case for his foreign policy would fail through inadequate explanation. He was not averse to playing to the gallery. His foreign policy would be 'popular' perhaps even 'populist'. There are those who see Canning as an eminently 'progressive' foreign secretary who changed Castlereagh's line of neutrality to positive support for constitutional governments and national independence. They assert that his main work was to destroy the 'neo-Holy Alliance' wherever it attempted to assert its influence.

The reality is different. If Castlereagh was less reactionary than his reputation suggests, Canning was less progressive. 1822 does not mark the clear break that some have imagined. There was an essential continuity between Castlereagh and Canning. If Castlereagh had lived, it is unlikely that things would have turned out to be different. They might have changed more slowly; perhaps they would have been better managed. The real change was more of style than of substance.

The reassuringly conservative Duke of Wellington was sent to Verona, taking the 'instructions' drawn up by Castlereagh. Canning continued Castlereagh's policy of co-operating with Austria over what was beginning to be called 'The Eastern Question'. He supported the final communiqué of the Congress which denounced the Greek revolt as a 'rash and criminal enterprise'. Canning also needed to review policy towards Spain. Ferdinand VII was now a prisoner in revolutionary hands. On his way to Verona, Wellington stopped in Paris and reported that Louis XVIII and his ministers were now determined to intervene in Spain to help Ferdinand. Canning instructed Wellington to declare that the British government could not support interference. Yet if Alexander could be persuaded by Britain and Austria that Russian support for the Greek rebels would shatter the Alliance and play into the hands of the revolutionaries everywhere, was it not logical for Alexander to demand that the Alliance prove its worth by destroying the revolutionary cause in Spain? Whatever he may have said in public, Canning regarded a French intervention in Spain, though unfortunate, as preferable to a Russian one.

Metternich was in a quandary. He wanted to see the Spanish Revolution crushed – but not by France or Russia. Yet a policy of non-intervention would only encourage trouble-makers in Austria's own territories. He tried to discredit both the French and Russian plans for intervention and to persuade the Congress to condemn the Spanish Revolution in a way that would demonstrate the unity of the Alliance and not upset the British. Castlereagh would probably not have objected to a series of rude notes from the Great Powers designed to frighten the Spanish revolutionaries into restoring some degree of power to Ferdinand, thus removing the case for intervention. Canning's reaction, however, was to condemn the policy of warning notes as 'insultive', more likely to inflame the Spaniards than to calm them. The Anglo-Austrian friendship that, despite ups and downs, had dominated Europe since 1815 was now at an end. The consequences were apparent immediately. Shortly after the Congress dissolved, France unilaterally invaded Spain. France did not ask for the consent of the Great Powers and only Russia approved of this action. The successful defiance of Europe, only seven years after 1815, represented what Castlereagh and Metternich had most feared. French intervention in Spain represented the victory of France and Russia over Britain and Austria. Canning's return to the Foreign Office had produced a grave reverse. Metternich concluded that the episode revealed that Britain was 'gangrenous to the bones with the revolutionary spirit' and had now no friends of consequence in the whole world.

There was some truth in Metternich's claims, yet Canning demonstrated his talent as a politician by presenting a defeat as a victory. The French invasion would bring the dispute between Spain and its colonies to a head. With Spain in its present condition any attempt at reconquest

would have to be given up. It was surely better that
Spanish America should be independent than that it should
fall under the indirect control of France. Thus good would
come out of evil. Canning's speeches were notable for their
emphasis on patriotism and national interest, as distinct
from Castlereagh's stress on the European balance. Canning's position was more representative of public opinion.
If Britain entered a war, it would be on grounds which
were clearly British. The country had a duty to maintain
the balance of power, and to aid the weak against the
strong, but it should never forget that it also had a duty to
itself. One consolation of the French invasion of Spain was
that it had demonstrated the bankruptcy of the Congress
System and brought the era of alliance diplomacy to an end.
Now that Verona had split 'the one and indivisible alliance'
things could get back to a 'wholesome state' again.[6] What
Canning meant by 'a wholesome state' can be summed up
as 'every nation for itself and God for us all'. Compared
to Castlereagh's stately vision of European harmony, Canning's ideal seems brash. In its approval of competition
and rivalry it contains a hint of a diplomatic version of
the economic histories of free trade and competition which
were gaining ground in the 1820s.

Espousal of self-interest should not be confused with doctrinaire isolationism. National interest would lead Britain
to intervene or not to intervene as each crisis presented
itself. The country had also to consider what means it
possessed to make any intervention effective. Canning was
no isolationist but a realist who appreciated the limitations
of British power. Britain's strength was maritime and
economic, not military. The country could act as a land
power only in limited circumstances and usually then in
conjunction with a Continental ally. Intervention in Spain,
either to support or to oppose France, would be neither
practical nor desirable; in the case of another country the
response might be different.

Although Canning's policies were really pragmatic rather
than ideological, he understood the political advantages of
concentrating on points of principle when making major
speeches. This was especially true of South America. In

one of the most famous speeches ever made by a British Foreign Secretary, Canning declared:

> If France occupied Spain, was it necessary, in order to avoid the consequences of that occupation, that we should blockade Cadiz? No, I looked another way: I sought materials for compensation in another hemisphere. Contemplating Spain, such as our ancestors had known her, I resolved that if France had Spain it should not be Spain with the Indies. I called the New World into existence to redress the balance of the Old.[7]

This can be interpreted in several ways. It can be construed as an admission of failure, a recognition of Britain's diplomatic isolation and her inability to prevent the invasion of Spain. The emphasis on the New World becomes a trick to divert attention from the wanton destruction of Castlereagh's finest legacy, the co-operation with Austria. If Canning had been honest he might have said that he was calling the New World into existence to redress the wreck of his own foreign policy. But Canning's powers of persuasion were such that few of his audience saw through him. Those with advanced views might see his comparison between the 'new world' and the 'old world' as one between youth and vitality on the one hand and sterility and decadence on the other. For traditionalists, however, this was a comforting comparison between the present situation and that in the early eighteenth century. Then Spain had been one of the greater powers in the world and Britain had gone to war to stop a French prince becoming King of Spain and the Americas. Since that time Spain's importance had declined. If France reduced Spain to satellite status the former would still not pose a serious threat to the overall balance of power in Europe – unless, that is, the country also had the resources of the Spanish Empire at its disposal. In other words, the French invasion of Spain gave Britain a direct interest in the cause of South American independence.

Canning was raising a non-existent threat. Despite their commitment to the monarchist principle, South America was too remote from Europe for the Continental powers to have either the means or the inclination to interfere. There were other reasons pushing Britain towards recognition of independence, especially the need to give legal sanction to the trade between Britain and South America. This would be in harmony with the trend towards the liberalization of British commercial policy; one of Castlereagh's last acts as Foreign Secretary had been to persuade the Cabinet to treat vessels flying the flags of the South American countries as legitimate traders. Canning's ultimate recognition of South American independence has been cited as evidence of 'progressive' views. The reverse may be true. Castlereagh's desire for good relations with the absolutist rulers of Europe was only part of his policy. Despite distaste for republican institutions, he appreciated the need for friendship with the United States. Whilst Canning may have been readier to part company with Metternich, he was actually more hostile to the United States. In large measure, Canning's policy towards South America was designed to thwart the ambitions of the United States.

Whilst the United States had been negotiating with Ferdinand VII for the purchase of Florida, its policy towards the South American revolt had been cautious. Once they had acquired Florida, however, the Americans became more interested in the rebel cause. Only recently they had felt threatened by the empires of Britain, France and Spain. Britain had now given up its claims to the lands south of the Great Lakes – the last serious obstacle to the westward expansion of the United States. Apart from some unimportant islands France had disappeared from the scene, whilst the Spanish Empire appeared to be disintegrating – a development which might allow the Americans to expand into the Vice-Regality of Mexico. This dramatic reduction of European power made it likely that the United States would dominate North and South America. Any independent states would become its clients. In 1822 the United States gave full recognition to the South American republics. American traders moved into these markets hoping to enjoy considerable advantages over European rivals.

Canning disliked the prospect of American hegemony whilst appreciating that the United States lacked sufficient strength to follow up its initiative. The rebels needed financial assistance and the Americans were in no position to lend money to anyone. Britain was stronger than the United States both militarily and financially, but had to put its bid for influence in quickly. Unless Britain gave full recognition to the new republics they might become satellites of the United States, a prospect no more acceptable than French dominance of the area. In the Autumn of 1824 Canning speculated that, sooner or later, Britain would find itself at war again with the United States; the attitude of the South American countries could make all the difference.

In October 1823 Canning began discussions with the French Ambassador, Polignac, in which Polignac conceded that France regarded the Spanish Empire as lost and would not send forces across the Atlantic. Canning also held discussions with Richard Rush, the American Minister in London. He did so against the background of President Monroe's message to Congress on 2 December 1823 embodying 'The Monroe Doctrine'. Monroe argued that as the United States did not involve itself in the affairs of Europe, so European powers should be prevented from meddling in the affairs of the Western hemisphere. Monroe promised to resist attempts to extend European power in America and specifically pledged himself not to permit European interference in the new republics. Whatever his long-term fears, Canning did not protest at Monroe's message and went out of his way to cultivate the Americans. He told Russia that Britain would shortly give full recognition of independence. Britain desired no part of the Spanish Empire for itself and would oppose even the covert transfer of colonial territory in America to the authority of another power. If such a possibility arose, Britain was ready to act in conjunction with the United States in warning off the power concerned.

Canning and John Quincy Adams, Monroe's Secretary of State, were playing a complicated game. Canning was using the new-found agreement with the United States to deter the Continental Powers from ideas of congresses and intervention. Adams was using his knowledge of British intentions, obtained via Rush, to persuade Monroe to make his support for the new republics more explicit and thus outbid Britain in the race for influence. But it was a game in which Canning had the better hand. For all its rhetoric, American policy could only be implemented by courtesy of Britain. In the last resort, the instrument that would stop France taking over the Spanish Empire was nothing so abstract as a doctrine. The reason why Polignac had given in to Canning was his fear of the Royal Navy. If the Americans pushed too hard, Canning could threaten to withdraw his objections to French involvement in the Spanish Empire. With a sense of self-congratulation he could declare 'the effect of the ultra-liberalism of our Yankee co-operators, or the ultra-despotism of the Aix-la-Chapelle allies, gives me just the balance that I wanted'.

Despite Canning's success, he advanced cautiously to full recognition. He approached the authorities in Madrid, offering to facilitate a peaceful transfer of power. It was only when his offer was rejected that he announced that British policy would be decided without reference to Spain. In the Summer of 1824, London merchants were demanding immediate recognition of the republics of Columbia, Buenos Aires and Chile. Canning prepared Cabinet papers in favour of recognition; he was supported by Liverpool but faced a rearguard action organized by Wellington. On 14 December 1824 Liverpool and Canning threatened resignation unless the Cabinet agreed to recognize Buenos Aires, Mexico and Columbia. The 'Ultra' party was forced to yield.

Canning wanted no extra territory for Britain but he did engage in a fierce conflict for commercial and diplomatic advantage. Perhaps he wanted to set up an 'informal empire' in South America and was determined to thwart the United States which had similar aspirations. Canning feared that the United States would try to exploit the fact that it was a republic to gain support from the new states. The British representative at the Congress of Panama in 1826 was instructed to prevent at all costs the emergence of any kind of all-American Confederacy headed by the United States. The danger was averted but in all the new states there was a struggle for supremacy between British and American factions.

Relations with Portuguese America were simpler than the complex saga of the Spanish Empire. On returning to Lisbon in 1821, King John VI appointed his son, Pedro, as Viceroy of Brazil with secret instructions that if anti-Portuguese feeling became too strong, Pedro was to declare independence and proclaim himself Emperor of Brazil. Pedro did so in October 1822. As Canning pointed out to the dubious Continental powers, Pedro had finally introduced the monarchial principle into the independent New World. Prospects seemed especially pleasing when Pedro in Brazil and John in Portugal granted parliamentary constitutions to their subjects. Once Pedro seemed secure, Britain signed a commercial treaty with Brazil, and in August 1825 Portugal recognized the independence of its American territories. Canning's policy in both Spanish and Portuguese America must be counted as a success. By 1826 British trade and influence dominated South America. Monarchial and aristocratic England had defeated the challenge of the United States, despite the Americans' early lead.

III

Despite Canning's success in South America, it was not the central concern of British foreign policy – which continued to be the maintenance of a broad equilibrium amongst the Great Powers of Europe. It must have been galling to Canning that, after his successful role in the birth of an independent Brazil, he should have then faced serious trouble in Portugal itself. He might regard the fate of metropolitan Spain with indifference but he could not take the same attitude to Portugal. General principles of 'non intervention' could not be applied there. Britain had treaty obligations to Portugal and the strategic, political and even historical significance of the Portuguese alliance was widely acknowledged in Britain. Any government which allowed Portugal to fall to forces hostile to Britain would be accused of betraying the national interest. Canning was

always careful to avoid such charges. Following the death
of King John, Pedro should have succeeded to the throne
of Portugal. After providing the country with a relatively
liberal constitution, Pedro abdicated in favour of his young
daughter, Maria. Neither the constitution nor the accession
of Maria pleased Pedro's brother, Miguel. In August 1826
there were risings in favour of Miguel, risings which
appeared to enjoy covert Spanish and French support.
No doubt the Continental powers would claim that it was
necessary to intervene in Portugal to stop the constitutional
disease spreading to Spain. It seemed that rulers holding
'Holy Alliance' views forgot their disapproval of usurpers
if there was a chance of overthrowing a liberal régime and
replacing it by an absolutist one.

In November 1826 Portuguese rebels, supported by
Spanish troops, invaded Portugal. Paralysed by disagreements the French government did nothing. The Portuguese
authorities appealed for assistance under the terms of the
Anglo-Portuguese alliance; Canning agreed. If the French
had been involved, an ugly situation might have arisen and
might even have led to war. The arrival of British forces
in Lisbon had the desired effect; the insurgents supporting
Miguel dispersed and Portugal returned to an uneasy calm.
British troops had been in action on the Continent for
the first time since Waterloo. Ever since 1815 there had
been talk of intervention in one place or another. From
the possibility of intervention in favour of absolutism,
British policy had moved through non intervention, to
intervention in favour of the constitutional cause. But, in
Portugal, at least, the constitutional cause was actually the
status quo cause and, whatever the ideology, intervention
to protect British interests was a policy several centuries
old. Second only in importance to the independence of
the Low Countries, the security of Portugal from Spanish
or Spanish/French domination was one of the cornerstones
of British foreign policy. In the case of Portugal, liberal
sentiment and Britain's national interest went hand in
hand, even if the significance attached to Portugal was
by now excessive. In South America there appeared to
be some conflict between the cause of freedom and British

interests, although certainly not between independence and economic interests.

The case of the Greek Revolt, the other great *cause célèbre* of the 1820s, was more complex. There, ideological considerations and national interest seemed to point in opposite directions. There were no close political ties with the Greeks. In so far as Greece was thought of at all, it was regarded as an integral part of the Turkish Empire. The Greek Revolt which began in April 1821 soon attracted the attention of Europe, if only because of the terrible cruelty of Greeks and Turks alike. Britain had no reason to welcome the revolt. If it succeeded the obvious beneficiary would be Russia, adept at exploiting its role as the protector of the Orthodox faith against Muslim oppression. An independent Greece under Russian protection would give the Czar his long-sought outlet onto the Mediterranean and threaten the British Empire at one of its most vulnerable points – the Eastern Mediterranean part of the route to India. After the defeat of France in 1815 many people regarded Russia as Britain's chief potential enemy. There seemed every reason to ignore reports of Turkish atrocities. The restoration of the integrity of the Turkish Empire appeared desirable, and ties with Austria pointed in the same direction. Metternich appreciated that the dismemberment of the multi-national Turkish Empire might lead to a similar fate befalling Austria. Even if the Greeks became independent, potential for increased trade was limited, certainly nothing compared to prospects in South America. The best thing to do was to play on the Czar's general fear of revolution in the hope that he would desist from sending help to the Greeks.

After the Congress of Troppau adjourned to Laibach, the signatories of the Troppau Protocol assured the Turks that they would give no assistance to the rebels. Back in Russia, however, Alexander came under pressure to help the Greeks. His commitment to the status quo was always lukewarm where Turkish territory was concerned and, if there was any chance of increasing Russian influence, liable to disappear completely. In October 1821 Castlereagh and Metternich addressed separate appeals to the Czar. The appeal from Metternich concentrated on the danger of assisting rebels and the need to preserve the status quo, whilst Castlereagh wrote of the practical dangers of a Turko-Russian war. But even Castlereagh did not consider giving direct help to the Turks. British intervention on their side was certain to bring in the Russians on the side of the rebels. Castlereagh was too attached to European peace to risk a general war for what, in the words of a later statesman, was essentially 'some damn fool affair in the Balkans'. For the time being Britain and Austria urged the Turks to make concessions to their Christian subjects and so rob the Czar of any excuse for intervention.

Yet supposing the Russians did intervene, supposing that, with or without Russian help, the Greeks managed to establish something resembling an effective state, what should Britain do then? Castlereagh's final 'instructions' envisaged a time when the Greeks might receive at least *de facto* recognition. In March 1823, Canning accorded the Greeks full belligerent status. A wave of sympathy for the Greeks was sweeping Europe; classical Greece had given birth to much of what was best about European civilization. The debt Europe owed to Hellas was incalculable. It was intolerable that the powers of Europe should allow the cradle of civilization to continue under barbarian oppression. The Phil-Hellene movement was popular in Britain and was led by the charismatic figure of Lord Byron. Given the special role of the classics in upper-class education, almost every person of taste and refinement was to some extent a Phil-Hellene. As a classicist himself, Canning felt the pull. The Foreign Enlistment Bill notwithstanding, it would prove impossible to stop idealistic young men and out-of-work officers joining the Greeks. The Phil-Hellenic movement cut across party lines and some of the most promising men in Canning's party supported the rebels. Canning himself possessed an acute sense of wind direction.

If the Greeks were going to win, it would be wise to identify with them soon. It was the story of the United States and South America over again. There might be elements in Greece unhappy with the prospect of Russian domination. Perhaps the best way to thwart the Russians would be to take up the Greek cause. As with South

America, Britain could be crucial in a military way, even
without direct assistance. In a country of peninsulas and
islands, naval power directly affected the outcome. The
interposition of units of the Mediterranean fleet between
the Turks and the rebels might be a tangible factor in
the establishment of a Greek state. Yet even if Greek
independence could be squared with the containment of
Russia, Britain's problems did not end there. Despite the
deterioration in relations with Vienna, Britain's more liberal
foreign policy had avoided any direct clash with Austria's
national interests. Britain may have denounced Austrian
intervention in Naples, but had not prevented it. It had
denounced the French intervention in Spain but had not
prevented it and, in any case, Metternich had had reservations about that particular episode. In Portugal, Britain
had acted in accordance with a long-standing tradition and,
in some senses, in support of legitimate authority. Even in
South America Canning had tried to persuade some of the
new states to become monarchies. There was a case for
believing that Canning was following conservative policy.
It followed that Liberal speeches did not mean much; they
were manufactured to appease public opinion and the
eccentrically English charade of Parliament. Whatever
ministers might say in public, important decisions were
still taken by men who understood the importance of
the Balance of Power and the central role of Austria in
maintaining it. Yet, if Britain supported the Greek rebels
this comforting conclusion would have to be discarded.
Greece was on the doorstep of the Austrian Empire and
the example it provided might prove fatal to the existence
of Austria as a state. Thus, more fundamental issues
were at stake than in previous differences between Britain
and Austria.

The Eastern Question must have seemed like a hideous
monster of unknown size rising from the sea. The full extent
of its horrors was not yet visible, but enough was above
the water to discern the chief features of the creature's
disgusting anatomy. For Britain, it was already clear that in
future one of the biggest dilemmas would be whether to try
to maintain the apparently moribund Turkish Empire or to

speed its demise in the hope that successor states would be influenced at least as much by Britain as by Russia. Either course entailed a risk of things going wrong. The implications seemed endless. Before returning to the Foreign Office, Canning had been on the verge of leaving for India to become Governor General. He had made an extensive study of India with its large Muslim population. The enthusiasm and tactlessness of some Christian missionaries was already provoking resentment, and British identification with the Greek – and hence anti-Islamic cause – might spark off massive disruption.

Understandably, Canning was reluctant to commit himself. The military situation in Greece had been transformed by the Sultan's appeal for assistance from Mahomet Ali, Pasha of Egypt. In February 1825 the Pasha's armies inflicted heavy defeats on the rebel forces. The Greek's bid for freedom was doomed unless outside powers intervened. Predictably, Russia was in favour of sending help, while Austria was totally opposed. Faced with the test of the Greek question, the Holy Alliance had disintegrated. Either by luck or by judgement, Canning had achieved a significant victory. So long as the Holy Alliance existed there was a danger that the Continental powers would join together against Britain. This had been the chief danger inherent in Canning's apparently more liberal foreign policy. The collapse of the Holy Alliance meant that a new grouping would emerge and British support would be sought by the rival Great Powers.

Canning hoped that Britain could extract concessions from both Russia and Austria so that eventually the Turks and Greeks could be presented with a united Great Power package which they would have to accept. In other words, the way to reduce the risks of the Greek question was to secure a solution by international agreement, but an agreement on terms largely worked out by Britain. Canning thought that the Russians would probably intervene in Greece in any case. If Russia was going to intervene, it was desirable that the country should do so on a basis previously agreed with Britain. The best way of containing Russia would be to act in concert and go to great lengths to appear to be a friend. The other course, support for Austria, would mean permitting the Turks to crush the Greek rebellion unhindered. The state of public opinion made a pro-Austrian policy out of the question. Yet even Austria might accept an Anglo-Russian solution as a lesser evil than unilateral Russian action. The success of Canning's policy depended on whether he could influence the Russians. Unexpected events in Russia assisted him. An uncertain succession after the death of Czar Alexander, followed immediately by a major attempt at revolution placed the new Czar, Nicholas, in a weak position. At this critical moment, Nicholas was delighted to receive a mission from Britain headed by Wellington. After offering his congratulations to Nicholas, Wellington broached a project of collaboration with Britain which would enable the Czar to begin his reign with a foreign policy success whilst avoiding the dangers in unilateral action.

On 4 April 1826 Britain and Russia signed the Protocol of St Petersburg, under which Britain and Russia would approach the Sultan with the suggestion that Greece become a dependency of the Ottoman Empire, still subject to nominal Turkish sovereignty but enjoying a substantial degree of autonomy. Russia promised not to seek territory for itself and together with Britain she would play the major role in determining the boundaries of the new dependency. The Protocol set the seal on the estrangement of Russia and Austria; it appeared to provide a painless way of containing Russian ambition; and offered a way out of the complexities of the Greek Revolt. Faced with defeat by the Egyptian armies, the Greeks had no option but to accept the terms of the Protocol. To Canning's dismay, however, the Turks rejected the Anglo-Russian compromise. Direct action to impose a settlement became inescapable. 'Internationalizing' the issue meant bringing in other Great Powers. As the Austrians were too sympathetic to the Turks, this meant bringing in the French. Although angry at its exclusion from the discussion in St Petersburg, the French government was subject to Phil-Hellene pressures and, after its success in Spain, was ready for further foreign adventures. Although the French refused to sign the Protocol – because this would seem too much like taking orders – it was agreed that a new treaty should be drawn up in which all the signatories would be on an equal footing. In terms of combinations amongst the five Great Powers, Britain had executed a graceful manoeuvre which had taken it from the Prusso-Austrian camp into the Franco-Russian camp.

IV

There was little change in foreign policy when Canning became Prime Minister in April 1827. He had so much experience of diplomacy that he probably wished to avoid any appointment which would leave the Foreign Office in the hands of a man likely to develop a distinct line of his own. If there was a change, it was more likely to result from the fact that the more conservative members of Liverpool's administration refused to take office in the new administration, whilst Canning began discussions with some leading Whigs with a view to them joining the government. Nevertheless, although Canning would determine policy, the appointment of the Earl of Dudley is surprising. When Castlereagh and Canning had been at the Foreign Office they had been amongst the most important men in the country. Dudley remains one of the most obscure figures ever to have been Foreign Secretary. His tenure of office was brief – little over a year – but during that period he served under three Prime Ministers: Canning, Goderich and Wellington.

Dudley was in sympathy with the latest turn in foreign policy. He disliked the Austrians and Germans generally. They seemed proud but without any real dignity; individually and collectively they displayed 'the utmost height of unchastized insolence' and yet were capable of 'the lowest point of sycophancy and submission'. The grandees in Vienna went around in barbarian stateliness which was in ludicrous contrast to the way they fawned for favours at Court.[8] He considered that Germans and Austrians had a natural propensity to despotic régimes and he expressed warm sympathy for Italian revolutionaries trying to rid their country of its Austrian masters.

Dudley's first task was to implement Canning's policy on Greece. On 6 July 1827, the Treaty of London was signed by Britain, France and Russia – Austria and Prussia refusing to have anything to do with it. The Treaty embodied the ideas of the Protocol of St Petersburg but treated France as an equal partner. The chief new provision was a secret article which pledged the signatories to use naval power to compel the Turks to accept a compromise peace along the lines decided upon in St Petersburg. On 21 October 1827 Admiral Codrington, supported by ships of the French and Russian navies, attacked and destroyed the Turkish fleet at Navarino, thereby guaranteeing the independence of Greece. By the time of Navarino, however, a major changed had occurred in British politics. Canning was dead and the new Prime Minister, Goderich, was a weak man, without experience in foreign affairs and only too well aware of his own inadequacies. Those who had opposed Canning in the past prepared to take their revenge on his heirs. Goderich resigned on 8 January 1828 and was replaced by Wellington.

Although Dudley remained at the Foreign Office, Wellington had no sympathy for the Greeks and the new season of Parliament began with a King's Speech describing the Battle of Navarino as 'an untoward event which was deeply lamented'.[9] Wellington spoke warmly of the Turkish Empire as the ancient ally whose strength and independence was vital to the general stability of Europe. From time to time, Dudley intervened in debates to assure the Lords that the foreign policy of the new government was the same as Canning's. He can have convinced no one. Wellington's prestige and influence were so great that few men in England dared stand up to him. Dudley certainly did not have the necessary qualities. Now that Wellington was dictating a policy more sympathetic to the Turks, the chances of Britain acting in concert with the Russians were diminished. Even after Navarino, the Turks still refused to negotiate with the Greeks. Russia proposed that Russia, Britain and France join up to put more pressure on the

Turks. Faced with Britain's changed policy Russia decided
to go ahead, either alone or in conjunction with France.
Shortly afterwards, Russian land forces invaded the Turkish
Empire, whilst French forces went ashore in Morea. In
Portugal, British troops sent by Canning to defend the constitutional cause were ordered not to interfere when there
was another rising in favour of Miguel. On 7 July Miguel
accepted the Crown of Portugal. In the space of a few
months British influence had suffered a disastrous decline.
An anti-British party had come to power in Portugal, whilst
Russia seemed poised to extract the maximum advantage
from the Greek crisis. It is understandable that Canning's
policy should have been criticized by conservatives, but the
attempt to change course at this stage meant that Britain
incurred the contempt of Liberals and Absolutists, Greeks
and Turks, Austrians and Russians, alike.

Matters did not improve when Dudley resigned and
was replaced by Aberdeen in June 1828. If British influence survived in the Eastern Mediterranean, it did so in
spite of government policy. In part, this was due to
Aberdeen's failure to send proper instructions to British
representatives in the area, notably to Stratford Canning
in Constantinople, and in part Stratford Canning's refusal
to pay much attention to the instructions he did receive
from London. Ultimately it was the Russians who brought
a solution to the Greek crisis. In the Summer of 1829 they
took Adrianople and Trebizond from the Turks, who now
had little alternative but to seek peace. The result was the
Treaty of Adrianople of 14 September 1829. Russia had
done what Canning had tried to prevent. The country
had acted alone; it had gone to war against Turkey and
had emerged victorious; it was therefore naturally inclined
to demand its own terms. It was the Treaty of Adrianople
which gave the Greeks their independence, a fact likely to
ensure Russian dominance of the new state. The Treaty
revealed more of the future complexities of the Eastern
Question. Russia gained a small area at the mouth of
the Danube, a guarantee of free passage for its shipping
through the Straits and increased influence in Moldavia
and Wallachia.The gains in Asia included Georgia and

Eastern Armenia and a possible claim on Circassia. This substantial increase in Russian territory was bound to increase the chances of future confrontation between Britain and Russia.

In short, the Treaty of Adrianople was a disaster for Britain. From this moment onwards, a party in Russia argued that, whilst there was no immediate prospect of the disintegration of the Turkish Empire, in the long run this objective was within Russia's grasp. The Russians can hardly be blamed for seizing the chance opened up for them. Canning's policy might have yielded happier results. The Russians were probably contemplating only a modest influence in Greece initially. Czar Nicholas was not prone to Alexander's fits of liberalism and even less inclined to assist rebels. He had been frightened of provoking the Austrians into intervention on the Turkish side and, properly handled, would have been prepared to make substantial concessions. There may have been times when fear of Russia was justified, but this was not one of them. It is ironic that the supposedly anti-Russian policy of the Wellington government should have resulted in such a resounding Russian triumph.

The government's Portuguese policy produced equally unsatisfactory results. Aberdeen contended that the use of British troops to defeat Dom Miguel would prove counter-productive. The constitutional cause would be identified with foreign interference and thus ensure its eventual defeat. Aberdeen claimed to be following a policy of strict neutrality – yet he allowed Miguel to fit out an expedition to attack islands in Constitutionalist hands, whilst preventing Queen Maria's forces from going to their defence. If the policy had protected British interests, there might have been something to have been said for it, but Miguel's government imprisoned many British subjects without trial and seized British shipping. In defiance of the Anglo-Portuguese trade treaty, duties were doubled on British goods. The Consul General declared that there was a 'root hatred in that party that now governs Portugal against everything Protestant and British'. The Wellington government decided that the only way to appease Miguel's anger was to accept him as King of

Portugal. Only the fall of the Tory government prevented recognition.

V

Yet the future of Greece and Portugal was unimportant compared to that of the Low Countries. The slightest hint of renewed French expansion in this area would cause panic in London. Castlereagh's chief objective had been to ensure that this threat should never arise again. If it did so, France would be faced with an immediate renewal of the wartime coalition of Britain, Russia, Austria and Prussia to thwart this move. But now the former allies were in disarray, France might break out of the carefully contrived barriers of 1815. The purpose of the Treaty of London, emphasizing co-operation between Britain, France and Russia, had been as much to limit French revisionism as to restrain the Russians. As Russia was now gaining more territory in the East, so France could take the opportunity provided to gain more territory in the West. In 1814 the former Austrian Netherlands had been united with the Dutch provinces under the rule of an Orange monarch. The Southern Netherlands had been part of France for twenty years. Many in Paris resented the loss of Belgium and were ready to stir up anti-Dutch feelings to regain the territory for France.

Charles X's Minister, Polignac, wished to replace the French Constitution with more absolutist arrangements. Polignac needed a foreign success to gain support for the destruction of the Charter. The French Ambassador in St Petersburg was instructed to propose a general reconstruction of Europe and the Middle East. The French plan involved the dissolution of the United Netherlands, French acquisition of the Belgian provinces, Prussian annexation of Dutch territory on the Rhine and – once the Turks had been expelled – the installation of a Dutch ruler in Constantinople as sovereign of a new Greek Empire. Britain was to be offered the Dutch colonies, but if this offer were to be refused, Britain would be confronted by a coalition of France, Prussia and Russia which would compel the country to accept or face European war. Political opponents in England accused Wellington and Aberdeen of fostering Polignac's rise to power and favouring his absolutist plans. Yet allegations made in *The Edinburgh Review* were poorly substantiated; Polignac's success would have been unwelcome to any British government. Fortunately the Russians agreed with *The Edinburgh Review*'s verdict that Polignac's proposals demonstrated 'an incapacity, wholly without example in any European minister or potentate from the days of the idiot kings'.[10] Russian rejection of Polignac's proposals, followed by the suspension of the French constitution, led to violence in Paris. By the end of July 1830, Charles X was in exile, Polignac under arrest and the Duke of Orleans had become King of the French.

Although Polignac's fall was welcome, the news from France was alarming. Europe seemed on the brink of another revolutionary explosion; this time Britain itself might not escape. Domestic and foreign issues coincided. Ministers were in the middle of an election campaign following the death of George IV. The demand for parliamentary reform, judged by many to be revolutionary, might increase in the light of events in France. Misjudgement in the handling of the situation could have serious consequences, yet Wellington and Aberdeen could not agree on what Britain's response should be. Wellington opposed recognition of the Orleanist régime until the matter had been discussed by a Congress of the Great Powers. He would not rule out armed intervention to deal with this manifestation of the revolutionary spirit in its most dangerous homeland. Aberdeen rejected intervention and argued that the behaviour of Charles X and Polignac had been so reprehensible that the states of Europe were relieved of any obligations to them. Delay in recognizing Louis Phillipe's government served no useful purpose and, by implying censure, would only endanger the peace of Europe. Aberdeen's argument that the moderate course of the Revolution in France was more like Britain in 1688 than Paris in 1792 overcame Wellington's doubts. Britain gave formal recognition to the new régime in August 1830.

Relations with Orleanist France were complicated by events in Belgium. The uprising which Polignac had done so much to encourage did not break out until after his fall. Organs such as *The Edinburgh Review* which approved of the changes in Paris were restrained in their comments on events in Belgium. The provisional government in Brussels was considering offering the throne of an independent Belgium to a relation of Louis Phillipe. The effect of this would be almost as bad as if the Belgian provinces had been incorporated into France. Although events in France did not necessarily infringe the treaties of 1814 and 1815, the treaties were most explicit on the obligation to maintain the integrity of the Kingdom of the Netherlands.

On 5 October 1830 King William of Holland called upon Britain, France, Russia, Austria and Prussia to send forces to the Southern Netherlands to preserve the work of the Congress of Vienna. Hitherto, Britain had generally been able to refuse requests for help on the grounds that it had never given specific promises of assistance – but firm promises had been given to the Dutch. If Britain failed to honour its obligations, the country would be giving the clearest indication yet that it was now indifferent to the maintenance of the central feature of the postwar settlement. Aberdeen was tempted to accede to the Dutch demands, especially as Prussia and Russia seemed sympathetic. But the appearance of British units in a Dutch army of reconquest would provoke such fury in Paris that the new government would find it hard to refuse to send help to the Belgian rebels, thus beginning a process likely to end in European war. Although the conference of representatives of the Great Powers meeting in London produced proposals for an armistice, the situation was still uncertain when Wellington's government fell in November 1830. The chief reason for the government's defeat was undoubtedly its opposition to reform, but its mediocre record in foreign policy, especially following after men of the stature of Canning and Castlereagh, further damaged its credibility. Lady Canning insisted that almost the last words her husband spoke were: 'I have laboured hard for the last few years to place the country in the high station which she now holds. Two years of the Duke of Wellington's government will undo all that I have done.'[11]

Notes: Chapter 4

1 *Hansard's Parliamentary Debates*, Vol. 32, pp. 356–61.
2 *Hansard*, Vol. 35, pp. 1196–1201.
3 *Hansard*, Vol. 40, pp. 368–9.
4 *Hansard*, Vol. 39, pp. 1090–3.
5 Ibid., Vol. 39, p. 1093.
6 H. W. V. Temperley, *The Foreign Policy of Canning, 1822–27: England, The Neo-Holy Alliance and the New World*, London, G. Bell & Sons Ltd., 1925, p. 324.
7 Quoted in C. Petrie, *George Canning*, London, Eyre & Spottis-woode, 1946, pp. 172–3.
8 *Letters of the Earl of Dudley to the Bishop of Llandaff*, (ed.) Edward Copleston, London, John Murray, 1841, p. 184.
9 *Hansard*, New Series, Vol. 38, p. 3.
10 *Edinburgh Review*, vol. 52, October 1830, p. 7.
11 Quoted in H. W. V. Temperley, *Life of Canning*, London, 1905, p. 267.

5

Coercion or Conciliation?
1830–1848

I

1830 appears an important turning point in nineteenth-century history, the occasion when the fabric of international relations established in 1815 was first seriously shaken. There may have been earlier rearrangements in South-Eastern Europe, but only now was there any modification of a highly sensitive boundary in the heart of Western Europe. There had been revolutions elsewhere but only in 1830 was there a change in régime in one of the Great Powers. To anxious conservatives it appeared that two Great Powers were affected; the July revolution in France was only marginally more alarming than the 'Whig revolution' in England. The postwar era of international relations was definitely over.

How much difference did this make to British foreign policy? Some historians have detected dramatic changes. After all, 1830 saw Britain faced with a situation apparently resembling that of 1792–3. Yet Britain did not go to war to overthrow the forces of revolutionary France, nor did it resort to arms to prevent changes in the Low Countries. Britain had expended huge amounts of blood and wealth to secure the restoration of the senior branch of the Bourbons and had been equally determined to guard against future French aggression by placing the whole of the Netherlands under the House of Orange. In 1830, however, obligations to the House of Bourbon and the House of Orange were cast aside. A usurper was accepted as King of the French and the widowed son-in-law of George IV became the ruler of territories which Britain had once been eager to present to the Dutch. Of course, 1830 was not 1793. Louis Phillipe was not Robespierre and an independent Belgium was less frightening than French annexation. Yet the two situations were sufficiently similar for the leaders of the other powers to contrast the weakness of Grey's government with the resolution of Pitt's. In terms of ancestry, British foreign policy in 1830 owed more to Fox than to Pitt.

One answer to the question posed above is that there was a fundamental change in foreign policy involving the implementation of ideas worked out a generation earlier. This interpretation would emphasize the significance of domestic politics and the change from 'reactionary' Tory principles to 'progressive' Whig ones. Some members of Grey's government, notably Lord Holland undoubtedly saw things in these terms. A Whiggish view of foreign policy would see Fox as a prophet, ridiculed in his own time, but vindicated by subsequent events. Fox had stood for friendship with revolutionary France and hostility to absolutism. In 1830 there were reasons for welcoming the revolution in Paris. What was emerging in Paris was not a new Jacobin Terror but a respectable constitutional monarchy. English and French values were sufficiently close for the two countries to function on the basis of similar institutions. The best men in France in 1789 had been aiming at a French 1688. Through a series of mistakes things had got out of hand – with deplorable consequences both for France and for Europe. The constitution of the restored Bourbons had been too limited and too obviously associated with allied victory. Now the French were getting it right. If 'reform in order to preserve' became the watchword in Paris as well as in London, the broken thread of Anglo-French co-operation could be resumed.

With such a government in Paris it might be safe to revise the peace treaties of 1814 and 1815. If Europe was to divide on ideological grounds, it made no sense to favour an absolutist régime in France. With a constitutional government in Paris, Britain and France should be natural allies, giving discreet but united assistance to the cause of freedom and standing together against despotism. With such co-operation, the ascendency of Metternich would be over. This Whig analysis represents the swan song of eighteenth-century enlightened aristocratic internationalism. The 1830s saw the final flowering of a cosmopolitan Whiggery, represented by the salons of Lady Holland in London and her opposite numbers in Paris. British and French politics were closely linked in the days of the July monarchy. There was close personal contact between British and French politicians and some Whigs had no qualms about intriguing with Frenchmen such as Thiers against their political enemies in England. Trips to Paris became frequent, a phenomenon enhanced by the rakish reputation of the French capital at a time of increasing respectability in Britain.

Yet it would be wrong to see 1830 as merely the posthumous triumph of C. J. Fox. There were more fundamental pressures at work. The 1830s was 'the decade of reform'. A reformed Parliament and an enlarged electorate required a new foreign policy. Metternich frequently deplored changes in British foreign policy since the death of Castlereagh as contrary to Britain's true interests. This view reveals as much about Metternich as about Britain. He believed that the interests of states were unchanging, an attitude based on the assumption of a static social order. Foreign policy is supposed to promote the national interest, yet the nature of that interest may be perceived differently by different groups, based on different economic motives, different value systems and even different ideas about the nature of states. If the social, economic and political balance should alter – as it undoubtedly was altering – the result was likely to be a different foreign policy, the diplomatic face of a new industrial and middle–class England.

These interpretations point to a substantial change in the priorities of British foreign policy around 1830. They seem plausible but imprecise. Beyond a Francophile tendency and a profusion of high sounding phrases, it is difficult to say what was distinctly Whiggish about Whig foreign policy. As the Whigs had been in opposition for fifty years they had been spared the necessity of turning their principles into specific policies. In any case, Grey's government was a coalition containing former Tories, Whigs and even some who might be considered Radicals. Tories and Radicals had their own ideas about foreign policy. A government of this kind, especially one preoccupied with domestic issues, could hardly be expected to follow a consistent foreign policy. Similarly, it is unwise to place too much emphasis on the alleged changes in British politics and society. Historians are now reluctant to use expressions like 'the triumph of the middle-classes' or 'the Industrial Revolution' without qualification. If things changed only gradually perhaps the corresponding changes in foreign policy would be equally modest. The 1832 Reform Bill did not deliver foreign policy into the hands of the middle-classes. In large measure, decisions were taken by men whose background differed little from that of those who had controlled foreign policy in the eighteenth century.

The options available to Britain in 1830 were the same as they had been since 1815, the same indeed as they were to remain until 1848 or even later. A few, on the extreme Right, believed Britain should uphold existing territorial arrangements and all existing governments. This 'dynastic conservatism' had usually been advocated by George IV and was still defended by ultra-Tory politicians such as Sir Richard Vyvyan. But even the most conservative postwar Foreign Secretaries shied away from the implication, inherent in this position, that Britain should send armed support to unpopular absolutist régimes. Most conservative thinkers stressed the excellence of the territorial arrangements of 1815, but were less concerned with the complexion of régimes established within those boundaries. They were critical of dynastic conservatism and insisted that Britain should only intervene in other states if its own national interests were threatened.[1] Each country was the best judge of its own institutions. The chief difference between the similar policies of Castlereagh and Canning had been that, whereas Castlereagh stressed his support for territorial conservatism, Canning's main emphasis was of opposition to dynastic conservatism.

On the left of politics, some would have no truck either with dynastic or territorial conservatism. They believed that Britain's true interests would be best served if it became the champion of the oppressed peoples of Europe and promoted national independence wherever it was denied. Such a policy would be popular and both inherently right and advantageous. National states would be liberal states, and liberal states would follow commercial policies beneficial to Britain. Taken to its logical conclusion, enthusiasm for liberty and national independence led to the complete over-throw of the 1815 settlement and the rejection of traditional Balance of Power theories.[2] It was hard enough to form an idea of the nature of the balance when there were only a few large states involved in the reckoning. Yet a Europe of nationalities would necessarily involve the dismemberment of at least one of the Great Powers and an overall increase in the number of significant states. In reality, the belief that some kind of *natural* balance would exist if the national principles were universally adopted rested on flimsy foun-dations. As a Europe of nationalities had never existed – with the partial and alarming exception of the Napoleonic period – it had to be taken as a matter of faith that, once everyone in Europe was a citizen of a state they wanted to belong to (assuming such a thing was possible), territorial disputes would cease and the new European order would embrace Free Trade and constitutional government and look to Britain as a friend and an example.

The foreign policy followed by the new government is best defined as occupying the ground between territorial conservatism on the right and liberal nationalism on the left, and including elements of both. This mixture of new and old was echoed at the personal level. The new Foreign Secretary, Lord Palmerston, was to emerge as the most important figure in the formulation of British foreign policy in the next generation. If the years since 1815 had been 'The Age of Castlereagh and Canning', the period from 1830 to 1865 was undoubtedly 'The Age of Palmerston'. Yet Palmerston was an unlikely harbinger of a new order. As an aristocrat and a minister under Liverpool, he was a distinctly eighteenth-century figure. His reputation as a dandy and philanderer scarcely fits with notions of bourgeois respectability. Indeed, Palmerston often encountered bitter criticism from those who regarded themselves as spokesmen for middle-class and industrial interests. Yet it would be wrong to conclude that nothing had changed. The Reform Bill made Parliament, and hence the Foreign Secretary, more responsible to the electorate. Decision makers in foreign policy, for all their aristocratic connections, were now subject to new pressures and many willingly subscribed to new values.

As a follower of Canning, Palmerston had been a proponent of the territorial conservatism line, a position rejected by some of his new colleagues. Palmerston's attitude was now changing into a new version of the Balance of Power theory. Article XVI of the Treaty of Chaumont had contained a commitment to maintain 'the Balance of Europe'. Palmerston thought that the peacemakers had done well but no treaty could hope to get the balance exactly right. In any case, the relative importance and strength of the different countries was bound to alter over the years. An inflexible commitment to the boundaries of 1815 was thus incompatible with the maintenance of a true balance between the powers of Europe. What was wanted was commitment to the spirit not the letter of the peace treaties. There would have to be periodic adjustments as circumstances required. Of course, a readiness to alter some of the existing frontiers of Europe was sure to anger the conservative powers, even though Palmerston wanted to retain most of the boundaries. It was also dangerous to arouse the hopes of those who wanted radical revisions – only to face their fury when it became clear that, in the last resort, Britain too was a conservative power. If things were mishandled, Britain could end up with no friends at all. Talk about the Balance of Power would be represented as another example of British hypocrisy – covering with high principle a selfish desire to promote change where it suited and to sustain the status quo where it did not. If the desired changes were to be achieved peacefully the Great Powers would have to agree. Britain would have to play an active part in European diplomacy. There would have to be frequent meetings or congresses to discuss the proposed changes, thus departing from Canning's dislike of congresses and reverting to Castlereagh's acceptance of them.

The meetings would be held not to uphold but to modify the Vienna settlement. What kind of changes should Britain support? National interest of the traditional kind required Britain to resist any changes which would assist France to escape from the *cordon sanitaire* placed around it in 1815. Changes likely to increase the power of Russia would be equally unwelcome. Such preoccupations were hard to square with newer arguments about the propriety and advantage of supporting liberal and nationalist movements. For public consumption, Palmerston might appear to incline towards the more modern arguments. The Foreign Secretary was increasingly concerned with his image. It suited him to be seen as the friend of progressive movements on the Continent. But there was often a substantial gap between rhetoric and reality. In any case, Palmerston never gave wholehearted endorsement to the new set of ideas. There was no guarantee that Palmerston would help revolutionary and nationalist movements. He might provide some diplomatic assistance but nothing more tangible. He might make public speeches but his diplomatic activities might seem muted and ineffective. He might do nothing at all. He might emerge as the champion of the status quo. Some, particularly in Poland, concluded that Palmerston was a kind of *agent provocateur* of absolutism. By fair words and hints of assistance he encouraged the oppressed to rise, only to leave them cruelly to their fate when their masters reasserted themselves. In reality, Palmerston's readiness to change the map of Europe to reflect new circumstances sprang from a desire to *maintain* the essence of the Balance of Power set up in 1815.[3] Whatever his position in domestic politics, Palmerston was a true Whig in foreign policy – in so far as a core of Whiggery is contained in the dictum 'reform in order to preserve'.

But it was not relations with European liberals and nationalists that posed the greatest problem. Palmerston might 'betray' them time and time again, but England was their only friend against the forces of repression. Sometimes

France seemed sympathetic, but events were to prove that
that country was even less trustworthy than Britain. What
mattered most in British diplomacy was relations with the
other Great Powers. Palmerston was sure to run foul of
the determination of Austria and Prussia to maintain the
letter of the 1815 settlements. Russian reaction was more
complicated. There was a strange similarity between British
and Russian foreign policy. Both were broadly committed
to the status quo, but both were prepared for alterations in
particular places. If Palmerston's public pronouncements
were more revisionist than his actual policy, the rhetoric
of Russian policy was more conservative than its practice.
But it would be hard to put this apparent congruence
to any specific use. Britain and Russia favoured changes
benefiting their own state interests, and these interests
rarely coincided. Russia wanted to keep things as they
were in Western Europe and encourage change in Eastern
Europe. The British position was the exact opposite. The
most sensitive relationship was with France. On hearing
of the fall of Charles X, Palmerston had declared that he
would 'drink the cause of Liberalism' all over the world.[4]
Both Whigs and Radicals were sympathetic to Orleanist
France. They appreciated, however, that an understanding
with Louis Phillipe would be difficult to achieve. In France,
the Left was associated with the patriotic cause and even
the modest move leftwards in 1830 had produced a more
assertive emphasis on France's national interests. Perhaps
Britain should make concessions to France because, if it
did not, popular support for Louis Phillipe would fade and
the régime would collapse. The result would be an extreme
government in Paris advancing demands totally incompatible with British interests and certain to provoke war.

Palmerston appreciated the strength of the pro-French
case. On occasion he could be its eloquent advocate. Yet
unlike some of his Whig colleagues, Palmerston was never
totally Francophile. With Whigs such as Holland, attitudes
to foreign policy were coloured by the memory of Fox's
sympathy for the French Revolution. Palmerston was a
former Tory who had been Secretary-at-War for the last
five years of the struggle against Napoleon. In his eyes,

whatever the complexion of the government in Paris, France remained France, a country with a tradition of rivalry with England and continuing ambitions which were incompatible with the interests of Britain. No political change could alter the geographical fact of France's proximity to the English coast. There were certain things Palmerston did not intend to give away in order to secure French friendship. He did not even wish to tie himself to a French alliance even if that were available on favourable terms. The essence of his policy was to play France and the other Great Powers off against each other, inclining one way and then the other as British interest directed.

II

In November 1830 a conference in London was trying to resolve the Belgian crisis. Palmerston at least knew what he wanted: an independent Belgium, free from French and Dutch alike.[5] Superficially, the reassertion of Dutch rule appeared compatible with British interests. It would keep the French out of the Low Countries and thus maintain one of the cardinal objectives of British foreign policy. Unfortunately matters were unlikely to end there. Insistence on the letter of the peace settlements might destroy their most admirable feature: the containment of France. Dutch success, especially if it involved armed assistance from the Northern powers, would inflame opinion in France and Louis Phillipe would be compelled to send his army to help the Walloons. In other words a 'right wing' policy could have horribly 'left wing' consequences which could be reversed only by a full scale war.

Palmerston would never buy French friendship the easy way by accepting French dominance in the Low Countries. What was required was a new barrier to French expansion. If Belgium was free and well governed, the French would have no excuse for intervention. Better still, if Belgium could be afforded a special neutral status, accepted by all the Great Powers, the British objective of a 'safe' Low Countries could be more completely realized than ever before. To achieve this it was essential that the Dutch received no military assistance. Indeed, the Dutch had to be dissuaded from crushing the Belgian revolt, even if they had sufficient means of their own. The French had to be persuaded not to send armies to help the Belgian rebels and to drop the idea of installing a French puppet on the throne of Belgium. The Belgians had to be persuaded not to make excessive territorial demands and to choose a king acceptable to Britain. The Dutch had to be persuaded to accept Belgian independence and a fair separation settlement. Much persuasion would be needed to induce the various parties to act in ways contrary to their real inclinations. On 20 January 1831 the principle of an independent Belgium was accepted by the representatives of the Great Powers. Palmerston exploited fears of general revolution; impending trouble in their own territories helped the Northern Powers to decide they could not help the Dutch. The Russians faced an uprising in Poland and revolutions in Italy deflected Austria away from involvement in the Low Countries.

Although they were useful distractions, Palmerston was not truly sympathetic to the Italian and Polish revolutions. If Palmerston's Belgian policy was one of trying to secure traditional ends to new means, elsewhere he was ready to keep to traditional means as well as ends. He urged the governments of Italy to introduce reforms, but in the last resort he supported Austrian hegemony south of the Alps. Austrian policy might be shortsighted, but a strong Austria was an essential element in the Balance of Power. The same applied to Russia. Palmerston defended Nicholas I's withdrawal of the Polish Constitution and the repressive measures taken by the Russian authorities. This produced heated exchanges in Parliament where Irish members, in particular, sympathized with the tribulations of their Polish co-religionists. Daniel O'Connell described the partition of Poland as one of the most disgraceful acts in modern history, the work of 'that outrageous public prostitute, the notorious Catherine, the grandmother of this Emperor'.[6]

Palmerston's solicitude for Russia was especially marked in the Dutch Loan affair and gave rise to bizarre allegations that he was a Russian agent. Under the terms of the Treaty of Vienna, the King of the United Netherlands agreed to take responsibility for a debt owed by the Russian government to the London Bankers, Hope & Co. Repayments would stop if the union of the Netherlands broke up. After the Belgian revolt, the Dutch expected the Russians to resume responsibility for the debt. Palmerston promised that future repayments would be made by Britain. The Russians would be more likely to accept the independence of Belgium if it involved them in no financial loss. The affair embarrassed the government, with Tories and Radicals uniting to condemn Palmerston. Sir Robert Peel denounced the proceedings as profligate and probably illegal.

Of course, if Palmerston could persuade the absolutist Courts that he was really on their side, he stood a better chance of inducing them to accept his solution to the Belgian crisis. The policy also provided a kind of insurance. If things went wrong and the French looked like gaining control, an anti-French coalition on 1814 lines would be required. It was wise to have the links ready, just in case. Ostentatiously cordial relations between Britain and the Northern Courts offered the best hope of restraining the French. Louis Phillipe had a stark choice to make. If he co-operated with Britain he might alter the 1815 treaties piecemeal and without war, gaining bits of increased prestige here and there. Yet to French eyes, the British seemed ready to offer very little, perhaps not enough to satisfy patriotic opinion in France. If he tried to secure more radical revisions than the British were ready to contemplate, Louis Phillipe would encounter the united opposition of Britain, Russia, Austria and Prussia. The only way of achieving anything would be by European war. The French might try to bluff their way through, but in the last resort they would back down. This was the real reason why the Belgian crisis was settled as Britain wanted. With Palmerston at the Foreign Office every ounce of advantage would be taken of the hold London had over Paris.

In January 1831 warnings from London induced Louis Phillipe to refuse an offer of the throne of Belgium made to his son, the Duke of Nemours. A candidate acceptable to Britain and France was found in Leopold of Saxe-Coburg. Unfortunately, Leopold was not satisfied with the territory provisionally allocated to Belgium and demanded Luxembourg as well. The Belgian claim on Luxembourg was to postpone a final settlement for several years. The King of Holland maintained that by demanding new territory Belgium had broken its side of the recent armistice. On 2 August 1831 Dutch troops entered Belgium and quickly defeated its small army. In response, a French army crossed the frontier to deal with the Dutch. This was the nadir of the crisis for Palmerston. Radicals wanted to send armed help to Leopold, whilst the Tories applauded the Dutch and insisted that Palmerston had been wrong to back Leopold's claim in Luxembourg. Worse still, Prussia and Austria took a renewed interest in the affair. Although ruled by the King of Holland, Luxembourg was part of the German Confederation. Its fate was of interest to Austria, the dominant power in the Confederation, and to Prussia whose Rhineland territories bordered upon it. Britain had become the pariah of Europe. France denounced Britain's betrayal of the Belgians by refusing to send direct military help against the Dutch. The Northern Courts were equally hostile to Britain's readiness to 'give away' territory which belonged to others.

Like Canning, Palmerston had a talent for salvaging something out of a disaster. He accepted the French presence in Belgium on the understanding that the French would withdraw if the Dutch returned to their own soil. Dutch withdrawal was achieved quickly, but owed more to French victories than to British diplomatic pressure. It looked as if Britain's worst fears would be realized when the French proved reluctant to pull their armies back. It took a direct threat of war to persuade them to honour their promises. A new effort was now made to solve the Belgian problem. Belgium was to receive the western half of Luxembourg only. The Dutch were to evacuate the fortress of Antwerp, whilst Belgium assumed responsibility for half the debt of the Kingdom of the United Netherlands. Although unhappy with the outcome, the Northern Powers signed the treaty embodying this agreement because they believed Palmerston's warning that if they did not the French armies would march again. The King of Holland refused to ratify the Treaty but, apart from keeping a beleaguered garrison in Antwerp, he could do nothing to stop its implementation. By the end of 1831 the Belgian question was largely resolved and Britain's main objective of keeping France out of the Low Countries had been achieved.

British policy changed after the partial settlement of the Belgium crisis. In August 1832 Palmerston described constitutional states as the natural allies of Britain, an advanced view compared to his recent pronouncements. This announcement was a coded way of saying that Britain wanted closer relations with France. Some Continental statesmen saw the passing of the Reform Bill as the first step in an English revolution and began to cold-shoulder Britain. Despite alarming moments during the Belgian crisis, and evidence that France was still ambitious, the country was now governed by men who appreciated that they had to co-operate with Britain. Failing the good offices of the Northern Courts, the only way to get the Dutch out of Antwerp was to act in concert with France. Palmerston agreed to a limited operation by the French army, reinforced by a blockade of Dutch ports by the Royal Navy. The Dutch soon surrendered. There was some heart-searching at the prospect of military action, however modest, in concert with a traditional enemy against a traditional ally. The Dutch forces in Antwerp surrendered in December 1832. A final settlement was achieved in April 1839. It was then that the first guarantees of neutrality were given which were to provide Britain with its *casus belli* in 1914. It is ironic that the resolution of a crisis which British diplomacy had handled with such skill should have sown the seeds of a harvest of blood three-quarters of a century later.

It is unfair to blame Palmerston for the First World War, but his solution to the Belgian problem can be faulted. The diversity of peoples and traditions found in the Low Countries had caused problems for centuries and, from the British point of view, most of the troubles had been caused by French aggression. 1815 had provided

Castlereagh with an opportunity to reunite the Southern
and Northern Netherlands which had been separated since
the sixteenth century. Whatever the names or specific territories, Castlereagh had produced a state which might be expected to play a 'Burgundian' role in European affairs. A
'Burgundian' or 'middle' state separating the French and
Germanic worlds usually suited England's interests. First
and foremost such a state constituted a barrier against
French aggression, but it could serve the same purpose
against aggression from any other quarter. By agreeing to
the division of the United Netherlands, Palmerston weakened that barrier. He fell into the trap of believing that
paper guarantees were as reliable as the reality of a strong
state. Although the threat came eventually from a quarter
no one had anticipated in 1839, future generations were to
pay a high price for Palmerston's naivety.

III

Russia was now about to supplant France as the chief object
of British suspicion. Mehemet Ali, the Pasha of Egypt, had
helped the Turks against the Greeks but the Pasha, considering his services ill-rewarded, invaded Syria and seemed
poised to capture Constantinople. The Czar, recently the
Christian champion against Muslim oppression, presented
himself as the saviour of the Turkish Empire, ready to send
his armies to help the Turks defeat the Egyptian rebels. Of
course, once the Egyptians had been dealt with, Russia could
compel the Sultan to accept arrangements which made him
the satellite of the Czar. The prospect of swallowing the
Turkish Empire whole rather than dismembering it piece by
piece appealed to St Petersburg. Rather than seek a head-on
collision with Russia, Palmerston fell back on Canning's old
policy of trying to 'internationalize' the Eastern Question.
If the Egyptian armies could be stopped by an international
force, the independence of the Turkish Empire would be
easier to sustain. Palmerston's request for naval squadrons
to be sent to Alexandria and to the Dardanelles, however,
was defeated in Cabinet. In later years he described this

decision as the worst mistake ever made whilst he was Foreign Secretary.[7]

The Sultan now had to call in the Russians. Events proceeded as Palmerston feared. Under the terms of the Treaty of Unkiar Skelessi, signed on 8 July 1833, the Czar and Sultan agreed not to take any step without consulting each other. Worse still, the Treaty contained a secret clause, discovered by a British agent, that Turkey would now reverse its traditional policy and allow Russian warships through the Straits at all times. Fear of a Russian presence in the Mediterranean ranked second only to preoccupation with the security of the Low Countries as a constant feature of British foreign policy. Palmerston concluded that, under the terms of Unkiar Skelessi, 'the Russian Ambassador becomes chief of Cabinet to the Sultan'.[8] Although this conclusion was unduly pessimistic, the Russian triumph at Unkiar Skelessi impressed Central Europe. The Austrians were not sorry to learn of Britain's humiliation, a just punishment for its recent behaviour. Where Austria led, Prussia followed. In October 1833, the Czar, the Emperor of Austria and the King of Prussia met at Munchengratz in Bohemia and issued a declaration pledging themselves to help any legitimate ruler facing trouble from liberal elements. Munchengratz looked like the beginning of an alliance directed against Britain and France. Palmerston had to face the fact that Europe was dividing into ideologically opposed blocs. Britain now needed France almost as much as France needed Britain.

There was not much that could be done in Poland, Germany or Italy but at least the Munchengratz powers could be thwarted in the Iberian Peninsula where the constitutional cause was reviving. France intended to intervene south of the Pyrenees but unilateral action on its part would be unwelcome. Intervention in conjunction with France would not only thwart the absolutists but would also check any excessive increase in French influence. A blind eye was turned to the large number of British officers joining Don Pedro, despite the provisions of the Foreign Enlistment Act. Don Pedro was able to establish his government in Portugal and Miguel left for comfortable exile in Vienna.

After Don Pedro's death, his daughter tired of constitutions and with the aid of her German husband, a Saxe-Coburg, reverted to absolutism. At least the Saxe-Coburgs were firm friends of Britain and an absolutist régime was more tolerable if it was pro-British. Spain posed a more difficult problem. Don Carlos was receiving help from Metternich and, on 22 April 1834, Britain, France, Spain and Portugal entered into a Quadruple Alliance. The Alliance marked the high point of Anglo-French co-operation and represented a firm riposte to Munchengratz. The undertaking to assist the constitutional cause in the Iberian Peninsula struck terror into the absolutists whose forces melted away, compelling Don Carlos to surrender. Victory in Spain compensated for humiliation in Turkey.

It would be wrong to make too much of events in Spain. British intervention was always of a limited kind and no British land forces set foot on Spanish soil. The Spanish troubles represented no more than shadow boxing between the Great Powers, allowing both sides to maintain that they were true to their principles whilst remaining confident that they could stop any escalation to a major European war. Outside parties knew that they were being exploited by their protégés and that there was not much different between absolutists and constitutionalists. British policy in Spain and Portugal seemed progressive but there was an element of artificiality about it, a charade designed to impress opinion in Britain and to give the French something to do to keep them out of real trouble.

Even with the change of direction in 1832, British policy was still essentially conservative. Protests issued at the treatment of the German Liberals who had tried to seize Frankfurt were almost apologetic in tone. Apart from a sense of relief amongst the much abused clerks in the Foreign Office, the departure of Palmerston and the appointment of Wellington as Foreign Secretary in the minority Tory government made little difference. During the Tory government, however, French influence had increased in Madrid and the continuing troubles in Spain gave France an opportunity to emerge as the chief protector of the constitutional cause. When Palmerston returned to the Foreign office in April 1835 he tried to continue his old policy of restraining France by appearing to co-operate with it. For geographical reasons, joint intervention in Spain would do more for France than for Britain. Palmerston tried to frighten off Metternich from giving serious support to the Carlists by an impressive, even belligerent, display of Anglo-French solidarity, but at the same time told the French that Britain and France should limit their involvement. To convince the French that Britain was serious, it was necessary to allow British volunteers to enlist in the service of Queen Isabella and a British legion was formed under the command of Colonel de Lacy Evans. This concession proved insufficient for a new French government under Adolphe Thiers which came to power in the summer of 1836, demanding intervention in Spain on a scale far beyond anything acceptable to Britain. Palmerston now did not know what he wanted in Spain. There was justice in J. A. Roebuck's complaint that after a three-hour 'explanation' of British policy towards Spain, Members of Parliament were more confused than ever.

IV

In Thiers, Palmerston encountered a formidable adversary. The demand for intervention in Spain was a clever move. Thiers had a good knowledge of British politics, even if he had no love of Britain. He knew that domestic opposition was likely to prevent Palmerston increasing the British commitment to Spain. The field would be left clear for France. Strong French action would outbid Palmerston's claim to be the champion of the liberal cause throughout Europe, a claim which in truth depended more upon words than upon deeds. France could regain its old position as the natural patron of liberty elsewhere and gain the support of a substantial 'fifth column' in Germany, Italy and beyond. Thiers was typical of thousands in France and elsewhere who tended to romanticize the achievements of the Revolution and Empire and felt that Europe in the 1830s was sadly lacking in excitement. To such men, Waterloo and

Vienna were tragic aberrations, yet with skill and resolution the future might yet belong to France.

Of course, if the glories of the past were to be restored, the settlements of 1814 and 1815 would have to be destroyed. Even events of 1830 had shown that they were capable of modification. Thiers was eager to accelerate the pace of change, to a rate Britain could not keep up with. Thiers saw through Palmerston's policy of friendship with France as a device for preventing the country from achieving its legitimate objectives. Palmerston had got the better of France over Belgium and Thiers was determined to prevent any repetition. He appreciated that it would be hard for France to break out of its straitjacket but thought that this could be done by deepening the divisions between the allies of 1814 and 1815. British disapproval of Munchengratz and Palmerston's support for the constitutional side of Spain, together with many liberal speeches, had gone some way to secure this end. France would be even better placed if she could establish an understanding with one or more of the absolutist powers. If Thiers could persuade them that France was less of a danger than Britain, then the way would be open for France to regain that long sought after freedom of manoeuvre. There were some plausible arguments to hand, notably building up common resentment at Britain's commercial and economic success. Thiers' policy was contradictory. It would be difficult, for example, to conciliate Metternich and take a strongly liberal line in Spain at the same time. But stranger things had happened in international relations and Palmerston had every reason to take fright at the prospect.

Fortunately, Metternich proved impervious to French blandishments. Louis Phillipe became alarmed at what seemed a risky policy and dismissed Thiers from office. Thiers' successors were cautious men and reverted to cooperation with Britain in the labyrinthine politics and squalid civil war dragging on in Spain. In Portugal Palmerston backed the moderate elements, while the French supported more extreme groups. In Spain the position was reversed with Britain backing the Radical 'exaltados'. Hitherto, Palmerston had been careful about the groups he supported, rarely linking Britain with positions more advanced than moderate liberalism. In Spain he demonstrated that, if circumstances required, a British government, would work with the extreme Left. Any revolutionary appeal possessed by Orleanist France was effectively out-trumped. By the summer of 1840 it looked as if the Spanish Civil War had ended when the leading Carlist General Marota, went over to the government side. Elements supported by Palmerston were victorious, both in Madrid and Lisbon.

But the antagonism between Britain and France which surfaced in 1836 did not go away. The two constitutional Great Powers viewed each other with suspicion. Neither did Thiers disappear from French politics; one day he would head a government again and make another bid to realize his objectives. Despite disapproval of each other's domestic policies, Britain and Austria had no real quarrel. The weak link in the Chaumont powers was between Britain and Russia. France had to exploit this weakness to achieve any of the things Thiers wanted. Some new instalment of the Eastern Crisis offered France the best chance of redrawing the map of Europe. Palmerston wanted a strong, pro-British and preferably reformed Ottoman Empire to provide an effective bulwark against Russian expansion. The Treaty of Unkiar Skelessi had turned the Sultan into a client of the Czar but left Egypt and Syria in the hands of the rebellious Mehemet Ali. The connection between France and Mehemet Ali provided Louis Phillipe with a real chance of rearranging the diplomacy of Europe. The current episode of the Eastern Crisis might be resolved in several ways. Turkish power could be reasserted by rejecting Mehemet Ali from his dominions and reimposing direct control from Constantinople. This outcome, especially if assisted by Britain, would help the Turks escape from tutelage to Russia. It would be unwelcome in St Petersburg but, if handled with care, the Czar might accept a reassertion of 'legitimate' authority. France would oppose the humiliation of Mehemet Ali and might consider sending him armed support. It might prove necessary to confront France with the united opposition of the other Great Powers to dissuade the country from anything foolish.

Alternatively, the entire Ottoman Empire might fall to Mehemet Ali, perhaps the only man capable of putting new life into it. At least under Mehemet Ali's control there was no danger that the Ottoman Empire would be a Russian puppet. Despite Palmerston's attempts to play down the Russian seizure of the British merchant ship *Vixen* and his assertion in December 1837 that Russia did as much as Britain to maintain world peace, the Russian menace seemed acute. Seen from London, Russian intrigue in Afghanistan provided the justification for the ill-fated British occupation of Kabul in 1839. Yet Mehemet Ali was too identified with France to be suitable for British purposes and strong backing for him would mean direct collision with Russia. Palmerston would have to align Britain alongside France and prepare for war against the Czar. France would thus achieve the long-sought division amongst the victors of 1815. The situation would have approximated to that of the Crimean War some fourteen years later. Yet at least in the Crimean War, the two German Great Powers avoided direct involvement. In 1840, Austria and Prussia might have joined Russia, creating a second Front on the Rhine. Significantly, the German song 'Wacht am Rhein' was written at that time. If Britain allied with France, it would have to sanction a French invasion of Germany. In effect, it would be encouraging the destruction of those features of the 1815 arrangements once considered the most admirable. For reasons of interest as well as tradition, Britain could not have acted with France in 1840.

Perhaps nothing dramatic would happen in the Near East. This, too, was hardly in Britain's interest. Russia's ambitions elsewhere had prevented it from taking maximum advantage from Unkiar Skelessi. No doubt it would do so when circumstances permitted. The more the Ottoman Empire came under Russian subjection, the harder it would be for Britain to object to the continuing control of Egypt and Syria by Mehemet Ali. It seemed only too likely that the Northern part of the Empire would be directed from St Petersburg whilst the Southern part, through the intermediary of Mehemet Ali, would be directed from Paris. France and Russia might establish a *modus vivendi*. Having excluded Britain from the Levant they would be united against its return. We may designate the first scenario as the 'British' solution, the second as the 'French' and the third as the 'Russian' – although the third also involved a useful 'second prize' for France. The eventual result approximated more closely to the 'British' solution than to any of the others. Although Palmerston could act decisively when required, he generally allowed others to take the initiative. A successful foreign policy which exploits opportunities as they arise often secures the best results by taking advantage of others' mistakes. In these matters there is an element of chance and, in 1840, Britain was lucky.

In the summer of 1839 the Sultan decided to send an army to expel Egyptian forces from Syria. He received tacit encouragement from the British and also from the Russians, who calculated that further military activities would place the Turks deeper in their debt. If the Sultan's armies were defeated, the Russians would come to his rescue and thus acquire extra influence. If the Turks defeated the Egyptians, the French would probably come to the aid of Mehemet Ali. A general war could result; Britain wanted both to prevent war and to stop either France or Russia gaining advantage. Palmerston proposed that an international conference settle the question and agreed that it should be held in Vienna. He believed that the Great Powers should insist on Mehemet Ali giving up Syria in return for Turkish confirmation of his position in Egypt, now to be made hereditary. Palmerston was anxious not to break with France, and units of the British and French navies were sent to the Dardanelles. This could be interpreted both as a warning to Russia as well as a demonstration of the value of sea power in protecting Constantinople from any attack by Mehemet Ali. The Russian response was cautious and the Czar seemed ready to accept the British line. If matters had ended there, things would have been simple. France could have backed down with little loss of face and British influences in Turkey would have increased without damaging relations with Russia. Unfortunately, the Sultan's army was defeated by Egyptian forces at the Battle of Nezib on 24 June 1839. The Russians were now more

likely to intervene and the French less likely to abandon a
protégé who was doing so well.

The successful resolution of the crisis demonstrates a
number of things about British foreign policy. Despite a
general commitment to non-intervention there were circumstances in which Britain was prepared to use force.
Other states could not dismiss British warnings as mere
bluff. It also demonstrates that Palmerston wished to act
in concert with other states. His policy in 1839 and 1840
– support for legitimate authority, armed intervention,
collaboration with Metternich and suggesting a congress
– seems to represent a return to the days of Castlereagh.
Yet this was not the intention. France may have been
discomfited by the outcome of the crisis but this was
really its own fault. At first the French indicated that
they would not object to the expulsion of Mehemet Ali
from Syria so long as he could keep Egypt – exactly what
Britain had proposed. When Adolphe Thiers returned to
power in March 1840, however, the French line hardened.
Palmerston had to decide whether or not to press the other
Great Powers to make some concession to Mehemet Ali –
perhaps allowing him to retain part of Syria – in order
to appease French national pride. Thiers thought he was
in a good position to force concessions. He calculated
that Britain's suspicion of Russia would compel Britain
to collaborate with France. But the collaboration would
now be on French terms. If Britain were to follow France
in support of Mehemet Ali, Palmerston would lose all
credibility with the Northern Courts; the solidarity of the
victors of 1815 would be broken; France would control the
diplomacy of Europe and the work of frontier revision
could begin in earnest. If Palmerston attempted to thwart
Thiers by stengthening links with the Northern Courts,
he would encounter powerful opposition at home, even
in Melbourne's Cabinet. Men such as Ellice and Holland
argued that it was essential to make concessions to France
because any short-term British success in the matter of
Mehemet Ali would only humiliate Louis Phillipe and
precipitate a revolution in France which would give power
to men who would make Thiers seem a moderate.[9] Thus,

Thiers believed that he possessed all of the attributes of a successful blackmailer.

The French position was weaker than it appeared and there were powerful arguments against making concessions to Thiers. Britain itself might have considered additional concessions to Mehemet Ali, but these would have been unacceptable to the other Powers – notably Russia. Had Palmerston given in to Thiers, unilateral Russian intervention would have been certain. This was Palmerston's biggest fear. His policy was primarily anti-Russian, although not overtly anti-Russian; it involved Canning's old strategy of collaborating with Russia in order to contain it. That collaboration had to be maintained at all costs, and this ruled out concessions to Thiers. British policy in 1840 was only coincidentally anti-French; from Christmas 1839 till the summer of 1840 Palmerston allowed matters to drift, hoping that the French might see sense and agree with the other Great Powers to impose a solution on Mehemet Ali. By June 1840, however, he decided that enough time had been wasted. The longer the delay in arranging an international agreement, the greater the chance of Russia acting on its own. If France would not join in, the other Great Powers would have to settle the Eastern Crisis in their own way. Britain, Russia, Austria and Prussia signed the Treaty of London on 15 July 1840; the treaty contained a provision for an ultimatum to be sent to Mehemet Ali.[10] France had to accept what had been decided or go to war. In the last resort the country could not face the prospect of fighting the other four Great Powers. The eventual expulsion of the Egyptians from Syria was achieved partly by a local uprising and partly by the actual involvement of British troops – on a modest scale – acting with an Austrian unit. Palmerston may not have intended to humiliate France, but Francophobia was never far from the surface in Britain and the Foreign Secretary was ready to profit from the way he had outmanoeuvred Thiers. Thiers was again dismissed by Louis Phillipe and again France backed down. This retreat did not bring about the immediate revolution which some of Palmerston's critics had predicted, although the Orleanist dynasty may have been damaged by the events of 1840. It acquired a reputation for weakness which was to dog it for the remainder of its existence. Yet Britain can hardly be blamed for this. What mattered most was that, although not solved, the Eastern Crisis would not now erupt again for a few years. French revisionist plans had been thwarted and Russian dangers successfully contained.

V

Palmerston's handling of Russia was even more intelligent than his dealings with France. Despite its apparent strength, Russia was financially weak and unilateral action would have been expensive. Palmerston could portray Russian collaboration with Britain as a return to the principles of 1814. In Russian eyes, the attraction of the Treaty of London was that it appeared to destroy the Anglo-French entente. In any case, the Treaty of Unkiar Skelessi was due to expire in 1841 and the Russians knew that the situation was now less favourable than in 1833. In 1840 France appeared to be humiliated, whilst Russia emerged with increased dignity if not real power. Despite the Russophobia in Britain, some basis for détente could still be found over the Eastern Question. The Russians would keep out of the Mediterranean if Britain would keep out of the Black Sea. A compromise of closing the Straits to foreign warships in time of peace provided the basis for a significant improvement in Anglo-Russian relations. The Straits Convention of 1841 appeared to establish a new era of harmony.

The Belgian crisis had been exclusively European and the troubles in Spain and Portugal largely European, though with some reverberations in South America. The Eastern Crisis involved European and non-European considerations in about equal proportions. In European affairs, despite the increased importance of public opinion and the need to give at least rhetorical support to the more respectable progressive movements, the pattern of interstate relations had changed little since the eighteenth century. The concept of the Balance of Power, though maddeningly vague, seemed to produce satisfactory results. Diplomacy was still conducted by men who had much in common. But the world was shrinking in the 1830s and Europeans, particularly the British were having more to do with non-Europeans. Frequently they came into collision with political entities based on value systems alien to their own. It was really policy towards the non-European world which underwent the greatest change in the 1830s.

At times the United States came close to rivalling France and Russia as an object of British suspicion. Although the United States was peopled largely by European stock, its political morals were not based on European values as understood by aristocratic diplomatists. There were hopes that a reforming government in Britain, containing men who revered the memory of Charles James Fox, would have narrowed the gap between the two countries. But if Britain was moving to the Left, so too was the United States. In 1829 the election of President Andrew Jackson, victor of the Battle of New Orleans, was a pointer to the future. At Jackson's Inauguration Ball, his supporters swarmed through the White House chewing tobacco and swigging whisky straight from the bottle. By the mid 1830s many American states had adopted universal male suffrage, whilst the bulk of the British political establishment thought that the reforms of 1832 had gone far enough. Despite some sense of a common heritage, popular sentiment in the United States was generally anti-British, a tendency likely to be increased by the growing number of settlers from Ireland, few of whom had reason to love England.

Britain and the United States were at odds over many issues. There were uncertainties about the exact line of the frontier with Canada which gave rise to unfortunate incidents. There was the emotive issue of slavery, still flourishing in the Southern States, but which Britain was now pledged to suppress throughout the world. There was American resentment at the British claim to a 'Right of Search' over shipping flying the American flag – tactlessly described by Palmerston as 'a piece of bunting'. There were individual *causes célèbres* such as the McLeod case. There was British anger at alleged American assistance to the Canadian rebels in 1837. The annexation of Canada was supposed to be a long-term American objective. Many, who on other grounds might have wanted Britain to withdraw from Canada, concluded that the American threat required Britain to stay. There were worries about American designs on Mexican territory, especially after the Texan revolt of 1835. The Monroe Doctrine annoyed some people, whilst others were still offended by the very existence of the United States. Sixty years after the event, British diplomats were still forbidden to attend any function celebrating American independence.

But unlike the triumph over France, matters did not come to a head with the United States. There might be protests and warnings but it is unlikely that Palmerston or his successors seriously contemplated war with the United States. This was partly because Canada was a hostage in American hands, partly because such a war would be difficult to win and would provide an opportunity for Britain's rivals elsewhere in the world and partly because, despite appearances to the contrary, there were good reasons not to quarrel. As a country, the United States was admired by many Radicals and there were still personal ties between individuals in Britain and their relations who had settled in America. Economic considerations relating to the cotton trade, and to British investment in North America, underlined the desirability of peace. Even the Monroe Doctrine was not an unmitigated evil and had the admirable effect of dissuading France from territorial ambitions in the Americas.

British foreign policy in the 1830s was characterized by tough talking, clever diplomacy and an ability to obtain a satisfactory result without recourse to more than a minimum of force. Much of this success was due to economic might and the long arm of the Royal Navy. Objectives were often secured by the despatch of a fleet, even if no landing was effected or a gun fired. Nevertheless, the 1830s were not a time of uninterrupted peace. The British Empire faced several major problems, including the abolition of slavery, the Great Trek and the Canadian rebellions. The Empire was expanding through a series of colonial wars

in India and elsewhere, but the most notorious war of the
period was the Opium War with China which broke out in
November 1839.

Whatever the brilliance of Palmerston's diplomacy in
some areas, the Opium War seems to reveal a less attractive
side. Britain went to war because the Chinese authorities
confiscated quantities of opium belonging to British merchants and imprisoned British subjects involved in the
contraband trade. The Chinese government had decided
that the consumption of opium was dangerous to the physical and moral welfare of its subjects. In the course of the
fighting, a number of Chinese war junks were sunk and British forces captured the city of Canton. Palmerston actually
repudiated a treaty negotiated by the British representative,
Charles Elliott, because the terms were too favourable to the
Chinese. Hostilities recommenced but eventually, under the
Treaty of Nanking, the Chinese agreed to cede Hong Kong,
compensate the British merchants, allow greater freedom to
British traders and pay an indemnity of $21 million.

Here, surely, is gun-boat diplomacy at its worst. Palmerston despatched a naval force to China as soon as he
heard of the actions of the authorities, before making any
attempt to resolve matters peacefully. Palmerston's critics
accused him of using the might of Britain to encourage
an evil trade and to spread the addiction of opium. The
Chinese would forget their former glories and become so
demoralized that they would be easy pickings for future
conquest. The British demand for exemption from Chinese
justice was in itself a violation of Chinese sovereignty.[11] To
moralists, convinced that European civilization was superior
to Oriental civilization, however sophisticated, and that
Christians should always behave better than non-Christians,
the Opium War was unforgivable because it put both
propositions in doubt.

Despite the denunciations of Tory paternalists, the reservations of some Radicals and the general condemnation
of posterity, the Opium War and the Eastern Crisis made
Palmerston popular with a broad section of the public for
the first time in his life. The last two years of the Whig
government witnessed an explosion of national truculence,

coupled with an implicit avowal that national self-interest was the only thing that mattered in foreign policy. The changed tone is manifest in articles in *The Globe*, written by Palmerston and extravagantly praising his own policies. They indicate a readiness to play to the gallery in a way quite different from his earlier style. The new mood was reflected in Palmerston's speeches during the 1841 election. He addressed crowds out of doors about the iniquities of France, ignoring the old convention that Foreign Ministers should always be circumspect about what they had said in public about other governments.

VI

In 1841, however, foreign policy success did not impress the electorate sufficiently. The Whigs were defeated and Peel formed a government with Aberdeen as Foreign Secretary. Aberdeen had been a none too successful Foreign Secretary under Wellington, but his record in the 1840s can be more readily defended. Aberdeen was naturally more conciliatory than Palmerston. His outlook was cosmopolitan and he was always eager to find a compromise solution to disputes. He had much in common with François Guizot, Chief Minister in France throughout the period of Peel's government, and certainly far easier to deal with than Thiers had been. In many ways Aberdeen was fortunate. He inherited a position in which Britain's prestige was higher than at any time since 1815. His adversaries, notably Palmerston, implied that he lacked the guile necessary in a successful Foreign Secretary. He was perhaps too transparent in his intentions and rarely engaged in tactics of bluff – unavoidable in international relations in some shape or another. Aberdeen thought that Palmerston's approach was too provocative and bound to involve Britain in major war. Palmerston argued that firmness protected the peace better than Aberdeen's apparent weakness.

By far the most successful feature of Aberdeen's policy was the resolution of disputes with the United States. In 1840 there was still a possibility that Britain and the United

States would one day find themselves at war. By 1846 this possibility had diminished markedly. In this sense the significance of Aberdeen's period at the Foreign Office was far greater than any of his contemporaries – even Palmerston's. It may not be too much to say that, by cementing relations with the United States, Aberdeen was the ultimate author of the survival of Britain in the world wars of the twentieth century. The most important milestone in the improvement of relations with the United States was the Ashburton Treaty of 1842 which settled the line of the disputed frontier. The Americans received more than half of the area formerly claimed by both sides – though less than an abortive arbitration award had allocated to them in 1831. Now Ashburton gave up the Right of Search in exchange for an American promise to co-operate with Britain in the suppression of the slave trade. Although the Ashburton Treaty removed the chief cause of friction, it did not resolve all ambiguities; there remained the problem of Oregon territory. Since 1827 this territory had been under the joint occupation of Britain and the United States, but there were more American than British settlers in Oregon. In the election of 1844, Democratic candidates coined the slogan 'Fifty-four Forty or Fight' indicating that the whole of the Oregon territory should be incorporated into the United States. Westwards from the Great Lakes, the frontier ran along the forty-ninth parallel. The American demand would mean a sharp turn to the North in the Rocky Mountains. President Polk repudiated the 1827 arrangements and claimed the entire territory. Despite his inflammatory speeches, Polk was ready for a compromise which extended the forty-ninth parallel frontier to the Pacific Ocean. Aberdeen's critics alleged that, by giving too much away under the Ashburton Treaty, Britain had only encouraged the Americans to ask for more on the Oregon question. They maintained that the proper solution was for the frontier lines to dip to the South rather than going straight across. On the other hand, Aberdeen could reply that the Ashburton Treaty had established the impression that Britain was a reasonable country to deal with and had finally abandoned its long-standing animus against its former colonies. Thus the ground was prepared for a sensible compromise over Oregon. Without the Ashburton Treaty war would have been much more likely.

If Aberdeen's American policy was his most important contribution to international relations, his dealings with France and Russia attracted more attention from contemporaries. Between 1830 and 1841 British foreign policy had passed through distinct 'French' and 'Russian' phases. Aberdeen was attempting something more difficult. He wanted to be on good terms with France and Russia at the same time. He hoped to build on the improvement in Anglo-Russian relations which resulted from Palmerston's handling of the Eastern Crisis in 1840. The Tories stood a better chance than the Whigs of maintaining the improvement. In 1841 it looked as if France was moving to the Right and accepting a fairly low profile in foreign affairs. With Guizot in charge and Aberdeen acting as honest broker, Orleanist France could be made 'respectable'. After coming face to face with the prospect of war in 1840, the Great Powers had received a salutary warning. Now prospects for a lasting peace looked encouraging.

In the 1830s the Russians had felt that Palmerston's entente with France was directed against them; they had no such fears regarding Aberdeen, who stressed that Britain and Russia had a common interest in limiting French naval power in the Mediterranean. Yet despite the friendship with Russia, relations between England and France were sufficiently close for Aberdeen and Guizot to speak again of an *entente cordiale*. The understanding between Aberdeen and Guizot bore fruit in informal agreements over the vexed question of finding husbands for the young Queen of Spain and her sister. In effect, Aberdeen was prepared to acknowledge a preponderance of French influence in Spain in return for French acceptance of British supremacy in Portugal. In 1845 Aberdeen agreed that the Queen's sister should marry a son of Louis Phillipe – but only after the Queen herself had married and produced an heir.

Yet Aberdeen's policy was based on insecure foundations. Improved relations with Russia did not extend to differences over Central Asia. The appearance of a British envoy in the Khanate of Khiva was regarded with suspicion in St Petersburg. Even the British disaster in Afghanistan did not bring the Russians the benefit they anticipated. British influence in Persia continued to increase, whilst in 1842 a British expedition arrived in Kabul to avenge the massacre of the previous year. Relations between Britain and Russia depended as much upon the Governor General of India as upon the Foreign Secretary. The Tory Governor, General Lord Ellenborough, was very anti-Russian and his policy of territorial expansion in India seemed to make a collision with Russia inevitable in the long run.

Aberdeen's policy towards France offended traditional prejudices on both sides of the Channel and was opposed in Cabinet. Aberdeen hoped to induce France to accept the fundamentals of the existing European order by treating the country with respect, perhaps making some concessions in unimportant matters. Like Palmerston's Whig critics in 1840, he was terrified of what might happen if the Oreleanist dynasty should fall. Aberdeen would take Guizot into his confidence, show him how British decisions were arrived at and make him understand the suspicion of Britain was no longer justified. If disputes arose, there was no reason why they should not be settled sensibly.

Yet was there really an underlying convergence of British and French interests? There were disagreements about the slave trade, about a proposed commercial treaty between France and Belgium, about Tahiti, and especially about the treatment of the British consul, Pritchard, following the French annexation of the Friendly Islands. Peel described the French behaviour as 'a gross insult' to Britain. France, which had been virtually eliminated as a colonial power in 1814, was creating a new Empire in North Africa. A return to the old colonial rivalries of the eighteenth century seemed likely. Yet in the 1840s neither Britain nor France really wished to advance far into Africa, although considerations of rivalry and prestige might have driven them on. The co-operation between Aberdeen and Guizot helped to postpone the partition of Africa for forty years.

The fundamental question about Aberdeen's policy was whether or not he was right to trust France. Was Guizot

really so Anglophile as he pretended? On occasion he
deliberately misled Aberdeen. Peel took a more sceptical
attitude. He believed that Guizot's first priority was to stay
in power; he would turn against England without hesitation
if this suited him. The French desire for 'respectability'
might be taken too far for comfort. The 'Citizen King'
wanted to be accepted as a legitimate monarch by the other
rulers of Europe. Aberdeen's idea was that he could win
French gratitude by sponsoring Louis Phillipe as a proper
king. But Orleanist France could do without sponsors and
could prove its respectability by a direct reconciliation with
the Northern Courts. Louis Phillipe was ready to crack
down on Radicals inside France and to return refugees who
had fled to Paris to escape the attentions of the Austrian
police. Since 1830, the various attempts to reassert French
power had all come to grief because the Northern Powers
regarded Orleanist France as too revolutionary to be associated with. Thus France faced the disagreeable alternative
of playing second fiddle to Britain or accepting diplomatic
isolation. But if France became a Northern Power itself
this would change. Guizot could just about pass muster
as a minister in an absolutist court. A France aligned
with Metternich might have to forget its old ambitions in
Germany but would be free to direct its energies against
Britain. Polignac and Charles X had tried this 'conservative'
way of escaping from the constraints of 1815, but had been
foiled by the 1830 Revolution. In 1845, however, there was
no reason to expect history to repeat itself.

Things might have been different if Aberdeen had remained at the Foreign Office. Guizot would have had less
reason to go all out to cultivate Austria. Yet the chances
are that French policy would have changed regardless of
events in Britain, thus exposing Aberdeen's policy as resting
on false premisses. Nevertheless, Palmerston's return to the
Foreign Office in June 1846 was unwelcome in Paris. He
was identified with the humiliation of France in 1840 and
was considered to be likely to take a tougher line than
Aberdeen on every issue. Yet there were compensations.
Rightly or wrongly, Palmerston was believed to be the
friend of revolutionaries in Europe. His return, however,

would cause great consternation in Vienna and increase the appeal of any overtures from Guizot.

VII

In 1846 and 1847 the usual Palmerston successes are missing. French fears about him were partially justified. Unlike Aberdeen, Palmerston would not accept French preponderance in Spain and began to work against Guizot by presenting himself as the champion of Spanish independence. If Palmerston succeeded, France would suffer another humiliation comparable to that of 1840. Not surprisingly, Guizot thought he was free to go back on his understanding with Aberdeen. He arranged the marriage of the Queen of Spain to a notoriously impotent husband. The Queen's sister was then married to a son of Louis Phillipe. There was thus every likelihood that a descendant of the King of the French would be the ruler of Spain. The two thrones could be united; an objective which had eluded the Sun King might be realized by 'Monsieur Poire'.

Palmerston tried to mobilize the Great Powers to thwart the French in Spain by claiming that Guizot's actions threatened the principle of the permanent separation of France and Spain enshrined in the Treaty of Utrecht. Metternich was unmoved by Palmerston's arguments. With Austria's approval, Guizot had achieved a notable victory and skilfully turned the tables on Britain. Metternich could view the situation with satisfaction. For so long denounced and reviled by liberals and radicals, he now enjoyed more influence than ever. The rupture between Britain and France was a disaster for the liberal cause elsewhere in Europe. Acting together, London and Paris could provide a minimum of protection for the opponents of Absolutism. Divided they could do nothing. In the autumn of 1846 Metternich sent Austrian troops to occupy the tiny republic of Cracow – the last remnant of an independent Poland – claiming that it was the source of nationalist agitation. The Austrian move was readily accepted in Berlin and St Petersburg. France and Britain issued feeble protests for the sake of form only; both Palmerston and Guizot were ready to sacrifice

Cracow without a second thought to gain a little favour with Metternich, now the undisputed arbiter of Europe.

Yet Metternich was not entirely convinced of Guizot's good faith. Despite historic links, Spain was a long way from Austria. Things were different where territory directly adjacent to Austria was concerned. Guizot and Metternich expressed sympathy for the grievances of the Catholic canons, or *Sonderbund*, in Switzerland. Yet mutual suspicions precluded any armed intervention and allowed the Protestant cantons, favoured by Palmerston, to achieve victory after a brief civil war. A similar but more complicated situation was found in Italy where Metternich was prepared to resort to traditional methods to uphold the status quo. This created problems for Guizot. If his chief object was to capitulate on his triumph in Spain and humiliate Palmerston even further, he would go along with Metternich. Yet French public opinion was not keen on the cultivation of Austria as an ally if this involved a crack-down on political refugees and refusal of demands for an extension of the franchise. At a time of economic difficulty, further support for Metternich seemed likely to produce trouble on the streets of Paris. Most fundamental of all, Guizot faced the inadequacy of the 'conservative' stratagem for escape from the restraints of the 1815 settlements which had given Austria a preponderant role in Italy. A desire to renew French influence in Italy came a close second to the wish for a fairer frontier on the North-East. For many Frenchmen, Italy was more important than ambitions to challenge British naval and colonial supremacy. Thus, if the Austrian position in Italy was threatened, France had a golden opportunity to reassert its influence by supporting Austria's opponents. This meant a radical, not a conservative, policy. Guizot's strategy failed because of all the Great Powers, Austria stood to lose most by the destruction of the Vienna settlement. What was Austria's greatest fear was France's greatest ambition – hardly the basis for co-operation. Guizot could support neither Britain nor Austria. All he could do was to initiate a similar but rival policy to that of Palmerston: talking to different rulers, different opponents and suggesting different reforms.

Metternich may have been gratified by the turn of events but the fact that Britain, France and Austria had now arrived at a three-way split was dangerous. There was nothing like disunity amongst the Great Powers to encourage revolutionaries. The first Revolution in the Year of Revolution came in January 1848 with an uprising in Sicily, and the more important French Revolution a month later was partly inspired by developments in Italy.

If Aberdeen had stayed at the Foreign Office, Britain and France might have acted together to promote moderate reform in Italy and thus head off the danger of revolution. Of course, the 1848 Revolution had causes far beyond the realm of diplomatic history, but diplomatic factors were present. Between 1846 and 1848, relations between the Great Powers departed from the well-trodden paths they had followed since 1815 and experienced a period of near anarchy. Aberdeen was right in thinking that Britain and France should stick together and solve their differences sensibly. Differences over the affairs of Spain should not have led to such ill feeling between the two nations. It is hard to decide whether Guizot or Palmerston were more blameworthy. Both behaved foolishly. Guizot paid a heavy price; Palmerston went unpunished – but in so far as he contributed to the diplomatic anarchy of 1846–8, his policy was a factor leading to revolution.

Notes: Chapter 5

1 C. Holbraad, *The Concert of Europe: A Study in German and British International Theory*, London, Longman, 1970, pp. 121–7.
2 Holbraad, op. cit., pp. 131–4.
3 Holbraad, op. cit., p. 139.
4 J. Ridley, *Lord Palmerston*, London, Constable, 1970, p. 103.
5 M. E. Chamberlain, *British Foreign Policy in the Age of Palmerston*, London, Macmillan, 1980, p. 35.
6 *Hansard*, 9 July 1833, Vol. 19, p. 442.
7 Ridley, op. cit., p. 160.
8 Ridley, op. cit., p. 161.
9 Chamberlain, op. cit., p. 43; pp. 115–16.
10 *Cambridge History of British Foreign Policy*, Vol. 2, p. 117.
11 W. E. Gladstone, in *Hansard*, 7 April 1840, Vol. 53, p. 811; p. 816.

6

Playing to the Gallery, 1848–1856

In the spring of 1848 Europe seemed to be undergoing an astonishing transformation. Of the five Great Powers, only Britain and Russia were unaffected by revolution. The other three experienced domestic discord and violence to such an extent that for a while their coherence as political entities was questionable. The collapse of authority in Paris, Berlin and Vienna created a power vacuum in which almost anything seemed possible – a united Italy, a united Germany, a revived Poland, an independent Bohemia, a Europe of constitutional governments, even a Europe of socialist republics. How should Britain respond to the most profound crisis that Europe had experienced since 1815? Perhaps there was little that Britain could or should do. Palmerston informed the Queen that his position towards events on the Continent was 'one rather of observation than of action'.

But this did not mean that Britain was indifferent to events in Europe. If Britain was to influence Continental affairs, the obvious course was to ally with another Great Power. In an important speech to Parliament on 1 March 1848, however, Palmerston came down against any alliance of this kind; Britain was strong enough to 'steer her own course'. Binding alliances were undesirable because Britain had no eternal allies and no perpetual enemies. It could

stand as the natural champion of justice and right when
these principles did not conflict with its own particular
interests.[1] As a general statement of intent, Palmerston's
speech was admirable. In any case, France, Austria and
Prussia were all too distracted to be worth considering
as allies. This left Russia, whose system of government
was unpopular with public opinion and whose ambitions
were regarded with widespread suspicion. Yet the speech
did not indicate what was meant by justice and right or,
indeed, how they should be championed. It also left open
the intriguing question of where justice and right ended and
national interest began. Palmerston did not tell his audience
how he intended to apply his general principles to specific
issues. He shed no light on some fundamental questions: did
Britain wish to maintain the existing territorial boundaries
of Europe, did it want to alter some boundaries and retain
the rest, or was a root and branch reconstruction required,
based on principles quite different from those which had
informed the peace makers in 1815?

Elsewhere, these questions would have been discussed
at a high level of academic refinement. In Britain, however, an aversion to theoretical discussion of foreign policy
was apparent. *The Edinburgh Review* produced articles
bemoaning this failure, but their content was historical
rather than analytical and lacked clear conclusions. Palmerston was not especially forthcoming and the historian
can only read between the lines of British foreign policy as
it emerged over the next eighteen months. British foreign
policy was essentially pragmatic and responded to issues
as they arose. Not surprisingly, therefore, of the three
options available, the second most accurately describes
Palmerston's foreign policy. There is much to be said for
pragmatism. More theoretical policies can lose contact with
the real world, but pragmatism too can have its dangers.
Those who were drawn either to the first or to the third
option believed that British policy was intellectually confused. They might discern in its inevitable inconsistencies
and illogicalities a peculiarly British tendency to hypocrisy
and double standards. If by his use of the term 'justice
and right' Palmerston meant liberal principles and a move

towards national unity (and this is debatable), it appeared
that he was prepared to apply these principles to France
and to Italy but to deny them to Germany and to Eastern
Europe. How could such a policy make sense?

One of Palmerston's most distinctive policies stemmed
from his refusal to take fright at events in France. French
foreign policy had experienced some strange vicissitudes
since 1815. Louis XVIII had not been a bad friend to
Britain, but Charles X and the Ultras had been attracted
by the *Alliance Russe*. This was also the preferred policy of
the extreme Republicans. For all its twists and turns, the
essence of Orleanist foreign policy had been the *Alliance
Anglaise*. In February 1848 Louis Blanc favoured a return
to a pro-Russian policy, but Palmerston went out of his
way to conciliate the new Republic and waited for more
moderate opinions to prevail. By the summer he could
congratulate himself that the Republic of Cavaignac was
as pro-British – perhaps more so – than Louis Phillipe and
Guizot had been. 1848 did not produce a European war
because Republican France did not pursue an expansionist
policy. It was the moderation of France that *The Edinburgh
Review* was applauding when it declared:

> At the present crisis, general war has hitherto been happily
> averted and this throughout a succession of chances unusu-
> ally critical and perilous. Sixty years ago Europe would have
> been infallibly plunged into flames from the Arctic Ocean
> to the Mediterranean, under one tenth of the temptations
> which sovereigns and peoples have now resisted.[2]

Friendship with the Republican government in France was
intended to turn it towards moderate paths. Palmerston
indicated that if the French people wanted a democratic
government, Britain would not stand in their way – provided
that this government pursued a sensible foreign policy.
Despite the traditional emnity and recurring crises, Britain
had found herself acting in concert with France with increasing frequency. Palmerston preferred not to make too much
of this but, for all his bouts of Francophobia, he did much
to promote the French cause. Once the Belgian question
was settled, the issues dividing Britain and France did not

involve vital national interests. British opinion might be
hostile to France, almost by force of habit, but a substantial
part of it wanted to help the oppressed peoples of the
Austrian and Russian Empires. It was obvious that more
could be achieved if London and Paris acted together rather
than against each other. Even the election of a Bonaparte as
President of the Second Republic in December 1848 seemed
unlikely to imperil continuing collaboration.

Dealings with France were relatively easy because it
was already a homogeneous nation state. It was harder to
decide what to do further East – Italy, Germany and
beyond – where the national principle did not apply.
The application of 'justice and right' would involve major
territorial changes. The course eventually followed is open
to criticism, both from the conservative and radical stand-
points. In Italy, Palmerston favoured a solution which was
distinctly 'progressive'. He supported the enlargement of
Piedmont, the most advanced part of Italy not under foreign
occupation. Palmerston was not convinced of the justice
of the Italian nationalist cause but an enlarged Piedmont
accorded with British interests. France had a traditional
interest in Italy which he did not care to see reasserted.
Yet in view of the need to conciliate Republican France,
he could hardly give unequivocal backing to reactionary
and repressive Austria. An enlarged Piedmont offered a
prospect of a Belgium-style solution to Northern Italy.
The idea of 'buffer states' was gaining ground; such states,
with a prosperous and contented population and backed
by international guarantees of neutrality, would separate
quarrelsome Great Powers such as France and Austria.
As a guarantor of their neutrality, Britain would influence
their policies and they would provide a valuable market
for British goods. Despite the *Sonderbund* troubles, Switzerland, the original buffer state, had proved a miracle of
stability and good sense. Palmerston's support for Piedmont
reflected a change in British opinion. Ottavio Barié's book
L'Inghilterra e il problema italiano del 1846–8, (Naples,
Edizion Scientifiche Italiane, 1960) stresses that scepticism
about Italian experiments in constitutional monarchy following the Bentinck episode had now disappeared and that

a new confidence in the Italian capacity to create liberal and stable régimes – rather than commercial ambitions – was the real basis of British attitudes.

Unfortunately, there were differences between Switzerland, Belgium and Northern Italy. Switzerland offers formidable physical obstacles against invasion. Belgium is more vulnerable but, in the 1830s, its former owners, the Dutch, only ranked as a second-rate power; Britain had intimidated them without much difficulty. In the 1830s, too, the French had sent an army into Belgium. Although Palmerston had opposed this, it had served his purpose in keeping the Dutch from returning. In 1848 Lamartine and Cavaignac were less resolute towards Italy than Louis Phillipe had been towards Belgium. Above all, Austria still possessed the attributes of a Great Power. After initial reverses, the Austrian armies were able to defeat the Piedmontese at Custozza on 25 July 1848.

Events further south also helped the Austrians. Following a revolution in the Papal States, Pius IX appealed for help from the Catholic powers. He received assistance from Austria and was also aided by French forces despatched by the new President. After an interlude of Anglo-French harmony, it looked as if, revolution or no revolution, the Second Republic was reverting to what amounted to Franco-Austrian collaboration, similar to the last phase of Guizot's policy. Such a policy could only work to Britain's disadvantage. In March 1849 the Piedmontese again declared war on Austria in an attempt to save the revolutionary cause in Italy from extinction. The Austrians repeated their recent victories by defeating the Piedmontese at Novara. Britain continued to demand that the Austrians should withdraw from Northern Italy and that Piedmont should receive more territory. After Custozza there was little chance of the Austrians paying any attention to this.

In diplomacy it is normally wise to be identified with the winning side. In Italy, Britain had backed the loser. Support for Piedmont and the Italian nationalists upset Austria. The new Emperor, Franz Josef, delivered a calculated insult when he excluded London from the list of capitals to receive special envoys announcing his accession. Britain was unable to protect the defeated Italians from Austrian wrath and could draw scant comfort from its handling of the Italian affair. Yet it was not all loss. There might be another time when the Austrians would not be victorious. However unsuccessfully, Britain had backed the side 'of justice and right'. French betrayal of the Italian cause meant that Britain now appeared as the only friend of liberals and nationalists. This might be put to good account in the future, especially if Piedmont were to develop on constitutional and progressive lines.

Really serious problems of interpretation arise when considering British policy north of the Alps. Here, the great question was the unification of Germany. Few historians now support the suggestion, advanced by Alexander Scarff, that Palmerston was implacably opposed to unification. W. E. Mosse insists that British statesmen of all parties desired the emergence of a strong German power capable of checking the ambitions of France and Russia. Mosse declares:

> A strong Germany would be the best safeguard against any repetition of the Napoleonic nightmare. Germany, moreover, having no interest in the Eastern question conflicting with those of England and might prove willing to oppose the encroachments of Russia. The new Germany, therefore, would assist in the defence of Belgium and the Straits. She would also free England from too exclusive a dependence on the French alliance which was popular on neither side of the Channel and ran counter to time honoured historical traditions. Whereas a French entente must always be precarious on account of French restlessness and political instability, the new Germany, especially if grouped around the Prussian monarch, would prove a solid and reliable partner. Such was the political 'Palmerstonian' basis of British policy.[3]

The unification of Germany fulfilled one of the chief criteria of British foreign policy since 1815 – it was arguably in the spirit, if against the letter, of the arrangements made at the end of the Napoleonic wars. The Vienna settlement had reduced the number of German states as compared to the eighteenth century and the German Confederation could be seen as the first step towards unification. In 1815 it had not been possible to complete the process because of the separate interests of Prussia and Austria, but the time had surely come to unite the peoples of the German Confederation into one state. Given the continued dangers of France and Russia, a united Germany would bring the Balance of Power in Europe to a state of virtual perfection.

Whatever it may have become later, in 1848 the impulse behind German unification was rightly seen as essentially liberal and as such was supported by public opinion in England. England and Germany would not only be liberal but teutonic and Protestant as well – natural allies against the alien values represented in Paris, St Petersburg and Rome. The union would be cemented by dynastic ties. Prince Albert was the very model of a German liberal and it was likely that several of the royal children would marry into German princely houses. With its natural ally, the new Germany, Britain could impose peace on East and West alike and decide the affairs of Europe. Whatever Castlereagh's intentions in 1815, the arrangements made for Central Europe had not served British interests. The German Confederation was weak and likely to prove a feeble obstacle to any renewal of French aggression. The main beneficiary of the old arrangement had been Russia. The conservative German order, personified by Metternich, formed a protective shield around Russian territory and had made it impossible to assist the Poles in 1830–31. With Germany liberal and Western orientated, Russia's protective barrier would be removed and the way would be open for a thorough-going revision of affairs in Eastern Europe. Perhaps British policy towards the unification of Germany should have been as straightforwardly progressive as it was towards Italy.

Yet there were other considerations. Russia, like Britain, appeared to favour German unification, and anything Russia wanted was unlikely to be in Britain's true interest. Of course, Russia's basic stance was conservative but might not Germany unite under autocratic rather than liberal leadership? Such a state in alliance with Russia would strengthen Russia's control over Poland, enlarge the protective shield against the West and allow Russia to influence the affairs of Western Europe directly, which was the exact opposite of the solution Britain preferred. Thus, whilst Britain might indeed welcome German unification, she would not welcome any German unification – only one which would be advantageous to itself.

The situation in 1848 raised the fundamental question of whether anything of the European order created in 1815 was to be maintained. Palmerston had no doubt that something should be preserved. The keystone of the old order was Austria. If a fresh start was to be made, Austria would have to be dismembered. Palmerston had no taste for this. Whilst the Austrians had to get out of Italy, elsewhere he wished them 'all the prosperity and success in the world'. If the German-speaking lands of the Austrian Empire were absorbed into a greater German national state, how could the rest of the Empire survive? Indeed, if all the lands included in the German Confederation were welded into a single unitary state, a country of vast extent would be created in the heart of Europe. In terms of the Balance of Power, such a state, whether liberal or otherwise, might prove too large and too powerful for the other countries of Europe to live with in comfort.

A united Germany might be acceptable if it did not include all of the German Confederation. Initially there were grounds for hope. A united Germany would probably be ruled by the liberal-minded professors who dominated the Frankfurt Parliament. Once they had consolidated into a single state all of the territory whose inhabitants regarded themselves as Germans, they would make no demands on areas where the people were not German and did not want to be citizens of a German state. In Italy some thought was given to this question. Mazzini imagined that there was no conflict between nationalism and internationalism, or between nationalism and liberalism. They represented facets of the same thing. Nationalism, representing the freedom of the peoples, was the macrocosm of liberty, whilst liberalism, representing the freedom of individuals, was the microcosm.

The two great German states, Prussia and Austria, had large numbers of non-German subjects. In Austria, the

German element represented only a quarter of the total population. Although Prussia was predominantly German, it had a substantial Polish minority. Would everything be all right, therefore, if a united Germany containing only Germans allowed the Poles of Posen, the Czechs of Bohemia, the Hungarians and Croatians to go their own way? The liberation of the largely Slavonic peoples of Eastern Europe from German rule might be the first step towards the union of all Slav people. *The Edinburgh Review* saw the implications of that:

> A full development of Panslavism would, of course, presume the supremacy of Russia; for since the inhabitants of this empire comprise fifty-three out of the seventy-eight millions numbered by the Slavonic race, it would be impossible to consummate the projected union without both including the population of Russia and acknowledging her natural presidency.[4]

Even if a Panslav union was a remote possibility in 1848, there was danger in a more modest rearrangement which would rectify the worst injustice of the existing system and restore Poland to the map of Europe. Radicals and Catholics might deplore the sufferings of the Poles, but an independent Poland would be the natural ally of France rather than of Britain. The historical and cultural ties between Poland and France were close. When Napoleon had redrawn the map of Europe he had established a Grand Duchy of Warsaw united with the German state of Saxony. The purpose of the Grand Duchy was to counter the influence of Austria and Prussia. Reduced in power and territory they were no longer able to dominate the smaller states of Western Germany which were then grouped together in the French-controlled Confederation of the Rhine. A return to this scenario was scarcely less appealing to Britain than the creation of a Panslav state dominated by Russia.

In the event, the Frankfurt professors did not turn out to be generous to the Slav peoples; territories ruled by German states should continue to be ruled by Germans, even if a majority of the inhabitants were non-German. The

German Liberals had one rule for themselves and another for the Czechs and the Poles. The German Liberals also demanded that the Duchies of Schleswig-Holstein, hitherto ruled by the King of Denmark, should be included in a united Germany. They secured the services of the Prussian army for a war against Denmark to win the duchies for Germany. The German claim on Schleswig-Holstein had more justice than the German position in Posen, but Britain never liked to see a strong power lengthening its North Sea coastline – which would happen if the duchies became part of a united Germany. If the duchies were lost, Denmark might be reduced to a German satellite. In reality the Germans would decided whether to open or close the Baltic to British shipping. During the Napoleonic wars Britain had risked damaging its reputation with other states by resorting to strong-arm tactics to maintain access. At least on the question of the Sound, Britain and Russia were in agreement. Intense and successful Anglo-Russian pressure was applied to the King of Prussia to persuade him to decline to take further orders from the Frankfurt Parliament. Frederick William IV subsequently accepted a peace treaty under which Schleswig-Holstein continued to be linked with Denmark – though the connection was a personal one with the King of Denmark ruling as Grand Duke.

This outcome was satisfactory, but Prussian behaviour was beginning to cause concern. In 1848 and 1849 Prussia showed the first signs of a restlessness which was to transform Europe. The readiness of Frederick William IV to throw in his lot with the German nationalists – if only for a while – was a dangerous portent. It is true that in 1849 the King rejected the Crown of a united Germany, offered to him by the Frankfurt Parliament. Some of the more cautious nationalists were already advocating a *Kleindeutsch* solution to German unification – a 'united' Germany which did not include any Austrian territory. Such a state could only be dominated by Prussia. The King of Prussia was not averse to all ideas on unification; in 1849 he established the Erfurt Union of princes under Prussian leadership. A Germany united under a Conservative Prussia could turn out to be a most uncomfortable and difficult state to deal with. In 1850, Britain was not sorry when pressures from Austria forced Prussia to dissolve the Erfurt Union.

Concern about Russia, however, was much greater. The prime purpose of Austria was to counterbalance Russia. This is why Palmerston wanted the Austrians to suppress the Hungarian revolt swiftly. He regretted that Austria found it necessary to ask the Russians for assistance. There was a danger that the Austrians would feel indebted to Russia for the help they received. Austria still had useful work to do in Europe north of the Alps but its role as a counterweight to French power in Italy was now redundant. Perhaps if revolutionary France had run true to form in 1848 and committed itself to a more expansionist foreign policy, British policy might have been more consistent. A major demonstration of French power in Italy was likely to have cured Palmerston of any enthusiasm for Italian nationalism and persuaded him to support the Austrian cause everywhere. Taking Europe as a whole, Britain's interests were still essentially conservative.

However attractive other arrangements might have appeared at first sight, on further reflection they offered no advantage. As far as Britain was concerned, at least to the north of the Alps, the revolutions of 1848 and their aftermath had raised issues which would have been better left undisturbed. A return to the old arrangements might not be ideal but at least this was preferable to most of the possible scenarios which had emerged briefly in 1848. Although there were a few loose ends to be tied up, the old European order was fast reasserting itself and the revolutionary dreams vanishing. With the unfortunate exception of the Russian involvement in Hungary, all the Great Powers confined themselves to the broad spheres of influence allotted to them in 1815. Despite all the wild schemes, the revolutions made no difference to the boundaries of Europe. They achieved even less than the revolutions of 1830, which at least produced Belgium. If Europe was so perfectly balanced that it always came back to something like the system of 1815, Britain had no cause to worry. Britain could keep to its own sphere of influence – the rest of the world. With Europe in perfect equilibrium, it could get on with its own business. Safe in its peaceful, industrious island, protected by the might of the Royal Navy, Britain could conclude that most of Europe should be left to the other Great Powers. It was precisely for this reason that Britain felt free to flaunt its power in areas where its sea power could be used to the greatest advantage.

II

In the years after 1848 British foreign policy entered a flamboyant period, the era of gunboat diplomacy *par excellence*. In April 1850 Palmerston sent the Mediterranean fleet into Piraeus to seize shipping to satisfy claims for compensation from the Greek government put forward by a Portuguese Jew whose house in Athens had been attacked by an anti-semitic mob in 1847. The victim of the attack, Don Pacifico, claimed to be a British subject and called for British assistance. As in the affair of the Spanish marriages, Palmerston believed that Aberdeen's conciliatory foreign policy had been mistaken. Aberdeen had allowed French influence to grow in Greece and as a result the Greek authorities had ignored the just claims of a British subject for compensation. Only the strongest action on Britain's part could induce other nations to afford it proper respect.

At the same time that British interests were so vigorously upheld, foreign policy appeared to be moving towards greater sympathy for the revolutionary cause in Central Europe. In September 1850, when General Haynau, an Austrian notorious for his savagery in Italy and Hungary, was attacked by a hostile crowd whilst on a visit to London, Palmerston sent an apology couched in such a way as to imply sympathy with the crowd rather than the General. In October 1851 the Hungarian leader, Kossuth, came to England to organize meetings protesting against Austrian and Russian rule in Central Europe. Palmerston actually arranged a meeting with Kossuth. The meeting was cancelled at the insistence of the Prime Minister, but the Foreign Secretary received a delegation of Kossuth's British supporters who presented him with an address describing the Emperor of Austria and the Czar of Russia as 'odious and detestable assassins'.

Inevitably the style and content of this foreign policy provoked controversy. One of its critics was Lord Aberdeen. In the debates on the 'Don Pacifico' incident, Aberdeen quoted Vattel to the effect that a prince should not interfere in the support of his subjects in foreign countries except in cases of grave injustice. Whilst the Greeks had been slow to compensate Don Pacifico, the sum he asked for exceeded the loss suffered, and he had not pursued the matter properly in the Greek courts. By resorting to force, Palmerston had endangered the tranquillity of Europe. Aberdeen was, however, less concerned about the violation of the Greek government's rights than by the lack of prior consultation with the other Great Powers. This was pure Castlereagh, a classic exposition of the view that there were two levels of European states – ordinary countries and Great Powers. Great Powers had more rights than other powers, but the system would only function if these Great Powers presented a common front to the rest of the world.

Aberdeen's theme was taken up by Sir James Graham. Graham argued that the Don Pacifico incident was typical; since his return to the Foreign Office Palmerston had caused appalling damage. His animosity to Guizot had led to the overthrow of the Orleanist dynasty and precipitated revolution throughout Europe. He had stirred up war and revolution in Italy by false allegations that Austria had designs on the independence of Piedmont. At every turn, obligations had been broken and friends betrayed. Other critics took a different tack. Cobden criticized the expense involved and claimed that diplomats often did more to cause disputes between states than to heal them. He deplored the bullying of the weak by the strong. If Britain itself committed injustice, how could it complain about the conduct of others? If disputes arose they should be settled by arbitration, not by force. Palmerston's policy of belligerence was alien to the best in both Tory and Whig traditions.

Palmerston's policy was attacked from various angles. F. J. C. Hearnshaw noted that the memoir- and letter-writers of the time – Guizot, Brougham, Stockmar, Metternich, Cobden, Malmesbury, Greville, Spencer, Walpole, Granville, Aberdeen, Bright, Gladstone and Disraeli – were all alarmed by one or more features of Palmerston's policy.[5] To pacifists he was a firebrand and warmonger; to the Whigs he was a meddler in things best left alone; to devotees of constitutional proprieties he was careless of his responsibilities to his colleagues and to the Crown; to the pundits he was a puzzle; to the Radicals he was a traitor; to foreigners he was living proof of all the charges ever made against the English national character. To some he was positively Satanic:

> Hat der Teufel einen Sohn
> So ist er sicher Palmerston

In his speech of 1 March 1848 Palmerston associated himself with the memory of George Canning, insisting that the first priority of policy must be 'the interests of England'. His *Civis Romanus Sum* speech of 25 June 1850, gave him the popular accolade of 'The Minister of England'. In this speech, his main contribution to the 'Don Pacifico' debates, Palmerston declared that it was his duty to protect fellow subjects living abroad. Like Roman citizens of old, a British subject, wherever he might find himself, should always feel confident that the watchful eye and strong arm of England would protect him against injustice.[6] The imperial theme was significant. Gladstone pointed out that a Roman citizen was a member of a privileged caste, a conquering race. Principles were asserted in his favour which were denied to the rest of mankind. Such, apparently, was to be Britain's relationship with other countries.[7] By definition, an imperial system implies that one power dominates the entire political system it operates within. By the beginning of the 1850s it could be argued that one political system embraced the entire world. In effect, Palmerston was claiming that Britain was not only 'above' the lesser states but above the Great Powers as well.

Although there were some changes, the view that the 1830s saw a revolution in British foreign policy can no longer be sustained. In the light of the extraordinary claims made by Palmerston perhaps the decisive break came at the beginning of the 1850s. Significantly, the 'Don Pacifico' debates resulted in the condemnation of Palmerston's policies by the House of Lords, but approval by the House of Commons, with extravagant praise for the Foreign Secretary from the Radical, J. A. Roebuck. What did the new style amount to? A policy of belligerent national assertiveness combined with calculated insults to Great Powers such as Austria and Russia implies a carelessness for such subtleties as the Balance of Power which had dominated British thinking as recently as 1848. British policy acquired a crude quality quite unlike the complex manoeuvrings of classical diplomacy in which Palmerston had once excelled.

Some of the critics thought that the explanation was to be found in Palmerston's own personality. In the past, senior Whigs such as Grey, Holland, Melbourne and Lansdowne had restrained his excesses Their generation was passing and the new party leader, Lord John Russell, was proving a disappointment; Russell found it hard to keep his Foreign Secretary in order. Palmerston's policy, formulated with virtually no reference to his colleagues, amounted to no more than a personal *folie de grandeur*, reflecting the arrogance, opportunism, impertinence and immorality which characterized the Foreign Secretary's private life. What chance had small nations of fair treatment or friendly sovereigns of protection from insult when British policy was in the hands of a man who treated his staff at the Foreign Office like dirt and who had even made an attempt upon the virtue of one of the Queen's companions?

Yet it is too simplistic to explain changes in foreign policy in purely personal terms. Palmerston was playing to the gallery more raucously than in any of his earlier campaigns to win public support, largely because of growing public interest in foreign policy. In a book devoted to foreign policy, it is easy to give the impression that questions about foreign affairs were always at the centre of political debate. Even during the Revolutionary and Napoleonic wars, many people were more concerned with domestic policies than with alliances and overseas campaigns. After 1815 this indifference increased. Perhaps England was undergoing too much change at home, adjusting to the transition from a rural to an urban and industrialized society, to have much energy left over for attention to foreign affairs. By 1850, however, the worst of the growing pains of industrialization had passed. Britain's immunity to the convulsions of 1848 suggested that the social tensions which had caused so much anxiety in the early 1840s were fading. There was now time to take stock of the world situation. Britain's economic lead over the rest of the world, as well as its general sense of superiority over other nations, reached the maximum about the time of the Great Exhibition of 1851. Perhaps this success entitled it to interfere in the affairs of other states who had shown themselves less competent. Britain was at the centre of international trade as its new factories made it 'the workshop of the world'. What went on elsewhere was of very material interest to people in Britain. In putting forward a foreign policy based on assertion of national interest, coupled with a dash of progressive ideology, Palmerston caught the mood of the time to perfection.

Palmerston's popularity with opinion out of doors served an important purpose. His policies were attacked not only by the Opposition but also by the anti-Palmerston faction amongst the Whigs. They were loathed by much of the political and social establishment. The furore about Palmerston's foreign policy also raised questions of prime constitutional importance. George III had enjoyed independent influence upon the formulation of foreign policy, but this had been lost through a combination of Canning's skill and George IV's indolence. Now, it seemed, a determined attempt was being launched to win it back. The central figure in the campaign was Prince Albert whose views were enthusiastically endorsed by the Queen.

Even if there was no deliberate campaign, circumstances still favoured the Court. The existence of a two-party system provides the most important check on the powers of the Crown, because the monarch has no alternative but to entrust the government to the leader of the largest party and to allow him to run the country in the way he thinks best. In the multi-party system, however, coalition governments have to be formed and the monarch can influence the composition and perhaps the policies of the new administration. The Tories had split in 1846 and Russell's government lacked talent and a clear sense of direction. The Court favourites were the Peelite Tories, now led by Aberdeen. Would the Peelites go into coalition with the Whigs or with the Stanley Tories? Whichever way they jumped they would be able to exact a high price in terms of the policies favoured by Albert. If things went Albert's way, Palmerston was sure to lose the Foreign Office. A strong following out of doors would be a useful weapon against any kind of 'establishment plot'.

Palmerston told his Cabinet colleagues little about his intentions and kept the Queen almost totally in the dark. On 14 August 1850 Prince Albert threatened him with dismissal unless he gave clear answers to inquiries from the Queen about his opinions and intentions on specific foreign policy issues. Having secured royal approval for a particular course of action, he promised not to alter it without further consultation. But Palmerston soon reverted to his old ways. Anger at his duplicity, coupled with fury at the insults offered to Austria and Russia in the Haynau and Kossuth affairs, ensured that his next indiscretion would bring his dismissal. The Court did not have to wait long. Palmerston expressed his warm approval on hearing that Louis Napoleon had overthrown the Second Republic. He did so privately, but his enemies pretend that he had given public blessing to the French *coup d'état* without consulting either the Queen or the Prime Minister. Public or private, Palmerston's response still looks extraordinary; it certainly destroyed the political base he had been so carefully erecting. By welcoming the *coup* he outraged Radical opinion, appalled by the President's betrayal of his trust. For Conservatives with long memories it seemed incredible that any British Foreign Secretary should approve of what was obviously the first step towards the re-establishment of a Napoleonic Empire in France. Palmerston's unseemly haste to ingratiate himself with the new régime in Paris offended that same British national pride which his recent speeches had done so much to promote. Palmerston's enemies had chosen their moment well. He was forced from office and on 19 December 1851 Earl Granville became Foreign Secretary.

The Queen now demanded to be consulted in the formulation of broad principles of foreign policy. Russell was able to deflect this demand but Granville was more willing than Palmerston to listen to royal advice. Broadly speaking, the royal view coincided with Aberdeen's conservative approach of maintaining good relations with all the Great Powers, but with special features. Victoria and Albert had no time for Italian nationalism and applauded Austria's efforts. Whereas Palmerston supported change in Italy and opposed it in Germany, they took the contrary view. Within Germany they showed a marked tenderness towards Prussia. They believed that the best arrangement in Germany would be for a league of Princes led by Prussia along the lines of the Erfurt Union. They regretted the dissolution of this union under Austrian pressure. Palmerston did not; if any power was to dominate Germany, Austria was the safest choice. Victoria and Albert refused to see Prussia as an oppressive state. Prussia was Protestant, dynamic and in some ways not illiberal. Catholic Austria was both more frivolous and more oppressive. Palmerston had got everything the wrong way round. He was in favour of constitutional government in places such as Italy, Spain and Portugal which were unsuited to this according to their history, religion and culture, yet he resisted constitutional government in North Germany where, with Prussian guidance and safeguards, it might have worked more satisfactorily.

III

Palmerston's policies are not, however, totally inexplicable in terms of the international situation. He seemed to be distancing himself from the old European order which had served Britain well in the past and which had been triumphantly restored after the chaos of 1848. But was the restoration real? Perhaps in the process of defeating the forces of revolution, the rulers of Europe had themselves undergone a change. The strongest argument in favour of the status quo had always been that, in the last resort, the Great Powers were conservative and each was reluctant to risk war by pushing its own interests beyond a point where they were certain to collide with the interests of another Great Power. But supposing the Great Powers lost their former caution and restraint – what would Britain do then? By the beginning of the 1850s the Great Powers were no longer satisfied powers; every one of them wanted more influence and, in some cases, more territory than each currently enjoyed. This was not new but they now seemed more determined to achieve their objectives, less willing to compromise. Above all, what they wanted could only be achieved at the expense of another Great Power. War between two or more Great Powers was increasingly likely. At least it was now obvious that the old European order was doomed and that it was pointless for Britain to try to maintain it much longer. In such an uncertain world, extremely nimble diplomatic footwork would be required if the situation were not to be turned to Britain's disadvantage.

This new climate requires an explanation. In part it was a matter of generations. The Napoleonic wars had brought relatively young men to the forefront of public affairs. Men as diverse as Palmerston, Wellington, Aberdeen and Metternich had all held important posts before 1815. Now their ranks were beginning to be thinned, partly by the events of 1848 and partly by death. They were being replaced by younger men without the same personal experience of war and revolution. The caution which had characterized the foreign policies of the Great Powers since 1815 had stemmed from the fear that war would lead to revolution. Yet the events of 1848 had suggested the revolution was something of a paper tiger. It could be defeated with properly disciplined armies; for those with eyes to see, the new railways and telegraphs provided governments with means of crushing local disturbances before they had a chance to spread. Perhaps with the spectre of revolution reduced to proper proportions, the Great Powers of Europe were simply reverting to their old selves. As in the days of Frederick and Catherine, they were now free to be as aggressive and unscrupulous as they pleased – eager to get the better of their rivals and ready to risk war in order to get what they wanted.

Yet between 1850 and 1870 the Great Powers behaved in a way that would have shocked the most cynical of Eighteenth-century rulers. 1848 was important in another way. Its true message was that liberalism and nationalism were distinct entities and that people tended to put their nationalism before their liberalism. Now that this connection was shown to be feeble the rulers of Europe had no reason to be coy about taking up nationalism. If they continued with their old negative approach, sooner or later, they would be overthrown by a better-organized version of an 1848 revolution. But if they stole some of the clothes of their former enemies, they might persuade their peoples to give them more wholehearted support. Nationalism, it seemed, was popular and if a ruler wanted to be popular it made sense for him to be a nationalist. If he gave a lead he might persuade people to forget their liberal demands or at least accept as genuine 'window dressing' constitutions which kept real power in the hands of the old ruling class. Thus in order to survive, a ruler simply had to embark on an aggressive, nationalist foreign policy and look for an opportunity to display his prowess in war.

In the long run these lessons were to be most completely accepted in Prussia. But Prussia provides only the most extreme example of a wider trend. Britain itself was not immune and popular endorsement of Palmerston's conduct over the 'Don Pacifico' incident becomes more explicable when seen in this context. Comparisons with Europe can be taken further. The upsurge of belligerent patriotism which Palmerston personified helped to reduce pressure for an extension of the franchise, to which he was opposed. Britain does not fit the Continental pattern completely. British belligerence was not directed towards places where it was likely to collide directly with the belligerence of other Great Powers. It might make life unpleasant for people of Asia, Africa or even Greece but it was unlikely to lead to European war. The ambitions of the other Great Powers, however, were directed inwards into Europe. The Continent had become too small to contain the pent up aggression within itself. For the time being the most assertive powers appeared to be Russia and France. Even in the relatively quiet times before 1848, Britain had viewed their activities with suspicion. It was preoccupation with France and Russia that was to lead Britain into really major war for the first time since 1815. Reversing the pattern of centuries, Britain allied itself with France and declared war on Russia on 28 March 1854.

There are a number of ways of looking at Britain's involvement in the Crimean War. It may have been a mistake, the result of diplomatic bungling. It would be foolish to accept without question that the war was the consequence of the flamboyant policies pursued by Palmerston between 1849 and 1851. Two years elapsed between his departure from the Foreign Office and the beginning of the Crimean War. Governments and Foreign Secretaries came and went in rapid succession. The Russell government fell in February 1852 and was followed by a minority Tory ministry under Lord Derby with Lord Malmesbury as Foreign Secretary. In December 1852 a new Whig-Peelite Coalition ministry was formed under Aberdeen. Although Palmerston had to be found a place as Home Secretary there was no intention of allowing him to influence foreign policy. The Foreign Office went to Lord John Russell and, in February 1853, to Lord Clarendon.

Granville and Malmesbury turned out to be competent Foreign Secretaries who continued Palmerston's policy of friendship with Louis Napoleon. France was very belligerent in 1852. There was talk of reviving French claims upon Belgium, even of an invasion of England. Malmesbury's long-standing friendship with the Prince President was important in preserving the peace. Aberdeen's record is less satisfactory; much damage was done whilst Lord John Russell was temporarily in charge of the Foreign Office. The government was faced with a dispute between France and Russia about the rival claims of Catholic and Orthodox Christians to control the Holy Places of Palestine. Under pressure from France, the Sultan in Constantinople decided that the Catholics were to have additional rights. The decree coincided with the proclamation of the Second Empire in France; Nicholas I of Russia refused to accept either.

If Aberdeen's foreign policy was more 'pacific' than Palmerston's, it seems extraordinary that Britain became involved in this 'churchwardens quarrel'. One way of considering foreign policy is in terms of crisis management. Periodic crises are unavoidable in international relations, and successful foreign policies take such crises in their stride. War may seem close, it may be threatened, but it is avoided; national interests are protected, prestige enhanced, a slight adjustment is made to the delicate Balance of Power and the air is cleared for a few years until the next crisis erupts. Aberdeen's government provides a classic example of what not to do in an international crisis.

In general, Palmerston had been adept in these matters. He thought it essential for other Great Powers to know where Britain stood and at what point it would consider its interests so seriously endangered that it would definitely fight to protect them. A strong, clear line was fairer to all concerned. A desire to avoid giving offence might result in other powers getting the wrong impression and taking steps in the mistaken belief that Britain would not object – only to discover their error when it was too late to retreat. Palmerston did not mind offending other powers – perhaps he took excessive pleasure in it – but his forthright language probably saved the peace of Europe both in the Belgian and the Mehemet Ali crises.

Aberdeen, Russell and Clarendon did not make themselves clear enough to Russia. Nicholas I convinced himself that Aberdeen would not oppose an extension of Russian power in South Eastern Europe and the Near East and might even participate in a Russian scheme for the partition of the Turkish Empire. The Czar was guilty of wilful self-deception but Britain should have taken more active steps to dispel his illusion. Following the dispute over the Holy Places, Nicholas had advanced his claim to be the

protector of the Orthodox Christians living in the Ottoman
Empire; on 9 February 1853 Russell accepted the Russian
claim. The move was soon regretted. It should have been
obvious that any kind of Russian 'protectorate' would
infringe the sovereignty of the Ottoman Empire. One of
the chief purposes of the Crimean War was to deny what
Russell had already conceded. Nicholas also believed that
Aberdeen's government hated Napoleon III and would
never act in concert with him. Again the Czar deceived
himself, but then Russell had declared that the blame for
the squabbles over the Holy Places lay with France and
that Russia had acted within its rights. Nicholas could
express genuine astonishment when in March 1853 the
British and French fleets sailed towards Turkey to stiffen
the Porte's resolve to reject the Russian demand for a
formal acceptance of the Czar's special position in relation
to the Orthodox Christians. The British, it seemed, had
capriciously changed their minds.

There are other contrasts between Palmerston and Aberdeen and Clarendon. Nineteenth-century Great Powers
did not go to war unless they thought they would win.
Faced with the opposition of all the other Great Powers,
they usually saw the wisdom of retreat. Thus, if France
was the likely disturber of the European peace, it was
prudent to form an alliance with Prussia, Austria and
Russia – as Palmerston had done in 1840. If the danger
came from Russia, the situation required a close union of
Britain, France, Austria and Prussia. If they had been united
it is unlikely that there would be war in 1854. Such a coalition would be hard to construct – it always was. But it was
not impossible; unfortunately it was beyond the skill of
Aberdeen's government.

Russian aggression should have played into Aberdeen's
hands. In June 1853, infuriated at the rejection of his
demands, Nicholas sent armies to occupy the Danubian
Principalities of Moldavia and Wallachia. The Austrians
were worried by the prospect of Russian control of the lower
Danube. Where Vienna led, Berlin would follow. Opposition to Russian occupation of the Principalities should have
provided a solid basis for a four-power coalition. On the

basis of past form, the crisis was now coming to its peak –
after which a compromise would emerge and the danger of
war disappear. This was the moment to call a Congress of
the Great Powers. In the absence of clear leadership, which
Britain might have been expected to provide, no Congress
was called. Instead, different schemes were worked out in
different European capitals.

This gave Russia an opportunity to divide the other
Great Powers. The two major proposals, one produced
in Constantinople (25 July 1853) and the other in Vienna
(28 July) differed markedly. The Vienna scheme, though
requiring a Russian withdrawal from the Principalities,
was 'softer' and would have allowed the Czar his protectorate over the Christians of the Ottoman Empire. This
scheme was welcomed by Nicholas, endorsed by Austria
and Prussia and accepted initially by Britain and France.
Upon reflection, however, they proposed amendments to
meet Turkish objections. Nicholas refused and was supported in his refusal by Prussia and Austria. The British
government's vacillation exposed it to renewed charges
of bad faith; above all, it destroyed prospects of unity
against Russia.

There was one final respect in which Aberdeen and
Clarendon diverged from the usual Palmerston pattern.
Palmerston normally managed to control the powers he
collaborated with; as shown in the Belgium crisis, he knew
how to make such powers accept compromises. In 1853,
however, Britain's eventual allies in war made most of the
running; decisions affecting British policy were taken in
Paris and Constantinople. The Turks were spoiling for a
fight; circumstances were especially favourable for them.
Whatever they did, once hostilities broke out, Britain and
France were sure to come to their aid. In the event, the
Turks declared war on Russia in October 1853 when the
Czar rejected an ultimatum for immediate evacuation of the
Principalities. The French also exploited British weakness.
Napoleon III wanted war and did everything to frustrate
a compromise settlement. It proved easy to drag Britain
along. When Russian forces attacked Turkey proper in
January 1854, Russophobia reached unprecedented heights

in England and the peace-loving Aberdeen found himself propelled into war. Despite all its wealth and power, the incompetence of Prime Minister and Foreign Secretary sadly diminished Britain's influence in the crucial year of 1853. With Palmerston at the Foreign office things might have been different. The Queen, though not exactly an admirer, thought that Palmerston would have prevented war.

Yet was the Crimean War unnecessary? There were some who detected a gigantic Russian plot to take control of most of the Euro-Asian landmass. Was Nicholas on the brink of achieving what Napoleon had failed to do – establishing a land power backed by sufficient resources to make it impervious to the influence of sea power? If so, Britain and France had cause for alarm. But it is hard to see the Russia of the mid-nineteenth century presenting any such threat. Of course, like the other Great Powers – and like Britain in the colonial world – Russia was out for what it could get. Its policy in the early 1850s was not inherently more aggressive than in the past. The Czar merely tried to expand his influence when an opportunity was provided for him by Louis Napoleon's disruptive intervention into the complex 'Holy Places' issue.

British foreign policy may have been totally wrongheaded. What would have happened if Aberdeen had opted for a pro-Russian policy? It is unlikely that there would have been war; France would not have taken Russia on without British backing. Perhaps Britain should have taken Russian proposals for a division of the Ottoman Empire more seriously. Generations of British statesmen were to insist that the Turks were an essential barrier to Russian expansion and that their Empire could in some way be 'revived'. Yet was such a revival possible? Turkish rule was becoming more offensive and the longer it lasted the more loudly its victims would call upon Russia for help. If Nicholas's proposals had been implemented, Russian influence and territory would have been increased, but some of the territory released from Turkish tyranny might have been turned into independent states not totally dominated by Russia. At least a question which was to fester for

another half century would have been settled once and
for all. A close understanding between Britain and Russia
would have made a difference to Europe in the 1860s. Such
a policy would have been risky, but hardly more so than the
Crimean War itself. A pro-Russian policy, however, did not
appeal to Palmerston. In part, Palmerston's Russophobia
sprang from his need for a following 'out of doors' and in
Radical circles in particular. Throughout the nineteenth
century, supporters of a 'progressive' foreign policy faced a
difficulty about Russia. On the one hand, sympathy for the
Christian victims of Turkish oppression made an extension
of Russian power in the Balkans seem desirable, or at any
rate preferable to the existing situation. On the other hand,
distaste for Russian methods in Poland, the state of society
in Russia itself and the general identification of Russia with
reactionary forces made the Czar seem detestable. Although
the balance between the two positions was to change later,
in the 1850s more was known about the bad 'Polish' side
of Russia than the good 'Balkan' side. Antipathy to Russia
led many Radicals to uphold the Turkish position in the
Balkans and to give their wholehearted support to the war.
This suited Palmerston. A robust assertion of 'the interests
of England' – a tune he could play very well – could be
combined with an ideologically attractive crusade against
a 'Czarist tyranny'. Careful exploitation of this position
might appeal to a wide range of political opinions. After
the set back of 1851, Palmerston's prospects were about to
improve again.

There may be links between Palmerston's behaviour in
December 1851 and his enthusiasm for war in 1854. Ever
since 1848 he had been convinced that Britain needed
good relations with whoever ruled France – hence his
approval of Louis Napoleon's *coup d'état*. Whatever they
may have thought about the details of his conduct, most
politicians agreed with his general analysis. When the
Derby ministry was formed in 1852, Wellington advised
the incoming Foreign Secretary: 'Mind you keep well
with France', and that at a time when the nephew of the
Duke's great adversary was proclaiming his intention of
restoring France to the pre-eminence it had enjoyed under

the First Empire. For fifty years the name Napoleon had conjured up visions of bloodshed and French conquest; was the whole business to begin again? Czar Nicholas reminded other monarchs that the arrangements of 1815 provided for the perpetual exclusion of all members of the Bonaparte family from the throne of France. In the event of a Bonapartist *coup*, the wartime coalition was to be resumed and the usurper expelled. The Czar was out of touch with contemporary opinion and others preferred to regard the clause as a dead letter. Nevertheless, Nicholas was entitled to be surprised by the enthusiasm with which Britain responded to the rise of Louis Napoleon, whose self-designated title 'Napoleon III' Russia properly refused to accept. In a sense Nicholas was right. The other powers' refusal to act when a Bonaparte established himself as ruler of France marked the disappearance of the last remnants of the solidarity of 1814.

Yet Louis Napoleon's Presidency and then his *coup* seemed to have saved France from social disaster and further bouts of revolution. Whatever his methods or his antecedents, such a man deserved some consideration. His régime stood for respect for property, efficiency and economic growth. There were promising opportunities for British investment in the expanding French railway network. France was undergoing something akin to the industrialization which had transformed Britain. A France committed to economic expansion would absorb large amounts of British exports. Despite his liking for bankers and entrepreneurs, the Emperor was sympathetic to the peasantry and to the poor and needy. Perhaps France had finally discovered a ruler who could bring together the divergent traditions which had divided the country for sixty years. These divisions had been the underlying reason behind the violent political oscillations which seemed to affect France more than other countries. These periodic convulsions never failed to produce alarm throughout Europe. After all the comings and goings since 1789, stability in France was in everyone's interest. Radicals might deplore the Emperor's betrayal of the Second Republic, but he was no old-style autocrat like Nicholas. His seizure of power had been endorsed by referendum. Further, the Emperor actually wanted to be friends with Britain. He had spent periods of exile in England and had been impressed. He had concluded that his uncle's greatest mistake had been to quarrel with Britain, a quarrel which deflected him from his true purpose – the reform of the institutions of France in the interests of progress and social harmony. Napoleon III would continue his uncle's work but avoid his fatal mistake. There was a perverse but striking attraction to the notion that the hesitant and often interrupted process of Anglo-French rapprochement could be most fully realized when France was again under a Bonaparte. At least Napoleon III seemed preferable to the Czar of Russia with his brutal government, stagnant economy and dangerous ambitions.

But did Napoleon III have no dangerous ambitions? France exemplified the combination of national assertiveness with a desire to serve some noble cause so typical of Europe after 1848. In France these aspirations were mixed up with romantic nostalgia for the days of Napoleon I and resentment at the boundaries of 1815. A Bonaparte Emperor could not disappoint his backers in the Army who expected him to make France glorious again. Nor could he afford to disappoint the French people who had similar expectations, deliberately fostered to win support for the *coup*. Failure to deliver the goods might encourage critical scrutiny of a constitution which claimed to be democratic but which produced an assembly without real power. If the deception were not to be discovered, a programme of distractions would have to be laid on. If Britain wanted Napoleon III to remain in power, it would have to allow him some foreign policy successes. This old argument, the same used for appeasing Louis Phillipe, now seemed more plausible. Palmerston had ridiculed it in 1840 but he accepted it now. Louis Phillipe had backed down but Napoleon III would fight. Louis Napoleon deceived himself if he was serious when he declared: *'L'Empire c'est la paix'*. The truth of the matter was, *'L'Empire, c'est la guerre'*. From the moment of the *coup* in December 1851, the honour of France and of the Bonaparte family required war with at least one of the victors of 1815.

Of course, neither the Emperor, nor the French people wanted a long war, a particularly bloody war, a costly war, or a war fought on French territory. Most emphatically, they did not want a war against all the other Great Powers. Against that combination they had lost in 1814, would have lost had they fought in 1840 and would certainly have lost in 1852 or 1853. Fortunately, time had put an end to any chance of such a coalition except, perhaps, in the mind of the Czar. France could probably attack one Great Power without the others coming to its aid. Even better, one of France's former conquerors might be persuaded to join it against another member of the 1814 coalition. The question was not whether there would be war but who would France attack – Britain, Austria, Prussia or Russia? An attack on either Prussia or Austria might bring in the other to the rescue. Russia was a possibility but how and where could it be attacked? Britain, with its very small peacetime army, was a tempting target. The battle of Waterloo appeared the greatest stain on the honour of France and that, too, pointed to Britain. The selection of Britain would have distressed the Emperor but he might have had no choice unless he discovered a more attractive alternative.

Palmerston's speedy recognition of the new régime in Paris indicated his desire to give the French no excuse for turning their pent-up resentment against Britain. If the desire for glory had to be found an outlet somewhere, could Britain direct it to a part of Europe where it could do little harm? Austria and Prussia were ruled out. They occupied territory too sensitive to contemplate deliberately exposing them to French attack. Russia, however, fitted the bill rather well – a long way away and unlikely to be able to inflict direct damage on Britain and France. Russia was so vast that whatever happened it would remain a Great Power; there was no need to contemplate altering the Pentarchy which had dominated a Europe for so long that it seemed a law of nature. Adjustment to areas such as the Black Sea, remote from the heart of 'civilized' Europe would surely not set up reverberations elsewhere. As a belligerent, Britain could keep its French ally in check and guarantee itself a central role in the eventual peace conference. Perhaps it had been foolish to deny the French their triumph for so long – especially if this could be arranged at the expense of a power Britain did not care for. Once the French had regained their military self-respect they might become more reasonable. This is not to say that the Crimean War was 'set up' by Britain or that it had lured France into war with Russia; France needed little persuasion. Yet alliance in war against Czarist Russia did provide an elegant way of coping with such a difficult entity as the Second Empire.

IV

The Crimean War was half-way between a full-scale 'European' war and a 'colonial' war. It was European in the passions it aroused and in the costs and casualties incurred. It was a colonial war in its remoteness and the fact that the enemy could not attack Britain or France directly or threaten their overseas possessions. War meant that military calculations would count for more in the formulation of policy than at any time since 1815. An alliance had to be formed with a power many instinctively regarded as Britain's natural enemy. Common military objectives and war aims had to be agreed upon. Ideally more powers should be persuaded to join the allied side.

Although the prime object of the war was to preserve the Ottoman Empire, the Turks themselves had little say in the matter. On 12 March 1854 France agreed that Turkish diplomacy and military activities should be kept under Anglo-French control. One disappointing feature was the reluctance of the other powers to join in a Grand Coalition against Russia – despite promises of financial assistance. Austria looked the most promising; the Russian presence in the Principalities threatened its whole position in South Eastern Europe. Yet Austria remembered Russian help in crushing the Hungarians in 1849 and saw the Czar as the embodiment of conservative values long ago rejected in London and Paris. For the time being, Austria would not go to war on either side, although concern about the

Principalities inclined the country to favour the allies. In Berlin pro-Russian sentiment was strong. An agreement between Austria and Prussia signed on 20 April 1854 disappointed the allies because any tendency in Vienna to move closer to Britain and France would be negated by Prussian influence pulling the opposite way. Hopes of Swedish, Danish or Spanish involvement proved abortive. The French had the finest army in the world and Britain had the best navy; if the Great Powers of the West stuck together there seemed little that could stand in their way.

But could the alliance stand the strains of a long war? A speedy victory would have been ideal but could such a victory be achieved against Russia? The experience of 1812 suggested otherwise. If there were reverses or the war became stalemated, cracks might appear in Anglo-French harmony. Napoleon III needed glory and he needed it quickly. Nostalgic as they were for the triumphs of Napoleon I, the French did not relish the other side of those triumphs – heavy casualties and crippling taxation. If the triumph was denied, or long in coming, the Emperor might execute a sudden *volte face*. Serious problems might surface if either Britain or France began to doubt the other's commitment. Whatever doubts statesmen may entertain before hostilities begin, once war starts they are well advised to forget their doubts and get on with the business of winning. Many members of Aberdeen's government had not forgotten their doubts. Lack of direction from the top and inadequate military organization gave a poor impression of British determination.

In part, Aberdeen's attitude is understandable. Russia was eager to prevent Austria joining the allies; in August 1854 it bowed to threats from Vienna and withdrew its armies from the Daubian Principalities which were then occupied by Austrian and Turkish forces. At the same time the Turks crushed a rising amongst their Christian subjects. The immediate danger to the integrity of the Ottoman Empire had passed; was there any point in going on? The conservatism characteristic of international relations between 1815 and 1848 would have produced a compromise settlement now. But protagonists of war

wanted no peace until Russia was defeated on the battlefield. They feared a uniquely favourable opportunity to
resolve the Eastern Question would be thrown away. A
compromise peace would not weaken Russia or strengthen
Turkey; Nicholas and his successors would soon be exploiting their advantages in the Balkans in the same old
way. Such a peace would change nothing. Truly formidable
barriers were needed to stand in the way of future Russian
advance. Such terms could only be imposed after decisive
allied victory. Further, a settlement without even one major
battle would not give Napoleon III the triumph he needed,
nor would it be welcomed by many in Britain who looked
forward to a convincing demonstration of the power of
British arms.

A hardening of the allied position became apparent in the
summer of 1854. Russia was required to abandon all claims
to the Danubian Principalities, agree to a European guarantee, grant complete freedom of navigation in the mouth
of the Danube, consent to a revision of arrangements
regarding access to the Black Sea and to renounce any kind
of protectorate over the Christian subjects of the Ottoman
Empire. Austria and Prussia were prepared to associate
themselves with these demands, but Russia rejected them
– as it was expected to. The only way to make Russia
accept these proposals would be to inflict military defeat.
This would be hard enough at the best of times but
doubly so if Austria and Prussia refused to back up their
support for the Four Points with military action. The task
of bringing Russia to its knees would fall on Britain and
France. British naval action might inflict some marginal
damage but little more. A land campaign on Russian
territory was essential, although there was a problem of
how and where to attack such a land-locked power. Various
possibilities were considered before the Crimean was select-
ed. Unlike colonial wars, large armies would be needed
and, despite assistance from the Turks, the invading forces
would depend on extended supply lines stretching back to
Britain and France. Ever the optimist, Palmerston clung to
the opinion he had expressed in 1836 – that one campaign
vigorously undertaken could defeat Russia and throw her

back fifty years. Yet, as the British army had changed little
since 1815, there was a danger that the allies had bitten off
more than they could chew.

Initially all went well. Allied armies landed and won at the
Battle of Alma on 20 September 1854. There were reports,
false as it turned out, that the fortress of Sevastopol, the key
to the Crimea, had fallen after less than a fortnight. The
Crimea was far from the centre of Russian power and the
Czar's forces experienced difficulties of communication as
serious as those facing the allies. The Crimea was Muslim
and Russian rule unpopular. Allied victory might produce
an independent Crimea – another buffer state – to limit
Russian influence in the Black Sea and keep the Russians
and Turks apart. The presence of a large Austrian army in
the Balkans compelled the Czar to divert military resources
away from the Crimea. On 26 January 1855 Piedmont
entered the war on the allied side; the tide seemed to be
flowing so strongly against Russia that Nicholas agreed to
begin peace negotiations on the basis of the Four Points.

Although some kind of victory was now certain, towards
the end of 1854 the direction of the war was subjected to
criticism in Parliament and in the country. The Crimean
War was the first major conflict to receive extensive newspaper coverage; in some respects it was the most 'open' war
ever fought. Although despatches took weeks to arrive in
England, newspapers and especially *The Times*, provided
their readers with more detailed and graphic accounts
of what was happening than they had done during the
Napoleonic wars. Compared to later wars, the true state
of affairs was not masked by censorship or distorted by
official propaganda. The newspapers carried unvarnished
reports of the bravery of the soldiers betrayed by the
incompetence of the generals and politicians. This was the
conclusion drawn from the news of the tragic Charge of
the Light Brigade (25 October 1854). Even more important
was public reaction to the revelations about sufferings of
British troops in the trenches before Sevastopol. The town
had not fallen at the initial assault and in November
1854 a prolonged siege began lasting until the Russians
surrendered on 8 September 1855. Newspaper readers

were shocked to learn that the British army had not made preparations for a winter campaign. The treatment of the sick and wounded was particularly deficient, although the arrival of Florence Nightingale and her band of nurses did bring some improvement.

For Richard Cobden and John Bright, opposed to the war from the first, vivid descriptions of the horrors involved only confirmed the need for an immediate peace. Cobden and Bright received some support in Radical and Nonconformist circles but the nation at large was more determined than ever. Aberdeen's position was difficult and similar to Asquith's in 1916 and to Chamberlain's in 1940. A peace-time Prime Minister leads the country into war – but with misgivings. The war goes badly or at least not so well as expected and the Prime Minister is blamed. At the same time he is appalled at the loss of life and expense his decision has caused. Aberdeen believed that as a man of blood he could not proceed with the building of a church he had had planned for his estate. Left to himself such a Prime Minister might conclude that he should cut his losses and accept a compromise peace. But this avenue is closed. His unpopularity arises not because he has gone to war but because he is not bellicose enough. Revelations about sufferings only make the public determined that sacrifices shall not be in vain. Thus, the worse the war, the more extreme the peace terms must be, the more extreme the peace terms, the less likely it is that the enemy will accept them; the war will go on, more sacrifices will be made, more extreme demands are advanced – and so on. The mood of the country in the closing days of 1854 marks the beginning of a process that will lead eventually to 'total war' and demands for 'unconditional surrender'.

More immediately, there will be demands that the war should be directed with more vigour. J. A. Roebuck's motion (28 January 1855) for a Select Committee to investigate the British Army in the Crimea – opposed by the government – was carried by a majority of 157, and Aberdeen resigned. On 6 February 1855, after a week of complicated negotiations, Palmerston became Prime Minister; his task was to 'win the war' and secure a peace which would make the sacrifices seem worthwhile. Palmerston was now a 'war leader', like Pitt the Elder in 1757, Lloyd George in 1916 and Churchill in 1940. All had a populist quality about them, a talent for mobilizing opinion 'out of doors'. All were unconventional figures and regarded with suspicion by the political establishment. All had experienced political eclipse at some stage in their career. Although possessing ministerial experience, none seemed likely to achieve the Premiership in peacetime. In most instances they were the Cabinet colleagues of the Prime Minister who had embarked upon the war but with whose policies and 'image' they were not wholly identified.

Palmerston's dismissal in 1851 had obviously been intended to put an end to any higher ambitions. The fact that he was now Prime Minister precluded any revival of royal influence over foreign policy or other spheres of government. War is a great political accelerator and often resolves in a few months questions which have perplexed politicians for generations. In one sense, the Crimean War marked the very end of that eighteenth-century world where the central question was the role of the Crown. It might have been otherwise. In 1855 Palmerston was 70 years old. Like Churchill in 1940, he faced the most demanding task of his life when he was well beyond what the late twentieth century considers the proper age of retirement,

Of course, the situation in 1855 was less grave than in 1916 or 1940, but there were still major difficulties to resolve. Palmerston had to gratify public opinion with victories and a triumphant peace, yet old considerations of a 'balanced' Europe could not be discarded entirely. Peace negotiations which opened in Vienna gave the Russians an opportunity to widen the split between the allies and the Austrians and Prussians. The participation of Piedmont, Austria's mortal enemy, in the war made Franz Josef less sympathetic to the allies. Above all, the negotiations revealed differences between Britain and France. If, in the run up to hostilities, France had been more belligerent than Britain, the position was now reversed. Disappointed of a speedy victory, Napoleon III was losing enthusiasm for the war. The next best thing to dramatic victory would be an audacious diplomatic *coup*. The advantages of the *Alliance Russe* were again canvased in Paris. What if France made a separate peace with Russia or even changed sides and attacked England when most of England's army was far away in the Crimea? The death of Nicholas I on 1 March 1855 made things no easier. Although more inclined to peace than his father, Alexander II could hardly begin his reign on a note of abject surrender. His representatives refused to make significant concessions on Russian naval strength in the Black Sea. Austria did not support Britain and Lord John Russell, representing the Palmerston government in Vienna, again demonstrated his diplomatic incapacity by accepting an Austrian proposal which would have left Russian preponderance in the Black Sea unimpaired. It was probably with some relief that Palmerston learned that the Vienna negotiations had broken up in June 1855.

Fortunately, the military situation began to improve; administrative reforms were undertaken and, following the death of Lord Raglan, the British forces were placed under the command of the more competent General James Simpson. On 28 May Palmerston urged Napoleon III to have no further thoughts of a compromise peace and not to allow 'diplomacy to rob us of the great and important advantages we are on the point of gaining'. The Russian position was weakened by the success of a British expedition to the Sea of Azov which prevented the Crimea from receiving assistance from the East. French enthusiasm for the war was rekindled by victory at Tcherhaya, and Napoleon III was flattered by a Royal Visit to France in August. The fall of Sevastopol in September brought the first stage of the war to a triumphant, if costly, conclusion. Would there be more stages? The trouble was that although Russia was 'down' it was not really 'out'. Should Britain settle for an advantageous, though probably not decisive, peace or should it proceed resolutely with more campaigns to see if more positive results could be achieved?

Palmerston's preference, supported by public opinion in Britain, was to go on with the war but, as far Napoleon

III was concerned, once Sevastopol had fallen, honour was satisfied. He believed, even acting together, that Britain and France could not cripple Russia permanently this could be achieved only in conjunction with powers possessing direct land borders with Russia. The Turks were the obvious choice. They had been brave enough but in other ways they had been a disappointment. There was scant sign of the reforms so often promised; financial aid and loans sent to the Sultan had been wasted or squandered on luxuries. The crucial question remained the attitude of Austria. If Austria would not join the war, there was little point in going on. Austria did not want war. Neither Austria nor France had any sympathy for the more extravagant projects passing through Palmerston's head. Britain would have no choice but to follow the Austrian and French lead. At the close of 1855 the Austrians presented an ultimatum to the Czar based on a slight hardening of the Four Points; the Russians accepted. The way was now open for peace talks, this time with a good prospect of success. On 25 February 1856 the representatives of the belligerent powers and of Austria met in Paris. The choice of the location was significant. The Congress of Paris marked the end of an epoch which had lasted since 1815, during which France, though a Great Power, was regarded as not quite respectable. France had now come in from the cold; Paris was now the centre of European diplomacy. The Emperor hoped that that Congress would be the first of many meetings which would enhance the prestige and actual power of France so that it could regain its rightful place as the arbiter of Europe.

The British representatives at the Congress of Paris were the Foreign Secretary, Lord Clarendon, and the diplomat, Lord Cowley. They appreciated that French opinion was turning against the British alliance and that the Emperor had no option but to seek peace. Clarendon knew that Britain had to accept a peace less decisive than she might have wished because, 'Whatever Palmerston in his jaunty way may say, we could not have made war alone: for we should have had all Europe against us at once and the United States would have followed'.[8] It was probably as well to come to terms as quickly as possible. The Congress worked with despatch and the Treaty of Paris was concluded on 30 March 1856. The Treaty satisfied most of Britain's objectives. The most important clause was for the neutralization of the Black Sea. The prospect of Russian ships in the Eastern Mediterranean was now lifted. The Russians would be unable to have any vessels of importance in the area because they promised 'not to establish or to maintain upon that coast (the Black Sea) any military or maritime arsenal'.[9] The other powers, including Russia, promised not to interfere in the internal affairs of the Turkish Empire. The Sultan agreed that his Christian subjects should enjoy equality before the law. The navigation of the Danube was opened to all nations. The Danubian Principalities acquired Bessarabia from Russia and the way opened for the union of the territory to form Rumania. The threat of Russian advance into the Balkans had been checked. The one weak feature of the otherwise excellent system of international relations, whose bases had been laid in 1815, had now been corrected. Thus the Crimean War and its outcome appeared to be a resounding success. Now that Napoleon III had had his moment of glory and the danger of Russia was contained there was no major issue left to disturb the tranquillity of Europe. The war had been popular in Britain; after a prolonged peace a certain amount of patriotic belligerence was understandable. But, however exhilarating the war had been at times, the Crimea did not really give Britain a taste for European war. Tranquillity and peace were still in Britain's interest. The trouble was that other nations had drawn rather different conclusions.

Notes: Chapter 6

1 *Hansard*, 3rd. Series, Vol. 97, p. 122.
2 *Edinburgh Review*, vol. 178, October 1848, p. 558.
3 W. E. Mosse, *The European Powers and the German Question, 1848–1871*, Cambridge, Cambridge University Press, 1958, p. 359.
4 *Edinburgh Review*, vol. 178, October 1848, p. 590.

5 F. J. C. Hearnshaw, *The Political Principles of some Notable Prime Ministers of the Nineteenth Century*, London, Macmillan, 1926, p. 45.
6 *Hansard*, 3rd. Series, Vol. 112, p. 444.
7 *Hansard*, 3rd. Series, Vol. 112, p. 543.
8 See J. Ridley, *Lord Palmerston*, London, Constable, 1970, pp. 449–52.
9 A. W. Ward and G. P. Gooch (eds), *The Cambridge History of British Foreign Policy 1783–1919*, Cambridge, Cambridge University Press, 1923, Vol. 2, 1815–1866, p. 389.

7

The Bluff Exposed, 1856–1865

The long-term implications of the Crimean War were alarming. As in 1848, there was a tendency to forget that what happened in one part of Europe set up reverberations elsewhere. The knock-on effects of the Treaty of Paris were especially extensive and long-lasting; much of European history between 1856 and 1870 can be explained in these terms.

Defeat made Russia behave differently. Whatever its 'revisionist' ambitions in the Balkans, it had been a major bulwark of the conservative order in Europe. Friend and foe alike had known that, in an emergency, Russia would use its armies in support of the territorial status quo in Central and Eastern Europe. Whatever they said in public, British ministers had not been entirely averse to Russia's role as policeman of Eastern Europe. But defeat in the Crimea made Alexander II appreciate that his country was backward compared to the industrializing powers of the West. Britain and France had devoted a smaller part of their resources to the war and had been operating far from their home bases, but they had still managed to inflict a serious defeat on the enemy. Unless Russia started to catch up, to improve industry, agriculture and communications, it would become a tempting target for aggression. Russia might find its territories dismembered and what was left reduced to quasi-colonial status.

It needed to turn inwards and concentrate on domestic reform and modernization. The rest of Europe would have to manage as best as it could. Russia entered a period of semi-isolationism, in sharp contrast to its earlier role. The Balance of Power does not depend solely on Great Powers restraining themselves from over-activity; it also requires that they should not be too inactive. Russia was now withdrawing, at least partially, from its 'assigned' role in the European state structure of 1815. For some purposes, Europe was moving from a system of five to one of four Great Powers. The consequences of this were incalculable. If Russia had played a bigger role in the 1860s, Prussia might have held back from its dramatic career of aggrandizement. Prussia's weakness was its geographical position in the middle of Europe; it was surrounded by other Great Powers and thus faced the possibility of having to fight a war on two fronts. Russian indifference to events beyond its own borders in the 1860s meant that Prussia was safe from attack in the East and thus could safely despatch its armies in other directions.

The Czar could no longer be relied upon to aid brother monarchs. Despite its apparent recovery from disaster in 1848, Austria was still inherently weak. Sooner or later its subject nationalities would rise again – perhaps with outside support. Austria's enemy, Piedmont, had used its involvement in the Crimean War to secure a place at the Congress of Paris and had skilfully used the occasion to draw international attention to its grievances against Austria. Napoleon III had listened to Piedmont's complaints with sympathy. St Petersburg would no longer respond to cries for help from Vienna. Apart from other considerations, Russia thought that Austria had betrayed it. Franz Josef had repaid Russian generosity in 1849 very poorly and, casting aside all considerations of conservative solidarity, had contributed substantially to the victory of Britain and France. Without Russian backing, the long-term prospects for Austria were bleak. If Austria collapsed that would be tantamount to the collapse of the old European order. Indeed, if Russia had supported Austria in 1859 or in 1866, the history of Europe would have been different. In other words, the reverberations of what had happened in the Crimea, seemingly so remote, echoed into the heart of Europe.

In so far as Russia did concern itself with the affairs of Europe, its approach became less ideological. Russia regarded the provisions of the Treaty of Paris as unfair and particularly hated the clauses which effectively prevented it from having a navy in the Black Sea. The resentment became an obsession.[1] An obsessed Great Power is dangerous. The Russians became so preoccupied with the Black Sea clauses that they seemed to lose sight of everything else. Their policy became erratic and unpredictable. They were ready to ally with any power – conservative or revolutionary – which might help them destroy the Treaty of Paris. From being one of the chief buttresses of the existing state system, Russia had changed into a revisionist, even a rogue, power.

If the transformation in Russian attitudes was to be repeated elsewhere, the result would be chaotic. Short-term alliances would be made for some short-term cynical purpose and after a few months the alliance would be dissolved and former friends would become enemies. Deception and double dealing would be the order of the day. It would be every state for itself and the devil take the hindmost. It did not require prophetic gifts to predict that the hindmost state would be Austria, whose fate had so concerned Britain in 1848. Austria was the symbol of the Old Order, an order gravely weakened by the 1848 Revolutions. The initial success of the revolutions had undermined the credibility of the conservative ideology of international relations. Yet their subsequent failure had reduced the credibility of the liberal ideology. There remained only the search for power. Even before the Crimean War, rulers had sought greater support at home by advancing more adventurous foreign policies; in part the war had been a consequence. But the war was more important than the revolutions in destroying the fundamentals of the European state system established in 1815. The stage was set for a period of international anarchy.

British statesmen were mistaken if they believed that victory in the Crimea and playing host to the Congress of

Paris would satisfy Napoleon III. For him the war was a means to an end, not an end in itself. It did not matter greatly where it was fought or even who the enemy was. It was important because France had made one of the victors of 1815 break ranks and come to blows against another. To conservatives, Britain had let down its natural allies by taking the wrong side. The prime purpose of the state system created in 1815 had been to contain France, but now British betrayal meant that the system no longer existed. France was free to break out again. Napoleon III had succeeded where Thiers had failed. The Crimean War was not about the Eastern Question at all. Its purpose was to create chaos, enabling France to revive its claims on areas nearer home – to the Rhineland, Northern Italy and even the Low Countries. If Britain was discomfited by this consequence of the war, it had no one to blame but itself. Shortly after the signature of the Treaty of Paris, perhaps even before, concern about France's intentions came to dominate British thinking. Thereafter, relations went through various phases, ranging from relative harmony to fear of impending invasion, but suspicion of Napoleon III lasted throughout the remainder of the Second Empire. Perhaps this suspicion was justified, yet it was also unfortunate, especially as it deflected attention from developments in Germany.

If France embarked on a career of expansion – through conquest, diplomacy or a combination of both – it would now enjoy advantages denied it since 1811. Paradoxically, the removal of the 'ideological' element in Russian policy also destroyed objections on principle to any alliance with the quasi-Revolutionary Second Empire. Above all, France and Russia were now revisionist powers, discontented with their lot. The obvious basis for Franco-Russian collaboration would be for France to help the Russians to secure the abolition of the Black Sea clauses; in return France would receive Russian support for its campaign to redraw the frontiers of Western Europe. This possibility was disturbing but, given their desire to concentrate on domestic reform, the Russians were reluctant to enter into commitments which might lead to war far from home. Nor would Napoleon III offer the Russians the kind of straightforward deal that might have tempted the Czar. As in much else, Napoleon wanted to have it both ways. He wanted to be friends with Russia but did not want to break off all links with Britain. For commercial and other reasons, British friendship was still desirable. It followed, therefore, that French approaches to Russia produced promises of neutrality in the event of war but nothing more tangible. In the short-term, Britain could be pleased but, as events turned out, the existence of a Franco-Russian alliance in 1870 would have saved Britain much trouble.

The Russian alliance was not the only line of advance open to France. The best way to change the map of Europe was for France to take up the cause of oppressed nationalities. Britain might talk of justice and right, but the French had armies which they could use. For the rulers of Piedmont the conclusion to be drawn from 1848 and 1849 was that they could not expel the Austrians without military assistance from an external power. France was the obvious source of help. A policy of providing assistance appealed to Napoleon III because France would appear the natural protector of the oppressed and the national states which emerged would be correspondingly grateful. They would be clients of France, supporting it in all important matters. The Emperor believed that Paris would become the centre of a 'Europe of the nationalities'; French culture, French finance, perhaps even French industry, would dominate a Europe rid of Austrian oppression.

In areas adjacent to France greater advantages might be secured. In return for assistance in gaining lost provinces, the beneficiaries of French help might cede to France some part of their existing territories. Such territories would have been part of France – and would have been quite content to have been so – under the First Empire. Their inhabitants would be either French-speaking, or at least, Francophile. If the logical conclusion of the Crimean War was an enlarged France, Napoleon III's policies would be vindicated. France would regain provinces that had been the country's by right and only denied it by the malice of the victors of 1815.

In July 1858 Napoleon III met with Count Cavour, Prime Minister of Piedmont. The terms of the secret Pact of Plombières stipulated that France would ensure the isolation of Austria whilst Piedmont would provoke war in Northern Italy – although preferably making Austria appear the aggressor. When the war began, France would send armies to rescue Piedmont and expel the Austrians from Lombardy and Venetia. Northern Italy would then be absorbed by Piedmont, whilst the rest of the country would be formed into a Confederation under the Presidency of the Pope. In return, France would receive the Piedmontese territories of Nice and Savoy. If war had not broken out within a year, however, the deal was off.

It is hard to think of any European statesman before 1848 or even 1856 being party to such an arrangement. For the first time since 1815 an agreement had been made between European states with the objective of fomenting war as a deliberate act of policy. There were time limits, concentration on short-term gains and indifference to long-term stability. Some historians have compared Napoleon III's style, both in his domestic and foreign policies, with that of Fascist dictators of the twentieth century. These comparisons may be unfair to the Second Empire, but in the Pact of Plombières, with its emphasis on war, its attempt to make the intended victim appear as the aggressor and its pay-off to France, one is certainly living in a world of extreme *realpolitik*. Napoleon III may have been outsmarted by Bismarck in the game of international ruthlessness, but he was no amateur in these matters himself.

For a time it looked as if the plan worked out at Plombières would fail – through the successful mediation of other powers or through Austria finding itself an ally. But war duly broke out within the year. On 29 April 1859 Austrian forces invaded Piedmont and on 12 May France entered the war. The French and Piedmontese drove the Austrians out of most of Lombardy. Unfortunately, the Austrians retained several strong positions in Northern Lombardy and still controlled the whole of Venetia. Napoleon III concluded that it would take a long campaign to expel the Austrians completely. The costs and casualties would not be welcomed in France where some sections of opinion had disliked the Italian war from the start. Worse still, Prussia had mobilized and threatened to come to Austria's aid. It is hard to say whether the Emperor displayed more cynicism in making or breaking the Pact of Plombières. He now abandoned his promises to Piedmont and sought an immediate peace with Austria. Under the terms of the Truce of Villafranca, Austria ceded Lombardy to France which, in turn, would convey it to Piedmont. The Austrians kept Venetia, however, and because France had not fulfilled its promises, the Piedmontese retained Nice and Savoy.[2]

The war of 1859 caused reverberations elsewhere in Italy and revolutions in the Duchies of Parma, Modena and Tuscany resulted in the overthrow of their pro-Austrian rulers. Plebiscites in the Duchies favoured union with Piedmont. Despite their anger at what they regarded as Napoleon III's betrayal at Villafranca, the Piedmontese finally gave up Nice and Savoy in return for French support over the plebiscites. But matters did not end there. In May 1860 Garibaldi arrived in Sicily and then crossed to the mainland and, with the support of the local population, overthrew the government of Naples. A tide of republican nationalism swept Italy and affected the Papal States, a development not to the taste of France or even Piedmont. A Piedmontese army was sent southwards but, on 26 October 1860, Garibaldi accepted Victor Emmanuel of Piedmont as King of Italy. Italy had been 'unified' in the space of a year. It is true that Austria still ruled Venetia and Rome remained outside the new kingdom. Paradoxically it was the presence of French forces, despatched to maintain the authority of the Pope, which prevented Italy from securing its historic capital. Yet the developments in Italy represented by far the most dramatic territorial change in Europe since 1815. Where Italy led perhaps Germany or even Poland might follow.

II

How was Britain to react to this turn of events? Its response was muted, especially when one considers that,

apart from an interlude in 1858 and 1859, Palmerston
was Prime Minister from 1855 until his death in October
1865. Indeed, the period of minority Tory government
under Lord Derby resulted from Palmerston behaving in
a manner regarded as too conciliatory. There are striking
similarities here with his dismissal in December 1851. On
14 January 1858, Felice Orsini tried to assassinate Napoleon
III at the Paris opera. The bomb thrown by Orsini had
been made in Birmingham and details of the assassination
plot had been worked out in England. These revelations
produced an outcry in Paris. Palmerston responded with
a Conspiracy to Murder Bill which would have tightened
the law considerably. The Bill was rejected, however, on
the grounds that Britain should remain a haven for political
refugees from other countries. Many felt it shameful that
Palmerston had responded to French pressure in such a
submissive fashion. The desire to stay on good terms
with France, apparent as much under Derby as under
Palmerston, did not reflect faith in the trustworthiness
of Napoleon III. On 29 September 1857 Palmerston told
Clarendon 'in our alliance with France, we are riding a
runaway horse and must always be on our guard'. The
full extent of French unscrupulousness revealed during the
next two years only served to confirm these suspicions.

In part, Britain's desire to keep a fairly low profile
in European affairs sprang from its commitments elsewhere. Several of these trouble spots required more military
involvement than the usual colonial campaign. Almost
immediately after the Congress of Paris, Britain found itself
in conflict with the Shah of Persia who was attempting to
reassert his influence in Northern India. Behind Persia was
the shadow of Russia, eager to avenge its recent defeats.
Persia was defeated without too much difficulty, but the
conflict complicated the situation in India, already made
difficult by the policies of Lord Dalhousie, including
the doctrine of 'lapse' and general insensitivity towards
Indian culture and religion. This discontent exploded in
the Indian Mutiny which began with the rising at Meerut
on 10 May 1857 and was followed by desperate struggles
at Delhi, Cawnpore and Lucknow. Fortunately for Britain,

the mutiny was confined to Northern India but it was not fully suppressed until July 1858. Britain had anticipated reducing its military establishment after the Crimean War but the Indian Mutiny prevented any significant savings. The lessons of the disloyalty of some of the Indian regiments could not be forgotten; for safety's sake, it would be necessary to keep more British troops in India. Unless there was to be an increase in defence spending, there would be fewer troops available for service elsewhere.

Palmerston feared that the Suez Canal project, backed by France but opposed by Britain, was part of a French bid to control Egypt and revive the country's influence further East. Napoleon III made no attempt to turn the Indian Mutiny to France's advantage. Palmerston was adamant in refusing offers of help from other European powers, declaring that Britain must put down its own rebellions 'off her own bat'. Further East still, however, Anglo-French collaboration was a reality. War between Britain and China arose out of the 'Arrow' incident of 8 October 1856 when the Chinese authorities arrested a British registered vessel. Napoleon III's anger was aroused by the execution of a French Roman Catholic missionary in Kwangsi. British and French forces seized Canton in November 1857. As a result of these and other military activities, new treaties were imposed upon the Chinese.[3] For the first time the importing of opium was legalized. Increased missionary activity was sanctioned and more ports were opened to foreign trade. Rules favourable to foreigners were stipulated for the conduct of trade, especially in the collection of custom duties. Rights of extra-territoriality were increased. The Chinese proposed that these terms should be reconsidered, whereupon Britain and France renewed the war. This time they fought their way to Peking where they fired and looted the Summer Palace. Even harsher terms were then imposed.

British and French collaboration in China at least had the merit of offsetting their growing estrangement elsewhere. Nor were these policies entirely selfish in that the two countries were ready for the nationals of other 'civilized' states to enjoy similar advantages to their own missionaries and traders. If the British and French were fairly 'open' in their attitude to China, Russian policy was more selfish. One of the consequences of the Crimea was that Alexander II tried to make up for his losses by expansion in the Far East The Russians were more interested in territory – to be annexed outright - than in trading rights or missionary activity. Taking advantage of the distracted state of China in 1860, the Czar compelled the Chinese to acknowledge his sovereignty over the territory to the east of the Ussuri River; Russia thus acquired an area of great strategic importance with a long coastline. It was on this coast that the Russians were later to build the railway terminus and naval base of Vladivostock.

This evidence of Russian recovery was not welcome in Britain. It also raised a question of wider significance. In the past it had appeared in Britain's interest to weaken the Chinese government – especially because the removal of the prohibition on the import of opium would help to turn a deficit on trade with China into a surplus. But if Chinese authority collapsed completely, Britain would have to take on all the expense of direct administration, if it did not wish to see the French or Russians taking over large areas for themselves. The only alternative was to reverse earlier policies and try to restore some authority to the Manchus. Thus, whatever its other disputes with the Chinese government, Britain had no sympathy with the Taiping rebellion affecting Southern China between 1851 and 1864. British soldiers, including the future General Gordon who had taken a prominent role in the capture of Peking, were 'lent' to the Chinese government to assist in the suppression of the rebellion.

Thus, Britain had enough preoccupations outside of Europe not to concern itself too closely with Italian developments. Whatever the suspicions of France, it was still essential to collaborate with that country. Indeed, Anglo-French relations reached a new level of harmony with the signature of the Cobden Treaty in March 1860. Since the Eden Treaty of 1786, the course of Anglo-French commercial relations had been far from smooth. The benefits of the Eden Treaty had hardly started to appear before the beginning of the Revolutionary and Napoleonic Wars. After 1815, the governments of Louis XVIII, Charles X and Louis Phillipe had all been protectionist and British imports faced prohibitive tariffs. The reduction on import duties imposed on goods entering Britain, started by Peel in 1842, had produced no corresponding reduction in France. The Second Empire was the first French régime since 1789 to express any interested in free trade, yet as late as 1858, only 1/2 of 1 per cent of Britain's exports went to France. Given the physical proximity of the two countries, this situation was manifestly absurd; how could there be a lasting improvement in relations so long as trade was so restricted? The proposal that the British government should persuade the French to agree to a commercial treaty was made by John Bright in a speech to Parliament on 21 July 1859.[4] In France the idea was taken up by Michel Chavalier.

Under the terms worked out by Richard Cobden and the French government, Britain undertook to abolish almost every duty on manufactured goods and to reduce the duties on French wines and brandies. France undertook to reduce duties on a long list of British goods to no more than 30 per cent *ad valorem* – and from 1 October 1864 no more than 25 per cent. The *ad valorem* duties would eventually be converted into specific duties by a Supplementary Convention. The treaty was accepted by Parliament by a majority of 116. In many ways the treaty initiated the golden age of Free Trade which was to last until the end of the 1870s. France embarked on a new phase of commercial policy and began to negotiate similar treaties with other states. In 1881 Gladstone declared that without the treaty there might have been war. At the very least, it helped to put an end to the periodic alarms and panics which had been a recurrent feature of Anglo-French relations.[5]

It is a tribute to the strength of free trade ideas that the treaty was concluded when, co-operation in China notwith-standing, relations were seriously strained. Although the British government did not wish to become involved, there were fears that the Italian Question could lead to general war. In 1860 defence spending was increased sharply. In the debates on the Cobden Treaty, Disraeli observed that, whilst the treaty implied confidence in peace, 'the estimates imply a strong expectation of war'.[6] Palmerston thought there was a danger of a sudden French attack upon England and thus embarked on an expensive programme of fortifying south coast ports. When warned that this policy might jeopardize the Cobden negotiations and provoke the resignation of several Cabinet Ministers, Palmerston replied crisply, 'It would be better to lose Mr. Gladstone than to run the risk of losing Portsmouth or Plymouth'.[7]

At the end of the Congress of Paris, Clarendon negotiated a surprisingly interventionist secret treaty, whereby Britain, France and Austria bound themselves to treat as a *casus belli* any future infractions of Turkish integrity and independence. Apparently the costs of the Crimean War – 25,000 dead and a bill of £50 million – had not deterred Britain from commitments which might involve the country in another European war.[8] Events in India were to change that. Nevertheless, membership of an alliance whose other members were on increasingly bad terms was bound to be an uncomfortable experience. As the situation in Italy deteriorated, Britain had to decide whether to back France or Austria or to embark on a distinctive policy of its own.

In one sense the country was already committed. In 1848 Britain had been a vociferous, if ineffective, advocate of the expansion of Piedmont. It would look odd to oppose such expansion once the French took it up and to insist that the Austrians must stay. By taking the allied side in the Crimean War and making a worthwhile contribution to the war effort, Piedmont had strengthened its claims on the Great Powers. Since 1848 Piedmont's armies had been improved, it had made considerable economic progress and had reformed its political system. Although Napoleon III might seek to profit from the situation in Italy, that was preferable to ambitions on Belgium or the Rhineland. The Emperor invited Palmerston and Clarendon to Compiègne to explain his policies and convince them of his good faith. Early in 1858 there seemed little danger that the Italian Question would lead to a crisis in Anglo-French relations.

Yet, all along, there were counter considerations. The traditional response to the prospect of a Franco-Russian alliance was for Britain to move closer to Austria. In the late 1850s, Britain was as anxious as ever to maintain Austria's strength. Lord Derby's government, formed in February 1858 with Malmesbury at the Foreign Office, was less sympathetic to the Italians and more favourable to Austria than Palmerston had been. Malmesbury rightly suspected that Napoleon III was involved in a secret intrigue with Piedmont; he was also reluctant to change any more of the 1815 boundaries. He tried to frustrate French and Piedmontese attempts to provoke a collision with Austria, advising the Austrians not to rise to the bait. Malmesbury saw his role as a mediator between Austria and France; it might have worked if France and Austria had really wanted peace but France was committed to war and the war party in Vienna was growing. By the spring of 1859, Malmesbury decided that Britain could not 'go on running from one to the other, like the old aunt trying to make up family squabbles'.[9] On 19 April, Austria finally lost patience and sent an ultimatum threatening the Piedmontese with war unless they disarmed immediately. Malmesbury was horrified and declared that Austria had forfeited any claim to British sympathy. Once war had started he sought to confine it to Northern Italy. Somewhat unfairly, he was accused of being pro-Habsburg and of wanting the German states to join the Austrian side. This issue became important during the British general election and was one of the factors in Derby's defeat. On 30 June 1859, Palmerston resumed the Premiership with Russell as his Foreign Secretary.

On recent form, a Palmerston ministry would be more sympathetic to France than Derby had been; yet Palmerston would never welcome an increase in French power unreservedly. The new government was further to the 'left' than any of its predecessors and some ministers were strongly committed to the Italian cause. A move towards Austria was unthinkable. Without departing from Malmesbury's policy of neutrality, Palmerston and Russell rejected his idea of maintaining the territorial status quo and adopted the slogan 'Italy for the Italians'. The policy was anti-Austrian but it was anti-French as well. The main concern about an enlarged Piedmont was that it would become just a

French satellite. It would be less worrying, however, if it felt as much indebted to Britain as to France. Palmerston had to out-trump French support for the Italians and discreetly draw attention to the underlying differences between France and Piedmont – all without involving Britain in any actual fighting.

Events played into Palmerston's hands. Piedmontese gratitude to France was shaken by the 'betrayal' of Villa-franca. The 'pay-off' of Nice and Savoy upset some Italian patriots. Above all, Napoleon III wanted only a modest extension of Piedmontese territory. A greatly enlarged Piedmont might be too powerful for France to control. It was precisely for this reason that the possibility appealed to Britain. Neither France nor Piedmont had anticipated the wave of radical nationalism which swept across Southern and Central Italy. In Britain the movement was welcomed and Guiseppe Garibaldi became a popular hero. The passage of Garibaldi and his followers from Sicily to the mainland under the eyes of ships of the British Mediterranean fleet was an important British contribution to Italian unification. Russell and Gladstone publicized the iniquities of the Bourbon government in Naples; news of its overthrow was received with delight. The Italy that eventually emerged was larger than Napoleon III had contemplated and quite well disposed to Britain. Thus Napoleon III's 'investment' in the Italian crisis produced a poor return. Once the champion of Italian liberty, the Emperor was now portrayed as a bitter foe who prevented the new kingdom from achieving the final stage of unification – Rome itself. The new Italian state was hostile to France, ready to ally with its enemies, a barrier to its expansion rather than a vehicle for its influence. In the long run, the Italian wars were even more damaging.

Britain could afford to view the situation with more satisfaction. Without using force, it had turned the tables on Napoleon III. But even Britain might have had second thoughts. The weakening of Austria, paving the way for the rise of Prussia, was hardly more fortunate for Britain than for France. The unification of Italy brought another member to the club of Great Powers. A Europe of six rather than five was capable of more combinations; there would be more intrigue and betrayal, and less stability. Britain itself had contributed to this instability. Russell's rhetoric disguised the shabbiness of some aspects of his policy. British disapproval of the French annexation of Nice and Savoy produced a sudden enthusiasm for the sanctity of treaties. Yet at the same time, Britain was encouraging the destruction of the state system of Southern and Central Italy. The Piedmontese invasion of the Papal States in October 1860 was without legal justification and condemned by all the powers except Britain. In a despatch of 27 October, Russell likened Victor Emmanuel to William of Orange who had invaded England in 1688 to bring liberty to its people.[10] Thus, in the name of liberty, one ruler could legitimately assist rebellion against another and then annex the territory concerned. It was implicit in this analysis that treaties did not matter. If adopted, the doctrine would have reduced Europe to chaos. Russell actually drafted another despatch encouraging Victor Emmanuel to attack Venetia and expel the Austrians. Such an attack would have brought Prussia into war yet, astonishingly, the despatch hints that Britain might provide armed assistance to Piedmont if it got into difficulties. Mercifully, the despatch was vetoed by Palmerston. To Continental observers, the contrast between attitudes to Nice and Savoy on the one hand and to the Papal States on the other showed Britain at its worst; some convenient 'principle' had to be found to disguise the calculation that a united Italy was a desirable counterweight to France. If the Pact of Plombières marked the nadir of morality in international relations, some of Britain's Italian policies were not far behind.

III

Britain had been fortunate in the Italian crisis. It had influenced the outcome without serious danger of being sucked into the war. Until 1860 it had done well in the unstable and selfish world which emerged from 1848 and the Crimea. Success had been due to diplomatic skill, to luck and the fact that Napoleon III was not so clever as people had imagined. The other powers had had to pay attention to Britain because of its naval presence in the Mediterranean. These advantages did not survive for long into the new decade; now Britain was to enjoy less good fortune than in the 1850s. Its diplomacy was conducted with less skill. Its opponents were more able than Napoleon III. Events in the non-European world were even more distracting. European crises tended to occur in the heart of the Continent, far from the sea, in areas where naval influence could not be brought to bear.

Fear of France led Britain to adopt a strange attitude to the Polish rising. The example of Italy inspired many Poles to try to regain their independence and reunite their partitioned country. Despite some concessions in 1861 and 1862, a major rising broke out in 'Russian' Poland in January 1863. The Russians responded with their customary brutality. Unfortunately for the Poles there was no parallel with Italy. There was no Polish Piedmont to act as the nucleus of a national state and soothe the fears of conservatives by stressing its monarchist credentials. The Russians could portray the Polish insurgents as dangerous republicans. Further, whereas Austria had been the only Great Power with an interest in the status quo in Italy, Russia was not the only Great Power with a stake in Poland. A rising in Russian Poland threatened the Prussians in Posen and the Austrians in Gallicia and Cracow. In the last resort, Prussia and Austria would support Russia over Poland. Also, compared to Italy, the Poles' potential friends in the West were a long way away. Yet without some external assistance the Polish cause was doomed.

In the past, both Palmerston and Russell had denounced Russian mis-government in Poland. After his unbounded enthusiasm for Italian liberty, Russell's response to the Polish rising was ambiguous – he accepted the Russian view of the Polish rebels, calling them 'the savage disciples of Mazzini'.[11] The Prime Minister and Foreign Secretary were both anxious not to damage relations with Prussia. Palmerston rejected a suggestion that Britain and France deliver a joint protest after the Prussians allowed Russian troops to cross into Posen to pursue Polish insurgents. Despite reluctance to imperil good relations with Russia, Napoleon III faced pressure from both Catholic and Radical elements in France urging him to help the Poles Yet, as Lord Napier pointed out, Britain had no interest in the creation of a powerful Catholic state, with strong ties to France, in the rear of Protestant Germany.[12] Whilst Britain wanted the Poles to be better governed it wanted them to remain under Russian sovereignty. Britain urged the Czar to proclaim a general amnesty and settle the rising as quickly as possible – before the French could acquire any influence.

Public opinion in Britain expected the government to do something to help the Poles; Palmerston acquiesced in French suggestions for a congress to discuss Poland. This response encouraged the Poles to continue fighting in the belief that Britain was sympathetic and, if Russia refused to co-operate, might actually send armed assistance. Palmerston had no intention of doing anything of the kind; as a result, a great deal of blood was shed to no avail. The Russians would only agree to a congress if the Black Sea Clauses were placed on the agenda. The Czar was playing for time; the longer the revolt lasted the more certain it was that Austria and Prussia would identify themselves with Russia. Britain and France would be powerless. If the two Western powers had been united earlier, the Poles might have got somewhere. Perhaps Britain, too, was playing for time. By the autumn, however, the rebels were weakening and Britain ended the pretence by rejecting a new French proposal for a congress. By now, Britain had decided that the sufferings of the Poles, though regrettable, were unavoidable and preferable to any obvious alternative. This equivocal attitude to the Polish crisis was based on a misconception. Napoleon III had no means of profiting from the Polish insurrection. The revolt was probably doomed from the start; Britain's involvement only ensured that more people died than need have been the case. After this earlier brilliance, Palmerston's handling of the crisis – handicapped as he was by the dogmatic and impatient Russell – still seems uncharacteristically inept.

Perhaps the uncertain handling of the Polish crisis resulted from preoccupation with the American Civil War. In the foreign policies of all states, some attention has to be paid both to the claims of self-interest and to those of moral probity and ideological rectitude. Palmerston, in particular, developed a talent for presenting his policies as combining the national interest with some higher good. This analysis could be advanced with some plausibility over Italian unification, but the perennial conflict between what was advantageous and what was right emerged starkly over America. Interest and morality seemed to point in opposite directions. If it was in Britain's interest that the South should establish its independence, moral considerations generally favoured the Union.

Despite Britain's preoccupation with the twists and turns of European diplomacy, there was an uncomfortable awareness of the power of the United States. The Atlantic Ocean gave that country a security against invasion, compared to which the English Channel was only a narrow ditch. Nowhere on earth was there such an extent of fertile agricultural land, nowhere such mineral resources. The political and social system encouraged initiative and promoted economic growth. The United States was more unified in every sense of the word than the far flung British Empire with its multiplicity of races, languages, religions and cultures. The sheer size of the country had once caused problems in communications; now the railroad offered the means of developing the resources of the West and of knitting the entire nation together more tightly. The American people generally enjoyed more freedom and higher standards than their counterparts in Britain – and far more than the peoples of Continental Europe. Numbers were rising rapidly. In short, the United States possessed such advantages that it seemed destined to overtake Britain in many fields well before the end of the nineteenth century.

The United States was not a great military or naval power but it could become one at short notice. Again, although not normally reckoned a Great Power, this assessment was less a reflection of weakness than of a reluctance to become involved in the affairs of Europe. The boundary disputes of the 1840s had mostly been resolved but nego-tiations with the Russians, beginning in 1859, for the purchase of Alaska, suggested unfulfilled territorial ambi-tions. Above all, there remained much anti-British senti-ment in the United States. This phenomenon grew with the arrival of more Irish immigrants; many claimed that the British government had been responsible for the recent famine and was thus guilty of mass murder. Then, Russell had been Prime Minister, and the fact that he was now Foreign Secretary did not improve Britain's standing in the eyes of many Americans. Thus, the war could appear as a providential means of preserving Britain's ascend-ancy in the non-European world. If the Southern states made good their attempt to secede from the Union, the former territory of the United States would be divided into two antagonistic nations; neither, it seemed, could pose much threat to Britain. Perhaps the rebellion which the Americans called their War of Independence was receiving its just reward. The destruction of the United States would avenge Britain's only major defeat in modern times. For monarchists the success of the United States had been an annoying exception to the general rule – amply proved by the experience of France and of Latin America – that, in large countries at least, republics were unworkable, syn-onymous with violence and bloodshed. Now the inherent defects of a republican system were revealing themselves. Whatever the public professions of regret, the news from America provoked an undercurrent of gloating. If the division of the United States was in Britain's interest, it followed that Britain should favour the South. The rebels appeared to have a good chance, but they were definitely the weaker side. A little help from Britain might make all the difference.

There were important economic reasons for favouring the South – it was cotton country, providing the raw material upon which the prosperity of a vital section of British industry rested. The Northern navy, however, soon block-aded Southern ports. Deprived of its cotton, Lancashire experienced bankruptcies and widespread unemployment.

If Britain helped to break the blockade, the factories of Lancashire could resume work and the rebels would acquire more money for their war effort. In broader terms, the economics of Britain and the South were complementary. The South favoured Free Trade and would take British manufactured goods in return for its cotton. A Northern victory, however, was to be deplored upon economic grounds. Many Union supporters wanted to divert the cotton of the South from Lancashire to the factories of New England. Worse still, the North favoured Protection – a high duty on imports to allow its own industries to develop. Free Trade was so much of an article of faith in some quarters that the evils of Northern Protectionism and the soundness of Southern Free Trade outweighed other more moral considerations.

It was also believed that the rebel leaders were gentlemen, whereas the Yankees were not. The plantation owners were the nearest equivalent to an aristocracy, or at least to a landed interest, to be found in North America. The landowners of England felt their position threatened – ironically by Lancashire millowners who made their fortunes from cotton – but they were still powerful and numerous in Parliament. Many believed – à la Metternich – that the best guarantee of peace between two nations was for their governors to subscribe to similar values. To some of the sympathizers, the South was an extension of the shires of England. The South professed to admire Britain; the North, with its Irish immigrants, was the hotbed of Anglophobia. The North was the land of upstarts, of dubious business ethics, of push and vulgarity – just the sort of society that some Radicals wanted to create in Britain. The success of the South would not only give Britain a firm friend but would provide a welcome check to the advance of democracy on both sides of the Atlantic.

There was even an ideological argument which might appeal to old fashioned Radicals: the issues which caused the Civil War had been States Rights and the South had been driven to secede because the dominant North tried to extend Federal power and erode the freedom of each state to arrange its affairs in its own fashion. In essentially

Lockeian terms, the early United States was presented as a voluntary body. Membership was contractual and each state, a commonwealth in its own right, could ask whether membership brought more disadvantages than advantages. If the disadvantages outweighed the advantages and a viable alternative existed in the shape of independence, then it had a right to go its own way. Any other conclusion was a justification for tyranny. These arguments were identical to those which had been used to justify American independence eighty years earlier. Whatever excuses the North might put forward, by wishing to strengthen central power and denying local rights – especially the right to secede – it was behaving as Britain had behaved in 1776. Lincoln was another George III. Britain should not compound its error of opposing freedom in the 1770s by opposing it again. Thus the true cause of liberty was the cause of the South. All in all, therefore, one might expect that cotton operatives, cotton shippers, cotton manufacturers, country gentlemen and at least some intellectuals – a formidable combination – would have been able to align British policy clearly behind secession.

Yet perhaps the success of the South was not consistent with British interests. The division of the United States into two hostile countries would make the Monroe Doctrine hard to sustain and expose the Americas to the colonial attentions of the Great Powers. Britain itself had no territorial ambitions in the Western hemisphere – the centre of her empire had shifted to Asia long before – but it was not indifferent to the fate of the Americas. Despite the panics and losses, Central and South America remained an important destination for British exports and investments; it is largely in this area that Gallagher and Robinson locate Britain's alleged 'informal empire' of the mid-nineteenth century.[13] The term 'informal empire' may exaggerate Britain's control over the governments of these territories, but it is undeniable that economic links were close and independent governments, nominal or real, saved the cost of administration and defence. Britain had no desire to take up these burdens, but might find that economic links and the profits that went with them could be imperilled if the territories were brought under the formal control of another European power.

France was definitely interested in territory in the Americas. Events in Italy and Poland had not turned out as the Emperor had intended. Napoleon III needed another 'triumph'. He would have preferred one in Europe, but he was ready to make do with one in Central America. The prospect of Napoleon III 'on the rampage' in Latin America was unappealing. If this was to be one of the consequences of the disruption of the United States, then it might be better to restore the Union with all possible speed. In 1863, taking advantage of the troubles in America, Napoleon III established a French-dominated empire in Mexico and persuaded Archduke Maximilian of Austria, younger brother of Franz Josef, to accept the throne. Maximilian and his wife were crowned on 10 July 1864. With the backing of a French army he made reasonable progress in extending his authority. Once the Civil War had ended, however, the American Secretary of State, William Seward, demanded the withdrawal of the French forces. Napoleon III complied and Maximilian was abandoned to his enemies. His execution on 19 June 1867 was a tremendous blow to French prestige. Britain might regret Maximilian's execution but not the failure of the attempt to establish a French client state in Mexico. If the American Civil War had gone the other way, Napoleon III might have succeeded.

There was also the consideration that, even if it lost the South, the North would still form a considerable power. In the North much patriotic feeling took the form of a belief that American popular democracy was superior to all other forms of government. If frustrated by the success of the South, this spirit would probably seek an outlet elsewhere. The thinly populated, defenceless British colonies would offer the Yankees a tempting target for conquest and the recovery of self-respect if the Civil War went against them. If the division of the United States carried with it the danger of the loss of Canada, the idea was best forgotten. Indeed, fears for the safety of British North America were a factor behind the proclamation of the Confederation of Canada in 1867.

Thus arguments, based on identification of national self-interest, did not always lead to clear cut conclusions. Yet most assessments of self-interests still pointed to the desirability of Southern success. Arguments based on morality generally favoured the North. Rightly or wrongly the war was perceived as being about slavery. Anti-slavery was a cause to which Britain was deeply committed. It could not support a cause whose real *raison d'être* was the maintenance of slavery, or oppose those who, whatever their other shortcomings, wished to bring emancipation to the South. This feeling was widespread out of doors, even amongst the Lancashire cotton workers suffering from the effects of the blockade.

This mood, championed by John Bright, helped to restrain those in the Cabinet who were more sympathetic to the rebels – a group including Palmerston, Gladstone and Russell. In a speech delivered at Newcastle-upon-Tyne on 7 October 1862, Gladstone described the Union cause as doomed; the Southerners had made an army and they were making a navy but they had done more than either: 'they had made a nation.'[14] But British help to the South was modest. In May 1861, Britain recognized the Confederacy's belligerent status – a step which caused anger in the North – yet stopped short of full recognition of independence and actually accepted the validity of the Northern blockade of the Southern ports. There was, however, a moment in the autumn of 1861 when Britain seemed about to go to war against the North. Two Southern agents, James Mason and John Slidell, slipped through the blockade with the intention of promoting the rebel cause in Europe and, if possible, of securing full diplomatic recognition for the Confederacy. After arriving in Cuba, Mason and Slidell embarked on a British mail steamer, the *Trent*. The *Trent* was stopped upon the high seas by a Union naval vessel; Mason and Slidell were taken off. This produced an outcry in Britain and Russell demanded the release of the prisoners and an apology to Britain. If the despatch had been sent as originally drafted, hostile reaction in the North might have made war unavoidable. But the Prince Consort, already a dying man, persuaded Russell to tone down the despatch;

Lincoln could now accept the British demands and the danger of war receded.

Much difficulty was caused by British shipyards accepting Southern orders to build vessels designed to break the blockade. The *Florida* and the *Alabama*, both built on the Mersey, proved quite effective. The Foreign Enlistment Act of 1819 forbade the building of armed ships destined for belligerents in a war in which Britain was neutral. The Union authorities claimed that the British government should accept responsibility and pay compensation. Palmerston refused; the British government had not connived at a departure from neutrality. The builders had tried to conceal the ships' destination and, in any case, the more successful vessel, the *Alabama*, did not receive its guns until after it had left British waters. As the war proceeded, however, Britain became more careful not to offend the North. In 1863 three more orders were placed. On this occasion the government was not to be deceived. One vessel, the *Alexandra*, was seized; ensuing court proceedings meant that it was detained until after the war was over. The other two, 'Laird rams', were purchased for use by the Royal Navy. Although the Civil War ended in 1865, relations with the United States remained strained. Gladstone's government agreed to submit the 'Alabama' affair to international arbitration. The arbitrators found in favour of the United States, and in 1872 Britain paid $15 million in compensation.

IV

In the early 1860s Britain seemed unconcerned at the rise of Prussia and the former was preoccupied with North America and with the ambitions of France and Russia. In many circles the rise of Prussia was actually approved of. The popular image of Germany was favourable, even sentimental. Writing in the 1920s A. A. W. Ramsey (1925) argued that the Victorian man in the street's notion of Germany was a place consisting of *Biergarten*, the Black

Forest, the Harz Mountains, and the Rhine; inhabited by maidens with large blue eyes and yellow plaits, who spent most of their time spinning; and by large stout men with untidy hair, drinking out of picturesque mugs, singing 'Ein feste Burg ist unser Gott'. The stereotypes proliferated: the German professor, untidy, impractical, kindly, slightly mad in a harmless way; the German Romantic hero, tender, brave and true.[15] The Germans were slightly absurd but they were preferable to the cynical, superficial, unstable yet threatening French. At a higher level, observers were impressed by the German contribution to the arts and sciences. The European intellectual centre of gravity had already moved from France to Germany. Yet the Germans enjoyed a political power inadequate to their elevated moral and intellectual character. They deserved to acquire the political power they now lacked. The rest of Europe would benefit from a powerful Germany which could somehow 'save' the other nations.[16]

The vision was attractive because it seemed so unlikely. The only German power that mattered was Austria and Austria was not seriously interested in German unification. 1848 had demonstrated the impracticability of the revolutionary road to unification. Prussia was a broken reed whose military prowess had never recovered from the catastrophe of 1806. Few people had any faith in either Prussia's military capacity or its general staying power. In August 1864 six months after Prussian forces invaded Denmark, Disraeli told the Prussian ambassador, 'Prussia is a country without any bottom, and in my opinion could not maintain a real war for six months'.[17]

From 1815 to 1862 Prussia had produced a few able rulers or statesmen. Where Disraeli went wrong was to assume that Prussia's feeble performance in international politics had been a true reflection of the country. The incapacity of a King such as Frederick William IV drew attention away from the great advances in civic administration, in economic organization, in communications and in military strength. It only needed someone with a fair degree of determination and acumen to set the machine in motion. Perhaps this would have happened in any case, but Otto von Bismarck, Prime Minister of Prussia in 1862, more than fulfilled these requirements. Yet even a strong Prussia was not seen as a threat. Suppose Prussia did bestir itself and Bismarck used unscrupulous methods to unite Germany under Prussian auspices, should Britain become alarmed? Some commentators stressed the common roots of the English and German peoples. In 1870 *The Times* urged its readers to support Prussia, not France, because 'blood is thicker than water'. Prussian success would be a victory for the entire Saxon race. Sir Charles Dilke, then an extreme Radical, declared 'Our true alliance is not with the Latin peoples, but with men who speak our tongue, with our brothers in America, and our kinsmen in Germany and Scandinavia',[18]

For most people, however, it was enough that they could not see how Prussia could be a threat. Perhaps Palmerston was more aware of the German danger than most of his contemporaries. In March 1863, Frederick VII of Denmark issued a Patent which declared Schleswig an integral part of his kingdom – although the special status of Holstein was acknowledged. In the months before the outbreak of war, British policy seemed the same as in 1848 – if anything more determined. On 23 July 1863 Palmerston made a remarkable speech in which he declared that, behind all the German outcry over Schleswig-Holstein was 'the dream of a German fleet and the wish to get Kiel as a German seaport'.[19] Perhaps Palmerston had a prophetic vision – of the Kiel canal and of the Anglo-German naval race, so crucial in leading to war in 1914. Britain usually took a tough line with potential naval rivals and Palmerston followed up his hints of future peril with a blunt warning that if any power or powers interfered with Danish independence, 'It would not be Denmark alone with which they would have to contend'.[20] This was taken to mean – especially by the Danes – that if Denmark was invaded, Britain would fight for Denmark.

Frederick VII died on 15 November 1863 and was succeeded by Christian of Glucksburg whose daughter, Alexandra, was now Princess of Wales. Frederick had had no direct heirs and although Christian was the rightful

King of Denmark proper, strictly speaking, different laws
of succession applied in the Duchies. The way was open,
therefore, for Frederick of Augustenburg to revive his family's claim to Schleswig and Holstein. Queen Victoria, who
had little time for Denmark or her daughter-in-law's family, supported the Augustenburgs. British public opinion,
however, indifferent to Salic or non-Salic laws of succession
and delighted with Princess Alexandra, favoured King
Christian. On 24 December 1863, Saxon and Hanoverian
troops occupied Holstein and proclaimed Frederick of
Augustenburg as Duke of Schleswig and Holstein. But
Prussia wanted the Duchies for herself whilst Austria felt
that the secession of Schleswig and Holstein from Denmark
would provide an unfortunate precedent for parts of its
own empire. In order to frustrate the Augustenburg claim,
Prussia and Austria decided upon direct intervention. They
demanded that Christian repudiate his predecessor's constitution. Fortified by what seemed firm assurances from
Britain, Christian rejected the ultimatum and, on 1 February 1864, Austro-Prussian armies invaded the Duchies and
then Denmark proper.

Britain did not provide the support the Danes had been
expecting. Compared to 1848, Russia was grateful to Prussia
for its co-operation in suppressing the Polish rising in 1863.
Anglo-Russian pressure which had forced Prussia to draw
back in 1849 would not now be available. Failing Russia,
the only hope was France. Russell proposed an approach
to Napoleon III whereby Britain and France would put on
a joint show of strength to warn Austria and Prussia – a
British fleet to Copenhagen and a French army to the Rhine
frontier. This idea was vetoed by Palmerston. Alarmed as
he was about the invasion of the Duchies, he was even less
inclined to give France a chance of following the annexation
of Nice and Savoy with the Prussian Rhineland.

It is unlikely that Napoleon III would have responded
favourably to Russell. He was preoccupied with his Mexican
project which he knew Britain would dislike. He felt let
down by Britain's behaviour over the Polish rising – which
contributed to his own loss of face at home and abroad.
Every few years French policy swung away from its normal

path of collaboration with England to an alternative position of trying to get a better deal with another Great Power. France had cultivated Russia and had also cultivated Austria – although Russia more than Austria because Austria was a status quo power and Russia, like France, was at least partially revisionist in relation to what was left of the settlement of 1815 and totally revisionist in relation to that of 1856. These initiatives had caused panics in Britain but they had had few tangible results. So far, France had not approached Prussia, perhaps because Prussia was not worth bothering about. Now Paris turned its attention to Berlin. It appeared that, apart from France itself, Prussia was now the most revisionist of the Great Powers; surely they could help each other. Like many Englishmen, Napoleon III did not see an enlarged Prussia as a threat. He believed that there was enough room in Europe for a substantially enlarged France to co-exist with a modestly extended Prussia. The Prussians could do what they liked in Schleswig-Holstein provided France received some 'compensation' in the Rhine. Napoleon III's belief that he could exact a price for accepting the expansion of Prussia was mistaken. He thought he could treat Prussia like a bigger Piedmont. In reality, Prussia did not need French help in its bid to dominate Germany. Bismarck can hardly be blamed for his unwillingness to pay for a service he did not require.

Britain was now more isolated than at any time since the Napoleonic wars. Prussia and Austria were at war with a small country which many believed Britain was pledged in honour to defend. France was eager to make a special arrangement with Prussia and would do nothing to damage its prospects in this direction. Russia stood aloof but inclined towards Prussia. It is sometimes asserted that the Schleswig-Holstein war reveals a steep decline in Britain's influence. This is true but simplistic. It is impossible to know how much influence Britain would have had in earlier crises if standing alone. Then, however, it had always enjoyed at least the partial collaboration of one or more of the Great Powers. The surprising thing about 1864 is that, given its isolated position, Britain wielded more power than it deserved. At Britain's behest, Austria recalled a squadron about to enter the Baltic. Britain also managed to convene a conference in London which arranged an armistice commencing on 12 May 1864. If this had been turned into a peace treaty, Palmerston and his colleagues might have emerged from the affair with their credit unimpaired. Yet their strong line at the conference encouraged the Danes to believe that, in the last resort, they could rely on Britain's armed intervention. Accordingly they refused to make concessions, no compromise was found, the armistice expired and war recommenced on 16 June. Again Danish expectations of British help were disappointed.

Some saw all this as a major reverse. For years Britain had witnessed the spectacle of a Prime Minister in 'left of centre' governments presenting himself as the embodiment of aggressive patriotism. One of the reasons for the eclipse of the Tory party was that its natural patriotic clothes had been stolen by Palmerston. Now Disraeli saw an opening and began a process which brought political dividends to the Tory party far into the future. He told Parliament that, by failing to maintain its avowed policy of upholding the integrity and independence of Denmark, Palmerston had destroyed Britain's reputation and influence in Europe. The implication was clear: a Tory government would not have left the Danes in the lurch. Whether a Tory government would have gone to war in June 1864 is another matter; nevertheless the government only just survived an opposition motion of censure.

Why did Palmerston behave so uncharacteristically? His government now included men who had opposed the Crimean War. In his party there were some who regarded war as the ultimate evil. Whatever the cause, the loss of life, the destruction of property, the increase in taxation and the inevitable interference with normal trade, far outweighed any possible benefits. So long as the authorities provided honest, cheap and efficient government and believed in Free Trade, did it matter who ruled in Schleswig-Holstein? June 1864 seems to mark the victory of the peace party in the Liberal party over their fire-eating leader. Despite his vigour, Palmerston was nearly eighty. Even he could not go on for ever and, as he appreciated, the future belonged to men with more 'advanced' opinions.

Yet was Palmerston such a fire-eater? In all his years as Foreign Secretary and Prime Minister he had never involved Britain in war with another Great Power – perhaps there would have been no war in 1854 if Palmerston had been in charge. On several occasions – notably in 1848–9 and in 1859–60 – he had allowed events to take their course and had skilfully protected Britain's interests by clever diplomacy. Palmerston was one of the most impressive practitioners of the art of crisis management the Courts of Europe had ever seen. He had been at his best in the 1830s but he had still been capable of remarkable displays of brilliance in the late 1840s and 1850s. He was now past his peak, although probably still a match for Napoleon III. Much of his success had always depended upon his threats and warnings being taken seriously; Palmerston was the master of bluff. In June 1864 the familiar tactics were used again. They did not work; Bismarck refused to be intimidated. Palmerston's gamble had failed.

It is tempting to condemn Palmerston's policy from the start. Yet as Kenneth Bourne points out in *The Foreign Policy of Victorian England 1830–1902* (Oxford University Press, 1970), with active intervention out of the question, it was the only policy which stood any chance of success. Bourne even hints that Palmerston's bluff might have worked. Bismarck's nerve might have failed him had not the Queen employed Granville to exploit the divisions in the Cabinet in order to frustrate what she considered to be the anti-German policy of 'those two dreadful old men', Palmerston and Russell. In reality, Bismarck was on surer ground than he supposed. Even if he had been given an entirely free hand, Palmerston would not have gone to war over Schleswig-Holstein and confided as much to Clarendon. Once it was clear that they could not expect help from Britain the Danes soon collapsed. On 1 August 1864 they signed a preliminary peace treaty by which the Duchies were ceded to Austria and Prussia.

Despite Palmerston's alarming speech in June 1863, the country quickly accepted the outcome of the Schlewig-Holstein war. The electorate cannot have been unduly distressed; Palmerston and the Liberals were returned to power at the General Election of 1865. In the election of 1857 Palmerston's conduct of the Crimean War and his generally belligerent foreign policy had been the central issue of the campaign. In 1865, however, domestic issues were more important. The electorate was not really voting for Palmerston as for the policies associated with his younger colleagues. There were some in the Liberal party who were glad that Palmerston's bluff had been called. Cobden said it was an end of an epoch; 'after the fiasco last Session on the Danish question' the Foreign Office would surely learn its lesson and not seek to involve Britain in Continental entanglements either to maintain the Balance of Power or to further dynastic objectives. Henceforward Britain would 'observe an absolute abstention from Continental politics'.[21]

Palmerston was still far from this conclusion. On 13 September 1865 he wrote to Russell explaining his view. He rejects any idea that Schleswig-Holstein should become an independent state. It is better for these two entities to be annexed by Prussia rather than become one of the many small states which 'encumber Germany and render it of less force than it ought to be in the general Balance of Power in the world' – very much the line he had taken in 1848. More remarkably, the problem with Prussia was not that the country was too strong but that it was too weak. Britain needed a strong Germany 'to control those two ambitious and aggressive powers, France and Russia, that press upon her West and East'.[22] This letter, written only a month before Palmerston's death on 18 October 1865, may be regarded as the last significant pronouncement of one of the masters of diplomacy and international relations. Perhaps Palmerston was fortunate to die in 1865; it would have been painful for him to have had to witness the events of the next five years – of which the Schleswig-Holstein war only gave a faint indication. Things may not have proceeded differently if Palmerston had lived longer. Isolationist pressures, both in the Liberal party and in the country, would probably have prevented him from trying to check the meteoric rise of Prussia even if he had been so inclined. Yet, despite the pro-Prussian sentiments of the letter to Russell, a man who had spoken as Palmerston had done in June 1863 might not have viewed the events of 1866 and 1870 with the detachment displayed by his successors, particularly Stanley and Granville. Perhaps the unification of Germany under Prussian leadership could still have been averted without war. Although in many ways an able man, Lord Clarendon was not in the same league as Palmerston and yet Bismarck later declared that if Clarendon had not died in June 1870 he could have prevented war arising from the Hohenzollern candidature for the Spanish throne.

V

Of course, what Palmerston might or might not have done is hypothetical but it does raise questions of fundamental importance. Should the politicians of the 1860s have realized that unless Britain used all the means at its disposal, including war, to prevent the emergence of a united Germany, the Balance of Power – established with such care in 1815 and preserved more or less intact – would be destroyed? Should they have foreseen that such a state, with the growing economic strength of the Zollverein behind it and equipped with the best army in the world, would outstrip Britain economically, challenge the country in the rest of the world and finally attempt an 'imperial' solution to the political problems of Europe? If they foresaw anything of the kind, their behaviour was deplorable. Perhaps, by standing aside as Prussia defeated Denmark, then Austria and finally France, they prepared the way for Britain's eventual eclipse as a Great Power. When Britain finally came face to face with the monster it had allowed to come into existence, it was forced to use up its accumulated reserves of strength.

Foresight is a virtue which historians can reasonably demand of their subjects, but how much foresight can be expected? To put it another way, how much hindsight can the historian properly employ? The view that Palmerston or his immediate successors should have gone to war to prevent the unification of Germany is hardly tenable. In Palmerston's case the suggestion is particularly inappropriate; in 1865 it is unlikely that Bismarck himself was fully committed to unification. It is not sensible to make men responsible for events fifty years and more after their deaths. All we can do is to judge their actions in the light of the evidence available to them. In 1865 there was little sign of the sinister side of Prussia or Germany. From Berlin, the British Ambassador, Lord Augustus Loftus, assured his masters that Prussia was essentially peaceful. Even when German unification was achieved in 1870, few thought it a bad thing. Britain's favourite Germans, the Liberals, were still strong and when the Crown Prince succeeded to the throne, more enlightened and more pro-British policies would be implemented. Even if it was not genuinely liberal, the new Germany appeared to subscribe to the correct ideas regarding economic policies. Despite the disappointment of many of Britain's hopes and the emergence of areas of disagreement, the expectation of 1848 that a united Germany would have few serious disputes with Britain and constitute an effective counter to France and Russia was actually fulfilled for twenty years after 1870. Britain had reason to regret the unification of Germany only in the 1890s. A war to prevent the rise of Prussia in the 1860s could have been unsuccessful and would certainly have been opposed by large sections of opinion. A major war in the 1860s, win or lose, would have nearly halved the century of European peace which Britain enjoyed after 1815 – with serious consequences in the economic, as in other spheres. In the 1870s most people thought that Britain's policy-makers had done well by preserving the neutrality of Belgium during the Franco-Prussian war, and above all by avoiding entanglement in Continental war. Palmerston had been an attractive figure but, in the decade or so after his death, the chances are that, if pushed, the average Englishman would have acknowledged that in these dangerous years it was just as well that such a flamboyant figure was no longer in charge.

Yet even if we excuse British foreign policy of culpable failure to perceive the dangers of the rise of Prussia, that does not mean that the 1860s were good years for British diplomacy. Many contemporaries thought that British policy after the death of Palmerston, perhaps after 1863, lacked a clear sense of direction. In 1870 the diplomat Sir Robert Morier complained that war could have been averted 'if for twenty-four hours the British people could have been furnished with a backbone'.[23] Modern commentators agree. Speaking of the behaviour of the British government, Richard Millman in *British Foreign Policy and the Coming of the Franco-Prussian War* (1965) declares 'what action Granville and the Cabinet did take was calculated to solve a dispute over fishing rights, not a controversy between two European powers of which war was a distinctly possible if not probable outcome'. Similarly, whilst Bourne concedes that the revulsion against Palmerstonian policies of bluster, bluff and occasional direct action was genuine enough, he also suggests that Palmerston's successors 'too readily made their idealism a cloak for timidity and inaction'.

Why then did the effectiveness of British foreign policy in the 1860s fall short of that of earlier decades. The most obvious reason is estrangement from France, particularly marked after 1863. Fear of France, though partially justified, was magnified beyond reason. Of course Napoleon III was ambitious and unscrupulous, but the mutual suspicion between London and Paris, which did so much to facilitate the rise of Prussia, can be blamed on British politicians as well. When it suited them they put the worst interpretation upon French behaviour, even when more innocent explanations were available. The widespread fears of impending French invasion in 1848, 1851 and 1860 – which Palmerston did so much to fan – rested on flimsy evidence. The French never moved a man or a ship to threaten England. In fact France proved surprisingly loyal. It had been conspicuously sympathetic during the Indian Mutiny and made no attempt to exploit the situation to its own advantage. The Cobden Treaty probably helped Britain more than France, yet the French had signed it because they believed that acceptance of Free Trade really would bring about British friendship.

France had supported Britain over the Trent affair and had helped to prevent war.

Yet France received small thanks for its help. Old prejudices remained powerful. Important opinion-forming institutions such as *The Times*, edited by John Delane from 1840 to 1877, were consistently anti-French. *The Times* was at the peak of its influence and, on the Continent, was seen as the official organ of the British government. This could do serious damage; on 5 December 1858, Palmerston wrote to Delane begging him to tone down his anti-French line. *The Times* argued that Britain should stay clear of any lasting alliances. In 1870 it declared that the time had passed when it could matter to England whether any Western power possessed a few square miles more or less, or the command of this or that fortress. It appeared that the only satisfactory relationship with France was one where France supported Britain in all its objectives, whilst Britain could thwart any plans the French worked out for their own advantage. It is hardly surprising that, from time to time, the French turned elsewhere.

British policy was based both on an excessive fear of French ambitions and on an excessive estimate of France's military capacity. In 1866, after the Battle of Sadowa, Clarendon still insisted 'There is no army in Europe to be compared to the French Army'. Most people in Britain would have agreed. Yet a few moments thought should have brought five simple points to mind. First, in the Crimean War, the French armies were, indeed, generally better than the British. Second, in the Italian Wars, however, the French had been only marginally better than the Austrians. Third, the Prussians were now beating the Austrians with ease. Fourth, it followed that the French would probably be beaten if they took on the Prussians. Fifth, a British army would probably do even worse.

The danger of Prussia was not appreciated until it was too late. Having backed down in 1864, British policy was isolationist for the rest of the decade. Britain now joined Russia as an almost indifferent spectator to events in Europe. Everything depended not on five Great Powers, but on three – three-and-a-half if one counts Italy. Of these powers, only Austria wanted to preserve the old European order, yet lacked the means to sustain this on its own. Austria was weakening fast, losing two major wars within seven years. In reality, there were only two Great Powers in Europe after 1866: France and Prussia. Both had grandiose designs for change. Europe was not large enough to contain both; the Franco-Prussian War of 1870 was to decide which would succeed. Five years after the death of Palmerston, Britain faced a united Germany and a Europe dominated by Bismarck.

British intervention in the Franco-Prussian War would have been neither practical nor desirable. The wars of 1866 and 1870 were fought far from the sea; Britain could have done little to influence the result in either. In the 1864 Danish crisis, however, sea-power could have been important – especially as Prussia had no navy. By failing to stand firm then and by not seeking arrangements with France – and by creating conditions in which such an arrangement was impossible – Britain was partly to blame for the reduction of influence it now experienced. Palmerston saw the danger for a while but failed to take appropriate action. Traditional anti-French prejudice overrode clear-sighted evaluation of the real position. Palmerston's successors had less excuse, yet were even more blinkered. Any history of British foreign policy which ends in 1865 must conclude on a sombre note. Ever since 1782, certainly since 1815, British foreign policy had been conducted with remarkable skill and in alliance with economic strength, political stability and naval power had enabled Britain to play a decisive and sometimes dominant part in European and world affairs. Despite the many crises, Europe had enjoyed an unusually long period of peace whilst experiencing social and economic change.

As Roy E. Jones (1974) has observed, 'strength is at the core of foreign policy'. The diplomatic skills of Castlereagh, Canning and Palmerston would have counted for little if Britain had lacked the resources necessary for an effective foreign policy. Jones identifies three major categories of resources: geography, mobilization and government. Geography includes the area of the state, its climate, soil and mineral deposits, as well as the size of population. But a large population on its own does not confer power. Similarly, mineral and agricultural resources require the application of capital and enterprise. Geography and mobilization still need proper co-ordination by a competent government enjoying a fair measure of popular acceptance. For much of the nineteenth century, Britain was well-placed in respect of all three factors.

Geographically, Britain was assisted by the fact that its homeland was rendered relatively secure by its surrounding moat. Any deficiencies in natural resources were made good by its overseas empire. Britain did not possess a population equal to Russia's, much less China's, but its numbers increased neither too rapidly nor too slowly to damage its economic strength. A long-established naval tradition enabled the country to acquire overseas bases and colonies – and above all to protect trade routes – with little effective opposition, either from European rivals or from indigenous peoples. Compared to other European countries, Britain accumulated capital earlier and deployed it more effectively. In the category of government, Britain also had many advantages. Jones points out that Britain possessed:

> A long tradition of centralised rule, an unusual measure of internal political stability, a skilled and mobile society, held in coherent form by a long established nationalism, a reverence for class and status and a fairly adaptable constitution able to bend to the political demands of new classes and new concentrations of internal wealth and influence. The apparatus of foreign policy was dominated by a small social elite which as a rule, was able to react flexibly to internal exigencies, unbound by fixed popular hatreds or crusades, and relieved of the anxieties of indistinct national boundaries.[24]

In 1865 Britain still possessed these advantages – indeed, the exploitation of the full benefits of Empire still lay in the future. But Britain's advantages were always relative rather than absolute; other countries were starting to catch up. Soon, the small size of the British homeland would become a positive disadvantage. This, together with a transformed diplomatic situation meant that in the last three decades of the nineteenth century, Britain's position in world affairs would be less comfortable than during the previous fifty years.

Notes: Chapter 7

1 F. R. Bridge and R. Bullen *The Great Powers and the European States System 1815–1914*, London, Longman, 1980, p. 88.
2 *The Cambridge History of British Foreign Policy*, Vol. 2, Cambridge, Cambridge University Press, p. 441.
3 ibid., p. 429.
4 *Hansard*, 3rd Series, Vol. 105, p. 190–203.
5 J. Morley, *Life of Gladstone*, 3 Vols., London, Macmillan, 1903, Vol. 2, p. 616.
6 J. Morley, *Life of Cobden*, London, Chapman & Hall, 1881, p. 753.
7 J. Ridley, *Lord Palmerston*, London, Constable, 1970, p. 496.
8 *The Cambridge History of British Foreign Policy*, Vol. 2, p. 394.
9 Earl of Malmesbury, *Memoirs of an Ex-Minister*, 2 vols., London, Longman 1884, vol. 2, p. 169.
10 *The Cambridge History of British Foreign Policy*, Vol. 2, p. 448.
11 ibid., p. 459.
12 ibid., p. 460.
13 J. Gallaher and R. Robinson, 'The imperialism of free trade', *Economic History Review*, Economic History Society, 2nd Series, vol. VI, 1953, pp. 1–15.
14 J. Morley, *Life of Gladstone*, op. cit., vol. 2, p. 80.
15 A. A. W. Ramsey, *Idealism and Foreign Policy: a Study of the Relations of Great Britain with Germany and France, 1860–1878*, London, John Murray, 1925, p. 37.
16 J. A. Crowe, *Reminiscences*, London, 1895, p. 377.
17 G. E. Buckle and W. F. Monypenny, *Life of Benjamin Disraeli, Earl of Beaconsfield*, 6 Vols., London, John Murray, 1910–1920, Vol. 4, p. 348.
18 A. A. W. Ramsay, *Idealism and Foreign Policy: A Study of the Relations of Great Britain with Germany and France, 1860–1878*, London, John Murray, 1925, p. 37.
19 *Hansard*, 3rd Series, vol. 172, p. 1252.
20 *Hansard*, 4 July 1864, New Series, Vol. 176, p. 751.
21 Ridley, op. cit., p. 574.
22 Ridley, op. cit., p. 582.
23 Ramsay, op. cit., p. 324.
24 R. E. Jones, *The Changing Structure of British Foreign Policy*, London, Longman, 1974, p. 17.

8

The Change in Foreign Policy

I

In Chapter 1 it was agreed that, despite the importance of some domestic factors, an external or 'state system' analysis probably provides the best means of understanding British foreign policy in the eighteenth century. On the face of it, by 1865 the situation had changed dramatically. Public opinion played some part in the formulation of foreign policy in the days of Carmarthen and Grenville. Yet it seems reasonable to suppose that the expansion of the electorate and the increasing information available in newspapers produced a situation in which foreign policy was at the centre of the political debate and subject to far greater public control. Without such control, the British government might have given more tangible help to the South during the American Civil War, or even gone to war in 1864. Foreign policy seems more 'ideological' than in the past. Perhaps the prolonged period of fluid party loyalties and unstable governments after 1846 created a situation in which administrations were especially likely to be influenced by pressure groups of various persuasions and interests. If there was a transition towards the increasing importance of domestic factors in the determination of foreign policy, the trend may have been unfortunate. Perhaps foreign policy is best conducted by real experts, professional diplomats and experienced ministers, well away from the glare of publicity.

In his 1907 Memorandum on British foreign policy, Sir Eyre Crow declared that the first interest of all countries is to preserve national independence, but that the second interest is to promote trade and prosperity. Considerations of security and trade may coincide but they can also diverge, and this was a problem in the 1860s. In some ways, Britain was more vulnerable than before – in part reflecting trends already visible in the eighteenth century. As populations increased, economic resources were developed and state power grew, so the nations of Europe 'pressed' even more tightly against each other. But it was not just existing trends. Until the beginning of the nineteenth century, human mobility depended – as it always had done – on wind power and animal muscle; there was an obvious limit to further improvements. Steam power created a new world, a world of shrinking distances. What one country did would now have a much greater impact upon others – hence the need for greater vigilance. In part, the aggression and paranoia, so characteristic of international relations in the 1850s and 1860s, can be explained in technological terms. The implications of many of the new inventions were disturbing in the extreme. Once the strongest argument for an isolationist foreign policy – that is, one in which 'first level' considerations are largely ignored – had been the belief that the Channel and North Sea, combined with a powerful navy, made Britain so immune from attack that it could afford to be indifferent to Continental developments and save money by keeping its land forces to a minimum. But steam power made Britain more vulnerable to attack; steam ships might deprive the country of its old strategic advantages. Compared to the days of sail, a hostile fleet could cross the Channel so quickly that no counter-measures could be taken. Given its tiny army and enormous colonial commitments, Britain might find itself conquered by a small invasion force.

Fears of invasion were reflected in fictional works such as Sir George Chesney's *The Battle of Dorking* (1871).[1] Nor was it just a matter of steam. Chesney spoke of devices like torpedoes which allowed a small fleet to destroy a much larger one. Naval technology was racing ahead. Entire fleets, once the envy of the world, could become obsolete overnight. On 15 March 1862, *The Times* noted that, although Britain had 149 first class warships, it would be madness to trust all but two of them to an engagement with the small Federal iron turret ship *Monitor* which had dominated the battle of Hampston Roads a few days earlier. Naval supremacy, Britain's chief defence against invasion, was more precarious than in the past. Even without the nightmare of conquest, terrible damage could be inflicted by lightning raids. Palmerston understood this; as early as 1845 he urged Peel to spend more money on national defence and, in particular, to fortify the naval dockyards against sudden attack. This policy was eventually implemented during Palmerston's last Premiership.

If Britain was not safe from attack, it had to take more interest in military developments on the mainland of Europe from where any attack would be launched. Again, steam was important – this time in the shape of railways. Instead of marching to meet the enemy – and thus arriving tired out – armies could now be taken into the battle zone by train. The pace of war was accelerating; this was not to Britain's advantage. In the past, wars usually started so slowly that there was enough time for Britain to expand its small peacetime forces, recruit some German mercenaries, despatch an expedition to the Continent and still be ready for when the fighting began in earnest. However, the trend now was towards ferocious but short wars which would be over before Britain could do anything about them. All the bluff in the world could not prevent others appreciating that Britain was not the power it appeared to be. If Britain was to retain its capacity to influence events on the Continent in the way it had done since 1815, it would have to expand its peacetime establishment – perhaps even going to the length of conscription – and also introduce changes in the organization, training and equipment of its forces which, by Continental standards, appeared increasingly inadequate. If trends in British foreign policy had been determined largely by the behaviour of other states, the

1860s should have seen a huge increase in spending on the armed forces and a readiness to intervene in European politics in order to maintain the Balance of Power.

Indeed, such was Britain's wealth that it could afford to spend at least as much on defence as its main rivals without appearing to impose a particularly heavy tax burden. There was no question of allowing the revolution in ship design to deprive Britain of its position as the leading naval power. A substantial building programme was undertaken, although there were times when the French were not far behind. In the army, too, there were reforms after the Crimean War, and in 1859 the launching of the Volunteer movement helped to increase the trained men available in an emergency. But in most military matters Britain lagged behind. Total government spending declined in the course of the 1860s, a decade of rapid economic growth. To a certain extent, the coat of foreign policy has to be cut in accordance with the cloth of military capacity. The Schleswig-Holstein crisis of 1864 saw Britain's last attempt to intervene in Western European politics for forty years. Thereafter, by adopting policies variously described as 'splendid isolation' or 'non intervention' but really meaning the same thing, Britain demonstrated that its policies were no longer primarily determined by interstate considerations. In 1864 Palmerston had insisted that the Balance of Power was an idea still worth defending. Yet indifference to the wars of 1866 and 1870 suggest that Britain had neither the means nor the inclination to maintain that Balance. By 1871 Europe was not in Balance; it was dominated by Germany.

II

The consequences of contemporary military developments may have worried Palmerston but, despite the occasional panics, their implications were appreciated only by a few. Perhaps Britain now placed too much emphasis on prosperity and not enough on security – the opposite to her role in the eighteenth century. In the 1860s the desire for economy was sufficient to stem bouts of strategic paranoia; several proposals for army reform were blocked by Parliament on grounds of costs. If Britain failed to respond adequately to a deteriorating military and strategic situation – or at least adequately in terms of the traditional preoccupation with the Balance of Power and the assumptions associated with a 'states system' approach to foreign policy – this may provide the proof of a decisive shift towards the increased importance of 'domestic factors' in the determination of policy. At the root of the change, we could expect to find fundamental factors such as the increasing strength of the middle-classes, the identification of the interests of Britain with those of finance and industry, the influence of Free Trade theories and of 'Cobdenism' generally.

In many circles, Free Trade was less of an economic policy than an article of faith; the magic formula of Free Trade would enable Britain to enjoy ever increasing prosperity and benefit all sections of the community. Thus the chief objective of foreign policy should be to promote the universal application of this formula. Enthusiastic advocates of Free Trade such as John Bright and Richard Cobden argued that it made redundant most of the traditional preoccupations of diplomats and foreign policy. Free Trade would bring peace as well as prosperity, a peace so profound that it would be unnecessary to bother any more with the Balance of Power, complex diplomatic manoeuvres, formal alliances, invasion scares or armaments races. All would vanish into thin air and with them would go most of the diplomatic profession. Diplomacy in the conventional sense was merely a game for aristocrats who wanted to live abroad at the public expense. The world of embassies, of chandeliers and parties aroused the contempt of those who subscribed to 'middle-class values'. Bright asserted:

> The more you examine this matter, the more you will come to the conclusion which I have arrived at, that this foreign policy, this regard for the Liberties of Europe, for 'the Protestant interests', this excessive love for 'the balance of power' is neither more nor less than a gigantic system of *out of door relief* for the aristocracy of Great Britain.[2]

The time had come for the aristocracy to receive the same kind of salutary shock which the New Poor Law of 1834 had given the paupers. If foreign policy was largely concerned with how one government deals with other governments, foreign policy itself would become unnecessary. In 1836 Cobden advanced his maxim: 'As little intercourse as possible betwixt *Governments*, as much connection as possible between the *nations* of the World.'[3]

In the 1830s, the ideas of Adam Smith, which first gained a following in the 1780s, had become economic orthodoxy. Even Palmerston subscribed to the new doctrines; when young he had studied Political Economy at its source in Edinburgh. By the 1850s, Tories and Liberals alike rejected the old idea that the amount of wealth in the world was finite and that one country could only grow rich at the expense of others. Increasing wealth in one state would promote the prosperity of its neighbours. The mutual benefits that would follow from reduction of duties would increase contacts between individuals from different countries and thus help to remove out-of-date prejudice and animosity.

Once, the opening of British markets to imports from abroad had seemed risky and dangerous. Yet if people in England found that they could buy some goods more cheaply than in the past, they would have more money to spend on other things, thus helping other sectors of the economy and re-absorbing into employment any labour displaced elsewhere. Further, the introduction of Free Trade policies would have a beneficial effect on exports. Other countries would no longer have any excuse for discriminating against British goods. Indeed, in the past they had often been unable to buy goods from Britain because they did not have the money. If they were allowed to send their food and raw materials to Britain, the money they received would return to Britain in the shape of increased orders for British manufactured goods.

If the whole world adopted Free Trade, the result would be the universal application of Smith's principle of the division of labour. Each country would concentrate on what it was best at, give up attempts at self-sufficiency

achieved at the cost of inefficiency and buy whatever was
needed in the cheapest market. The repeal of the Corn Laws
in 1846 marked a significant step towards the realization of
this dream. Rightly or wrongly, the prosperity of Britain in
the 1850s and 1860s was attributed to Free Trade policies.
Apparently other countries had reason to follow suit. The
full benefits of Free Trade might be delayed by high
transport costs, providing a form of protection to inefficient
industries, but railroads and steamships would change that.
Sooner or later, the abandonment of self-sufficiency and
reliance on imports for food or other essentials would
mean that the economies of the various states of Europe,
ultimately of the world, would become so interdependent
and integrated that war between them would become
unthinkable and impossible.

There were other areas where Free Trade was expected
to be equally beneficial. Under the now despised Mercantile
System the object had been to acquire colonies whose
economic potential would be exploited for the exclusive
benefit of the mother country. All European countries had
much the same attitude and it is hardly surprising that
rivalries for colonies had been a major cause of war in
the eighteenth century. The political economists viewed the
colonial system inherited from the past with disapproval.
There was no reason why the free flow of trade should be
interfered with. Colonial producers should be able to sell
their sugar with equal freedom. The whole system of tariffs,
bounties and preferences was inefficient and, as the 1840
Select Committee pointed out, many of the duties produced
less revenue than they cost to administer. But if foreigners
were to be admitted to the trade of the British Empire on
equal terms with British subjects, if colonial preferences
were to be abolished and navigation laws repealed – above
all, if the empire were no longer to be regarded as the source
of exclusive economic benefit – what point was there in
having an empire? Men such as Goldwin Smith answered
'none'. The empire was a burden. British taxpayers had
to find the money for its defence and for the salaries
of governors and officials. These taxes inevitably put up
British costs and made British goods less competitive. In

effect, Britain was shouldering a disadvantage to which the traders of other countries, operating in the same colonial markets, would not be subject.

It would, therefore, be pointless to engage in wars, either with Europeans or non Europeans, to acquire more colonies. If Britain was sensible it would get rid of its existing colonies. Perhaps, like the diplomatic service, the real reason for keeping colonies and the colonial service was to provide jobs for the relations of politicians. In any case, the empire could not last. The independence of the United States, which had done more good than harm to the British economy, was an example which other colonies would follow. Silly aristocratic ideas of prestige and grandeur were the real cause of war. If hard-headed calculation became the order of the day, no one would want empires, and an important cause of earlier wars would disappear.

Perhaps, even if other countries persisted in protectionist policies, Britain should adopt Free Trade unilaterally. This argument seems plausible because, as A. N. Imlah (1969) shows, after a difficult period in the early 1840s, Britain enjoyed an increasing surplus on its balance of payments due to rising income from foreign investments and could thus afford to ignore an adverse balance on its visible trade.[4] Some of the proponents of Free Trade anticipated the later arguments of Schumpeter (1951), that the psychological satisfaction of trade and money-making outweighed the appeal of military adventurism and annexation for the sake of annexation.[5] There was an element of genuine internationalism, even of pacifism, amongst the free traders. By increasing taxation and unproductive expenditure, war necessarily interfered with the free flow of trade and economic activity, both internally and externally. If such freedom provided the best way of increasing wealth and happiness, war could never be justified upon economic grounds. If the promotion of economic growth became the first end of public policy, it followed that war, or any policy involving the risk of war, was wrong because the loss in terms of missed economic growth would outweigh for the maintenance of such uncertain concepts as the Balance of Power made no sense to people who subscribed to these views.

Yet, as D. C. M. Platt (1968) demonstrates, in *Finance, Trade and Politics in British Foreign Policy 1815–1914*, the implications of Free Trade for foreign policy were complex, even contradictory. In one sense, Free Trade values represented the values of men who believed that British governments had been insufficiently concerned with the needs of trade. Such people resented the contemptuous treatment which British merchants living overseas had received at the hands of aristocratic ambassadors who considered that their task was to represent one government to another government and had nothing whatever to do with trade. In so far as doctrinaire Free Traders allowed that the diplomatic service should continue at all, they wanted to make the promotion of British trade a higher priority and hoped to achieve this by recruiting more men of middle-class background. On the other hand, Free Traders were suspicious of government involvement in any aspect of economic activity. The demand that government assist British trade has a curiously mercantilist ring about it – would not this involve helping some British merchants against others and lead to allegations of favouritism and corruption? Further, if British embassies were used to gaining favours with foreign governments for British merchants, would not other embassies do the same for their nationals – with all the mercantilist consequences of rivalry and friction that would necessarily ensue? The Free Trade answer, that foreign policy should be used to help British foreign trade as a whole, not individual merchants, did not provide a satisfactory answer, any more than did the assertion that British merchants did not require unfair advantages compared with the traders of other nations. Open markets and competition upon equal terms sounded well enough in theory but what looked equal to some might look very unequal to others.

However fervently advocated by Cobden and Bright, Free Trade did not produce all the expected results. The British Empire was not dismantled; extra territory was

acquired. Foreign policy did not 'wither away' as some anticipated. Nor did Free Trade remove all rivalries between
states; it actually created new suspicions and antagonisms.
Even in a Free Trade era, it was necessary to maintain a
foreign policy which was 'traditional' in that it regarded
other powers as rivals and potential enemies. It is possible
to turn Cobden's ideas on their head and argue that the
logical implication of Free Trade was a highly aggressive
and interventionist foreign policy, at least in some parts
of the world. This is the core of Bernard Semmel's *The
Rise of Free Trade Imperialism*, (Cambridge, Cambridge
University Press, 1970). According to Semmel it was hardly
surprising that foreign observers found Britain's enthusiasm
for Free Trade less benign than its advocates claimed.
Although Britain might be satiated from a territorial point
of view, it was not satiated commercially; here it was
insatiable. Diplomacy was now preoccupied with opening
up ever-widening markets to Britain's trade and investments. The country's burgeoning industrial economy created pressures on patterns of world trade which, in reality,
were more acute than anything experienced in the relatively
stagnant eighteenth century. The Mercantile System was
not discarded because it was unfair to foreigners. In th
days when Britain had lagged behind the Dutch, protectionism was needed to stop the Dutch enjoying all of the
economic advantages of the British Empire. But Britain
no longer lagged behind. Logically, Free Trade is the
theory of the strong and efficient, Protectionism of the
weak and inefficient. What had once been defences behind
which Britain could make the most of its limited home and
colonial markets had now become shackles preventing it
from realizing its full potential. Britain now fixed its eyes
not just on its home market, or upon its empire, but upon
the entire world. In effect, it offered to open its own markets
in return for access to the markets of the rest of the world.
This was really a one-side deal. Britain might now import
foreign food and raw materials but that was about as far
as it would go. British manufactured goods were generally
cheaper than foreign ones, so there was little chance that
imports would make much impression upon either home or

empire markets. Yet cheap British exports in the markets of other countries would wipe out entire industries. In these places it was hard to accept the belief that unemployment in one sector was always balanced by more employment in another. The gain in employment would be in the factories of Britain. Such was the momentum of the British economy, the sophistication of skills, marketing and financial services, that other countries had little chance of establishing their own industries – certainly not if British goods were to come in duty free. Old and new economic policies were not dissimilar. In both instances, the real objective was to corner a large share of the world's wealth and ruin rivals. Once the British had not denied they were selfish – just like everyone else. Now they pretended to be altruistic, whereas in reality they were more selfish than ever. The adoption of Free Trade made Britain as many enemies as friends, enemies who would have been delighted to see the country humiliated and weakened.

Semmel's work builds upon the classic article by J. Gallagher and R. Robinson 'The Imperialism of Free Trade', published in the *Economic History Review* of 1953. Gallagher and Robinson assert the virtual primacy of economic calculations in all aspects of British foreign policy. Although they do not attempt to link their theories directly to Britain's apparent isolation from Europe, it is not difficult to suggest such a link. Perhaps Britain was relatively indifferent to European developments because its trade was moving elsewhere – in other words, Europe mattered less. More likely, European trade still mattered, but British politicians were confident that other governments would protect the lives and property of British subjects and to allow them to compete freely and fairly for business. The same held good in other parts of the world where political power belonged to those who might be expected to subscribe to European notions of behaviour. Here, it was sufficient to use British diplomatic influence to establish some degree of 'informal control'. Yet there were countries which refused to open their markets to British traders, subjected those traders to various kinds of harassment, or were either unable or unwilling to give adequate protection to British property. The problem was what to do in such places. Clearly, they needed to be charmed or bullied into taking a more reasonable attitude. This, in turn, would require the services of more diplomats and an enlarged Foreign Office in London. The problem was particularly difficult in Africa and Asia. Obviously diplomatic pressure had to be tried, but if that failed should Britain proceed to sanctions, threats of forces, military demonstrations, even outright invasion, occupation and annexation? Free Traders did not want to go this far. They preferred to see diplomatic pressure have the desired result – they were therefore particularly dependent upon the Foreign Office. Yet in the last resort most would go as far as was necessary to secure the right conditions for trade; in some circumstances this could be achieved only by outright annexation. Thus those who in general terms might be hostile to the idea of Empire could advocate an expansion of British rule in particular cases. They would not justify intervention or annexation in crude 'Mercantilist' terms – Britain would not seek exclusive advantage and would admit traders of other nations. Yet the innocuous sounding concept of 'Free Trade' could be used as a battering ram for Britain to thrust its way into the markets of countries such as China by force, if necessary. Again, if British trade and industry were so far ahead of its rivals, the actual result of 'opening up' new areas would be to benefit Britain greatly and other countries hardly at all.

Thus, we have an explanation for the paradox that, contrary to expectations, the new economic thinking did not result in the abandonment of the British Empire. Despite the discouraging example of the American Revolution, there was a revival of interest in colonies of settlement. The generation of economists which flourished during the Napoleonic Wars and its aftermath had been pessimistic about the future. Under the influence of Malthus they expected population growth to outstrip food supplies, leading to much higher prices. People would have to spend more of their income on food; they would have less available to buy manufactured goods; demand would collapse; and the industrial sector would be wiped out. At the same time, an overfull labour market would drive down wages, resulting in a further contraction of demand. Even if Britain did not suffer a major demographic crisis, it was sure to experience economic catastrophe. Malthus's arguments were also applied to capital. As capital increased, investment opportunities would diminish, rates of return would decline and eventually economic growth would cease altogether. The next generation of economists was more optimistic. Although supporters of Free Trade, men such as Wakefield and J. S. Mill approved of colonies and believed that they could help Britain avoid the economic stagnation and probable collapse anticipated by their predecessors. Emigration to the colonies would reduce the upward pressure on food prices – fewer mouths to feed – and alleviate the downward pressure on wages – fewer people looking for employment in Britain. The development of colonies would also provide an outlet for capital, avoiding the problem of a glut of capital in Britain and the consequent fall of rates of return. Further, the development of efficient agriculture in the colonies would provide food to export back to Britain, lowering domestic food prices and maintaining purchasing power for other things. The emergence of prosperous societies in the colonies would also provide markets for British manufactured goods, helping to keep up profits and maintain growth.

In a Free Trade world there was no need for this emigration and capital to go to territories under British rule. In theory, many of the same benefits would accrue if their destination was the United States or if new areas of settlement were independent from the first. Yet emigrants, especially the more respectable ones, preferred to go to places which enjoyed the stability and security of British rule. Trade would also expand more rapidly if some kind of political connection, reinforced by ties of language, institutions and sentiment, were retained with Britain. Perhaps the position was really one of 'Non-tariff Mercantilism' – although there was no intention of binding colonies of settlement to Britain by the type of restrictions characteristic of the old system. Such restrictions only caused resentment and had been a major cause of the

American Revolution. An empire bound together by natural rather than artificial ties would have greater real unity. A Free Trade empire would also be compatible with the demand that colonies of settlement should enjoy a large measure of self-government. Self-governing colonies would bear the costs of their own administration and at least part of their defence costs. Thus the British taxpayer would be relieved of the burdens of Empire, whilst continuing to enjoy its advantages. In short, the new economic ideas did not make Britain any less expansionist than in the past.

III

The imperialistic implications of the doctrine of Free Trade were strengthened by another ideological and essentially domestic factor. In the past, most people accepted that self-interest determined foreign policy. Perhaps nothing had changed. Social and economic change might alter perceptions of what was in the national interest, but the career of Palmerston demonstrates that frank espousals of national selfishness could still pay political dividends. Yet there were always some who believed that policy should reflect some higher ideals. The ideals varied widely over time and have been discussed in earlier chapters. They could be of the Right or of the Left – the ideal of defending aristocratic civilization against the forces of evil and revolution, the ideal of the Balance of Power, the ideal of constitutional government, the ideal of nationalism, the ideal of anti-slavery – to name but a few. Of all ideologies in nineteenth-century Britain, the most powerful was Christianity. Many people believed that all activities of government, including foreign policy, should be based upon Christian principles. Nineteenth-century Christianity did not turn its back upon the world; it proclaimed that huge efforts were needed to save souls and bodies. As the state could do much to assist this work there was no more appropriate career for a Christian than to be a politician actively seeking high office. In a society where the churches were powerful, a policy which could be presented as 'godly' would attract extra support. This influence of religion upon politics had been increasing ever since the end of the eighteenth century. The Evangelical movement, by far the most effective Christian pressure group, had a large following in Parliament. The Evangelicals enjoyed considerable support amongst the aristocracy, but the real strength of organized religion lay in the middle-classes or, even, in some areas, in the working-classes. The expansion of the electorate might further enhance the influence of religion in general and, in particular, create important Nonconformist pressure groups.

It was one thing to say that foreign policy should be directed in accordance with Christian principles and another to secure general agreement as to what actual policies embodied those principles. In foreign policy terms, the Evangelicals' influence was conservative. They supported the wars against Revolutionary France, holding that the social order was God-given and hence it was blasphemous to seek to change it. Yet the Evangelicals were also strongly anti-Catholic and disliked policies based upon collaboration with either Austria or with the restored Bourbons in France. In later years, their Protestantism made them likely to approve of the rise of Prussia – although not of Bismarck's methods. The Evangelicals – who were very strong in the armed forces – had no objection to war as such, but they were bound to condemn unjust wars. For the most part they believed that the wars Britain became involved in were justified; but there could be exceptions. Although not himself an Evangelical, Gladstone shared many Evangelical attitudes. In 1840, whilst still in his 'stern unbending Tory' phase, he denounced the Opium War as incompatible with Christianity and asserted the right of the Chinese government to resist the importation of opium by force.

Nonconformist groups were more likely to criticize British foreign policy on Christian grounds. Whilst generally supporting the Whigs and Liberals they made strange companions for a man such as Palmerston. They approved of the attempts of the peoples of Europe to throw off oppression. Their ideal was one of constitutional nation states and they opposed collaboration with absolutist governments. But their sympathy with the oppressed did not go to the lengths of urging that Britain should go to war on their behalf. Many Nonconformists took an isolationist attitude to foreign policy and were liable to be unenthusiastic about Europe. Some deeply disapproved of war and most of the opposition to the Crimean War came from this quarter. Like the Free Traders, Christian pressure groups believed they knew best; strong opinions might lead to strong actions. If Free Traders argued that force might be justified to compel other states to admit British traders, some Church groups approved of force to suppress evils such as the Slave Trade or to overcome the refusal of non-Christian rulers to admit Christian missionaries. They considered missions so vital that they sometimes adopted an 'end justifies the means' approach. If millions could be saved from damnation, should one be too scrupulous about the ways in which they were to be brought into the Christian fold? Here, the Chinese wars presented an acute dilemma. Some Evangelicals argued that Chinese defeat would allow Britain to insist that large numbers of Christian missionaries should be allowed to enter China. Of course dealing with non-Christian rulers was never easy. The Gospel might be spread more effectively if heathen lands came under British rule and were administered directly by the Colonial Office. For many years the dominant influence in the Colonial Office was James Stephen, Under Secretary from 1836 to 1847 and himself a prominent Evangelical. The nineteenth-century Colonial Office supported missionary activities – in contrast to the eighteenth century when missionary activity had been disapproved of as likely to cause trouble.

IV

Whatever else was happening to foreign policy, therefore, Britain was not really moving into an era of isolationism and non-intervention. The 'low profile' approach to European affairs was only one facet of a transition in which policy became less Eurocentric. It became more concerned with the rest of the world and, in parts of the Globe, more aggressive and interventionist. Yet the full validity of the Gallagher-Robinson thesis depends upon two things: first, that British policy really was more affected by commercial considerations than in the past; second, that the former stately pace of foreign policy accelerated to one of near frenzy. So much had to be done if Britain was to come anywhere near to achieving the Gallagher and Robinson dictum of 'trade with informal control if possible; trade with rule were necessary'. The adoption of such an objective required a dramatic change both in attitudes and personnel.

D. C. M. Platt (1968) exposes some of the deficiencies of the Gallagher and Robinson thesis. The notion that the middle of the nineteenth century saw a dramatic increase in the priority given to economic considerations presupposes that there was once a time when economic objectives were relatively unimportant. Platt quotes Pitt the Younger's remark 'British policy is British trade' to indicate how long-standing this preoccupation had been. Virtually all British Foreign Secretaries attested to the importance they attached to commercial considerations. Nor were these empty words; at least until the middle of the nineteenth century, British merchants enjoyed more consistent support from their government than their rivals elsewhere. Perhaps commercial factors did become more important as British trade and industry expanded, but there were some factors pointing in the opposite direction. Platt cites Harold Nicolson's argument in *Diplomacy* (London, Oxford University Press, Home University Library of Modern Knowledge, 1950) that originally British diplomats in the Middle East and Far East were agents of the Levant and East India Companies. When their role changed to that of representing their national government, however, they reacted against their old links with commerce, believing that it 'implied a lowering of their own status from sovereign representatives to commercial travellers'. More fundamentally, how were the doctrines of Free Trade and *laissez-faire* to be interpreted by the makers of foreign policy? Gallagher and Robinson claim that they led to a more active policy. In opposition to 'trade with informal control if possible; trade with rule where necessary', Platt offers 'equal favour and open competition for British finance and trade overseas' as the touchstone of British policy during the century after 1815. The second definition does not mention 'control' and implies that Free Trade doctrines produced less dramatic results. Platt goes as far as to assert:

> Noblemen, bored, dispirited and inexperienced in matters of commerce and finance, found in *laissez-faire* exactly the rationalization they were looking for; they could avoid a distasteful contact with the persons and problems of traders and financiers merely by referring in perfect good faith, to the traditions of non-intervention, Free Trade, and open competition... Most politicians and officials were continually aware of the importance to Britain of a thriving trade overseas. But social convention in a class bound society, was certain to act as a barrier to unqualified trade promotion while, in the century before 1914, a much more formidable barrier existed in the ideology both of *laissez-faire* and of what Keynes once called its 'most fervent expression', Free Trade.[6]

This argument would be of little value if the personnel involved in foreign policy had undergone a substantial change by 1865. But whatever was happening elsewhere in government, the composition of the Foreign Office remained overwhelmingly aristocratic. Although the ability of entrants may have improved, their social background had changed little. If not a peer himself the Foreign Secretary was usually a member of an aristocratic family, as were virtually all ambassadors and officials at the Foreign Office. The Consular Service did concern itself with trading matters to some extent and recruited its members from a wider social circle, but there was a rigid division between the Diplomatic Service and the Consular Service and consuls remained the second-class citizens of the diplomatic world. If the Foreign Office remained immune to what some historians see as the aristocratization of government in the last quarter of the nineteenth century, that was only because it had been aristocratic all along. There was still a good defence to be made for this state of affairs. More than in the eighteenth century, entry into the Foreign Office required knowledge of foreign languages, a facility unlikely to be acquired without one or two years' residence abroad – an expensive item for any family. Above all, there was the argument that diplomatic relations would proceed more smoothly if like could speak to like. As most of the governments of Europe were still dominated by aristocrats with a powerful belief in the superiority brought by ancient lineage it made sense to send men of good family as ambassadors to cities such as Vienna and St Petersburg. It may be objected, perhaps, that the treatment of British foreign policy in this book has been too Eurocentric. Yet most of the people involved in foreign policy were decidedly Eurocentric and disliked the prospect of a diplomatic posting outside Europe, partly because the climate and society would be less agreeable than in a European capital, and partly because there would be more commercial and less political work to perform. It was in this world of high politics that most diplomats and Foreign Secretaries believed that their skills would be most usefully and most honourably employed.

If we discount as minimal changes in the social composition of the diplomatic and foreign service, and go along with Platt's implicit argument that the nineteenth century did not see any conscious increase in the importance of economic considerations on foreign policy, it is still possible that changes in domestic politics produced a radically different balance of factors in the determination of policy. It has been suggested before in this book that the period 1848–65 witnessed a degree of public interest in foreign policy greater than that found earlier or later in the nineteenth century. There seems reason to believe that this interest was shared by many MPs at the time. The fragmentation of traditional political parties, and the succession of weak governments during the same period, presented back-bench MPs with unique opportunity to influence foreign policy – in other words, the situation appears ideal for a dramatic increase in the 'internal' input in the formulation of British foreign policy.

Yet the limitations on the executive in matters of foreign policy remained surprisingly few. Formal parliamentary sanction was not required for a declaration of war – even in the case of major conflicts such as the Crimea. Parliament was told of the decision to enter war either before or after hostilities had broken out – usually afterwards. Nor did the constitutional position on treaties favour Parliamentary debate. Treaties were laid before Parliament after they had been ratified – and in the case of most treaties no debate took place. Thus really important treaties were largely outside parliamentary control. Only when the treaty concerned involved a change in the law of England or an alteration in customs duties – as did the Cobden Treaty – was parliamentary consent required. Because the position of the legislature in relation to the executive was particularly strong in financial matters, critics of foreign policy concentrated their attacks less upon a policy itself than upon its costs. In 1865, as in 1782, Parliament was not an appropriate body for the conduct of international diplomacy – and this was appreciated universally. Valerie Cromwell declares:

> At the last resort, the House always proved willing to give way should a minister insist on the inconvenience of answering a particular question, of providing desired papers or even of debating at all... Suggestions on the lines of a standing Foreign Affairs Committee were only intended as a regular retrospective check on the Executive, and not as a policy making body.[7]

It was frequently argued that prolonged tenure of the Foreign Office could be corrupting. This was a line taken by the Tory *Quarterly Review* when it conducted a sustained campaign against Palmerston's foreign and domestic policies. The Foreign Office brought out the worst in men of 'restlessness and ambition'.

> It alone has the privilege not only of excluding all Parliamentary interference, but even of refusing information to the Legislature until its policy has reached the point which it may itself select as likely to render it either convenient or at worst

innocuous. This enables it to finish its work in silence or it in general makes known the results to Parliament at a time when its members can only raise a retrospective question and upon a retrospective discussion, no Parliament ever has condemned, probably no Parliament ever will condemn an Administration.[8]

The *Quarterly Review* made no suggestion as to how the 'immunities' enjoyed by the Foreign Secretary could safely be removed. In reality, the only restraint acting upon a Foreign Secretary was self-restraint; without that he was no more than a 'chartered libertine'. Cabinet colleagues were no better placed to monitor foreign policy than back-bench MPs. The vast mass of foreign business, the constant windings of diplomatic correspondence, the delicate but vital shadings received in letters, in discussions with foreign envoys and in communications with foreign courts – all required an expertise which ordinary politicians did not possess. In the last resort, foreign policy was managed by the Prime Minister and the Foreign Secretary with very little outside interference.

It has been claimed by H. W. V. Temperley and L. S. Penson in *A Century of Diplomatic Blue Books 1814–1914*, (Cambridge University Press, 1938) that 'it is literally true to say that as Parliament became more democratic, its control over foreign policy declined'.[9] Parliamentary control over foreign policy depended on the availability of unbiased information; whereas, earlier in the century, parliamentary papers dealing with diplomatic matters were produced as a result of initiatives on the part of Parliament, later, they were produced without prompting by the Foreign Office. In the first case, Parliament could stipulate the material it wished to see; in the second, the Foreign Office exercised a degree of discretion. Although Sheila Lambert has demonstrated the shortcomings of the Temperley–Penson thesis by proving that there was no significant difference between the two types of Blue Book,[10] the notion that Parliament, as representing public opinion, exercised greater control over foreign policy in 1865 than in 1782 must be treated with caution – exactly in the way that it is unlikely that Trade organizations were notably more influential.

V

As compared to 1782, therefore, there had been – at most – a modest increase in the domestic input to foreign policy. Whatever Marxists may suppose, British foreign policy was not simply a manifestation of the interests of financiers and industrialists. Public opinion, though important on occasion, was usually 'managed' by figures within the political establishment. But had nothing changed? The changes were less than have been imagined but they did exist. Perhaps the most important development occurred at what Spanier calls his third or 'decision making' level. There was greater professionalism at all levels. In the old days, the Foreign Office had provided employment for young men of good family, many of whom would probably soon leave government service, take up their seats in Parliament, and apply themselves to running their country estates. In the meantime, they wanted to 'rag about in the office, to play practical jokes on each other, to smoke cigars in the Nursery, as the clerks' room was called, and to ogle the pretty girls who worked in the dressmaker's establishment in Fludyer Street, at the back of the Foreign Office building in Downing Street'. Such an atmosphere did not make for efficiency. Canning and Palmerston managed to increase staff and introduce a better sense of office management – although in Palmerston's case earning the resentment of the clerks.

The old Foreign Office building was unsuitable in every way and Palmerston waged a long campaign for a new one which would provide proper accommodation and suitably impressive reception rooms. When Palmerston returned to power in 1859 he found that his Conservative predecessors had decided to build a new Foreign Office and had commissioned a neo-Gothic design from Gilbert Scott. Palmerston vetoed Scott's plans; the rooms would be too dark for the clerks to see properly. But architecture is more than a matter of convenience; it involves a statement of values. Palmerston wanted the new building to be in the Classical style. Even in his popular days he obviously believed that there was something especially 'eighteenth century' about diplomacy. Further, by rejecting Gothic, he was implicitly identifying Britain with the Latin rather than with the Germanic world.

Although the relationship between Foreign Secretary, the diplomatic service and Foreign Office staff varied according to the personalities involved, a number of general features can be discerned. There were few experts attached to the Foreign Office. Most of the clerks were copyists whose work was judged according to its accuracy and legibility. Such a training was unlikely to encourage original thinking in the event of promotion. All decisions of importance were taken by the Foreign Secretary himself. Most Foreign Secretaries drafted their own despatches. Despite the improvements in the running of the Foreign Office, Britain's widening role in the world brought a corresponding increase in business, much of which fell upon the shoulders of one man. The job was the most onerous in the Cabinet. Palmerston normally spent eight hours a day at the Foreign Office – quite apart from the time he spent in the House of Commons. After Parliament rose, he returned to the Foreign Office and worked into the early hours, standing at a special desk designed to stop him falling asleep. Even though Palmerston possessed a remarkably robust constitution, sheer exhaustion must have been a factor in some errors of judgement.

Until the 1840s, pressures on the Foreign Secretary had been fewer because slow communications made it essential to delegate some decision making to ambassadors. Despatches took two or three days to reach Paris or Brussels, between ten days and a fortnight to reach Berlin, Vienna, Lisbon, Madrid or St Petersburg, about a month to reach Constantinople or Washington, three months to reach South America and six months to reach China. Thus, the Ambassador of Constantinople, a particularly sensitive post, had the authority to summon the Royal Navy to the Dardanelles, whilst the High Commissioner of the Far East could declare war on China on his own initiative. Figures such as John Ponsonby, Frederick Lamb, William Russell and Howard de Walden, occupants of key embassies over long periods, had a major influence upon foreign policy.

If crucial decisions were taken by a small number of men, it is important to consider what kind of pressures they had to work under. For some the pressure became too great. Whatever the immediate cause of Castlereagh's suicide, it would be foolish to ignore the possibility that the enormous work load of the Foreign Office may have been a factor. Yet we are concerned less with the personal effects of work than with its implications for the quality of decisions. There were times when pressure was greater than others and greatest of all in times of crisis, crises which could develop into major wars. In his article 'Crisis Management: History and Theory in International Conflict' (1979), P. S. Lauren declares:

> One of the most fascinating of all subjects in diplomatic history and international politics is that of crises. Crises break out suddenly, they threaten vital interests, demand quick decisions, place leaders under extreme stress, flood communication channels, raise enormous risks and uncertainties, and they dramatically approach the critical threshold between war and peace. In the last regard one of the questions that has occupied the attention of historians, political scientists, psychologists, generals and citizens alike is why some crises lead to war while others are somehow defused and resolved by successful management among the protagonists. What, they have asked, either allows or actually encourages statesmen to keep a crisis within certain bounds, to reach some kind of mutually acceptable settlement, and to prevent the eruption of armed conflict.[11]

With the exception of the Crimean War, the various crises between 1815 and 1865 did not produce major conflict between the Great Powers. On the whole British foreign policy had served Britain and Europe well. Certainly mistakes were made; perhaps the Crimean War could and should have been avoided or – more doubtfully – Britain should have been more resolute in response to the rise of Prussia. Yet in 1865 Britain was infinitely stronger than in 1782 and, in reality, the fundamentals of the European social and economic fabric were more secure. The situation was not perfect; some, at least, found it paradoxical that Britain should enjoy such power in world affairs whilst a significant part of her domestic population lived in poverty. Equally, it would be foolish to credit British foreign policy alone either for the influence Britain wielded or for the comparative peace enjoyed after 1815. Foreign policy and diplomacy were only the tip of an iceberg; without the strength of the navy, the resources of empire, or financial and industrial might, a man such as Palmerston would have been ridiculous. In some instances, objectives may have been achieved not because of, but despite foreign policy and diplomacy. But foreign policy was never so incompetent as to deny Britain its period of near world pre-eminence after 1815. For all his faults, Castlereagh played a major part in creating a European order which brought peace. Canning and Palmerston saw the wisdom of altering the letter of that order to maintain its spirit. By and large, these men believed in the virtues of traditional diplomacy and possessed a strong sense of the limitations of what they should attempt to achieve. Their ideal remained a peaceful and balanced Europe; according to Palmerston this doctrine was actually 'founded in the nature of man'. It was very eighteenth century, very Enlightenment. Perhaps the aspirations of eighteenth-century optimists and *Philosophes* were most completely realized in the European diplomacy of the period between 1815 and 1848.

Perhaps the success owed more to war weariness than to higher values. Of course, it could not go on for ever. Palmerston tried to compromise with the new forces, both at home and abroad; for a while he was successful. By the time of his death in 1865 events were slipping out of his control. Britain's prestige was still high and the country had great days still ahead of it. In particular, Britain's empire was to grow massively before the end of the century. But in the 1860s Britain was being pushed out of Europe and the very first signs of its slow economic decline became visible. If there was ever a 'British' period in the history of international relations, this must be dated 1815–1864, with a necessary preparatory build up during the Revolutionary and Napoleonic Wars.

At its best, this 'British' period was marked by a sense of realism, by a desire to settle disputes peacefully and by an ability to reconcile national interest with a concern for Europe as a whole. The contrast between the 'British' period and the ensuing 'German' period is striking. Bismarck made a cult of Blood and Iron, of unscrupulousness and national selfishness. British policy was sometimes guilty of these things, but there was something more which gave it a degree of decency lacking in later epochs. Castlereagh summed it up best: 'The Great Powers feel that they have not only a Common interest, but a Common duty to attend to.' The duty would be easier to fulfil if there was a growing congruence amongst the major countries of Europe. In 1782 Britain had something in common with the *ancien régime* states on the Continent, although it differed from them in important ways. In most respects, the gap between England and the Continent had narrowed by 1865. Communication was easier both physically and bureaucratically. Governments were entering into all kinds of agreements about postal services, telegraphs and railways, whilst the field of international law was widening. Britain's success encouraged other countries to emulate its policies and institutions. As Norman Stone shows in *Europe Transformed, 1878–1919*, (London, Fontana, 1983) the 1860s saw the triumph of the ideas of Classical Liberalism. Industrialization was spreading to the Continent. Everywhere the influence of the middle-classes was growing. Governments were making administration more efficient and parliaments reached their peak in public esteem. Such societies could not really be described as war mongering, and large sections of the population regarded all aspects of militarism with aversion. Despite the wars, the reversals and convulsions, the general trend appears progressive, a movement towards responsible, constitutional government. Men such as Palmerston, Napoleon III and Bismarck may seem devious and self-seeking, but they also had better qualities. They were models of propriety and prudence compared to many twentieth-century decision makers. In 1865 there was reason to hope that, despite their rivalries, the states of Europe and their leaders had enough in common to shun general, as distinct from local, war and to seek no more than adjustments – however dramatic these appeared to contemporaries – in the overall order which had served so well since 1815. The retreat from Liberalism and the return to Protectionism, with all that that implied, was still over a decade in the future.

The generally successful management of diplomatic crises clearly requires an explanation. Here, as Lauren points out, the traditional methods of diplomatic historians are inadequate. They stress the unique features of each crisis and describe it in detail; the method is descriptive rather than analytical. Yet it is dangerous to go too far in the opposite direction and produce models of crisis management which are 'scientific' to the extent of ignoring historical circumstances altogether. One factor of great importance was the time available to policy-makers to respond to developments elsewhere. The longer the time available, the better and more sensible the final decision was likely to be. As we have seen, steam power was significantly accelerating the pace of international relations; this was compounded by the invention of the telegraph even though the full effects of the transformation were revealed later than is sometimes supposed. It was not until 1850 that the first submarine cable was laid across the Channel. The incomplete telegraph networks between the capitals of Europe were largely responsible for the difference between the proposals drawn up in Vienna and those drawn up in Constantinople on the eve of the Crimean War.

The telegraph was a mixed blessing for foreign policy. It helped to make events elsewhere more accessible to newspaper readers. It diminished the degree of discretion left to ambassadors and reduced the chances of trouble being caused by misunderstandings or ill-advised personal initiatives. It is in the 1830s, the last decade before railways, telegraph and steam ships made a significant impact, that one can discern the final period when international relations were conducted at a 'natural' rate. There was plenty of time for reflection and reconsideration. The build up to diplomatic crises before the 1850s was gradual. Despite occasional panics, declaration of war out of the blue, sudden and unexpected attacks and angry responses leading to immediate hostilities were virtually impossible. Even at the worst of these crises, some aspects of diplomacy were functioning normally and unhurriedly – an atmosphere totally different from the obsessive concern with railway timetables and the despatch of telegrams which characterized the governments of Europe from the 1860s onwards. If the quality of decisions was not so good as it had been, this was due in part to the environment in which those decisions had been taken.

As noted earlier, the idea of 'compensation elsewhere' for the Great Powers, whether at the expense of the smaller European powers or of non-European peoples, although unfair to the victims, reduced the chances of war between the five Great Powers. By 1865 possible areas of 'compensation' had largely been used up in Europe – although Napoleon III foolishly supposed that they had not – but the concept had a longer career ahead of it elsewhere. In some ways, 1865 was not the end of an era at all. Many of the assumptions and patterns of behaviour which had dominated international relations since 1815 continued for another generation. Yet, if not the end of an era, it was the beginning of the end. The innate aggressiveness, the will to expand, which foreign policy-makers of the past had sometimes encouraged but usually restrained, would soon burst forth and destroy the achievement of the afterglow of the eighteenth century and all that it had stood for at its best.

Notes: Chapter 8

1 Reprinted in C. Emsley and I. Donnachie, *Collection of Nineteenth Century and Twentieth Century Documents*, The Open University, Course A301, 'War and Society', Unit 5, pp. 48–52.
2 T. Rogers (ed.) *Speeches of John Bright M.P.*, 2 vols. London, Macmillan, 1869, Vol. 2, p. 105.
3 R. Cobden, *The Political Writings of Richard Cobden*, 2 vols., London, William Ridgway, 1867, vol. 1, pp. 282–3.
4 A. H. Imlah, *Economic Elements of the Pax Britannica: Studies in British Foreign Trade in the Nineteenth Century*, Second edition, New York, Harvard University Press, 1969, Ch. VI, 'The Success of British Free Trade Policy', pp. 156–98.

5 J. A. Shumpeter, *Imperialism and Social Classes*, translated by H. Norden, Oxford, Basil Blackwell, 1951, pp. 117–25.
6 D. C. M. Platt, *Finance, Trade and Politics in British Foreign Policy 1815–1914*, Oxford, Clarendon Press, 1968, p. 353.
7 V. Cromwell, 'The Private Member of the House of Commons and Foreign Policy in the Nineteenth Century' in *Liber Memoralis, Sir Maurice Powicke*, Louvain, Editions Nauwelaerts, 1965, p. 218.
8 *Quarterly Review*, 1857, vol. 10, p. 252.
9 H. W. V. Temperley and L. M. Penson, *A Century of Diplomatic Blue Books 1814–1914*, Cambridge, Cambridge University Press, 1938, p. ix.
10 S. Lambert, *Bills and Acts. Legislative Procedure in Eighteenth Century England*, Cambridge, Cambridge University Press, 1971.
11 P. S. Lauren 'Crisis Management: History and Theory in International Conflict', *International History Review*, 1979, p. 543.

Bibliography

CHAPTER 1

Eighteenth Century Background
Useful, not excessively fanciful studies, whose conclusions may be applied to the eighteenth century, include Watson, A., *Diplomacy* (London: Methuen, 1982); Nicolson, H., *Diplomacy* (Second Edition, London: Oxford University Press, 1950); Spanier, J., *Games Nations Play: Analyzing International Politics* (London: Nelson, 1972). Perhaps the best balance between 'theory' and 'history' is to be found in Hinsley, F. H., *Power and the Pursuit of Peace: Theory and Practice in the History of Relations between States* (Cambridge: Cambridge University Press, 1963).

For contemporary attitudes to international relations, see Hinsley, op. cit.; Anderson, M. S., 'Eighteenth-Century Theories of the Balance of Power', in R. Hatton and M. S. Anderson, (eds) *Studies in Diplomatic History: Essays in Memory of David Bayne Horn* (London: Longman, 1970); Gullick, E. V., *Europe's Classical Balance of Power* (New York: Cornell University Press, 1955); Meineke, F., *Machiavellism* (London: Routledge & Kegan Paul, 1957). On specifically British aspects, see Langford, P., *The Eighteenth Century, 1688–1815, Modern British Foreign Policy* (London: A & C Black, 1976); Ward, A. and Gooch, G. P., (eds) *The Cambridge History of British Foreign Policy*, 3 Vols. (Cambridge: Cambridge University Press, 1922–3); Horn, D. B., *Great Britain and Europe in the Eighteenth Century* (Oxford: Clarendon Press, 1967); Williams, J. B., *British Commercial Policy and Trade Expansion, 1750–1850* (Oxford: Clarendon Press, 1972); Imlah, A. H., *Economic Elements in the Pax Britannica* (Cambridge, Mass.: Harvard University Press, 1958).

For 'organizational aspects' see Horn, D. B., *The British Diplomatic Service, 1689–1789* (Oxford: Clarendon Press, 1961); Jones, R., *The Nineteenth-Century Foreign Office: An Administrative History* (London: Weidenfeld & Nicolson, 1971); Gibbs, G. C., 'Laying treaties before Parliament in the eighteenth century', in Hatton, R. and Anderson, M. S., *Studies in Diplomatic History*, op. cit.

CHAPTER 2

The End of the American War and its Aftermath
Military aspects of the closing stages of the war are covered in Mackesy, P., *The War for America 1775–83* (London: Longman, 1964). The fullest

study of diplomacy of the American war is in Bemis, S. F., *The Diplomacy of the American Revolution: the Foundations of American Diplomacy* (Bloomington, Indiana: Indiana University Press, 1967). For attitudes of European powers to Britain, see Madariaga, de I., *Britain, Russia and the Armed Neutrality of 1780* (London: Hollis & Carter, 1962), Pinon, R., 'Vergennes et la grande lutte contre l'Angleterre 1774–1789', *Revue d'histoire diplomatique*, vol. 43 (1929), pp. 37–64; Conn, S., *Gibraltar in British Diplomacy in the Eighteenth Century* (New Haven: Yale University Press, 1942); Coquelle, P., *L'alliance franco-hollandaise contre l'Angleterre 1735–1788* (Paris: Plon-Nourrit et cie, 1902). For the peace negotiations, see Morris, R. B., *The Peacemakers* (New York: Cornell University Press, 1965); Harlow V. T., *The Founding of the Second British Empire 1763–1793* (London: Longman, Green & Co., 1952); Woodburn, J. A., 'Benjamin Franklin and the peace treaty of 1783', *Indiana Historical Magazine*, vol. 30 (1934), pp. 223–37; Robinson, S., 'Richard Oswald, peacemaker', *Ayrshire Archeological and Natural History Collection*, 2nd series, vol. III (1955), pp. 119–32. The most recent biography of Fox is Derry, J. W., *Charles James Fox* (London: Batsford, 1972). Shelburne's role as a speculative thinker is considered in Brown, P., *The Chathamites: A Study in the Relationship between Personalities and Ideas in the Second Half of the Eighteenth Century* (London: Macmillan, 1967). The role of the peace proposals in the political developments of 1782–4 is examined in Norris, J., *Shelburne and Reform* (London: Macmillan, 1963), and in Cannon, J., *The Fox-North Coalition* (Cambridge: Cambridge University Press, 1969).

Foreign Policy 1783–1786

The choice of Carmarthen as Foreign Secretary is explained in Ehrman, J., *The Younger Pitt, the Years of Acclaim* (London: Constable, 1969) which also has admirable coverage of the overall development of British foreign policy in the 1780s. See also Browning, O., (ed.) *The Political Memoranda of Francis, Fifth Duke of Leeds* (London: Camden Society, 1884). Useful, though slightly dated, analysis of Pitt's policy during these years is to be found in Clapham, J. H., 'Pitt's first decade, 1783–1792', in Ward, A., and Gooch, G. P., *The Cambridge History of British Foreign Policy*, Vol. 1, 1783–1815 (Cambridge: Cambridge University Press, 1922). See also Anderson, M. S., 'European diplomatic relations, 1763–1790', in *New Cambridge Modern History*, vol. 8 (Cambridge: Cambridge University Press, 1965). See also Ritcheson, C. R., *Aftermath of Revolution: British Policy towards the United States 1783–1795* (Dallas, Texas: Southern Methodist University Press, 1969).

Commercial Treaties

For general consideration of Britain's trading position see Parry, J. H., *Trade and Dominion: the European Overseas Empires in the Eighteenth Century* (London: Weidenfeld & Nicolson, 1966) and Williams, J. B., *British Commercial Policy and Trade Expansion 1750–1850* (Oxford: Clarendon Press, 1972). For commercial treaties, see especially Ehrman, J.,

The British Government and Commercial Negotiations with Europe 1783–93 (Cambridge: Cambridge University Press, 1962); Holland Rose, J., 'The Franco-British Commercial treaty of 1786', *English Historical Review*, vol. XXIII (1908), pp. 709–24; Bourden, W., 'The English manufacturers and the commercial treaty of 1786 with France', *American Historical Review*, vol. 39 (1924), pp. 665–74; Brace, S., 'The Anglo-French Treaty of Commerce of 1786: a reappraisal', *Historian* vol. 9 (1947), pp. 151–62; Henderson, W. O., 'The Anglo-French Commercial Treaty of 1786', *Economic History Review*, 2nd series, vol. 10 (1957), pp. 104–12.

The Dutch Crisis
The most interesting modern treatment is in Cobban, A., *Ambassadors and Secret Agents: The Diplomacy of the First Earl of Malmesbury at the Hague* (London: Jonathan Cape, 1954). Related material is to be found in Cobban, A., 'British Secret Service in France 1784–92', *English Historical Review*, vol. LXIX (1954), pp. 226–61. Earlier studies include Holland Rose, J., 'Great Britain and the Dutch question in 1787–1788', *American Historical Review*, vol. 14 (1909), pp. 262–83; Holland Rose, J., 'The missions of William Grenville to the Hague and Versailles in 1787', *English Historical Review*, vol. XXIV (1909), pp. 278–95; Adams, E. D., *The Influence of Grenville on Pitt's Foreign Policy 1787–1798* (Washington D.C.: Carnegie Institute, 1904). For the role of Prussia in the Dutch crisis, see Wittichen, F. K., *Preussen und England in der europaischen Politik, 1785–1788* (Heidelberg: C. Winter, 1902); Lodge, R., *Great Britain and Prussia in the Eighteenth Century* (Oxford: Clarendon Press, 1923). For the Austrian dimension, see Salomon, S., 'England und der deutsche Furstenbund von 1785', *Hist. Vierteljahrsschrift*, 6 (1903), pp. 221–42.

Nootka Sound and Ochakov Crises
For Nootka Sound, see Norris, J. M., 'The policy of the English cabinet in the Nootka Crisis, *English Historical Review*, vol. LXX (1955), pp. 563–80; Manning, W. R., *The Nootka Sound Controversy* (Washington D.C.: American Historical Association, 1905); Cullet-Bois, R. R., 'La Controversia del Nootka Sound', *Humanidades*, vol. 20 (1930), pp. 341–74; Mills, L., 'The real significance of the Nootka Sound Incident, *Canadian Historical Review*, vol. 6 (1925), pp. 110–25. For the wider context, see de Parrel, C., 'Pitt et l'Espagne', *Revue de l'histoire Diplomatique*, vol. 64 (1950), pp. 58–98; Lynch, J., 'British Policy and Spanish America 1783–1808', *Journal of Latin American Studies* (1969), pp. 1–30; Cook, W. L., *Flood Tide of Empire: Spain and the Pacific Northwest 1543–1819* (Newhaven: Yale University Press, 1973); Williams, G., *The British Search for the North West Passage in the Eighteenth Century* (London: Longman, 1962). For the Ochakov crisis, see especially, Ehrman, J., 'The Younger Pitt and the Ochakov Affair', *History Today*, vol. 9 (1959), pp. 462–72; Webb, P. L. C., 'Sea power in the Ochakov Affair', *International History Review*, vol. 2 (1980), pp. 13–33. See also Ehrman, J., *The Younger Pitt: the Reluctant Transition*

(London: Constable, 1983). This second volume of Ehrman's biography of Pitt also covers the outbreak of the French wars and contains an excellent bibliography. For the wider context of relations with Russia, see Anderson, M. S., *The Eastern Question, 1774–1923* (London: Macmillan, 1966); Gerhard, D., *England und der Aufstieg Russlands* (Munich and Berlin: R. Oldenbourg, 1933).

Relations with France 1789–1793
See Ehrman, J., *Pitt*, Vol. 2, op. cit.; Ward, A. and Gooch, G. P., *Cambridge History of British Foreign Policy*, Vol. 1, op. cit., Stoker, J. T., *William Pitt et la Révolution française 1789–1793* (Paris: Librairie du Recueil Sivey, 1935); Chardon, A. H., 'Fox et la Révolution française (Paris: Bossard, 1918); Baker, E., 'Edmund Burke et la Révolution française', *Revue philosophique*, vol. 128 (1939), pp. 129–60; Laprade, W. T., *England and the French Revolution 1789–1797* (Baltimore, Maryland: John Hopkins University Press, 1909); Dechamps, J., *Les Îles Britanniques et la Révolution française 1789–1803* (Bruxelles: Renaissance du Livre, 1949); Holland Rose, J., 'The Compte d'Artois and Pitt in December 1789', *English Historical Review*, vol. XXX (1915), pp. 322–4.
    For the outbreak of hostilities, see Fenn, P. T., *Anglo-French Diplomacy in 1792–3: A Study in the Psychology of Revolution* (New Haven: Concord University Press, 1925); Holland Rose, J., 'Documents relating to the rupture with France in 1793', *English Historical Review*, vol. XXVII (1912), pp. 117–23 and pp. 324–30; Holland Rose, J., 'Protest of Talleyrand against his expulsion from England, 1st January 1793', *English Historical Review*, vol. XXI (1906), pp. 330–2; Williams, D., 'The Missions of David Williams and James Tilly Matthews to England, 1793', *English Historical Review*, vol. LIII (1938), pp. 651–68.

The War of the First Coalition and Attempts at Peace 1793–97
For military and naval aspects of the opening stages of the war, see Webb, P. L. C., 'The rebuilding and repair of the fleet 1783–1793', *Bulletin of the Institute of Historical Research*, vol. 50 (1977), pp. 194–209; Burne, A. H., *The Noble Duke of York: the Military Life of Frederick Duke of York and Albany* (London: Staples Press, 1949); Holland Rose, J., 'Pitt and the campaign of 1793 in Flanders', *English Historical Review*, vol. XXIX (1909), pp. 744–9. The classic survey is Mahan, A. T., *The Influence of Seapower on the French Revolution and Empire*, 2 Vols (London: Sampson & Low, 1891–6). See also, Albion, R. G., *Forests and Seapower: The Timber Problem of the Royal Navy, 1652–1862* (Cambridge, Mass.: Harvard University Press, 1926).
    For relations with Russia, see Steinberg, E., 'The making of an Anglo-Russian alliance', *Russian Review*, vol. I (1945), pp. 45–9; on the Anglo-Russian convention of 1793, Lobanov-Rotovsky, A. A., *Russia and Europe 1789–1815* (Durham, N. Carolina: Duke University Press, 1947); Lord, R. H., *The Second Partition of Poland: A Study in Diplomatic*

History (Cambridge, Mass.: Harvard University Press, 1916); Dennis, A. L. P., *Eastern Problems at the Close of the Eighteenth Century* (Cambridge, Mass.: Harvard University Press, 1901). On British subsidies, see Sherwig, J. M., *Guineas and Gunpowder: British Foreign Aid in the Wars with France 1793–1815* (Cambridge, Mass.: Harvard University Press, 1969). On British contacts with French royalists, see Mitchell, H., *The Underground War against Revolutionary France: The Missions of William Wickham 1794–1800* (Oxford: Clarendon Press, 1965); Gabory, E., *L'Angleterre et la Vendée*, 2 Vols (Paris: Perrin et Cie., 1930–1); Hutt, M., 'Spies in France 1793–1808' *History Today*, vol. 12 (1962), pp. 158–67. See also Godechot, J., *La Grande Nation: l'Expansion Révolutionnaire de la France dans le Monde de 1789 à 1799*, 2 Vols (Paris: Aubier, 1956); Fryer, W. R., *Republic or Restoration in France 1794–7* (Manchester: Manchester University Press, 1965); Biro, S. S., *The German Policy of Revolutionary France: A study in French Diplomacy during the War of the First Coalition 1792–7*, 2 Vols (Cambridge, Mass.: Harvard University Press, 1957); Guyot, R., *Le directoire et la paix de l'Europe; des traités de Bâle à la deuxième coalition* (Paris: F. Alcan, 1901); Sorel, A., 'Les Négotiations avec l'Angleterre en 1796', *Journal des Savants* (1902), pp. 121–34; Ballot, C., *Les Négotiations de Lille* (1797, Paris: E. Cornely et Cie., 1910).

The Second Coalition
See Sherwig, J. M., 'Lord Grenville's plan for a concert of Europe 1797–1799', *Journal of Modern History*, vol 34 (1962), pp. 284–93; Bonnard, G., 'The invasion of Switzerland and English public opinion, January–April 1798' *English Studies* (February 1940), pp. 1–26; Rodger, A. B., *The War of the Second Coalition, 1798–1801* (Oxford: Clarendon Press, 1964); Glover, R., 'Arms and the British diplomat in the French revolutionary era', *Journal of Modern History*, vol. 29 (1957), pp. 199–212; Perkins, B., *The First Rapprochement: England and the United States 1795–1805* (Philadelphia: University of Pennsylvania Press, 1955); Waliszewski, K., *Paul the First, the Son of Catherine the Great* (London: William Heinemann, 1913); Piechowiak, A. B., 'The Anglo–Russian expedition to Holland in 1799', *Slavonic and Eastern European Review*, vol 41 (1962–3), pp. 182–95; Ford, G. S., *Hanover and Prussia, 1795–1803: A Study in Neutrality* (New York: Columbia College Press, 1903); Elliott, D. C., 'The Grenville Mission to Berlin, 1799', *Huntington Library Quarterly*, vol. 18 (1954–5), pp. 129–46.

CHAPTER 3

The Collapse of the Second Coalition and the Peace of Amiens
For the League of Armed Neutrality, see Richmond, A. A., 'Napoleon and the armed neutrality of 1800', *Journal of the Royal United Services Institute*, vol. 14 (1959), pp. 186–94. A variety of works are devoted to

the Peace of Amiens: Bowman, H. M., 'Preliminary stages of the peace of Amiens', *University of Toronto Studies in History and Economics*, vol. I (1901), pp. 77–105; Gill, C., 'The relations between England and France in 1802', *English Historical Review*, vol. XXIV (1909), pp. 61–78; Sorel, A., 'Comment la paix d'Amiens fut appliquée', *Séances Trav. Acad. Sci. mor. pol.*, n.s. 59 (1903), pp. 670–96; Gauton, L., *Essai sur les antécédents du blocus continental. La rupture de la paix d'Amiens 1802–3* (Paris: F. Alcan, 1903); Dechamps, J., 'La rupture de la paix d'Amiens', *Revue des études napoléoniennes*, vol. 44 (1939), pp. 172–207; Beeley, H., 'A project of alliance with Russia in 1802', *English Historical Review*, vol. XLI (1934), pp. 497–502. Other material is found in more general works, such as Driault, J. E., *Napoléon et l'Europe*, 5 Vols (Paris: F. Alcan, 1910–27), Vol. 1, *La Politique extérieure du Premier Consul 1800–1803*; Ziegler, P., *Addington*, (London: Collins, 1965); Yonge, C. D., *The Life and Administration of Robert Banks, 2nd Earl of Liverpool*, 3 Vols (London: Macmillan & Co., 1868).

The War of the Third Coalition 1803–6
Although Ehrman's study of Pitt the Younger is not yet complete, useful material for this period can be found in Holland Rose, J., *William Pitt and the National Revival* (London: G. Bell & Sons, 1911); Holland Rose, J., *Napoleonic Studies* (London: G. Bell & Sons, 1904), especially 'Pitt's plans for the settlement of Europe'; Mackesy, P., *The War in the Mediterranean 1803–1810* (London: Longman, Green & Co., 1957); Coquelle, P., *Napoleon and England 1803–1813* (English edition by G. D. Knox) (London: G. Bell & Sons, 1904); Driault, J. E., op. cit., Vol. 2, *Austerlitz: La Fin du Saint-Empire*; Glover, R., *Britain at Bay: Defence against Napoleon 1803–1814* (London: George Allen & Unwin, 1973); Mowat, R. B., *The Diplomacy of Napoleon* (London: E. Arnold & Co., 1924); Ebbinghaus, T., *Napoleon, England und die Presse 1800–1813* (Munich and Berlin: R. Oldenbourg, 1914) Guyot, R., 'Pitt et Napóleon, d'après M. J. Holland Rose', *Revue des études napoléoniennes*, vol. 6 (1914), pp. 41–50; Wheeler, H. F. B., and Broadley, A. M., *Napoleon and the Invasion of England: The Story of the Great Terror*, 2 Vols (London: John Lane, 1907); Bryant, A., *The Years of Endurance* (London: Collins, 1942).

The abortive peace negotiations of 1806 are fully examined in Butterfield, H., *Charles James Fox and Napoleon: The Peace Negotiations of 1806* (London: Athlone Press, 1962). See also Lloyd, E. M., 'The Anglo–French peace negotiations of 1806', *English Historical Review*, vol. XXVII (1912), pp. 753–4; Perry, J. W., *Charles James Fox* (London: Batsford, 1972); Chardon, A. H., *Fox et la Révolution française* (Paris: Bossard, 1918).

The Continental System, The Orders in Council and their Economic Implications
The classic study is Hecksher, E. F., *The Continental System* (Oxford: Clarendon Press, 1922). Also extremely valuable is Crouzet, F., *Le Blocus*

continental et l'économie britannique, 2 Vols (Paris: Presses Universitaires de France, 1958). Other works include Heymann, E., *Napoleon und die Grossen Machte 1806* (Berlin and Leipzig: W. Rothschild, 1910); Parkingson, C. N., (ed.) *The Trade Winds: A Study in British Overseas Trade during the French Wars 1793–1815* (London: George Allen & Unwin, 1948); Parry, J. H., *Trade and Dominion* (London: Weidenfeld & Nicolson, 1966); Holland Rose, J., 'England's commercial struggle with Napoleon', in F. A. Kirkpatrick, (ed.) *Lectures on the History of the Nineteenth Century* (Cambridge: Cambridge University Press, 1904), pp. 59–78. Biographical information may be found in Rollo, P. V. J., *George Canning* (London: Macmillan & Co., 1965); Marshall, D., *The Rise of George Canning* (London: Longman & Co., 1938); Temperley, H. W. V., *Life of Canning* (London: James Finch & Co., 1905); Collyer, C., 'Canning and the Napoleonic Wars', *History Today*, vol. 11 (1961), pp. 227–31.

For relations with Scandinavia, see Carr, R., 'Gustavus IV and the British government 1804–9;, *English Historical Review*, vol. LX (1945), pp. 36–66; Møller, E., *England øg Danmark-Norge* (Copenhagen: Karl Schonberg Forlag, 1910–12); Reddaway, W. F., 'Canning and the Baltic in 1807', *Baltic Countries*, Vol. 2 (1936), pp. 13–23; Ryan, A. N., 'The Defence of British trade with the Baltic', *English Historical Review*, vol. LXXIV (1959),pp. 443–6. For Russia, see Driault, J. E., op. cit., Vol. 3, *Tilsit: France et Russie sous le premier empire. La question de Pologne 1806–9*, Vol. 4, *Le Grand Empire, 1809–1812*; Holland Rose, J., 'A British agent at Tilsit', *English Historical Review*, vol. XVI (1901), pp. 712–18. Anderson, M. S., 'The Continental System and Russo–British relations during the Napoleonic Wars', in K. Bourne and D. C. Watt, (eds), *Studies in International History* (London: Longman, 1967). For Turkey and the Middle East, see Ghorbal, S., *The Beginnings of the Egyptian Question and the Rise of Mehemet Ali* (London: G. Routledge & Sons, 1928); D'Ivray, J. D., 'La première occupation anglaise en Egypte 1807', *Revue des études napoléoniennes*, vol. 19 (1922), pp. 110–18; Marriott, J. A. R., 'The Egyptian factor in European diplomacy, 1798–1898',*Edinburgh Review*, vol. 240 (1924), pp. 32–50; Shupp, P. F., *The European Powers and the Near Eastern Question 1806–7* (New York: Columbia University Press, 1931); Holland Rose, J., 'Napoleon and sea power', *Cambridge Historical Journal*, vol. 1 (1923–5), pp. 138–57. A very important general work is Anderson, M. S., *The Eastern Question* (London: Macmillan, 1966).

Spain and the Spanish Empire

On the military side, the most important work is Glover, M., *The Peninsular War 1807–1814* (London and Newton Abbot: David & Charles, 1974). See also, (anon) 'Miranda and the British Admiralty, 1804–6',*American Historical Review*, vol. 6 (1901), pp. 508–30; Crawley, C. W., 'French and English influence in the Cortes of Cadiz, 1810–14', *Cambridge Historical Journal*, vol. 6 (1939), pp. 176–208; Rydyard, J., 'British Mediation between Spain and her colonies, 1811–13', *Hispanic*

American Historical Review, vol. 21 (1941), pp. 29–50. Holland Rose, J., 'Canning and the Spanish patriots in 1808', *American Historical Review*, vol. 12 (1907), pp. 39–52; Robertson, W. S., 'The juntas of 1808 and the Spanish colonies', *English Historical Review*, vol. XXXI (1916), pp. 573–85.

The United States and the War of 1812

The most important works are Horsman, R., *The Causes of the War of 1812* (Philadelphia: University of Pennsylvania Press, 1961) and Horsman, R., *The War of 1812* (London: Eyre & Spottiswoode, 1969). Other works include Beirne, F., *The War of 1812* (New York: E. P. Dutton, 1948); Willson, B., (pseudonym) *America's Ambassadors to England 1785–1928* (London: Dickson, 1928). Perkins, B., 'George Canning, Great Britain and the United States, 1807–9', *American Historical Review*, vol. 63 (1957), pp. 279–95; Updyke, F. A., *The Diplomacy of The War of 1812* (Baltimore, Maryland: John Hopkins Press, 1915); Mills, D., 'The Duke of Wellington and the peace negotiations at Ghent in 1814', *Canadian Historical Review*, vol. 2 (1921), pp. 19–32; Mahan, A. T., 'The negotiations at Ghent in 1814', *American Historical Review*, vol. 11 (1906), pp. 68–87.

The Fourth Coalition and the Peace

This period remains dominated by the work of Sir Charles Webster. Webster, C. K., *The Foreign Policy of Castlereagh 1812–15: Britain and the Reconstruction of Europe* (London: G. Bell & Sons, 1921); Phillips, W. A., *The Confederation of Europe. A Study of the European Alliance 1813–23* (London: Longman, Green & Co., 1914), is rather old fashioned but still worth reading. Kissinger, H. A., *A World Restored: Metternich, Castlereagh and the Problems of Peace* (London: Weidenfeld & Nicolson, 1957), is admirable though perhaps too uncritical of Metternich. Important biographical information may be found in Gray, D., *Spencer Percival: The Evangelical Prime Minister, 1762–1812* (Manchester: Manchester University Press, 1963); Bartlett, C. J., *Castlereagh* (London: Macmillan, 1966). Robson, W. H., 'New Light on Lord Castlereagh's Diplomacy', *Journal of Modern History*, vol. 3 (1931), pp. 198–218, is disappointing.

More specific studies include Stearns, J., *The Role of Metternich in Undermining Napoleon* (Urbana, Illinois: University of Illinois Press, 1948); Buckland, C. S., *Metternich and the British Government from 1809–1813* (London: Macmillan & Co., 1932). See also, Buckland, C. S., *Fr. von. Gentz's Relations with the British Government 1809–12* (London: Macmillan & Co., 1933).

For Italy, see (anon) 'Naples and Napoleon', *Edinburgh Review*, vol. 202 (1905), pp. 456–73; Lackland, M. M., 'Lord William Bentinck in Sicily 1811–12', *English Historical Review*, vol. XLII (1927), pp. 371–96; Lackland, M. M., 'The failure of the constitutional experiment in Sicily 1813–14', *English Historical Review*, vol. XLI (1926), pp.

210–35; Wiskemann, E., 'Lord William Bentinck: precursor of the Risorgimento', *History Today*, vol. 1 (1952), pp. 492–9; Crawley, C. W., 'England and the Sicilian constitution of 1812', *English Historical Review*, vol. LV (1940), pp. 251–74; Rosselli, J., *Lord William Bentinck and the British Occupation of Sicily 1811–1814* (Cambridge: Cambridge University Press, 1956). For the Low Countries, see Aspinall, A., 'The Rupture of the Orange Marriage Negotiations', *History*, vol. 34 (1949), pp. 44–60; Renier, G. J., *Great Britain and the Establishment of the Kingdom of the Netherlands 1813–1815* (London: G. Allen & Unwin, 1930). For Russia, see Anderson, M. S., 'British public opinion and the Russian campaign of 1812', *Slavonic and Eastern European Review*, vol. 34 (1956), pp. 408–25; Barnes, G. M., 'Alexander I's visit, June 1814', *Cornhill Magazine*, vol. 159 (June, 1939), pp. 776–93. For a French view, see Driault, J. E., op. cit., Vol. 5, *La chute de l'empire: la légende de Napoléon 1812–1815*.

The diplomatic aspects of the closing stages of the war are covered in Escoffier, M., 'Les Instructions de Lord Castlereagh, plénipotentiaire britannique au congrès de Châtillon, 1813', *Revue des études napoléoniennes*, vol. 5 (1914), pp. 85–99; Scott, F. D., *Bernadotte and the Fall of Napoleon* (Cambridge, Mass.: Harvard University Press, 1939). For the peace treaties, see especially Webster, C. K., *The Congress of Vienna*, new edition (London: G. Bell & Sons, 1934) and Nicolson, H., *The Congress of Vienna: A Study in Allied Unity 1815–1818* (London: Constable & Co., 1945); Craemer, A. R., 'Peace 1814', *Current History*, 1949, pp. 427–31; Peterson, S., 'Political inequality at the Congress of Vienna', *Political Science Quarterly*, vol. 60 (1945), pp. 532–54; Marcham, F. G., 'Castlereagh: the balance of power in Europe', *Current History*, vol. 27 (1954), pp. 337–41; Ganière, P., 'Pourquoi en 1815, Napoléon s'est il rendu aux Anglais', *Historia*, 1957, pp. 59–65.

CHAPTER 4

The Castlereagh Era 1815–22

The most important study is Webster, C. K., *The Foreign Policy of Castlereagh 1815–22: Britain and the European Alliance* (London: G. Bell & Sons, 1925). Other valuable studies by Webster include 'Castlereagh and the Spanish colonies', *English Historical Review*, vol. XXVII (1912), pp. 78–95 and vol. XXX (1915), pp. 631–45; *Castlereagh and the Independence of Latin America 1812–30: Select Documents*, 2 Vols (London: Ibero-American Institute of Great Britain, 1938); 'Castlereagh et le système du congrès 1814–1822' *Revue des études napoléoniennes*, Vol. 15 (1919), pp. 70–82. See also, *Cambridge History of British Foreign Policy*, op. cit., Vol. 2; Kissinger, H., op. cit.; Phillips, W., op. cit.; Schenk, H. G., *The Aftermath of the Napoleonic Wars: The Concert of Europe, an Experiment* (London: Kegan Paul, Trench, Trubner & Co., 1947) (provocative but neglects conventional diplomatic material);

Pirenne, J. H., *La Sainte Alliance 1815–1818*, 2 Vols (Neuchatel: Editions de la Baçonniere, 1946–9), (emphasis on Anglo-Russian rivalry); Bourquin, M., *Historie de la Sainte Alliance* (Geneva: Georg, 1954). For a more thematic approach, see Holbraad, C., *The Concert of Europe: A Study in German and British International Theory 1815–1914* (London: Longman, 1970).

More specific studies include Lescott, T. H. S., 'The beginnings of the Anglo-French alliance', *Contemporary Review*, vol. 109 (1916), pp. 732–9; Dechamps, J., *Chateaubriand en Angleterre* (Paris: Editions Albert, 1934); Daudet, E., *L'ambassade du duc Deçazes en Angleterre, 1820–21* (Paris: Plon-Nourrit et Cie., 1910); Wemyss, A., 'L'Angleterre et la terreur blanche de 1815 dans le Midi', *Annales du Midi*, vol. 72 (1961), pp. 287–310; Woodward, E. L., 'Les caractères generaux des relations franco-anglaises', *Revue d'histoire moderne*, vol. 13 (1938), pp. 110–25, Boyce, M., *The Diplomatic Relations of England with the Quadruple Alliance 1815–30* (Iowa City: The University Press, 1918); Gleason, J. H., *The Genesis of Russophobia in Great Britain: A Study of the Interaction of Policy and Opinion* (Cambridge, Mass.: Harvard University Press, 1950); Crawley, C. W., 'Anglo-Russian relations 1815–1840', *Cambridge Historical Journal*, vol. 3 (1929), pp. 47–73; Robinson, L. G. (ed.), *Letters of Dorothea, Princess de Lieven, during her Residence in London 1812–34* (London: Longman & Co., 1902); Bindoff, S. T., 'Great Britain and the Scheldt 1814–1839', *Bulletin of Institute of Historical Research*, vol. 12 (1934), pp. 60–3; Wertheim, B., *Britain and Spain Since 1700: The lost British Policy* (London: United Editorial, 1938).

For relations with the United States, see Tatum, E. H., *The United States and Europe 1815–23: A Study in the Background of The Monroe Doctrine* (Berkeley, California: University of California Press, 1936); Lawson, L. A., *The Relation of British Policy to the Declaration of the Monroe Doctrine* (New York: Columbia University Press, 1951); Perkins, B., *Castlereagh and Adams: England and the United States 1812–23* (Berkeley, California: University of California Press, 1964); Griffin, C. C., *The United States and The Disruption of the Spanish Empire 1810–22: A History of the Relations of the United States with Spain and with the Rebels* (New York: Columbia University Press, 1937); Goebel, D. B., 'British-American Rivalry in the Chilean Trade 1817–20', *Journal of Economic History*, vol. 2 (1942), pp. 190–202; Kaufmann, W. W., *British Policy and the Independence of Latin America, 1804–24* (New Haven: Yale University Press, 1951); Perkins, D., 'Europe, Spanish America and the Monroe Doctrine', *American Historical Review*, vol. 27 (1922), pp. 207–18; Rippy, J. F., *Rivalry of the United States and Great Britain over Latin America 1808–1830* (Baltimore, Maryland: John Hopkins Press).

The Canning Era
The period of Canning's tenure of the Foreign Office is covered mainly in the works of Temperley, H. W. V. – notably Temperley, H. W. V., *The Foreign Policy of Canning 1822–27: England, The Neo–Holy Alliance and*

the New World (London: George Bell & Sons, 1925). See also, Temperley, H. W. V., 'Canning and the conferences of the four allied governments at Paris 1823–26', *American Historical Review*, vol. 30 (1925), pp. 16–43; 'The Later Policy of George Canning', *American Historical Review*, vol. 11 (1906) pp. 779–97, 'British secret diplomacy from Canning to Grey', *Cambridge Historical Journal*, vol. 6 (1938), pp. 1–32. For the continuity between Castlereagh and Canning, see Green, J. S. S., 'Wellington and the Congress of Verona, 1822', *English Historical Review*, vol. XXXV (1920), pp. 200–11; Lackland, H. M., 'Wellington at Verona' *English Historical Review*, vol. XXXV (1920), pp. 374–80; Nichols, I. C., 'The Eastern Question and the Vienna Conference, 1822', *Journal of Central European Affairs*, vol. 21 (1961), pp. 53–66. For a recent biography of Canning, see Hinde, W., *George Canning* (London: Collins, 1973).

For Canning and the Americas, see Perkins, D., *The Monroe Doctrine 1823–26* (Baltimore, Maryland: John Hopkins Press, 1927); Perkins, D., *The Monroe Doctrine 1826–7* (Baltimore, Maryland: John Hopkins Press, 1933); Pratt, E. J., 'Anglo-American commercial and political rivalry in the Plata 1820–1830', *Hispanic American Historical Review*, vol. 11 (1931), pp. 302–35; Swan, J. E., 'Canning: the new world: the old', *Current History*, vol. 27 (1954), pp. 342–6; Ferns, H. S., *Britain and Argentina in the Nineteenth Century* (Oxford: Clarendon Press, 1960); Lanning, J. T., 'Great Britain and Spanish recognition of the Hispano-American states', *Hispanic American Historical Review*, vol. 10 (1930), pp. 429–56.

For the affairs of Portugal, see Cowell, C. M., 'The attitude of the British government to the Portuguese Revolution of 1826–34', *Bulletin of the Institute of Historical Research*, vol. 5 (1928), pp. 114–17. For the Greek Revolt and associated questions, see Penn, V., 'Philhellenism in Europe 1821–28', *Slavonic Review*, vol. 16 (1938); pp. 638–53; Lang, D. M., 'The Decembrist Conspiracy through British eyes', *American Slavic and East European Review*, vol. 8 (1949), pp. 262–74; Graves, P. P., *Briton and Turk* (London: Hutchinson & Co., 1941); Marlowe, J., *Anglo-Egyptian Relations 1800–1853* (London: Cresset Press, 1954); Zegger, R. E., 'Greek Independence and the London committee', *History Today*, vol. 20 (1970), pp. 236–45; Bailey, F. E., *British Policy and the Turkish Reform Movement: A Study in Anglo Turkish Relations 1826–53*, (Cambridge, Mass.: Harvard University Press, 1942). Dakin, D., *British and American Philhellenes During the War of Greek Independence* (Thessalonika: Institute for Balkan Studies, 1955); Crawley, C. W., *The Question of Greek Independence, A Study in British Policy in the Near East 1821–1833* (Cambridge: Cambridge University Press, 1930).

1827–30
See Gordon, Sir A., *The Earl of Aberdeen* (London: Sampson, Low & Co., 1893); Aberdeen, Earl of, *Correspondence of Lord Aberdeen and Princess Lieven* (London: Cambden Society, 3rd Series, Nos 60 and 62, 1938–9); Copleston, E. (ed.), *Letters from Dudley* (London: John Murray, 1840); Morgan, G., *Anglo-Russian Rivalry in Central Asia* (London: Cass,

1981); Ingram, E., *The Beginning of The Great Game in Asia 1828–34* (Oxford: Clarendon Press, 1978; Fleming, D., *John Capodistrias and the Conference of London 1828–31* (Thessalonika: Institute for Balkan Studies, 1970), Khan, M. A., 'The Russophobia óf Lord Ellenborough 1828–30', *Asiatic Society, Pakistan Journal*, vol. VIII (1963), pp. 73–82; Beales, A. C. F., 'Historical Revision LXVIII: Wellington and Louis-Philippe, 1830', *History*, vol. XVIII (1930), pp. 352–56.

CHAPTER 5

1830–48
The Whig Government 1830–41
The most important work on this period remains Webster, C. K., *The Foreign Policy of Palmerston, 1830–41: Britain, The Liberal Movement and the Eastern Question*, 2 Vols (London: G. Bell & Sons, 1951). Additional information may be found in Bourne, K., *Palmerston: The Early Years 1784–1841* (London: Allen Lane, 1982); Ridley, J., *Lord Palmerston* (London: Constable, 1970); Southgate, D., *The Most English Minister* (London: Macmillan, 1966). Webster was generally sympathetic to Palmerston and his outlook is revealed in papers such as 'Lord Palmerston at Work, 1830–41', *Politica*, vol. I (1934), pp. 129–44; 'Palmerston and the liberal movement, 1830–41' *Politica*, vol. 3 (1938), pp. 299–323; 'Palmerston, Metternich and the European system, 1830–41', *Proceedings of the British Academy for 1934* (1936), pp. 125–58; 'Urquhart, Ponsonby and Palmerston', *English Historical Review*, vol. LXII (1947), pp. 327–51. Some writers are still very critical of Palmerston, notably Henderson, G. B., 'The foreign policy of Lord Palmerston', *History*, vol. XXII (1937–8), pp. 335–44; and Stapleton, A. G., *Intervention and Non Intervention in the Foreign Policy of Great Britain, 1790–1865* (London: John Murray, 1866).

For relations with France, see Poutras, C. H., 'Sur les rapports de la France et de l'Angleterre pendant la Monarchie de Juillet', *Revue d'Histoire Moderne* (1927), pp. 455–68; Guyot, R., *La première entente cordiale* (Paris: F. Rieder, 1926); Duhame, J., *Louis Philippe et la première entente cordiale* (Paris: P. Horay, 1951); Artonne, A., 'La politique extérieure de Palmerston de 1830 à 1841', *Revue de l'Historie Diplomatique*, vol. LXVIII (1953), pp. 72–91 and vol. LXVIII (1954), pp. 71–154; Bastide, C., 'The Anglo-French entente under Louis Philippe', *Economica*, vol. VII (1927), pp. 91–8; Lacour-Gayet, G., 'L'ambassade de Talleyrand à Londres', *Revue des Etudes historiques*, vol. LXXXVII (1921), pp. 153–70; Hall, J. R., *England and the Orleans Monarchy* (London: Smith, Elder & Co., 1912). For the Low Countries, see De Lannoy, F., *Les origines diplomatique de l'indépendence belge: La Conférence de Londres 1830–31* (Louvain: C. Peeters, 1903); Colby, C. W., 'The earlier relations of England and Belgium', *American Historical Review*, vol. 21 (1916), pp. 62–72; Swain, J. E., 'Talleyrand

and the independence of Belgium: a study in Anglo–French Relations', in Murray, J. J. (ed.), *Essays in Modern European History* (Bloomington, Indiana: Indiana University Press, 1951), pp. 113–54; Thomas, D. H., 'The use of the Scheldt in British plans for the defence of Belgium neutrality 1831–1914', *Revue Belge de Philologie et d'Histoire*, vol. 41 (1963), pp. 449–70. More generally, Kossman, E., *A History of the Low Countries 1789–1945* (Oxford: Clarendon Press, 1978).

For Spain and Portugal, see Bullen, R., 'Party politics and foreign policy: Whigs, Tories and Iberian affairs, 1830–36', *Bulletin of the Institute of Historical Research*, vol. 51 (1978), pp. 37–59; Bullen, R., 'England, Spain and the Portuguese question in 1833', *European Studies Review*, vol. IV (1974), pp. 1–22; Bullen, R., 'France and the problem of intervention in Spain 1834–6', *Historical Journal*, vol. 20 (1977), pp. 363–94; Mosely, P. E., 'Intervention and non-intervention in Spain 1838–9', *Journal of Modern History*, vol. 13 (1941), pp. 195–217.

An extensive literature on the Eastern crisis includes Dodwell, H. H., *The founder of Modern Egypt. A study of Muhammad Ali* (Cambridge: Cambridge University Press, 1931); Rodkey, F. S., 'Lord Palmerston and the rejuvenation of Turkey, 1830–41', *Journal of Modern History*, vol. I (1929), pp. 570–93 and vol. 2 (1930), pp. 193–225; Temperley, H. W. V., 'British policy towards parliamentary rule in Turkey 1830–1914', *Cambridge Historical Journal*, vol. 4 (1933), pp. 156–91; Rodkey, F. S., *The Turco–Egyptian Question in the Relations of England, France and Russia 1832–41* (Urbana, Illinois: University of Illinois Press, 1923); Verete, M., 'Palmerston and the Levant Crisis, 1832', *Journal of Modern History*, vol. 24 (1952), pp. 143–51; Baker, R. L., 'Palmerston on the Treaty of Unkiar Skelessi', *English Historical Review*, vol. XLIII (1928), pp. 83–9; Puryear, V. J., 'L'opposition de l'Angleterre et de la France au traité d'Unkiar-Iskelessi en 1833', *Revue Historique*, vol. CLXXXII (1938), pp. 283–310; Rodkey, F. S., 'The views of Palmerston and Metternich on the Eastern Question in 1834', *English Historical Review*, vol XLV (1930), pp. 308–16; Bolsover, G. H., 'Lord Ponsonby and the Eastern Question, 1833–39', *Slavonic and East European Review*, vol. 13 (1934), pp. 98–118; Bolsover, G. H., 'Palmerston and Metternich on the Eastern Question in 1834', *English Historical Review*, vol. LI (1936), pp. 237–56; Bolsover, G. H., 'David Urquhart and the Eastern Question, 1833–7: a study in publicity and diplomacy', *Journal of Modern History*, vol. 8 (1936), pp. 444–67; Barker, G. F., 'Bowring and the Near Eastern Crisis of 1838–40', *English Historical Review*, vol. LXXXIX (1964), pp. 761–74; Waddington, F., 'La politique de Lord Palmerston et le traité de 15 juillet 1840', *Revue d'histoire diplomatique*, vol. XLIX (1935), pp. 1–27, and 174–201; Mosley, P. E., *Russian Diplomacy and the opening of the Eastern Question in 1838 and 1839* (Cambridge, Mass.: Harvard University Press, 1934); Rodkey, F. S., 'Anglo-Russian negotiations about a permanent quadruple alliance 1840–41', *American Historical Review*, vol. 36 (1931), pp. 34–49; Garnett, R. (ed.), 'A letter of Lord Palmerston on the Egyptian question of 1840', *English Historical Review*, vol. XVIII (1903), pp. 125–30.

For reactions to Polish risings, see Ureisser, H. G., 'Polonophilism and the British working class 1830–45', *Polish Review*, vol. XII (1967), pp. 78–96; Weisser, H. G., 'The British working class and the Cracow uprising of 1846', *Polish Review*, vol. XIII (1968), pp. 3–19.

For developments in the Far East, see Greenberg, M., *British Trade and the Opening of China, 1800–42* (Cambridge: Cambridge University Press, 1957); Graham, G. S., *The China Station: War and Diplomacy, 1830–1860* (Oxford: Clarendon Press, 1979); Waley, A. D., *The Opium-War through Chinese eyes* (London: George Allen & Unwin, 1958), Vol. 1, *The Period of Conflict 1834–60*; Costin, W. C., *Great Britain and China, 1833–60* (Oxford: Clarendon Press, 1937); Sargent, A. J., *Anglo-Chinese Commerce and Diplomacy* (Oxford: Clarendon Press, 1907); Kuo, Phn-Chia, 'A critical Study of the First Anglo-Chinese War, with Documents' (Shanghai: The Commercial Press, 1935); Chang, Hsin-Pat, *Commissioner Lui and the Opium War* (Cambridge, Mass.: Harvard University Press, 1964), Fairbank, J. K., 'Chinese Diplomacy and the Treaty of Nanking, 1842', *Journal of Modern History*, vol. 12 (1940), pp. 1–30; Owen, P. E., *British Opium Policy in China and India* (Newhaven, Conn: Yale University Press, 1934).

The Peel Government 1841–6

For relations with North America, see Bourne, K., *Britain and the Balance of Power in North America*, op. cit.; Soulby, H. G., *The Right of Search and the Slave Trade in Anglo-American Relations, 1814–62* (Baltimore, Maryland: John Hopkins Press, 1933); Gordon, H. T., *The Treaty of Washington, concluded August 9th, 1842, by Daniel Webster and Lord Ashburton* (Berkeley, California: Berkeley University Press, 1908); Watt, A., 'The case of Alexander MacLeod', *Canadian Historical Review*, vol. 12 (1931), pp. 145–67; Baldwin, J. R., 'The Ashburton-Webster boundary settlement', *Canadian Historical Association Report for 1937* (1938), pp. 121–33; Kurtz, H. I., 'The undeclared war between Britain and America 1837–42', *History Today*, vol. XII (1962), pp. 777–83 and 873–80; Adams, E. D., 'Lord Ashburton and the Treaty of Washington', *American Historical Review*, vol. 17 (1912), pp. 764–82; Callahan, J. M., *American Foreign Policy in Canadian Relations* (New York: The Macmillan Company, 1937); Jones, W. D., 'Lord Ashburton and the Maine boundary negotiations', *Missisippi Valley Historical Review*, vol. XL (1953), pp. 477–90; Merk, F., *The Oregon Question: Essays in Anglo-American Diplomacy* (Cambridge, Mass.: Harvard University Press, 1967); Clarke, R. C., 'Aberdeen and Peel on Oregon, 1844', *Oregon Historical Quarterly*, vol. XXXIV (1933), pp. 236–40; Commager, H. S., 'England and the Oregon Treaty of 1846', *Oregon Historical Quarterly*, vol. XXVII (1927), pp. 18–38; Jones, W. D., *The American Problem in British Diplomacy, 1841–1861* (London: Macmillan, 1974).

For the foreign policy of the Peel government, see sections on France, the Far East and North America above. See also Goryanov, G. M., 'The secret agreement of 1844 between Russia and Great Britain', *Russian Review*, vol. I (1912), pp. 97–115; Daudet, E., 'La reine Victoria en

France (1843)', *Revue des Deux Mondes* (1902), pp. 357–88; MacLean, D., 'The Greek revolution and the Anglo-French entente 1843', *English Historical Review*, vol. XVIC (1981), pp. 117–29; Cunningham, A. B., 'Peel, Aberdeen and the Entente Cordiale', *Bulletin of the Institute of Historical Research*, vol. XXX (1957), pp. 189–206; Poulthas, C., 'The relations of Guizot and Aberdeen, 1837–52', in *Journées Franco-Anglaises de 1937, Revue d'Histoire Moderne*, vol. XIII (1938), pp. 197–211; Jones Parry, E., 'A review of the relations between Guizot and Lord Aberdeen 1840–52', *History*, vol. XXIII (1938), pp. 25–36; Jones Parry, E. (ed.), *The Aberdeen–Lieven Correspondence 1832–48* (London: Cambden Society, 1938).

The Return of Palmerston
For the period 1846–8 see Ridley, J., op. cit.; Eckniger, K., *Lord Palmeston und der Schweizer Sonderbundskrieg* (Berlin: Ebring, 1938); Imlah, A. G., *Britain and Switzerland 1845–60: A Study of Anglo-Swiss Relations During Some Critical Years for Swiss Neutrality* (London: Longman, 1966); Halévy, E., 'Palmerston et Guizot', *Revue des Sciences Politiques*, vol. LIX (1936), pp. 321–46; Johnson, D., *Guizot: Aspects of French History 1787–1874* (London: Routledge & Kegan Paul, 1963); Syme, S. A., 'The Minto mission to Italy, 1847–8', *Italian Quarterly*, vol. VIII, 30 (1964), pp. 35–65; Taylor, A. J. P., *The Italian Problem in European Diplomacy 1846–9* (Manchester: Manchester University Press, 1934); Jones Parry, E., *The Spanish Marriages 1841–46* (London: Macmillan & Co., 1936); Bullen, R., *Palmerston, Guizot and the Collapse of the Entente Cordiale* (London: Athlone Press, 1974); Bullen, R., 'Guizot and the *Sonderbund* Crisis', *English Historical Review*, vol. LXXXVI (1971), pp. 497–526.

CHAPTER 6

The 1848 Revolutions
For the 1848 Revolutions, see Greer, D. M., *L'Angleterre, la France et la Révolution de 1848: le troisième ministère de Lord Palmerston au Foreign Office 1846–51* (Paris: Rieder, 1925); Lefèvre, A., 'La reconnaissance de la Seconde Republique par l'Angleterre', *Revue d'histoire diplomatique*, vol. LXXXII (1968), pp. 213–31; De Groot, E., 'Contemporary political opinion and the revolution of 1848', *History*, n.s., XXXVIII (1953), pp. 134–54; Sandford, K. A. P., *Great Britain and the Schleswig-Holstein Question 1848–1864: A study in Diplomacy, Politics and Public Opinion* (Buffalo, N. Y.: Buffalo University Press, 1975); Soutag, R. J., *Germany and England: Background of the Conflict, 1848–94* (New York: Harper & Row, 1969); Hjelholt, H., *British Mediation in the Danish-German Conflict, 1848–50*, 2 Vols. (Copenhagen: Historisk-filosofiske meddelelser udgivet af Det Kongelige Danske Videnskabernes Selskab, 1965–6); Weber, F. G., 'Palmerston and Prussian liberalism, 1848', *Journal of*

Modern History, vol. 35 (1963), pp. 125–36; Mosse, W. E. E., *The European powers and the German Question 1848–71 with special reference to England and Russia* (Cambridge: Cambridge University Press, 1958); Fischer-Ane, H. R., *Die Deutschland-Politik des Prinzgernahls Albert von England 1848–52* (Coburg and Hanover: H. Schroedel, 1953); Sproxton, C., *Palmerston and the Hungarian Revolution* (Cambridge: Cambridge University Press, 1919); Szenczi, N. J., 'Great Britain and the War of Hungarian Independence 1848–9', *Slavonic Review*, vol. XVIII (1939), pp. 556–70; Floresan, R. R., 'Stratford Canning, Palmerston and the Wallachian Revolution of 1848', *Journal of Modern History*, vol. 35 (1963), pp. 227–44; Barie, O., *L'Inghilterra e'il problema italiano nel 1848–9: dalle revoluzioni alla seconda res Faurazione* (Milan: CEUM, 1965).

For developments of the early 1850s, see Thomas, D. H., 'The Reaction of the Great Powers to Louis Napoleon's rise to power in 1851', *Historical Journal*, vol. XIII (1970), pp. 237–50; Lefèvre, A., 'L'Angleterre et l'avènement du Second Empire, février-décembre, 1852', *Revue d'Histoire diplomatique*, vol. LXXXIII (1968), pp. 142–56; Hyamson, A. M., 'Don Pacifico', *English Jewish Historical Society* (1958), pp. 1–39; Preston, A., and Major, J., *Send a Gunboat: A Study of the Gunboat and its Role in British Policy, 1854–1964* (London: Longman, 1967).

The Crimean War
For the Crimean War, see Martin, B. K., *The Triumph of Lord Palmerston: A Study of Public Opinion in England before the Civil War* (London: G. Allen & Unwin, 1924); Aubrey, O., 'La France et Napoléon III, l'Alliance anglaise', *Revue des Deux Mondes* (1937), pp. 286–318; Henderson, G. B., 'The Diplomatic Revolution of 1854', *American Historical Review*, vol. 44 (1937), pp. 22–56; Fouques-Dupare, J., 'Les aspects diplomatiques de la guerre de Crimée', *Risorgimento*, vol. VIII (1956), pp. 1–13; Herkless, T. L., 'Stratford Canning, the Cabinet and the outbreak of the Crimean War'. *Historical Journal*, vol. 18 (1975), pp. 497–523; Floresan, R. R., 'The Rumanian principalities and the origins of the Crimean War', *Slavonic and Eastern European Review*, vol. XLIII (1964), pp. 46–67; Henderson, N., 'Lord Stratford de Redcliffe and the Crimean War', *History Today*, vol. 2 (1952), pp. 729–37; Temperley, H. W. V., 'Stratford de Redcliffe and the Origins of the Crimean War', *English Historical Review*, vol. XLVIII (1933), pp. 387–414 and vol. XLIX (1934), pp. 265–98; Bailey, F. E., *British Policy and the Turkish Reform Movement*, op. cit.; Puryear, V. J., *International Economics and Diplomacy in the Near East: A Study of British Commercial Policy in the Levant 1834–1853* (Stanford, California: Stanford University Press, 1935); Puryear, V. J., *England, Russia and the Straits Question, 1844–56* (Berkeley, California: University of California Press, 1931); Puryear, V. J., 'New Light on the origins of the Crimean War', *Journal of Modern History*, vol. 3 (1931), pp. 219–34; Henderson, G. B., *Crimean War Diplomacy* (Glasgow: Collins, 1947); Schroeder, P., *Austria, Great Britain*

and the Crimean War (Ithaca, N. Y.: Cornell University Press, 1972); Schmitt, B. E., 'The diplomatic preliminaries of the Crimean War', *American Historical Review*, vol. 25 (1920), pp. 36–67; Temperley, H. W. V., *England and the Near East: The Crimea* (London: Longman & Co., 1936); Taylor A. J. P., 'John Bright and the Crimean War', *Bulletin of John Rylands Library*, vol. 36 (1954), pp. 501–21; Henderson, G. B., 'The two interpretations of the Four Points, December 1854', *English Historical Review*, vol. LII (1937), pp. 48–66; Henderson, G. B., 'The Pacifists of the fifties', *Journal of Modern History*, vol. 9 (1937), pp. 314-41; Temperley, H. W. V., 'Austria, England and the ultimatum to Russia, 16 February 1855', in *Wirtschaft und Kultur Festschrift Alfons Dopsch* (Vienna and Leipzig: Brunn, 1938); Henderson, G. B., 'The European Concert June 1854–July 1855', *Cambridge Abstracts* (1934), pp. 61–2; Mosse, W. E., 'The triple treaty of 15 April 1856', *English Historical Review*, vol. LXVII (1952), pp. 203–29; Rupprecht, F., *Der Pariser Frieden von 1856* (Wurzburg: A. Rosstentscher, 1934); Temperley, H. W. V., 'The Treaty of Paris and its Execution', *Journal of Modern History*, vol. 4 (1932), pp. 387–414 and 523–43; Charles-Rouz, F., 'La Russie et l'alliance Anglo-française après la guerre de Crimée, *Revue historique* (1909), vol. CI, pp. 272–315. For domestic aspects, see Anderson, O., *A Liberal State at War* (London: Macmillan, 1967).

CHAPTER 7

France and Italy

For relations with France, see Bradshaw, D. F., 'A decade of British opposition to the Suez Canal project 1854–64', *Transport History*, vol. 9 (1978), pp. 15–23; Packe, M. St. J., *The Bombs of Orsini* (London: Secker & Warburg, 1957); Hearder, H., 'Napoleon III's threat to break off diplomatic relations with England during the crisis over the Orsini attempt in 1858', *English Historical Review*, vol. LXXVII (1957), pp. 478–81'; Sherer, P., 'British reaction to the French annexation of Nice and Savoy', *International Review of Historical and Political Science*, vol. 2 (1965), pp. 31–40; Wright, S., 'The Origins of Napoleon III's free trade', *Economic History Review*, vol. IX (1938), pp. 64–7; Dunham, A. L., 'The origins of the Anglo-French Treaty of 1860', *Nineteenth Century*, vol. XCII (1922), pp. 786–96; Dunham, A. L., *The Anglo-French Treaty of Commerce* (Ann Arbor, Mich.: University of Michigan Press, 1930); Morazé, P., 'The treaty of 1860 and the industry of the North', *Economic History Review*, vol. XI (1940), pp. 18–28; Dawson, W. H., *Richard Cobden and Foreign Policy* (London: George Allen & Unwin, 1926).

For the unification of Italy, see Beales, D. E. D., *England and Italy, 1859–60* (London: Thomas Nelson & Sons, 1961); Davis, J., 'Garibaldi and England', *History Today*, vol. 32 (1982), pp. 21–6; Blakiston, N., *Inglesi e Italiani nel Risorgimento* (Catania: Bonanno, 1973); Jazzay, M., 'La questione italiana nei rapporti anglo-austricci durante la crisis del

1859', *Rassegna Storia del Risorgimento*, vol. 52 (1965), pp. 557–78; Simpson, F. A. 'England and the Italian war of 1859', *Historical Journal*, vol. V (1962), pp. 111–21; Beales, D. E. D., 'Gladstone on the Italian question, January 1860', *Rassegna Storia del Risorgimento*, vol. XLI (1954), pp. 96–104; Taylor, A. J. P., 'European mediation and the Agreement of Villafranca 1859', *English Historical Review*, vol. LI (1936), pp. 52–78.

The American Civil War

For the American Civil War, see Beloff, M., 'Great Britain and the American Civil War', *History*, n.s., vol. 37 (1952), pp. 40–8; Jones, W. D., 'The British Conservatives and the American Civil War', *American Historical Review*, vol. 58 (1953), pp. 527–43; Whitridge, A., 'British Liberals and the American Civil War', *History Today*, vol. XII (1962), pp. 688–95; Hernon, J. M., 'British sympathies in the American Civil War: a Reconsideration', *Journal of Southern History*, Vol. XXXIII (1967), pp. 356–67; Reid, R. L., 'William E. Gladstone's insincere neutrality during the Civil War', *Civil War History*, vol. XV (1969), pp. 293–307; Jenkins, B., *Britain and the War for the Union*, Vol. 1 (Montreal: McGill, Queen's University Press, 1974); Bourne, K., 'British preparation for war with the North, 1861–2', *English Historical Review*, vol. LXXXVI (1961), pp. 805–61; Adams, E. D., *Great Britain and the American Civil War*, 2 Vols (London: Longman & Co., 1925); Merli, F. J., *Great Britain and the Confederate Navy 1861–5* (Bloomington, Indiana: Indiana University Press, 1970); Khagigia, A., 'Economic factors and British neutrality, 1861–5', *Historian*, vol. XXV (1963), pp. 451–65; Whitbridge, A., 'The Trent Affair, 1861', *History Today*, vol. IV (1954), pp. 394–402; Wheeler-Bennett, J., 'The Trent Affair: How the Prince Consort saved the United States', *History Today*, vol. XI (1961), pp. 805–16; Poolman, K., *The Alabama Incident* (London: William Kimber, 1958); Wardle, A. C., 'Mersey-built blockade runners in the American Civil War', *Mariners Mirror*, vol. XXVIII (1942), pp. 179–88; Leston, R. J., *Confederate Finance and Purchasing in Great Britain* (Charlottesville, Virginia: Georgetown University Press, 1975).

The East

For the non-European world, see Hibbert, C., *The Great Mutiny, India, 1857* (London: Allen Lane, 1978); Wong, J. T., 'The building of an informal British Empire in China in the Middle of the nineteenth century', *Bulletin of John Rylands Library*, vol. 59 (1977), pp. 472–85; Steeds, D., and Nish, I. H., *China, Japan and Nineteenth Century Britain* (Dublin: Irish University Press, 1977); Leavenworth, C. S., *The Arrow War with China* (London: Sampson, Low & Co., 1901); Barker, G. F., 'Sir John Bowring and the *Arrow* war in China', *Bulletin of John Rylands Library*, vol. XLIII (1961), pp. 293–316; Lumby, E. W. R., 'Lord Elgin and the burning of the Summer Palace', *History Today*, vol. X (1960), pp. 479–517; Banno, M., *China and the West 1858–61* (Cambridge, Mass.: Harvard University Press, 1964).

The Polish Rising

For the Polish Rising, see Kutolowski, J. F., 'English radicals and the Polish insurrection of 1863–4', *Polish Review*, vol. XI (1966), pp. 3–28; Kutolowski, J. F., 'Mid-Victorian public opinion, Polish propaganda and the uprising of 1863', *Journal of British Studies*, vol. 8 (1969), pp. 86–110; Pasicka, K. S., 'The British press and the Polish insurrection of 1863', *Slavonic and Eastern European Review*, vol. XLII (1963), pp. 15–37; Mosse, W. E. E., 'England and the Polish insurrection of 1863', *English Historical Review*, vol. LXXI (1956), pp. 28–55; Harley, J. H., 'Great Britain and the Polish insurrection of 1863', *Slavonic Review*, vol. XVI (1937), pp. 155–67 and vol. XVI (1938), pp. 425–38.

The Rise of Prussia

For Britain and the rise of Prussia, see Picot, M. L., *England und Preussens deutsche Politik 1854–66* (Munster: University of Munster, 1935); Burckhardt, H., *Deutsch-England-Frankreich: die politischen Beziehungen Deutschlands zu den beiden westeuropaischen Grossmachten 1864–6* (Munich: Wilhelm Fink, 1970); Steefel, L. D., *The Schleswig-Holstein Question* (Cambridge, Mass.: Harvard University Press, 1932); Sempel, C., *England und Preussen in der Schleswig-Holsteinischen Frage* (Berlin: Ebring, 1932); Voigt, J. H., 'Englands Aussenpolitik wahrend des deutsch-danischen Konflicts 1862–4' *Zeitschrift Gessellschaft Schleswig-Holsteinische Geschichte*, vol. LXXXIX (1964), pp. 61–194; Møller, E., 'Det engelske Kabinet øg den Dansk-Tyske Strid 1863–4', *Hist. Tidsskaft* (Denmark), 11th Series, IV (1954), pp. 232–312, (with English summary); Lubrich, F. J. P. H., *Hannover und die schleswig-holsteinische Frage, 1863 bis 1864* (Gottingen: Gottingen University Press, 1937); Carr, W., *Schleswig-Holstein 1815–64* (Manchester: Manchester University Press, 1963).

See also, Mosse, W. E., *The Rise and Fall of the Crimean System* (London: Macmillan & Co., 1963); Kennedy, P. M., 'Idealists and Realists, British Views of Germany, 1864–1939', *Transactions of the Royal Historical Society*, 5th Series, Vol. 25 (1975), pp. 137–56; Mander, J., *Our German Cousins: Anglo-German Relations in the 19th and 20th Centuries* (London: John Murray, 1974).

CHAPTER 8

The Change in Foreign Policy

For 'institutional' aspects see Temperley, H. W. V., and Henderson, G., 'Disraeli and Palmerston in 1857 or, the dangers of explanations in Parliament'. *Cambridge Historical Journal*, vol. VII (1942), pp. 115–26; Cromwell, V., 'The losing of the initiative by the House of Commons', *Transactions of the Royal Historical Society*, 5th series, vol. XVIII (1968), pp. 1–24; Middleton, C. R., *The Administration of British Foreign Policy 1782–1846* (Durham, North Carolina: Duke University

Press, 1977). Bindoff, S. T., 'The unreformed Diplomatic Service 1812–1860', *Transactions of the Royal Historical Society*, 4th Series, vol. XVIII (1935), pp. 143–72; Lambert, S., 'A century of Diplomatic Blue Books', [review article], *Historical Journal*, vol. 10 (1967), pp. 125–31; Hughes, E., 'Civil service reform 1853–5' *History*, vol. XXVII (1942), pp. 51–83. Cecil, A., 'The Foreign Office' in A. W. Ward and G. P. Gooch (eds.), *The Cambridge History of British Foreign Policy*, 3 Vols. (Cambridge: Cambridge University Press, 1923), Vol. 3, pp. 539–617; Tilley, J., and Gaselee, S., *The Foreign Office* (London: G. P. Putnam & Sons, 1933); Hertslet, E., *Recollections of the Old Foreign Office* (London: John Murray, 1901); Ashton-Gwatkin, F. T., 'The British Foreign Service: a discussion of the development and formation of the British foreign service' (Syracuse, New York: Syracuse University Press, 1950); Jones-Parry, E., 'Under Secretaries of State for Foreign Affairs, 1782–1855', *English Historical Review*, vol. XLIX (1934), pp. 56–77; Anderson, O., 'The janus face of mid-nineteenth century radicalism: the administrative reform association of 1855', *Victorian Studies*, vol. VIII (March 1965), pp. 231–42.

For general assessments of British foreign policy in the nineteenth century, see, Porter, B., 'British foreign policy in the nineteenth century', *Historical Journal*, vol. 23 (1980), pp. 192–202; Hayes, P., *The Nineteenth Century 1814–1880* (London: A & C Black, 1975); Bourne, K., *The Foreign Policy of Victorian England* (Oxford: Clarendon Press, 1970); Bryant, A. W., 'Factors underlying British foreign policy', *International Affairs*, vol. XXII, No. 3 (July 1946), pp. 338–51; Davies, G., 'The continuity of British foreign policy', *University of Toronto Quarterly*, vol. XV, No. 3 (April 1946), pp. 242–55; Petrie, C. A., *Diplomatic History 1713–1933* (London: Hollis & Carter, 1946); Seton-Watson, R. W., 'The foundations of British policy', *Transactions of the Royal Historical Society*, 4th series, vol. XXIX (1947), pp. 47–67; Webster, C. K., 'Fundamentals of British foreign policy', *International Journal*, vol. III, No. 4, Autumn 1948, pp. 320–26; Davies, G., 'The Pattern of British Foreign Policy 1815–1914', *Huntington Library Quarterly*, vol. VI, No. 3 (May 1943), pp. 367–77; Jones-Parry, E., 'British foreign policy in the nineteenth century', *History* new series, vol. XXIII (1939), pp. 322–30.

For Imperial and commercial issues, see Penson, L., *The Colonial Background to British Foreign Policy* (London: G. Bell & Sons, 1930); Bailey, F. E., 'The economics of British foreign policy, 1825–1850', *Journal of Modern History*, vol. XII, No. 4 (December 1940), pp. 449–484; Hyde, F. E., *Mr Gladstone at the Board of Trade* (London: Cobden-Sanderson, 1934). Lingelbach, A. L., 'Huskisson and the Board of Trade;, *American Historical Review*, vol. 43 (1937–8), pp. 759–74; Brown, L. M., *The Board of Trade and the Free Trade Movement 1830–1842* (Oxford: Clarendon Press, 1958); Rogge, H., *England, Freidrich List und der deutsche Zollverein* (Wurzberg: Greifswald, 1939); Gallagher, J., and Robinson, R., 'The imperialism of free trade, *Economic History Review*, 2nd series, vol. VI (1953), pp. 1–15; Macdonagh, O., 'The anti-imperialism of free trade;, *Economic History*

Review, 2nd series, vol. XIV (1962), pp. 489–501; Platt, D. C. M., 'The imperialism of free trade: some reservations', *Economic History Review*, 2nd Series, vol. XXI (1968), pp. 296–306; Platt, D. C. M., 'The role of the British consular service in overseas trade 1825–1915', *Economic History Review*, 2nd Series, vol. XV (1963), pp. 494–512; Imlah, A. H., *Economic Elements in the Pax Britannica* (Cambridge, Mass.: Harvard University Press, 1958); Platt, D. C. M., *Finance, trade and politics in British foreign policy, 1815–1914* (Oxford: Clarendon Press, 1968); Platt, D. C. M., *Business Imperialism 1840–1930* (Oxford: Clarendon Press, 1977); Bartlett, C. J. (ed.), *Britain Pre-eminent: Studies in British World Influence in the Nineteenth Century* (London: Macmillan, 1969); Bartlett, C. J., *Great Britain and Sea Power 1815–1853* (Oxford: Clarendon Press, 1963); Porter, B., *The Lion's Share: a short history of British Imperialism 1850–1970* (London: Longman, 1975).

For ideological and theoretical aspects see Dawson, W. H., *Richard Cobden and Foreign Policy* (London: George Allen & Unwin, 1926); Armitage-Smith, G., *The Free Trade Movement and its Results* (London: Blackie & Son, 1898); Nelson, B. H., 'The slave trade as a factor in British foreign policy 1815–62', *Journal of Negro History*, vol. XXII, No. 2 (April 1942), pp. 192–209; Semmel, B., *The rise of Free Trade Imperialism* (London: Cambridge University Press, 1970); Summerton, N. W., 'Dissenting attitudes to foreign relations, peace and war 1840–1890', *Journal of Ecclesiastical History*, vol. 28 (1977), pp. 151–178; Tyrell, A., 'Making the millenium: the mid-nineteenth century peace movement', *Historical Journal*, vol. 21 (1971), pp. 338–352; Winch, D., *Classical Political Economy and Colonies* (London: G. Bell & Sons, 1965); Holbraad, C., *The Concert of Europe: a study in German and British International Theory 1815–1914* (London: Longman, 1970); Jones, R. E., *The Changing Structure of British Foreign Policy* (London: Longman, 1974); McClelland, C. A., *Theory and the International System* (New York: Columbia University Press, 1966); Taylor, A. J. P., *The Trouble Makers: dissent over foreign Policy, 1792–1939* (London: Hamish-Hamilton, 1957); Hinsley, F. H., *Power and the Pursuit of Peace* (Cambridge: Cambridge University Press, 1963); Knorr, K., and Rosenan, J. N., *Contending Approaches to International Politics* (Princeton: Princeton University Press, 1969); Wallace, M. D., 'Alliance polarization, cross cutting and international war, 1815–1864', *Journal of Conflict Resolution*, vol. XVIVI (1973), pp. 575–604; Small, M., and Singer, J. D., 'Alliance aggregation and the onset of war, 1815–1914', in J. D. Singer (ed.), *Quantitative International Politics* (New York: Free Press, 1968).

Index